BIG TREES

BIG TREES

THE FLORIDA REGISTER

Daniel B. Ward

Robert T. Ing

Sponsored by the
Division of Forestry
Florida Department of Agriculture and Consumer Services

With participation by the
Department of Botany, University of Florida

Published by the
Florida Native Plant Society
1997

COVER: Florida's largest live oak (Quercus virginiana). The Cellon Oak,
3 miles south of LaCrosse, Alachua County. Circumference of trunk = 360 inches;
height = 85 feet; branch spread = 175 feet × 155 feet. With botany class,
University of Florida. (Photo by T. Ann Williams, April 1992.)

Library of Congress Catalog Card Number 97-60578
Copyright © 1997
Daniel B. Ward
ISBN 1-885258-06-2

TABLE OF CONTENTS

LIST OF PLATES

PREFACE

It has long been recognized that big trees are of exceptional interest to many people. Since 1941 the American Forestry Association (now American Forests), Washington, D.C., has retained records and published listings of trees that were the largest in the United States—the "National Champions." And since 1978 the Division of Forestry, Florida Department of Agriculture and Consumer Services, has maintained similar records for the state of Florida—the "Florida Champions."

This report of the Florida Champion Tree Survey is the product of an intensive six year effort by Dr. Daniel B. Ward and Dr. Robert T. Ing, supported by personnel of the district offices of the Division of Forestry and other participants, to locate and measure the largest trees of all species in the state of Florida. It has drawn upon the records of big trees accumulated by the Division in former years, as updated and confirmed during the present study, and has been greatly expanded to include information regarding many larger trees of species presently represented in the files as well as trees of species for which no data were otherwise available.

The Survey documents 610 native and 243 non-native trees, for a total of 853 listed trees. For each individual tree, information is given as to its common and scientific name, its measurements in terms of circumference of trunk, height, and spread of canopy, its location, owner, and nominator, and its rank as a champion or other status among the elite trees of Florida.

Of these documented trees, 151 of the native species and 13 of the non-natives are National champions, while 106 of the natives and 118 of the non-natives are Florida champions.

These trees represent 228 of the approximately 290 native species recognized as actually or potentially of tree stature within the state. A further 133 of Florida's numerous non-native tree species are also included, though their numbers are limited by the requirement that non-natives attain appreciable size before meriting inclusion.

Based upon these tree records, separate studies addressed other factors in the life of these giant trees. For 129 trees of 82 species, remeasurements made during the study permitted estimates of growth rates, while use of the accumulated measurements as a data set gave a quantitative ranking as to height of the different species. Of the 186 trees that were found to have died since measurement in former years, information was gathered as to the forces that terminate the life of these ancient trees.

But this Survey is not complete. To facilitate further work, this report also explains how a tree is measured, and how it may be nominated as a potential champion. An appreciable number of native tree species and perhaps an even larger number of non-native species have not been included for lack of some sharp-eyed observer to locate and nominate them. Many of the trees absent from this study are of small stature and have thus been overlooked even though they are the largest of their kind. Many are surely to be found in the Florida Keys, whose unique tropical habitat will cause them to be not only Florida champions but National champions. And many champions are surely to be found in areas of the state that have not yet received adequate attention; fully 26 of our 67 Florida counties are the home of no more than one or two trees nominated as potential champions.

We thus encourage all those who value our natural heritage and especially those with love for our beautiful trees, to seek out and nominate further exceptional trees of great size. These trees, yet to be found and measured, will rank among our future champions.

James F. Testin
Champion Tree Program Coordinator
Florida Division of Forestry

FOREWORD

Florida is blessed by an abundance of natural beauty—from its coastal beaches and coral reefs to its freshwater lakes and springs, from its agricultural croplands to its still-wild parks and preserves. But the single natural feature that most often attracts the admiration of visitors to our state and loyalty by our citizens are its trees.

The trees of Florida are a wonder. We have more species of trees than any other state. They are of species native to the state and of species brought here for ornamental and horticultural purposes. They range from hardy species of the Florida panhandle to delicate tropical species found only in the warmest corners of our Florida Keys. Many of them, the citrus and the pine in particular, are of great economic importance to the state. But many of the others, though individually not dominant, are so beautiful and so interesting that the visitors they attract also give us great benefit and value.

And now we find that within our Florida forests and parklands we have many individual trees that are the largest of their kind. The Florida Division of Forestry has long been interested in tracking and recording these giants. The purpose of this work has had three goals. The first is simply the gathering of scientific facts in this area of forestry; there was previously little information on record regarding many of these species—how large they grow, how long they live, and what causes their death. The second may perhaps best be called pride of heritage, the instinctive impulse of all of us to value and protect those rare things we receive from those who lived before us. And the third is the opportunity of people throughout the state to learn of the uniqueness of the trees around them, and thus to encourage protection both of these trees and the environment they represent.

One of the satisfactions of my present position within the government of the State of Florida is the opportunity it provides to oversee and encourage the work of many individuals who are dedicated to the protection of our state's natural beauty. I wish to commend the personnel of the Division of Forestry for their faithful management of its Champion Tree Program over the years. I am especially grateful to Dr. Daniel B. Ward and Dr. Robert T. Ing of the University of Florida for their participation in this program, by their meticulous documentation of our big trees and by the preparation and publication of the Florida Champion Tree Survey, as reported here.

Bob Crawford
Commissioner of Agriculture
Florida Department of Agriculture
and Consumer Services

INTRODUCTION

There is something magical about a big tree. A tree of great size conveys stability and permanence by its massive trunk, majesty in its towering height, and protective shelter beneath its spreading branches. It may serve mankind in many ways: the innumerable uses for its timber and its fruits; the value of its influence on weather, conservation of soil, and purification of air; the home it provides to cherished birds and other wildlife. Its great bulk evokes near-forgotten memories of the awe it held for the vanished druid, while the venturesome child scaling its limbs unknowingly recapitulates the life of his distant primate ancestor. To stand beneath a giant tree is to experience a reverence whose depth and intensity cannot be surpassed by contact with any other living thing.

We shall present in this report of the Florida Champion Tree Survey a summation of current information on the largest trees in Florida: their names, both scientific and common; their dimensions; where they grow; and to whom they belong.

And of these many big trees, which are the true champions, the very largest individuals of their kind? Which trees are the Florida champions, the largest of their species within the state although perhaps surpassed elsewhere in the nation? Which trees are the National champions, the largest known anywhere in the United States?

To answer these questions we must travel throughout Florida. We must explore its swamps and forests, visit its parks and preserves, travel its back roads, prowl the quiet streets of its historic towns, and peer over the fences of its private estates. We must enlist the assistance of foresters and land managers who know the nooks and crannies of their properties. We must, to a great extent, rely on the enthusiasm and knowledge of the many residents of Florida who love their beautiful trees.

We will find many trees that are giants of their kind, some of them well known, even famous, and others wholly secluded and overlooked. We will discover entire groves of trees all of which are larger than any of their species known elsewhere. Even more often we will stand beneath a solitary leviathan, the sole survivor of a time now past, sometimes a "wolf" tree bypassed by loggers because of a hollow trunk or other flaw, others magnificent specimens in full maturity preserved by protective owners or by chance. We will be told of history, of hangings, of Indian treaties—even of fantasy, as we encounter a giant tree beneath whose roots reportedly lies a treasure of great value, and another rumored to be guarded by a resident ghost.

We will be especially interested in those trees that are native to Florida—that is, those species already growing in Florida before the influence of European man. But we will also record trees of species that have been brought to Florida more recently, particularly the many tropical species that now grace our South Florida lawns and parkways.

We will obtain records of many individuals of some tree species and only one or a few of others. In some cases all large trees of a certain species will wholly elude us, and remain to be discovered by someone more persistent or fortunate.

Our trees will be measured for circumference of trunk, height, and spread of branches. Their measurements will permit us, by use of a simple formula, to compare them with one another and to rank them in size.

Then we will designate which of Florida's big trees are its National champions, which are its Florida champions, and which merely merit respect and protection because they are among the elite in size and rarity.

We have organized our information into chapters, each addressing a separate aspect of interest. The greatest part of this report is our INVENTORY, the actual record of the 853 largest trees now alive in Florida. It is here that we document the scientific and common name of the tree, who nominated it, its owner, its location, the measured dimensions of its trunk circumference, height, and crown spread, and any related information. It is here that we rank the trees of each species as to overall size, and here that we designate which is the champion.

But as we traveled the state in search of the big trees recorded by other workers in the years before our Survey began, we were saddened at how many of them are now gone. Often we were awed by their measurements; many of these vanished patriarchs were larger than any tree of the same species now alive. We gathered these data as our GIANTS OF YESTERYEAR, in their memory. Where we could, we noted HOW THEY DIED, a record of the forces that destroy big trees.

Though many of the big trees recorded in years past were no longer living, we found most of them still alive. We compared their present dimensions with those measurements taken years, even decades, before by other workers, to obtain a unique yardstick, the RATES OF GROWTH they attained in the years of their full maturity.

We then ranked the LARGEST AND SMALLEST champion trees throughout the state. Some of our trees are impressively tall; we documented seventeen individual trees above 120 feet in height. Of these, six are above 130 feet tall. And the tallest tree we have found in the entire state—a loblolly pine—towers to 145 feet.

Though most Florida trees are only modest in size of trunk, we measured a few with truly massive girths. Seven of our trees are greater than 400 inches in circumference—over ten feet in diameter. Three of these giant trees are our native bald cypress, rare individuals that by happenstance survived the brutal logging of former years that removed nearly all of these stately monarchs, for their near-imperishable wood. These few survivors are awesomely ancient; they may be 2000, a few perhaps 3000 years old, although their hollow centers usually makes accurate age-counts impossible.

We also ranked our trees for the size of their crown spread, the edge-to-edge distance beneath the entire canopy. We found six trees with a crown spread greater than 140 feet; of these, four are magnificent live oaks. But the two very largest are species not native to Florida—two kinds of fig with secondary root-trunks that descend from the spreading branches and give stability to the canopy that no native tree can attain.

Then, at the other end of the scale, we ranked those trees with the title of Champion that are the smallest in trunk size, in height, and in crown spread. Though these trees are modest, they are each the largest of their kind, and we are no less proud of them.

We made a calculation that we believe is unique in the realm of forestry, our SPECIES RANKED BY HEIGHT. We devised a procedure for ranking tree species—not individuals—as to their height. We knew, as do all others who work with Florida trees, that certain species are relatively tall, others relatively short. But nowhere is there available a quantitative measure of the height of the species. The multitude of seedlings, immature saplings, and young adults, and the complications of excluding these smaller individuals from the data set, has limited workers to general statements of height. For our data set we chose the many trees nominated as champions, and on that basis we have been able to give a numerical, quantitative height for each species.

Then, we asked, what is the size of the average National champion in Florida? What is the size of the average Florida champion? Our analysis of THE "AVERAGE" CHAMPION has given us answers. We found that the National champions and the Florida champions, on average, are of identical proportions. But the Florida champions, we learned, are much the larger. We attribute this difference to the many small tropical species that enter the United States only in South Florida, and the many northern species, though smaller in Florida than in more boreal areas, that still loom large in our flora.

As we traveled the state our attention was called not only to large trees, but occasionally to LARGE VINES. Though at first we smiled, for a vine is certainly not a tree, we then realized that the data that had come to us are otherwise wholly unavailable, and are worthy of inclusion in our Survey.

Because of the intense interest we found in many communities as to the kinds and locations of their champions, we tabulated each of the species in a COUNTY TREE-FIND LIST. If one employs this LIST, the names of species found in each county are a quick guide to the appropriate listing in the INVENTORY.

In one sense the people involved in this Survey are as important as the trees, for without the efforts of scores of volunteers over the years to document and record the trees, and the willingness of landowners and agencies to protect and preserve them, Florida would now be tree-poor indeed; we have assembled in one place all these NOMINATORS AND OWNERS. We give special thanks in our ACKNOWLEDGMENTS to the over one hundred persons who either accompanied us in the field or who at our request sought out and measured trees of particular interest.

Finally, we brought together in an APPENDIX the necessary instructions as to how trees are measured and nominated for championship status and other topics related to our Survey.

Come with us as we revisit these marvelous trees.

INVENTORY OF BIG TREES

The following INVENTORY consists of those Florida trees nominated as potential champions and believed living at the date of completion of the Florida Champion Tree Survey. Each is ranked as to its status as "National Champion," "Florida Champion," "Florida Challenger," or "Honorable Mention." Where individuals have formerly held the ranking of champion but have been displaced following nomination of a larger tree, the former rank is retained but marked as "Emeritus." For those individuals that are believed to surpass the current National champion but are yet to be so designated by **American Forests**, the provisional title of "National Champion (nominee)" is assigned.

Each tree bearing the rank of Champion is marked in the left margin by a star—solid if a National champion (★), and in outline if a Florida champion (☆).

For convenience in handling and clarity of understanding, the species believed present in Florida in pre-Columbian times are listed together as "Native." Those species believed introduced at a later date by the agency of man or by fortuitous circumstances are separately listed as "Non-native." Nominations have been accepted for any native species of tree form, while for non-native species only those individuals are listed whose point score is 100 or greater.

The INVENTORY also contains "Title vacant" entries of those native tree species for which no nominations have been made or for which all previously nominated trees are deceased by the date of survey. The tabulation of native trees thus is also a complete listing of the 290 species of trees native to Florida.

Measurements are given for each tree included in the INVENTORY—of circumference (in inches, at 4.5 feet), of height (in feet), and of average crown spread (in feet). Total point scores are also given, following the standard **American Forests** formula (see Appendix E: HOW TO MEASURE A CHAMPION TREE).

The point scores obtained by application of the **American Forests** formula are the gauge used for ranking the individual trees within each species, except in the rare case (see Appendix G) where volume measure is used. The tree with the largest point score is always assigned the rank of Champion. Occasionally two or more trees may receive point scores so similar the difference may lie within the error of measurement; in such case the rank of Co-champion is given to each. The tree next in point score immediately below the Champion (or Co-champions) is then assigned the rank of Challenger; this tree may rise to the higher title if mishap befalls the Champion. All other trees of the INVENTORY are given Honorable Mention, a congratulatory but noncommittal term used for worthy but non-winning contestants.

Each entry in the INVENTORY is accompanied by the name of the owner; the address of the owner (if different from that of the tree) is not provided, but is retained in file as part of the basic nomination documentation. (A listing of all owners is provided in NOMINATORS AND OWNERS.) The location of each tree is given, generally with street address or other specific description, and with city/town and county designations. (Where location is a park or preserve, with the owner a governmental entity, the location is generally designated as if it were the owner.) Map coordinates are also given, based on the U. S. Public Lands Survey System grid of sections (and quarter-sections where possible), township, and range.

The name of the person(s) who first brought the tree to the attention of the Champion Tree Survey, and the year of its nomination, is provided. Where the tree has been measured more than once, the person(s) responsible for updating the record, and year of update, is also provided. (All persons who have nominated or updated trees are listed in NOMINATORS AND OWNERS.)

Most entries are accompanied by a comment paragraph in which supplementary information is provided. This may include measurements obtained at earlier dates, or other pertinent observations. If the tree has been acknowledged as a National champion by **American Forests**, that will be indicated. Where a tree of the same species outside of Florida has been designated the National champion, the point size of the current title

holder is given for comparative purposes. For those species for which no champion has been nominated, data are provided as to the range of the species within Florida and its known size as obtained from herbarium records or other sources.

The comment paragraph will often contain information about the tree that has been provided by landowners, nominators, or other persons. These data will be accompanied by citation of the informant and date. There may also be reference to a published authority (see SELECTED REFERENCES). Where a source is not otherwise indicated, the present investigators are responsible.

Part I.—**NATIVE TREES**

Acacia choriophylla Benth.
Cinnecord

(1)

★ **National Champion**.

Size:			
	Circumference:	14	inches
	Height:	20	feet
	Crown spread:	24	feet
	Total points:	40	points

Owner / location: Phillip Elliott / Cedar Lane, Sugarloaf Key, Monroe Co. [sec 3, T67S, R27E]

Nominator(s) / date: David M. Sinclair, Michael J. Cullen / 1986

Comments: Acknowledged by American Forests (1996 listing).

Acacia farnesiana (L.) Willd.
Sweet Acacia, Huisache

(1)

☆ **Florida Champion**.

Size:			
	Circumference:	28	inches
	Height:	21	feet
	Crown spread:	44	feet
	Total points:	60	points

Owner / location: Steve Chappell / 901 W. 75th St., Marathon, Monroe Co. [sec 14, T66S, R29E]

Nominator(s) / date: Vincent P. Condon / 1994

Comments: The larger of two trees at this location.

This species, associated with aboriginal sites in South Florida, was undoubtedly introduced in pre-Columbian times, and is thus native. Not included in the Checklist of Trees Native to Florida (Ward, 1991).

National champion: Texas (203 points).

(2)

Florida Challenger.

Size:			
	Circumference:	21	inches
	Height:	20	feet
	Crown spread:	32	feet
	Total points:	49	points

Owner / location: Steve Chappell / 901 W. 75th St., Marathon, Monroe Co. [sec 14, T66S, R29E]

Nominator(s) / date: Vincent P. Condon / 1994

Comments: The smaller of two trees at this location.

Acacia macracantha
Humb. & Bonpl. ex Willd.
Long-spine Acacia

Title vacant.

Size:		
	Circumference:	
	Height:	
	Crown spread:	
	Total points:	

Owner / location:

Nominator(s) / date:

Comments: Native in southeast peninsular Florida (Dade County) and the Florida Keys (Ramrod Key).

Several trees with heights of 5—6 meters and with trunk diameters of 8—10 centimeters were discovered in 1963 on Ramrod Key (Ward, 1967). This species is recognized as a tree by American Forests (1996 listing), but as a "species without a champion."

Acacia tortuosa (L.) Willd.
Wild Poponax, Huisachillo

Title vacant.

Size:		
	Circumference:	
	Height:	
	Crown spread:	
	Total points:	

Owner / location:

Nominator(s) / date:

Comments: Native in coastal southwest peninsular Florida (Collier County).

This tree has been found only on aboriginal shell mounds, where it is associated with *Acacia farnesiana*. Both species may share the same history, as pre-Columbian introductions to Florida. On Chokoloskee Island, Collier County, plants have been observed with a height of 4 meters (Ward, 1968). In its range outside of Florida this species seldom attains the stature of a tree. Not included in the Checklist of Trees Native to Florida (Ward, 1991).

National champion: Texas (28 points).

Acer floridanum (Chapm.) Pax
= *Acer barbatum*, misapplied
Florida Maple

(1)

☆ **Florida Champion.**

Size:			
	Circumference:	83	inches
	Height:	83	feet
	Crown spread:	45.5	feet
	Total points:	177	points

Owner / location: Andrews Wildlife Management Area / 3 mi. s. of Fanning Springs, Levy Co. [n.w. 1/4 of sec 7, T11S, R14E]

Nominator(s) / date: Dennis Andrews, Robert W. Simons / 1983

Update: Archie W. Gaylard, Daniel B. Ward / 1994

Comments: Earlier measurements: circ. = 82 in., ht. = 85 ft., spread = 51 ft. (Andrews & Simons, 1983).

National champion: Georgia (255 points).

Acer leucoderme Small
Chalk Maple

Title vacant.

Size:		
	Circumference:	
	Height:	
	Crown spread:	
	Total points:	

Owner / location:

Nominator(s) / date:

Comments: Native in central panhandle Florida.

Herbarium records (FSU, Nov 1996) indicate this species, on the Apalachicola River bluffs near Chattahoochee, Gadsden County, to reach a height of 8 meters, with a trunk circumference of 12 centimeters.

National champions: South Carolina, two trees (95 points, 93 points).

Acer negundo L.
Box Elder

(1)

☆ **Florida Champion.**

Size:			
	Circumference:	80	inches
	Height:	74	feet

Crown spread:	65	feet
Total points:	170	points

Owner / location: Paul Smysor / s.w. corner of N.W. 8th Ave. & N.W. 13th St. overpass, Gainesville, Alachua Co. [n.e. 1/4 of sec 6, T10S, R20E]

Nominator(s) / date: Robert T. Ing, Daniel B. Ward / 1991

Comments: The larger of two large trees at this location.

National champion: Michigan (356 points).

(2)

Florida Challenger.

Size:			
	Circumference:	72	inches
	Height:	65	feet
	Crown spread:	44	feet
	Total points:	148	points

Owner / location: Paul Smysor / s.w. corner of N.W. 8th Ave. & N.W. 13th St. overpass, Gainesville, Alachua Co. [n.e. 1/4 of sec 6, T10S, R20E]

Nominator(s) / date: Robert T. Ing, Daniel B. Ward / 1991

Comments: The second largest tree at this location, just w. of the Florida champion.

Acer rubrum L.
Red Maple

(1)

☆ **Florida Champion.**

Size:			
	Circumference:	155	inches
	Height:	92	feet
	Crown spread:	49	feet
	Total points:	259	points

Owner / location: Welaka State Forest / just w. of fire tower, 2 mi. s. of Welaka, Putnam Co. [s.e. 1/4 of sec 15, T12S, R26E]

Nominator(s) / date: Ned D. Neenan / 1993

Comments: National champions: Tennessee (433 points); Michigan (431 points).

(2)

Emeritus Florida Champion.

Size:			
	Circumference:	130	inches
	Height:	95	feet
	Crown spread:	57.5	feet
	Total points:	239	points

Owner / location: Colin C. Wells / between Fla. 39 and Withlacoochee River, 3 mi. s.e. of Dunellon, Citrus Co. [s.e. 1/4 of sec 7, T17S, R19E]

Nominator(s) / date: Bruce Hill / 1985

(3)

Emeritus Florida Champion.

Size:			
	Circumference:	122	inches
	Height:	107	feet
	Crown spread:	38	feet
	Total points:	239	points

Owner / location: Duval START Center / e. bank of Ortega River, s.w. Jacksonville, Duval Co. [sec 26, T3S, R25E]

Nominator(s) / date: Larry T. Figart / 1987

(4)

Emeritus Florida Champion.

Size:			
	Circumference:	146	inches
	Height:	81	feet
	Crown spread:	47.5	feet
	Total points:	239	points

Owner / location: June Houchins / Merck's Landing, Georgetown, Putnam Co. [sec 37, T13S, R26E]

Nominator(s) / date: Ned D. Neenan / 1988

(5)

Florida Challenger.

Size:			
	Circumference:	113	inches
	Height:	94	feet
	Crown spread:	66	feet
	Total points:	224	points

Owner / location: Conservation Fund, Inc. / w. of Jammes Rd., 700 ft. n. of jct. with Morse Ave., s.w. Jacksonville, Duval Co. [n.e. 1/4 of sec 24, T3S, R25E]

Nominator(s) / date: Buford C. Pruitt, Susan McMurray / 1989

(6)

Honorable Mention.

Size:			
	Circumference:	95	inches
	Height:	90	feet
	Crown spread:	32	feet
	Total points:	193	points

Owner / location: Ventura Ranch / 4 mi. n. of Rutland, 10 mi. w.n.w. of Wildwood, Sumter Co. [s.w. 1/4 of sec 21, T18S, R21E]

Nominator(s) / date: David L. Fogler / 1994

(7)

Emeritus Florida Champion.

Size:			
	Circumference:	98	inches
	Height:	75	feet
	Crown spread:	63.5	feet
	Total points:	189	points

Owner / location: Fred B. Miller / ca. 3 mi. n.e. of

Baldwin, Duval Co. [n. 1/2 of sec 18, T2S, R24E]

Nominator(s) / date: Jim Bryan / 1985

(8)

Honorable Mention.

Size:			
	Circumference:	88	inches
	Height:	71	feet
	Crown spread:	65	feet
	Total points:	175	points

Owner / location: Roberts Oldsmobile, Inc. / 605 Wells Rd., Orange Park, Clay Co. [sec 50, T4S, R26E]

Nominator(s) / date: William L. Rutherford / 1986

Update: Robert W. Ray / 1994

Comments: Earlier measurements: circ. = 76 in., ht. = 67 ft., spread = 58 ft. (Rutherford, 1986).

Acer saccharinum L.
Silver Maple

(1)

☆ Florida Champion.

Size:			
	Circumference:	46	inches
	Height:	64	feet
	Crown spread:	39	feet
	Total points:	120	points

Owner / location: City of Chattahoochee / Apalachicola River bottom, w. edge of Chattahoochee, Gadsden Co. [n.e. 1/4 of sec 32, T4N, R6W]

Nominator(s) / date: Robert T. Ing, Daniel B. Ward / 1995

Comments: National champion: Iowa (461 points).

Acoelorrhaphe wrightii (Griseb. & Wendl.) Becc.
= *Paurotis wrightii* (Griseb. & Wendl.) Britt.
Paurotis Palm

(1)

★ National Champion.

Size:			
	Circumference:	12.5	inches
	Height:	32	feet
	Crown spread:	4	feet
	Total points:	46	points

Owner / location: Mounts Bldg. / 531 N. Military Trail, W. Palm Beach, Palm Beach Co. [sec 36, T43S, R42E]

Nominator(s) / date: Michael Zimmerman / 1989

Comments: Tree was reported to have a "spread" of 28 feet based on full width of 69 stems (M. Zimmerman, Dec 1989); reduced here to 4 feet, the approximate spread of a single stem's foliage.

Acknowledged by American Forests (1996 listing).

(2)

★ **National Co-Champion** (nominee).

Size:	Circumference:	10	inches
	Height:	34	feet
	Crown spread:	4	feet
	Total points:	45	points

Owner / location: Fairchild Tropical Garden / 10901 Old Cutler Rd., Miami, Dade Co. [n.e. 1/4 of sec 7, T55S, R41E]

Nominator(s) / date: Don Evans, Daniel B. Ward / 1995

Comments: Tree has 45—50 full-grown stems plus many shorter ones
National champion: Florida (46 points).

Aesculus pavia L.
Red Buckeye

(1)

☆ **Florida Co-Champion**.

Size:	Circumference:	25	inches
	Height:	36	feet
	Crown spread:	11	feet
	Total points:	64	points

Owner / location: Foley Timber & Land Co. / e. bank of Steinhatchee River, 11 mi. s.s.w. of Mayo, Lafayette Co. [s. 1/2 of sec 5, T7S, R11E]

Nominator(s) / date: Jerry N. Livingston / 1994

Comments: National champions: Michigan (168 points); Virginia (165 points).

(2)

☆ **Florida Co-Champion**.

Size:	Circumference:	27	inches
	Height:	30	feet
	Crown spread:	19	feet
	Total points:	62	points

Owner / location: Myrtle E. Dudley / 0.3 mi. n. of Fla. 26, 4 mi. e. of Newberry, Alachua Co. [s.e. 1/4 of sec 31, T9S, R18E]

Nominator(s) / date: Robert W. Simons / 1979
Update: Robert T. Ing, Daniel B. Ward / 1991

Comments: Miss Dudley (born 1901) says the tree "has been here as long as I can remember" (R. T. Ing & D. B. Ward, Oct 1991). Earlier measurements: circ. = 24 in., ht. = 25 ft., spread = 19 ft. (Simons, 1979).

(3)

Florida Challenger.

Size:	Circumference:	19	inches
	Height:	26	feet
	Crown spread:	22	feet
	Total points:	51	points

Owner / location: Millie Tyre / s.w. corner of Fla. 100 & Magnolia Ave., Florahome, Putnam Co. [n.w. 1/4 of sec 10, T9S, R24E]

Nominator(s) / date: Ned D. Neenan / 1993

Agarista populifolia (Lam.) Judd
= *Leucothoe acuminata* (Ait.) G. Don
Pipestem

(1)

☆ **Florida Champion**.

Size:	Circumference:	10	inches
	Height:	27	feet
	Crown spread:	14.5	feet
	Total points:	41	points

Owner / location: C. G. Money / between Orange Springs Country Inn and Orange Creek, Orange Springs, Marion Co. [sec 25, T11S, R23E]

Nominator(s) / date: Robert T. Ing, Daniel B. Ward / 1991

Comments: This species is usually not thought to be a tree. Its usual habit is to ascend from the base by long, slender, scarcely self-supporting stems. Occasional individuals, however, develop erect axes and reach tree stature and size. Not included in the Checklist of Trees Native to Florida (Ward, 1991).

This specimen could also be considered a national champion since no others have been nominated from other states. But, since this species was not included by Little (1979), it is not acknowledged by American Forests (1996 listing).

Alnus serrulata (Ait.) Willd.
Hazel Alder

(1)

☆ **Florida Champion**.

Size:	Circumference:	11	inches
	Height:	23	feet
	Crown spread:	19	feet
	Total points:	39	points

Owner / location: St. Joseph Land & Development Co. / bank of Crooked Creek, 7 mi. s.s.w. of Chattahoochee, Gadsden Co. [s.e. 1/4 of sec 36, T3N, R7W]

Nominator(s) / date: Robert T. Ing, Daniel B. Ward / 1995

Comments: National champions: New York (55 points); Texas (57 points); Virginia, three trees (59 points, 57 points, 54 points).

Alvaradoa amorphoides Liebm.
Mexican Alvaradoa

(1)

★ **National Champion.**

Size:	Circumference:	25	inches
	Height:	15	feet
	Crown spread:	9	feet
	Total points:	42	points

Owner / location: Camp Owaissa Bauer / 17001 S.W. 264th St., 3 mi. n. of Homestead, Dade Co. [s. 1/2 of sec 30, T56S, R39E]

Nominator(s) / date: John G. Cordy, Jim Eggert / 1983

Update: American Forests, source unstated / 1991

Update: Carol L. Lippincott / 1993

Comments: Earlier measurements: circ. = 12 in., ht. = 35 ft., spread = 14 ft. (Cordy & Eggert, 1983); circ. = 22 in., ht. = 35 ft., spread = 14 ft. (A.F., 1992 listing). Tree survived Hurricane Andrew (Aug 1992), but with height reduced to 15 ft. (C. L. Lippincott, July 1993).

Acknowledged by American Forests (1996 listing).

Amelanchier arborea (Michx. f.) Fern.
Downy Serviceberry

(1)

☆ **Florida Champion.**

Size:	Circumference:	18	inches
	Height:	40	feet
	Crown spread:	17	feet
	Total points:	62	points

Owner / location: Charles E. Salter / 2206 Durward Ride, Tallahassee, Leon Co. [n.e. 1/4 of sec 19, T1N, R1E]

Nominator(s) / date: Robert T. Ing, Daniel B. Ward / 1993

Comments: Cultivated tree, planted about 1970 (C. E. Salter, Sept 1993).

National champion: Virginia (181 points).

Amorpha fruticosa L.
Indigo-bush

Title vacant.

Size:	Circumference:		
	Height:		
	Crown spread:		
	Total points:		

Owner / location:

Nominator(s) / date:

Comments: Native in north and central Florida.

A single-stemmed, erect plant, but only dubiously reaching a size sufficient to merit treatment as a tree. Herbarium records (FLAS, Jan 1995) indicate this species, near Fanning Springs, Dixie County, to reach a height of 5 meters. Since this species was not included by Little (1979), it is not acknowledged by American Forests (1996 listing).

Amphitecna latifolia (Mill.) Gentry
= *Enallagma latifolia* (Mill.) Small
Black Calabash

Title vacant.

Size:	Circumference:		
	Height:		
	Crown spread:		
	Total points:		

Owner / location:

Nominator(s) / date:

Comments: Assignment of this species as native to Florida rests on uncertain evidence. It is presently known in the state only in cultivation or in situations suggesting recent escape. However, an early publication (C. S. Sargent, 1894) reported trees to have been known since 1859 at two locations on the west shore of Biscayne Bay. One may surmise, in view of the inconsequential utility of this plant to European man, it was a pre-Columbian introduction from the West Indies where it appears to be native.

Herbarium records (FLAS, Jan 1995; FTG, Dec 1995) indicate this species, on Sanibel Id., Lee County, to reach a height of 7 meters, and in Cutler Hammock, Dade Co., to attain 8 meters. This tree is treated by American Forests (1996 listing) as a "species without a champion."

Amyris balsamifera L.
Balsam Torchwood

Title vacant.

Size:	Circumference:		
	Height:		
	Crown spread:		
	Total points:		

Owner / location:

Nominator(s) / date:

Comments: Native in southern peninsular Florida (Dade County).

Rare; a solitary "small tree" was observed in Matheson Hammock, Dade County (G. Avery notes, Sept 1966). This species is recognized as a tree by American Forests (1996 listing), but as a "species without a champion."

Amyris elemifera L.
Torchwood

(1)

★ National Champion.

Size:			
	Circumference:	18	inches
	Height:	22	feet
	Crown spread:	15	feet
	Total points:	44	points

Owner / location: Lignumvitae Key State Botanical Site / Lignumvitae Key, Monroe Co. [n.w. 1/4 of sec 2, T64S, R36E]

Nominator(s) / date: Michael J. Cullen, David M. Sinclair / 1986

Update: Robert Rose / 1993

Comments: Earlier measurements: circ. = 16 in., ht. = 22 ft., spread = 15 ft. (Cullen & Sinclair, 1986); height & spread were not remeasured (R. Rose, Jan 1993).

Acknowledged by American Forests (1996 listing).

(2)

Florida Challenger.

Size:			
	Circumference:	18	inches
	Height:	15	feet
	Crown spread:	9.5	feet
	Total points:	35	points

Owner / location: Biscayne National Park / s. end of Totten Key, Dade Co. [s.w. 1/4 of sec 21, T58S, R41E]

Nominator(s) / date: Clifford Shaw, Jim Tilmant / 1975

Update: Diane Riggs / 1995

Comments: Earlier measurements: circ. = 12 in., ht. = 24 ft., spread = 13 ft. (Shaw & Tilmant, 1975).

Following Hurricane Andrew, 24 Aug 1992, this tree, with other champions on Totten Key, was presumed dead (J. M. Parks & R. Curry, Nov 1993). It did survive, but with height and crown spread appreciably reduced (D. Riggs, July 1995).

Annona glabra L.
Pond Apple

(1)

★ National Champion.

Size:			
	Circumference:	125	inches
	Height:	44	feet
	Crown spread:	47	feet
	Total points:	181	points

Owner / location: Parrot Jungle and Gardens / 11000 S.W. 57th Ave., Miami, Dade Co. [n.e. 1/4 of sec 12, T55S, R40E]

Nominator(s) / date: Carol L. Lippincott / 1989

Comments: Acknowledged by American Forests (1996 listing).

(2)

Florida Challenger.

Size:			
	Circumference:	92	inches
	Height:	48	feet
	Crown spread:	46	feet
	Total points:	152	points

Owner / location: F. E. Boe / 2124 E. Main St., Pahokee, Palm Beach Co. [sec 4, T42S, R37E]

Nominator(s) / date: Michael J. Greenstein, Norman E. Masencup / 1994

(3)

Honorable Mention.

Size:			
	Circumference:	25	inches
	Height:	36	feet
	Crown spread:	14	feet
	Total points:	65	points

Owner / location: Lignumvitae Key State Botanical Site / at waterhole, Lignumvitae Key, Monroe Co. [n.w. 1/4 of sec 2, T64S, R36E]

Nominator(s) / date: Robert Rose, Vincent P. Condon / 1995

Comments: The larger of two trees at this location.

(4)

Honorable Mention.

Size:			
	Circumference:	25	inches
	Height:	31	feet
	Crown spread:	20	feet
	Total points:	61	points

Owner / location: Key Largo Hammocks State Botanical Site / n. end of Key Largo, Monroe Co. [sec 24, T59S, R40E]

Nominator(s) / date: Jeanne M. Parks / 1989

(5)

Honorable Mention.

Size:			
	Circumference:	24	inches
	Height:	32	feet
	Crown spread:	15.5	feet
	Total points:	60	points

Owner / location: Lignumvitae Key State Botanical Site / at waterhole, Lignumvitae Key, Monroe Co. [n.w. 1/4 of sec 2, T64S, R36E]

Nominator(s) / date: Robert Rose, Vincent P. Condon / 1995

Comments: The smaller of two trees at this location.

Aralia spinosa L.
Devil's-walkingstick

(1)

☆ **Florida Champion.**

Size:	Circumference:	15	inches
	Height:	40	feet
	Crown spread:	14.5	feet
	Total points:	59	points

Owner / location: San Felasco Hammock State Preserve / n. of Fla. 232, 8 mi. n.w. of Gainesville, Alachua Co. [sec 8, T9S, R19E]

Nominator(s) / date: Robert W. Simons, Daniel B. Ward / 1991

Comments: San Felasco Hammock has been the location of a series of National champion *Aralia spinosa*. Two National co-champions were nominated in 1974; these were deposed in 1976 by a near-by larger tree; about 1980 this tree died and was replaced in 1982 with an 81-point National champion; by 1990 the replacement was also dead and National championship status was transferred to smaller trees outside of Florida (R. W. Simons, Mar 1994).

National champion: Tennessee (98 points).

(2)

Florida Challenger.

Size:	Circumference:	11	inches
	Height:	38	feet
	Crown spread:	14	feet
	Total points:	53	points

Owner / location: O'Leno State Park / 0.2 mi. w. of River Rise, Alachua Co. [s.e. 1/4 of sec 15, T7S, R17E]

Nominator(s) / date: Robert T. Ing, Daniel B. Ward / 1993

Ardisia escallonioides Schlecht. & Cham.
Marlberry

Title vacant.

Size:	Circumference:		
	Height:		
	Crown spread:		
	Total points:		

Owner / location:

Nominator(s) / date:

Comments: Native in central and southern peninsular Florida.

Herbarium records (FLAS, Jan 1995) indicate this species, at Pinecrest, Monroe County, to reach a height of 20 ft. This species is recognized as a tree by American Forests (1996 listing), but as a "species without a champion."

Asimina obovata (Willd.) Nash
Flag Pawpaw

Title vacant.

Size:	Circumference:		
	Height:		
	Crown spread:		
	Total points:		

Owner / location:

Nominator(s) / date:

Comments: Native in central peninsular Florida.

Herbarium records (FLAS, Jan 1995) indicate this species, at Silver Glen Springs, Marion County, to reach a height of 4 meters. This species is recognized as a tree by American Forests (1996 listing), but as a "species without a champion."

Asimina parviflora (Michx.) Dunal
Small-flowered Pawpaw

(1)

★ **National Champion.**

Size:	Circumference:	21	inches
	Height:	24	feet
	Crown spread:	16.5	feet
	Total points:	49	points

Owner / location: Lake Jem County Park / 3.5 mi. n.e. of Astatula, Lake Co. [n.w. 1/4 of sec 14, T20S, R26E]

Nominator(s) / date: H. Terrell Davis / 1980

Update: Robert W. Simons, Daniel B. Ward / 1993

Comments: Earlier measurements: circ. = 17 in., ht. = 23 ft., spread = 20 ft. (Davis, 1980).

This species is usually reported to be a shrub; a plant of tree size is indeed very rare. Not included in the Checklist of Trees Native to Florida (Ward, 1991).

This tree was originally reported as *Asimina triloba* (Davis, 1980), and was previously assumed to be Florida champion for that species. But the much smaller leaves and the copious reddish-brown pubescence on the twigs and petioles is unlike that species and is characteristic of *A. parviflora* (D. B. Ward & R. W. Simons, July 1993).

Acknowledged by American Forests (1996 listing).

Asimina triloba (L.) Dunal
Pawpaw

Title vacant.

Size:	Circumference:		
	Height:		
	Crown spread:		

Total points:

Owner / location:

Nominator(s) / date:

Comments: In Florida the native range of *Asimina triloba* is restricted the the central Panhandle, where it seldom reaches the size and stature of a tree. Herbarium records (FLAS, Jan 1995; FSU, Nov 1996) indicate this species, at Aspalaga Landing, Gadsden County, to reach a height of 35 ft., with a trunk circumference of 44 in.

National champion: Mississippi (160 points).

Ateramnus lucidus (Sw.) Rothm.
= *Gymnanthes lucida* Sw.
Crabwood, Oysterwood

(1)

★ **National Champion.**

Size:			
	Circumference:	17	inches
	Height:	33	feet
	Crown spread:	8	feet
	Total points:	52	points

Owner / location: Key Largo Hammocks State Botanical Site / n. end of Key Largo, Monroe Co. [sec 26, T59S, R40E]

Nominator(s) / date: Jeanne M. Parks / 1989

Comments: Acknowledged by American Forests (1996 listing).

(2)

Emeritus National Champion.

Size:			
	Circumference:	14.5	inches
	Height:	24	feet
	Crown spread:	11	feet
	Total points:	42	points

Owner / location: Lignumvitae Key State Botanical Site / Lignumvitae Key, Monroe Co. [n.e. 1/4 of sec 3, T64S, R36E]

Nominator(s) / date: Michael J. Cullen, David M. Sinclair / 1986

Update: Robert Rose / 1993

Comments: Earlier measurements: circ. = 13 in., ht. = 24 ft., spread = 11 ft. (Cullen & Sinclair, 1986); height & spread were not remeasured (R. Rose, Jan 1993).

Avicennia germinans (L.) L.
= *Avicennia nitida* Jacq.
Black Mangrove

(1)

★ **National Champion** (nominee).

Size:			
	Circumference:	101	inches
	Height:	43	feet
	Crown spread:	57	feet
	Total points:	158	points

Owner / location: Mound Key Archaeological Site / n. end of Mound Key, Estero Bay, Lee Co. [sec 36, T46S, R24E]

Nominator(s) / date: Larry Fooks, Arden Arrington / 1996

Comments: Trunk was measured at 1.5 ft., the minimum circumference; circumference was 113 in. at 4.5 ft. (L. Fooks, Mar 1996).

(2)

★ **National Champion.**

Size:			
	Circumference:	81	inches
	Height:	56	feet
	Crown spread:	31.5	feet
	Total points:	145	points

Owner / location: Ricardo Cadenas / s.e. of Tarpon Basin, Key Largo, Monroe Co. [s.e. 1/4 of sec 22, T61S, R39E]

Nominator(s) / date: Vincent P. Condon / 1995

Comments: Acknowledged by American Forests (1996 listing).

(3)

Florida Challenger.

Size:			
	Circumference:	40	inches
	Height:	49	feet
	Crown spread:	46	feet
	Total points:	101	points

Owner / location: Hugh Taylor Birch State Park / 3109 E. Sunrise Blvd., Ft. Lauderdale, Broward Co. [s.e. 1/4 of sec 36, T49S, R42E]

Nominator(s) / date: Jim Higgins / 1995

Comments: A former National champion, now deceased, attained a height of 61 ft.

Baccharis halimifolia L.
Common Saltbush, Groundsel-tree

(1)

☆ **Florida Champion.**

Size:			
	Circumference:	18	inches
	Height:	10	feet
	Crown spread:	7.5	feet
	Total points:	30	points

Owner / location: Jenkins Middle School / N. 19th St., Palatka, Putnam Co. [n.e. 1/4 of sec 1, T10S, T26E]

Nominator(s) / date: Ned D. Neenan / 1990

Update: Ned D. Neenan / 1993

Comments: Earlier measurements: circ. = 18 in., ht. = 17 ft., spread = 17 ft. (Neenan, 1990).

National champion: Georgia (42 points).

Betula nigra L.
River Birch

(1)
☆ **Florida Champion.**

Size:			
	Circumference:	88	inches
	Height:	92	feet
	Crown spread:	63	feet
	Total points:	196	points

Owner / location: Soterra, Inc. / e. bank of Apalachicola River, 0.5 mi. s. of Int. 10, 6 mi. s.w. of Chatta-hoochee, Gadsden Co. [s.e. 1/4 of sec 26, T3N, R7W]

Nominator(s) / date: Robert W. Simons, Angus K. Gholson, Robert K. Godfrey / 1993

Comments: National champion: Alabama (293 points).

(2)
Florida Challenger.

Size:			
	Circumference:	82	inches
	Height:	89	feet
	Crown spread:	62.5	feet
	Total points:	187	points

Owner / location: (unknown) / Wannee, e. bank of Suwannee River, 5 mi. s.w. of Bell, Gilchrist Co. [sec 7, T9S, R14E]

Nominator(s) / date: Jerry N. Livingston, Sammy Poore / 1988

(3)
Honorable Mention.

Size:			
	Circumference:	72	inches
	Height:	75	feet
	Crown spread:	42.5	feet
	Total points:	158	points

Owner / location: (unknown) / Troy Springs, w. bank of Suwannee River, 11 mi. e.s.e. of Mayo, Lafayette Co. [sec 36, T5S, R13E]

Nominator(s) / date: Jerry N. Livingston, Owen McCall / 1987

(4)
Emeritus Florida Champion.

Size:			
	Circumference:	67	inches
	Height:	65	feet
	Crown spread:	43.5	feet
	Total points:	143	points

Owner / location: Andrews Wildlife Management Area / just e. of Suwannee River, 4 mi. s.w. of Fanning Springs, Levy Co. [n.w. 1/4 of sec 12, T11S, R13E]

Nominator(s) / date: Dennis Andrews, Robert W. Simons / 1983

Update: Archie W. Gaylard, Daniel B. Ward / 1994

Comments: Earlier measurements: circ. = 65 in., ht. = 65 ft., spread = 43 ft. (Andrews & Simons, 1983).

Bourreria ovata Miers
Bahama Strongback

(1)
★ **National Champion.**

Size:			
	Circumference:	24	inches
	Height:	28	feet
	Crown spread:	23	feet
	Total points:	58	points

Owner / location: Key Largo Hammocks State Botanical Site / n. end of Key Largo, Monroe Co. [sec 24, T59S, R40E]

Nominator(s) / date: Jeanne M. Parks, Wayne Hoffman / 1990

Update: Jeanne M. Parks / 1993

Comments: Tree is in good health; not remeasured (J. M. Parks, May 1993).

"Strongback" is the Bahamian name, given because of presumed stimulative medicinal uses; in Florida, often mis-cited as "strongbark."

Acknowledged by American Forests (1996 listing).

(2)
Florida Challenger.

Size:			
	Circumference:	6	inches
	Height:	15	feet
	Crown spread:	21	feet
	Total points:	26	points

Owner / location: Biscayne National Park / s. end of Totten Key, Dade Co. [s.w. 1/4 of sec 21, T58S, R41E]

Nominator(s) / date: Diane Riggs / 1995

Bourreria radula (Poir. in Lam.) G. Don
Rough Strongback

(1)
★ **National Champion.**

Size:			
	Circumference:	22	inches
	Height:	23	feet
	Crown spread:	18.5	feet
	Total points:	50	points

Owner / location: Marjorie Butcko / 810 Florida St., Key West, Monroe Co. [n.e. 1/4 of sec 6, T68S, R25E]

Nominator(s) / date: Vincent P. Condon / 1995

Comments: Acknowledged by American Forests (1996 listing).

Bucida spinosa (Northr.) Jennings
Ming-tree, Spiny Black Olive

(1)
☆ **Florida Champion.**

Size:			
	Circumference:	55	inches
	Height:	28	feet

Crown spread:	32	feet
Total points:	91	points

Owner / location: City of Hollywood / 1020 N. North Lake Dr., Hollywood, Broward Co. [n.e. 1/4 of sec 14, T51S, R42E]

Nominator(s) / date: David A. Spicer / 1990

Comments: Although usually assumed to be only in cultivation or escaped from cultivation, this tree is seemingly native in south peninsular Florida (Dade County). Not recognized as a native tree by Little (1979), nor by American Forests (1996 listing). Not included in the Checklist of Trees Native to Florida (Ward, 1991).

Bumelia anomala (Sarg.) R. B. Clark
Alachua Buckthorn

(1)

☆ **Florida Champion.**

Size:	Circumference:	16	inches
	Height:	27	feet
	Crown spread:	21	feet
	Total points:	48	points

Owner / location: Paynes Prairie State Preserve / e. of headquarters, 2 mi. s.s.e. of Gainesville, Alachua Co. [sec 22, T10S, R20E]

Nominator(s) / date: Robert W. Simons / 1991

Comments: A *very* rare tree! Two trees are known at this location (2nd tree: circ. = 14 in.); about 15 small trees are growing on rims of sinks in the Preserve headquarters area (planted by Simons in 1979). One tree is present at Blue Springs, Madison Co.; 5 trees are known along Silver River, Marion Co. (D. B. Ward & R. T. Ing, Oct 1991.)

This small population was acknowledged to be a distinct species by Godfrey (1988) and Ward (1991), but is otherwise almost wholly unknown. This individual could also be considered a National champion since the species is endemic to Florida. But, since this name was treated as a synonym of *Bumelia tenax* by Little (1979), it is not acknowledged by American Forests (1996 listing).

Bumelia celastrina HBK.
Saffron Plum, Tropical Buckthorn

(1)

☆ **Florida Champion.**

Size:	Circumference:	33	inches
	Height:	29	feet
	Crown spread:	33	feet
	Total points:	70	points

Owner / location: Beachview Golf Club / s.w. of jct.

Donax St. & Periwinkle Way, e. Sanibel Id., Lee Co. [n. 1/2 of sec 30, T46S, R23E]

Nominator(s) / date: Richard W. Workman, Jeffrey S. Mangun / 1991

Comments: National champion: Texas (93 points).

(2)

Florida Challenger.

Size:	Circumference:	34	inches
	Height:	25	feet
	Crown spread:	26	feet
	Total points:	67	points

Owner / location: County of Monroe / Planning Dept., 5100 College Rd., Stock Island, Monroe Co. (n.e. 1/4 of sec 34, T67S, R25E]

Nominator(s) / date: Vincent P. Condon / 1994

(3)

Honorable Mention.

Size:	Circumference:	15	inches
	Height:	23	feet
	Crown spread:	13	feet
	Total points:	41	points

Owner / location: Lignumvitae Key State Botanical Site / Lignumvitae Key, Monroe Co. [n.w. 1/4 of sec 2, T64S, R36E]

Nominator(s) / date: Ken Roundtree, Frank L. Zickar / 1986

(4)

Not ranked; possibly still alive, but not verified for many years.

Size:	Circumference:	27	inches
	Height:	23	feet
	Crown spread:	17	feet
	Total points:	54	points

Owner / location: National Key Deer Refuge / Cactus Hammock, s. end of Big Pine Key, Monroe Co. [n.e. 1/4 of sec 1, T67S, R29E]

Nominator(s) / date: Robert W. Simons, Mary Lee Eletz / 1979

Comments: This tree has not been seen in recent years; a recent search of part of the hammock did not find it (T. Wilmers, June 1993).

Bumelia lanuginosa (Michx.) Pers.
Woolly Buckthorn, Gum Bumelia

(1)

☆ **Florida Champion.**

Size:	Circumference:	26	inches
	Height:	43	feet
	Crown spread:	19.5	feet
	Total points:	74	points

Owner / location: James A. Corbett / bluff above
Suwannee River, l.5 mi. w. of U.S. 129, 6 mi. s. of
Jasper, Hamilton Co. [n.w. 1/4 of sec 7, T1S, R14E]

Nominator(s) / date: Robert T. Ing, Daniel B. Ward /
1993

Comments: National champion: Texas (190 points).

(2)

Florida Challenger.

Size:			
	Circumference:	13	inches
	Height:	20	feet
	Crown spread:	18	feet
	Total points:	38	points

Owner / location: Ravine State Gardens / Twigg St.,
Palatka, Putnam Co. [s.e. 1/4 of sec 12, T10S, R26E]

Nominator(s) / date: Ned D. Neenan / 1993

(3)

Honorable Mention.

Size:			
	Circumference:	13.5	inches
	Height:	14	feet
	Crown spread:	22	feet
	Total points:	33	points

Owner / location: John H. Sameck / 2620 N.W. 8th St.,
Gainesville, Alachua Co. [s.w. 1/4 of sec 29, T9S,
R20E]

Nominator(s) / date: Robert T. Ing, Daniel B. Ward /
1992

Bumelia lycioides (L.) Pers.
Smooth Buckthorn

(1)

★ National Champion (nominee).

Size:			
	Circumference:	17	inches
	Height:	58	feet
	Crown spread:	23	feet
	Total points:	81	points

Owner / location: Martin Marietta Materials, Inc. / w.
end of Satsuma Rd., Chattahoochee, Gadsden Co.
[n.e. 1/4 of sec 5, T3N, R6W]

Nominator(s) / date: Angus K. Gholson, Robert T. Ing,
Daniel B. Ward / 1995

Comments: National champion: Missouri (68 points).

Bumelia tenax (L.) Willd.
Tough Buckthorn, Tough Bumelia

(1)

★ National Champion.

Size:			
	Circumference:	41	inches
	Height:	41	feet
	Crown spread:	28	feet
	Total points:	89	points

Owner / location: Amelia Island State Recreational Area
/ s. tip of Amelia Id., Nassau Co. [sec 31, T1N, R29E]

Nominator(s) / date: Buford C. Pruitt / 1987

Comments: Acknowledged by American Forests (1996
listing).

(2)

Florida Challenger.

Size:			
	Circumference:	31	inches
	Height:	36	feet
	Crown spread:	32	feet
	Total points:	75	points

Owner / location: Rollins State Park / ranger's resi-
dence, s.e. side of Ft. George Id., Duval Co. [sec 37,
T1S, R29E]

Nominator(s) / date: Buford C. Pruitt / 1984

Bursera simaruba (L.) Sarg.
Gumbo-limbo

(1)

★ National Co-Champion.

Size:			
	Circumference:	125	inches
	Height:	41	feet
	Crown spread:	48	feet
	Total points:	178	points

Owner / location: St. Mary's Catholic Church / 1010
Windsor Lane, Key West, Monroe Co. [s.w. 1/4 of sec
1, T68S, R25E]

Nominator(s) / date: William S. Hubard, Beverlee Wang /
1992

Comments: Acknowledged by American Forests (1996
listing).

(2)

★ National Co-Champion.

Size:			
	Circumference:	99	inches
	Height:	64	feet
	Crown spread:	57	feet
	Total points:	177	points

Owner / location: City of Ft. Lauderdale / Snyder Park,
3299 S.W. 4th Ave., Ft. Lauderdale, Broward Co.
[s.w. 1/4 of sec 22, T50S, R42E]

Nominator(s) / date: Kathy Preston, Frank L. Zickar / 1995

Comments: Acknowledged by American Forests (1996
listing).

(3)

★ National Co-Champion.

Size:			
	Circumference:	108	inches
	Height:	55	feet
	Crown spread:	51.5	feet
	Total points:	176	points

Owner / location: Willard Scott / 15687 Captiva Dr., Captiva Id., Lee Co. [center of sec 34, T45S, R21E]

Nominator(s) / date: Jeffrey S. Mangun / 1992

Comments: Acknowledged by American Forests (1996 listing).

(4)

Florida Challenger.

Size:	Circumference:	102	inches
	Height:	48	feet
	Crown spread:	55	feet
	Total points:	164	points

Owner / location: National Key Deer Refuge / Watson Hammock, w. side of Big Pine Key, Monroe Co. [s.w. 1/4 of sec 9, T66S, R29E]

Nominator(s) / date: Michael K. Hennessey / 1992

(5)

Honorable Mention.

Size:	Circumference:	104	inches
	Height:	32	feet
	Crown spread:	57	feet
	Total points:	150	points

Owner / location: Charles Deering Estate / 16701 S.W. 72nd Ave., Miami, Dade Co. [s.e. 1/4 of sec 26, T55S, R40E]

Nominator(s) / date: Roger L. Hammer, William G. Miller / 1993

Byrsonima lucida (Mill.) DC.
Locust-berry, Byrsonima

(1)

★ National Champion.

Size:	Circumference:	30	inches
	Height:	31	feet
	Crown spread:	37.5	feet
	Total points:	70	points

Owner / location: Key West Botanical Garden Society / Botanical Garden, Stock Island, Monroe Co. [n.e. 1/4 of sec 34, T67S, R25E]

Nominator(s) / date: Eloise Boon, Vincent P. Condon / 1995

Comments: Acknowledged by American Forests (1996 listing).

(2)

★ National Co-Champion (nominee).

Size:	Circumference:	31	inches
	Height:	35	feet
	Crown spread:	16.5	feet
	Total points:	70	points

Owner / location: National Key Deer Refuge / s. of road,

1 mi. e. of bridge, No Name Key, Monroe Co. [s.w. 1/4 of sec 18, T66S, R30E]

Nominator(s) / date: T. Ann Williams, Vincent P. Condon / 1995

(3)

Florida Challenger.

Size:	Circumference:	32	inches
	Height:	22	feet
	Crown spread:	26	feet
	Total points:	61	points

Owner / location: Fred Guarnieri / 14 Colson Dr., Cudjoe Key, Monroe Co. [s.w. 1/4 of sec 29, T66S, R28E]

Nominator(s) / date: Patricia L. McNeese / 1995

(4)

Honorable Mention.

Size:	Circumference:	28	inches
	Height:	22	feet
	Crown spread:	29	feet
	Total points:	57	points

Owner / location: Cristopher K. Harlan Trust / E. Fifth Ave., Key West, Monroe Co. [n.w. 1/4 of sec 32, T66S, R28E]

Nominator(s) / date: Dianna L. Stevenson, Vincent P. Condon / 1995

Calyptranthes pallens Griseb.
Spicewood, Pale Lidflower

(1)

★ National Champion.

Size:	Circumference:	49	inches
	Height:	40	feet
	Crown spread:	24	feet
	Total points:	95	points

Owner / location: Viscaya Museum & Gardens / Miami, Dade Co. [sec 14, T54S, R41E]

Nominator(s) / date: Carol L. Lippincott / 1993

Comments: Acknowledged by American Forests (1996 listing).

(2)

Emeritus National Champion.

Size:	Circumference:	18	inches
	Height:	33	feet
	Crown spread:	18.5	feet
	Total points:	56	points

Owner / location: Key Largo Hammocks State Botanical Site / n. end of Key Largo, Monroe Co. [sec 24, T59S, R40E]

Nominator(s) / date: Jeanne M. Parks / 1989

Update: Jeanne M. Parks / 1993

Comments: Tree is in good health; not remeasured (J. M. Parks, Oct 1993).

Calyptranthes zuzygium (L.) Sw.
Myrtle-of-the-river

Title vacant.

Size: Circumference:

          Height:

          Crown spread:

          Total points:

Owner / location:

Nominator(s) / date:

Comments: Native in south peninsular Florida (Dade County).

Trees 6–7 m. tall have been observed along the Gumbo-limbo Trail, Everglades National Park, Dade County (G. Avery notes, Mar 1967). This species is recognized as a tree by American Forests (1996 listing), but as a "species without a champion."

Canella winterana (L.) Gaertn.
Wild Cinnamon

(1)

★ **National Champion.**

Size:	Circumference:	21	inches
	Height:	29	feet
	Crown spread:	15	feet
	Total points:	54	points

Owner / location: Key Largo Hammocks State Botanical Site / n. end of Key Largo, Monroe Co. [sec 24, T59S, R40E]

Nominator(s) / date: Jeanne M. Parks / 1989

Comments: Acknowledged by American Forests (1996 listing).

(2)

Florida Challenger.

Size:	Circumference:	12	inches
	Height:	20	feet
	Crown spread:	15	feet
	Total points:	36	points

Owner / location: National Key Deer Refuge / e. side of No Name Key, Monroe Co. [s.e. 1/4 of sec 18, T66S, R30E]

Nominator(s) / date: Chad Bryant / 1993

Capparis cynophallophora L.
Jamaica Caper

(1)

★ **National Champion.**

Size:	Circumference:	25	inches
	Height:	15	feet
	Crown spread:	20	feet
	Total points:	45	points

Owner / location: (unknown) / n. end of Buck Key, just e. of Captiva Id., Lee Co. [sec 35, T45S, R21E]

Nominator(s) / date: David Fox, Dee Slinkard / 1984

Comments: Acknowledged by American Forests (1996 listing).

Capparis flexuosa L.
Limber Caper

Title vacant.

Size: Circumference:

          Height:

          Crown spread:

          Total points:

Owner / location:

Nominator(s) / date:

Comments: Native in coastal central and south peninsular Florida.

Herbarium records (FLAS, Jan 1995) indicate this species, near Turtle Mound, Volusia County, to reach a height of 3.5 meters. This species is recognized as a tree by American Forests (1996 listing), but as a "species without a champion."

Carica papaya L.
Papaya

(1)

★ **National Champion** (nominee).

Size:	Circumference:	27	inches
	Height:	17	feet
	Crown spread:	11	feet
	Total points:	47	points

Owner / location: Marie Selby Botanical Gardens / 800 S. Palm Ave., Sarasota, Sarasota Co. [n.w. 1/4 of sec 30, T36S, R18E]

Nominator(s) / date: Richard W. Workman / 1995

Comments: This species was recognized as a tree by American Forests, as a "species without a champion" (1996 listing). It is widely present in South Florida hammocks (where it is native) and is a vigorous member of the post-hurricane regrowth.

This species is considered "native" since trees in Everglades hammocks have small fruits, unlike modern cultivated varieties, and papaya seeds are found in Calusa Indian middens. Papaya is, of course, "introduced" in that its original home was Central America, but it was surely brought to Florida prior to advent of European man.

Carpinus caroliniana Walt.
Blue Beech, Hornbeam

(1)

☆ **Florida Champion.**

Size:			
	Circumference:	60	inches
	Height:	43	feet
	Crown spread:	52	feet
	Total points:	116	points

Owner / location: Suwannee River Water Management District / Holton Spring, Holton Creek Wildlife Management Area, n. side of Suwannee River, 3 mi. e. of Noble's Ferry bridge, 10 mi. s.w. of Jasper, Hamilton Co. [s.w. 1/4 of sec 31, T1N, R13E]

Nominator(s) / date: Robert W. Simons, Daniel B. Ward / 1993

Comments: Near-by trees 44 in. and 41 in. circ. (R. W. Simons & D. B. Ward, Aug 1993).

National champion: New York (178 points).

(2)

Florida Challenger.

Size:			
	Circumference:	47	inches
	Height:	45	feet
	Crown spread:	39	feet
	Total points:	102	points

Owner / location: J. A. Bielling / 1.25 mi. s. of Fla. 238, 10 mi. w.s.w. of Lake Butler, Union Co. [s.e. 1/4 of sec 9, T6S, R18E]

Nominator(s) / date: Timothy S. Worley / 1993

(3)

Emeritus Florida Champion.

Size:			
	Circumference:	30.5	inches
	Height:	51	feet
	Crown spread:	25	feet
	Total points:	88	points

Owner / location: Aycock Trust Co. / 8 mi. s. of Mayo, Lafayette Co. [n.e. 1/4 of sec 23, T6S, R11E]

Nominator(s) / date: Jerry N. Livingston / 1989

Carya aquatica (Michx. f.) Nutt.
Water Hickory

(1)

★ **National Champion.**

Size:			
	Circumference:	228	inches
	Height:	101	feet
	Crown spread:	85	feet
	Total points:	350	points

Owner / location: St. Johns River Water Management District / Barr's Landing, e. shore of Lake George, 1 mi. s. of county line, 4 mi. w.n.w. of Seville, Volusia Co. [n.w. 1/4 of sec 39, T13S, R27E]

Nominator(s) / date: Betty Rich / 1981

Update: Robert W. Simons, Daniel B. Ward / 1993

Comments: This tree was originally reported as *Carya illinoinensis* (Rich, 1981), and was recently assumed to be the Florida champion for that species. But the fruits are small, with prominent longitudinal wings, and the leaflets are narrowly lanceolate; the tree is clearly *C. aquatica* (R. W. Simons & D. B. Ward, June 1993).

Earlier measurements: circ. = 219 in., ht. = 104 ft., spread = 90 ft. (Rich, 1981).

Acknowledged by American Forests (1996 listing).

(2)

Florida Challenger.

Size:			
	Circumference:	149	inches
	Height:	112	feet
	Crown spread:	66	feet
	Total points:	278	points

Owner / location: Louis Atkins / 0.5 mi. w. of Apalachicola River, 6 mi. n.n.e. of Blountstown, Calhoun Co. [n.w. 1/4 of sec 36, T2N, R8W]

Nominator(s) / date: Jake Almond / 1990

Carya cordiformis (Wangenh.) K. Koch
Bitternut Hickory

(1)

☆ **Florida Champion.**

Size:			
	Circumference:	73	inches
	Height:	120	feet
	Crown spread:	41.5	feet
	Total points:	203	points

Owner / location: Tall Timbers Research, Inc. / Fla. 12, 15 mi. n.n.e. of Tallahassee, Leon Co. [s.w. 1/4 of sec 16, T3N, R1E]

Nominator(s) / date: W. Wilson Baker, Charles E. Salter, Daniel B. Ward / 1995

Comments: National champion: Virginia (342 points).

Carya floridana Sarg.
Scrub Hickory

(1)

★ **National Champion.**

Size:			
	Circumference:	62	inches
	Height:	47	feet
	Crown spread:	48	feet
	Total points:	121	points

Owner / location: John B. Combs / w. side of U.S. 27, e. end of Lake Josephine, 6 mi. s. of Sebring, Highlands Co. [n.w. 1/4 of sec 34, T35S, R29E]

Nominator(s) / date: Jim Thorsen, Robert W. Simons / 1992

Comments: Acknowledged by American Forests (1996 listing).

Carya glabra (Mill.) Sweet
Pignut Hickory

(1)

★ **National Co-Champion** (nominee).

Size:			
	Circumference:	177	inches
	Height:	109	feet
	Crown spread:	90	feet
	Total points:	309	points

Owner / location: Mary Ann Lee / 5629 Weller Ave., Jacksonville, Duval Co. [s. 1/2 of sec 41, T2S, R27E]

Nominator(s) / date: Charles R. Mould / 1980

Update: Robert T. Ing, Daniel B. Ward / 1993

Comments: Earlier measurements: circ. = 168 in., ht. = 104 ft., spread = 80 ft. (Mould, 1980).

National champions: Tennessee (298 points); Maryland (247 points).

(2)

★ **National Co-Champion** (nominee).

Size:			
	Circumference:	195	inches
	Height:	86	feet
	Crown spread:	101	feet
	Total points:	306	points

Owner / location: Elizabeth Butts / e. side of U.S. 17, just n. of Doctors Lake bridge, Orange Park, Clay Co. [n.e. 1/4 of sec 44, T4S, R26E]

Nominator(s) / date: Robert W. Ray / 1991

(3)

Florida Challenger.

Size:			
	Circumference:	161	inches
	Height:	76	feet
	Crown spread:	113	feet
	Total points:	265	points

Owner / location: George Carty / 1 mi. w. of U.S. 301, 0.25 mi. s. of Fla. 328, 5 mi. s. of Ocala, Marion Co. [sec 16, T16S, R22E]

Nominator(s) / date: Gary T. Beauchamp / 1982

Update: Jeff Overby / 1993

Comments: Earlier measurements: circ. = 153 in., ht. = 90 ft., spread = 114 ft. (Beauchamp, 1982).

(4)

Honorable Mention.

Size:			
	Circumference:	119	inches
	Height:	116	feet
	Crown spread:	50	feet
	Total points:	248	points

Owner / location: Prairie View Trust / Sugarfoot Hammock, e. of Int. 75, 200 yds. s. of S.W. 20th Ave. overpass, Gainesville, Alachua Co. [sec 10, T10S, R19E]

Nominator(s) / date: Robert W. Simons, Daniel B. Ward / 1994

Carya pallida (Ashe) Engl. & Graebn.
Sand Hickory

Title vacant.

Size:		
	Circumference:	
	Height:	
	Crown spread:	
	Total points:	

Owner / location:

Nominator(s) / date:

Comments: Native in panhandle Florida.

Herbarium records (FLAS, Jan 1995) indicate this species, at Rock Bluff, Liberty County, to reach a height of 70 ft. with a trunk diameter of 15 in.

National champions: New Jersey (254 points); Maryland (252); North Carolina (250 points).

Carya tomentosa (Poir. in Lam.) Nutt.
Mockernut Hickory

(1)

☆ **Florida Champion.**

Size:			
	Circumference:	125	inches
	Height:	98	feet
	Crown spread:	77	feet
	Total points:	242	points

Owner / location: Mrs. Allen B. Tyree / 1.5 mi. s. of Fla. 6, w. of Alapaha River, 9 mi. s. of Jennings, Hamilton Co. [s.e. 1/4 of sec 23, T1N, R12E]

Nominator(s) / date: Robert W. Simons, Daniel B. Ward / 1993

Comments: National champion: Mississippi (314 points).

(2)

Florida Challenger.

Size:			
	Circumference:	82	inches
	Height:	103	feet
	Crown spread:	51.5	feet
	Total points:	198	points

Owner / location: Three Rivers State Recreation Area / s. of campground, 2 mi. n. of Sneads, Jackson Co. [s.e. 1/4 of sec 15, T4N, R7W]

Nominator(s) / date: Robert T. Ing, Daniel B. Ward / 1995

Casasia clusiifolia (Jacq.) Urban
= *Genipa clusiifolia* (Jacq.) Griseb.
Seven-year Apple

Title vacant.

Size: Circumference:

             Height:

             Crown spread:

             Total points:

Owner / location:

Nominator(s) / date:

Comments: Native in coastal south Florida.

Herbarium records (FLAS, Jan 1995) indicate this species, on Newfound Harbor Key, Monroe County, to reach a height of 25 ft.

This species (as *Genipa clusiifolia*) was recognized as a tree by American Forests, as a "species without a champion" (1996 listing).

Castanea alnifolia Nutt.
= *Castanea floridana* (Sarg.) Ashe
Southern Chinquapin, Florida Chinquapin
(1)

☆ **Florida Champion.**

Size:			
	Circumference:	76	inches
	Height:	41	feet
	Crown spread:	45	feet
	Total points:	128	points

Owner / location: Earl Cain / Horton St., Fort White, Columbia Co. [n.e. 1/4 of sec 33, T6S, R16E]

Nominator(s) / date: Joe McGrath / 1985

Update: Robert T. Ing, Daniel B. Ward / 1993

Comments: Earlier measurements: circ. = 69 in., ht. = 30 ft., spread = 60 ft. (McGrath, 1985).

The tree form of this species has been named *Castanea alnifolia* var. *floridana* Sarg., but the difference may be developmental rather than genetic.

National champion: Arkansas (132 points).

Castanea ashei (Sudw.) Ashe
= *Castanea pumila* (L.) Mill. var. *ashei* Sudw.
Ashe Chinquapin
(1)

★ **National Champion.**

Size:			
	Circumference:	85	inches
	Height:	55	feet

	Crown spread:	60	feet
	Total points:	155	points

Owner / location: John Mathe / old road parallel to Fla. 20, 0.8 mi. e. of Fla. 315, Interlachen, Putnam Co. [n.w. 1/4 of sec 14, T10S, R24E]

Nominator(s) / date: John Mathe / 1990

Update: Robert W. Simons, Daniel B. Ward / 1993

Comments: *Castanea ashei* is a tree-form analog of the northern, shrubby *C. pumila* (L.) Mill., the name to be used if the two are treated as conspecific.

Earlier measurements: circ. = 84 in., ht. = 60 ft., spread = 63 ft. (Mathe, 1990). Larger of two trees on this property.

Acknowledged (as *Castanea pumila*) by American Forests (1996 listing).

(2)

Florida Challenger.

Size:			
	Circumference:	72	inches
	Height:	42	feet
	Crown spread:	39	feet
	Total points:	124	points

Owner / location: John Mathe / old road parallel to Fla. 20, 0.8 mi. e. of Fla. 315, Interlachen, Putnam Co. [n.w. 1/4 of sec 14, T10S, R24E]

Nominator(s) / date: Robert W. Simons, Daniel B. Ward / 1994

Comments: Smaller of two trees on this property. When property was acquired, about 1960, owner says there were five trees, one, now dead, appreciably larger than the surviving trees.

Catalpa bignonioides Walt.
Catalpa
(1)

☆ **Florida Champion.**

Size:			
	Circumference:	145	inches
	Height:	45	feet
	Crown spread:	65	feet
	Total points:	206	points

Owner / location: City of White Springs / just w. of town hall, White Springs, Hamilton Co. [n.w. 1/4 of sec 7, T2S, R16E]

Nominator(s) / date: Clay Wachob, Doug Longshore / 1993

Comments: National champion: Illinois (459 points).

(2)

Emeritus Florida Champion.

Size:			
	Circumference:	102	inches
	Height:	65	feet

Crown spread:	53.5	feet
Total points:	180	points

Owner / location: Lawrence J. Hamilton / 923 S.E. 4th St., Gainesville, Alachua Co. [s.w. 1/4 of sec 9, T10S, R20E]

Nominator(s) / date: Duane R. Durgee, Lawrence J. Hamilton / 1990

(3)

Emeritus Florida Champion.

Size:	Circumference:	105	inches
	Height:	34	feet
	Crown spread:	46	feet
	Total points:	151	points

Owner / location: Mrs. Allen B. Tyree / 1.5 mi. s. of Fla. 6, w. of Alapaha River, 9 mi. s. of Jennings, Hamilton Co. [s.e. 1/4 of sec 23, T1N, R12E]

Nominator(s) / date: Charles R. Marcus / 1983

Update: Robert W. Simons, Daniel B. Ward / 1993

Comments: Earlier measurements: circ. = 106 in., ht. = 43 ft., spread = 54 ft. (Marcus, 1983).

(4)

Honorable Mention.

Size:	Circumference:	95	inches
	Height:	39	feet
	Crown spread:	41	feet
	Total points:	144	points

Owner / location: Harold Tyree / s. side of Fla. 6, 1 mi. e. of jct. with Fla. 141, 8 mi. s. of Jennings, Hamilton Co. [n.e. 1/4 of sec 16, T1N, R12E]

Nominator(s) / date: Doug Longshore / 1993

Celtis laevigata Willd.
Sugarberry

(1)

☆ **Florida Champion**.

Size:	Circumference:	234	inches
	Height:	67	feet
	Crown spread:	83	feet
	Total points:	322	points

Owner / location: Harold Tyree / s.e. of jct. Fla. 141 & Fla. 6, 8 mi. s. of Jennings, Hamilton Co. [s.e. 1/4 of sec 16, T1N, R12E]

Nominator(s) / date: Charles R. Marcus / 1983

Update: Doug Longshore / 1993

Comments: Earlier measurements: circ. = 192 in., ht. = 70 ft., spread = 82 ft. (Marcus, 1983).

Tree was originally reported as *Celtis occidentalis* (hackberry), a species that does not grow south of northern Georgia.

National champion: South Carolina (411 points).

(2)

Emeritus Florida Champion.

Size:	Circumference:	130	inches
	Height:	100	feet
	Crown spread:	85	feet
	Total points:	251	points

Owner / location: San Felasco Hammock State Preserve / Split Rock, n. side of Fla. 232, 8 mi. n.w. of Gainesville, Alachua Co. [sec 37, T8S, R19E]

Nominator(s) / date: Robert W. Simons / 1974

Update: Robert W. Simons / 1984

Update: Robert W. Simons, Daniel B. Ward / 1996

Comments: Earlier measurements: circ. = 115 in., ht. = 108 ft., spread = 81 ft. (Simons, 1974); circ. = 130 in., ht. = 108 ft., spread = 86 ft. (Simons, 1984).

(3)

Honorable Mention.

Size:	Circumference:	128	inches
	Height:	81	feet
	Crown spread:	84.5	feet
	Total points:	230	points

Owner / location: J. T. Howle / 2725 Market St., Jacksonville, Duval Co. [sec 12, T2S, R26E]

Nominator(s) / date: Richard W. Gorden, Joseph E. Dunbar / 1987

Update: Robert T. Ing, Daniel B. Ward / 1993

Comments: A substantial tree, in good health; not remeasured (R. T. Ing & D. B. Ward, Oct 1993).

(4)

Honorable Mention.

Size:	Circumference:	143	inches
	Height:	65	feet
	Crown spread:	55	feet
	Total points:	222	points

Owner / location: Russell Lante / 11529 S.W. 99th Ave., Gainesville, Alachua Co. [n.w. 1/4 of sec 1, T11S, R17E]

Nominator(s) / date: Winifred Lante / 1993

(5)

Honorable Mention.

Size:	Circumference:	118	inches
	Height:	71	feet
	Crown spread:	70.5	feet
	Total points:	207	points

Owner / location: James A. Corbett / 1/4 mi. n. of Suwannee River, 1.5 mi. w. of U.S. 129, 6 mi. s. of Jasper, Hamilton Co. [n.w. 1/4 of sec 7, T1S, R14E]

Nominator(s) / date: Robert T. Ing, Daniel B. Ward / 1993

(6)

Emeritus Florida Champion.

Size:	Circumference:	113	inches
	Height:	70	feet
	Crown spread:	36	feet
	Total points:	192	points

Owner / location: Ruth Hayworth / 2812 Tallevast Rd., Tallevast, Manatee Co. [n.w. 1/4 of sec 32, T35S, R18E]

Nominator(s) / date: Mark Bakeman / 1981

Update: William J. Schilling / 1994

Comments: Earlier measurements: circ. = 101 in., ht. = 70 ft., spread = 61 ft. (Bakeman, 1981).

(7)

Emeritus Florida Champion.

Size:	Circumference:	110	inches
	Height:	60	feet
	Crown spread:	77.5	feet
	Total points:	189	points

Owner / location: Jeffrey McInnis / n. side of Fla. 349, 1.5 mi. w. of U.S. 129 (at O'Brien), 6 mi. n.w. of Branford, Suwannee Co. [n.e. 1/4 of sec 24, T5S, R13E]

Nominator(s) / date: Stuart Moore / 1980

Update: Robert T. Ing, Daniel B. Ward / 1993

Comments: Earlier measurements: circ. = 105 in., ht. = 62 ft., spread = 72 ft. (Moore, 1980).

Celtis pallida Torr.
Spiny Hackberry

(1)

★ National Champion.

Size:	Circumference:	10	inches
	Height:	23	feet
	Crown spread:	27	feet
	Total points:	40	points

Owner / location: Ding Darling National Wildlife Refuge / n. side of Sanibel-Captiva Rd., Sanibel Id., Lee Co. [n.w. 1/4 of sec 18, T46S, R22E]

Nominator(s) / date: Richard W. Workman / 1995

Comments: This species is most often a spindly shrub. It was not included in the Checklist of Trees Native to Florida (Ward, 1991), nor recognized by Little (1979).

Acknowledged by American Forests (1996 listing).

Celtis tenuifolia Nutt.
Georgia Hackberry

Title vacant.

Size:	Circumference:
	Height:

	Crown spread:
	Total points:

Owner / location:

Nominator(s) / date:

Comments: Native in panhandle Florida.

Herbarium records (FLAS, Jan 1995; FSU, Nov 1996) indicate this species, near Niceville, Okaloosa County, to attain a height of 10 ft., and near Marianna, Jackson County, of 4 meters.

National champions: Virginia, two trees (49 points, 49 points).

Cephalanthus occidentalis L.
Buttonbush

(1)

☆ Florida Co-Champion.

Size:	Circumference:	42	inches
	Height:	19	feet
	Crown spread:	7.5	feet
	Total points:	63	points

Owner / location: James E. Wing / just s.e. of Santa Fe River, 1.5 mi. n.n.e. of High Springs, Alachua Co. [s.w. 1/4 of sec 23, T7S, R17E]

Nominator(s) / date: Robert W. Simons / 1977

Update: Robert W. Simons, Robert T. Ing, Daniel B. Ward / 1991

Comments: Earlier measurements: circ. = 49 in., ht. = 23 ft., spread = 22 ft. (Simons, 1977). Still alive, but in very poor condition (R. W. Simons, R. T. Ing & D. B. Ward, Nov 1991). Two other trees with similar dimensions are also present at this location.

National champion: California (87 points).

(2)

☆ Florida Co-Champion.

Size:	Circumference:	34	inches
	Height:	25	feet
	Crown spread:	17	feet
	Total points:	63	points

Owner / location: James E. Wing / just s.e. of Santa Fe River, 1.5 mi. n.n.e. of High Springs, Alachua Co. [s.w. 1/4 of sec 23, T7S, R17E]

Nominator(s) / date: Robert W. Simons, Robert T. Ing, Daniel B. Ward / 1991

Comments: The second of three trees of similar size at this location.

(3)

☆ Florida Co-Champion.

Size:	Circumference:	30	inches
	Height:	27	feet

| Crown spread: | 25 | feet |
| Total points: | 63 | points |

Owner / location: James E. Wing / just s.e. of Santa Fe River, 1.5 mi. n.n.e. of High Springs, Alachua Co. [s.w. 1/4 of sec 23, T7S, R17E]

Nominator(s) / date: Robert W. Simons, Robert T. Ing, Daniel B. Ward / 1991

Comments: The third of three trees of similar size at this location.

Cercis canadensis L.
Redbud

(1)

☆ **Florida Champion.**

Size:	Circumference:	32	inches
	Height:	67	feet
	Crown spread:	21.5	feet
	Total points:	104	points

Owner / location: Prairie View Trust / Sugarfoot Hammock, 200 yds. s. of jct. S.W. 62nd St. & 20th Ave., Gainesville, Alachua Co. [sec 10, T10S, R19E]

Nominator(s) / date: S. Craig Lowe, Daniel B. Ward / 1994

Comments: National champion: Tennessee (178 points).

(2)

Florida Challenger.

Size:	Circumference:	45	inches
	Height:	40	feet
	Crown spread:	39.5	feet
	Total points:	95	points

Owner / location: Mildred Thomas / jct. S.W. 4th Ave. & S.W. 4th St., High Springs, Alachua Co. [sec 3, T8S, R17E]

Nominator(s) / date: Robert T. Ing, Daniel B. Ward / 1991

Comments: Tree was planted by Mrs. Thomas in 1947. A slightly larger tree on the same property (Bordyn, 1981), now dead, was previously the Florida champion.

Cereus robinii (Lemaire) Benson
Key Tree Cactus

(1)

★ **National Champion.**

Size:	Circumference:	11	inches
	Height:	23	feet
	Crown spread:	1	feet
	Total points:	35	points

Owner / location: National Key Deer Refuge / Cactus Hammock, s. end of Big Pine Key, Monroe Co. [n.w. 1/4 of sec 6, T67S, R30E]

Nominator(s) / date: Michael K. Hennessey / 1992

Comments: This "tree" is a vertical stem with no branches.

Acknowledged by American Forests (1996 listing).

(2)

Florida Challenger.

Size:	Circumference:	12	inches
	Height:	17	feet
	Crown spread:	2	feet
	Total points:	31	points

Owner / location: National Key Deer Refuge / Cactus Hammock, s. end of Big Pine Key, Monroe Co. [n.e. 1/4 of sec 1, T67S, R29E]

Nominator(s) / date: Vincent P. Condon / 1995

Chamaecyparis thyoides (L.) BSP.
Atlantic White Cedar

(1)

☆ **Florida Champion**

Size:	Circumference:	113	inches
	Height:	87	feet
	Crown spread:	31	feet
	Total points:	208	points

Owner / location: Ocala National Forest / Morman Branch, tributary of Juniper Run, Marion Co. [sec 37, T15S, R26E]

Nominator(s) / date: Robert W. Simons, David S. Maehr / 1984

Update: Daniel B. Ward /1985

Comments: Trunk has been deeply scratched by black bears as a territorial marker; not remeasured (D. B. Ward, July 1985). (See also: Ward & Clewell, 1989.)

National champion: Alabama (284 points).

(2)

Florida Challenger

Size:	Circumference:	109	inches
	Height:	71	feet
	Crown spread:	35	feet
	Total points:	189	points

Owner / location: Blackwater River State Forest / n. side of river, just e. of Fla. 4, 11 mi. n.w. of Crestview, Okaloosa Co. [n.e. 1/4 of sec 22, T4N, R25W]

Nominator(s) / date: Clifford Faulkner / 1984

(3)

Emeritus Florida Champion

Size:	Circumference:	121	inches
	Height:	56	feet
	Crown spread:	33	feet
	Total points:	185	points

Owner / location: Blackwater River State Forest / n. side of river, e. of road, 3.5 mi. n. of Harold, 11 mi. n.e. of Milton, Santa Rosa Co. [sec 6, T2N, R26W]

Nominator(s) / date: James T. Harrelson / 1981

Update: Kenneth L. Oser / 1994

Comments: A "wolf" tree, rejected by loggers. Earlier measurements: circ. = 120 in., ht. = 52 ft., spread = 34 ft. (Harrelson, 1981).

Chionanthus virginicus L.
Fringe-tree

(1)

★ National Co-Champion.

Size:			
	Circumference:	42	inches
	Height:	41	feet
	Crown spread:	31	feet
	Total points:	91	points

Owner / location: Telford Spring County Park / n. bank of Suwannee River, 16 mi. s.w. of Live Oak, Suwannee Co. [e. 1/2 of sec 25, T4S, R11E]

Nominator(s) / date: Buford C. Pruitt / 1987

Comments: Acknowledged by American Forests (1996 listing).
    National co-champion: Virginia (94 points).

Chrysobalanus icaco L.
Coco Plum

Title vacant.

Size:			
	Circumference:		
	Height:		
	Crown spread:		
	Total points:		

Owner / location:

Nominator(s) / date:

Comments: Native in coastal central and south Florida.
    Herbarium records (FLAS, Jan 1995) indicate this species, in Matheson Hammock, Dade County, to reach a height of 15 ft. This species is recognized as a tree by American Forests (1996 listing), but as a "species without a champion."

Chrysophyllum oliviforme L.
Satinleaf

(1)

★ National Champion.

Size:			
	Circumference:	73	inches
	Height:	41	feet
	Crown spread:	34	feet
	Total points:	123	points

Owner / location: U.S. Dept. Justice / 3031 Brickell Ave., Miami, Dade Co. [n.e. 1/4 of sec 14, T54S, R41E]

Nominator(s) / date: Clifford Shaw, Albert H. Hetzell / 1976

Update: William G. Miller, John T. Valenta / 1993

Comments: Earlier measurements: circ. = 65 in., ht. = 42 ft., spread = 37 ft. (Shaw & Hetzell, 1976).
    Acknowledged by American Forests (1996 listing).

(2)

Emeritus National Champion.

Size:			
	Circumference:	72	inches
	Height:	33	feet
	Crown spread:	41	feet
	Total points:	115	points

Owner / location: Richard Dean / s.w. corner, jct. Davie Rd. & S.W. 57th St., Davie, Broward Co. [s.e. 1/4 of sec 34, T50S, R41E]

Nominator(s) / date: David A. Spicer / 1991

(3)

Honorable Mention.

Size:			
	Circumference:	25	inches
	Height:	26	feet
	Crown spread:	12	feet
	Total points:	54	points

Owner / location: Key Largo Hammocks State Botanical Site / n. end of Key Largo, Monroe Co. [sec 24, T59S, R40E]

Nominator(s) / date: Jeanne M. Parks / 1989

Citharexylum fruticosum L.
Fiddlewood

(1)

★ National Champion.

Size:			
	Circumference:	17	inches
	Height:	27	feet
	Crown spread:	12	feet
	Total points:	47	points

Owner / location: Lignumvitae Key State Botanical Site / Lignumvitae Key, Monroe Co. [n.e. 1/4 of sec 3, T64S, R36E]

Nominator(s) / date: Ken Roundtree, Frank L. Zickar / 1986

Comments: Acknowledged by American Forests (1996 listing).

Cliftonia monophylla (Lam.) Britt. ex Sarg.
Buckwheat-tree

(1)

★ National Champion.

Size:			
	Circumference:	73	inches
	Height:	58	feet

Crown spread:	30	feet
Total points:	139	points

Owner / location: St. Marks National Wildlife Refuge / s.w. of jct. U.S. 98 & U.S. 319, 3 mi. n. of Panacea, Wakulla Co. [s.w. 1/4 of sec 1, T5S, R2W]

Nominator(s) / date: Frank Zantek, Doug Scott, Mark M. Milligan / 1990

Comments: Acknowledged by American Forests (1996 listing).

Clusia rosea Jacq.
Balsam Apple

(1)

★ **National Champion.**

Size:	Circumference:	25	inches
	Height:	40	feet
	Crown spread:	37	feet
	Total points:	74	points

Owner / location: Hugh Taylor Birch State Park / 3019 E. Sunrise Blvd., Ft. Lauderdale, Broward Co. [s.e. 1/4 of sec 36, T49S, R42E]

Nominator(s) / date: Jim Higgins / 1995

Comments: There is reason for doubt that this species is a Florida native. Although specimens were collected in the Florida Keys (probably on Big Pine Key) in the 1840s and wild-growing plants have been encountered on five other keys since the 1950s, in each case they may well have been waifs from early habitations. No self-sustaining populations are now known within the state.

Acknowledged by American Forests (1996 listing).

Coccoloba diversifolia Jacq.
Pigeon Plum

(1)

★ **National Champion.**

Size:	Circumference:	84	inches
	Height:	49	feet
	Crown spread:	21.5	feet
	Total points:	138	points

Owner / location: Simpson Park / jct. S. Miami Ave. & S.E. 15th Rd., Miami, Dade Co. [sec 12, T54S, R41E]

Nominator(s) / date: Harold J. Nett / 1965

Update: William G. Miller, John T. Valenta / 1993

Comments: Earlier measurements: circ. = 66 in., ht. = 45 ft., spread = 28 ft. (Nett, 1965).

Acknowledged by American Forests (1996 listing).

(1)

Florida Challenger.

Size:	Circumference:	45	inches
	Height:	37	feet
	Crown spread:	19	feet
	Total points:	87	points

Owner / location: Lignumvitae Key State Botanical Site / Lignumvitae Key, Monroe Co. [n.w. 1/4 of sec 2, T64S, R36E]

Nominator(s) / date: Ken Roundtree, David M. Sinclair / 1986

Update: Robert Rose / 1993

Comments: Earlier measurements: circ. = 41 in., ht. = 37 ft., spread = 19 ft. (Roundtree & Sinclair, 1986); height & spread were not remeasured (R. Rose, Jan 1993).

Coccoloba uvifera (L.) L.
Sea Grape

(1)

★ **National Champion.**

Size:	Circumference:	149	inches
	Height:	62	feet
	Crown spread:	66	feet
	Total points:	228	points

Owner / location: Banyon Bay Apartments, Inc. / 703 N.E. 63rd St., Miami, Dade Co. [n.e. 1/4 of sec 18, T53S, R42E]

Nominator(s) / date: Don McGarthy / 1971

Update: Roger L. Hammer, Daniel B. Ward / 1994

Comments: Earlier measurements: circ. = 98 in., ht. = 57 ft., spread = 69 ft. (D. McGarthy, 1971).

Acknowledged by American Forests (1996 listing).

(2)

Florida Challenger.

Size:	Circumference:	60	inches
	Height:	40	feet
	Crown spread:	44	feet
	Total points:	111	points

Owner / location: Tarpon Bay Marina / n. end of Tarpon Bay Rd., Sanibel, Lee Co. [s.w. 1/4 of sec 23, T46S, R22E]

Nominator(s) / date: Robert T. Ing, Daniel B. Ward / 1994

(3)

Honorable Mention.

Size:	Circumference:	40	inches
	Height:	43	feet

Crown spread:	71	feet
Total points:	101	points

Owner / location: Hugh Taylor Birch State Park / 3109 E. Sunrise Blvd., Ft. Lauderdale, Broward Co. [s.e. 1/4 of sec 36, T49S, R42E]

Nominator(s) / date: Jim Higgins / 1995

Coccothrinax argentata (Jacq.) Bailey
Silver Palm

(1)

★ National Co-Champion.

Size:	Circumference:	19	inches
	Height:	29	feet
	Crown spread:	6	feet
	Total points:	50	points

Owner / location: Bahia Honda State Park / Bahia Honda Key, Monroe Co. [n.w. 1/4 of sec 35, T66S, R30E]

Nominator(s) / date: John A. Baust / 1979

Update: Monay Markey / 1993

Comments: Earlier measurements: circ. = 19 in., ht. = 27 ft., spread = 6 ft. (Baust, 1979).

Acknowledged by American Forests (1996 listing).

(2)

★ National Co-Champion.

Size:	Circumference:	21	inches
	Height:	25	feet
	Crown spread:	7	feet
	Total points:	48	points

Owner / location: Bahia Honda State Park / Bahia Honda Key, Monroe Co. [s.w. 1/4 of sec 26, T66S, R30E]

Nominator(s) / date: Clifford Shaw, George Avery / 1976

Update: Monay Markey / 1994

Comments: Earlier measurements: circ. = 22 in., ht. = 22 ft., spread = 6 ft. (Shaw & Avery, 1976).

Acknowledged by American Forests (1996 listing).

Colubrina arborescens (Mill.) Sarg.
Coffee Colubrina

Title vacant.

Size:	Circumference:		
	Height:		
	Crown spread:		
	Total points:		

Owner / location:

Nominator(s) / date:

Comments: Native in south peninsular Florida and the Florida Keys.

Often a shrub. Herbarium records (FLAS, July 1995) indicate this species, on Bahia Honda Key, Monroe County, to attain a height of 2 meters. This species is recognized as a tree by American Forests (1996 listing), but as a "species without a champion."

Colubrina cubensis (Jacq.) Brongn.
Cuban Nakedwood

Title vacant.

Size:	Circumference:		
	Height:		
	Crown spread:		
	Total points:		

Owner / location:

Nominator(s) / date:

Comments: Native in south peninsular Florida (Dade County) and Florida Keys.

Herbarium records (FLAS, July 1995) indicate this species, in Fuchs Hammock, Dade County, to reach a height of 5 meters. This species is recognized as a tree by American Forests (1996 listing), but as a "species without a champion."

Colubrina elliptica (Sw.) Briz. & Stern
Nakedwood, Soldierwood

(1)

★ National Champion.

Size:	Circumference:	22	inches
	Height:	41	feet
	Crown spread:	13	feet
	Total points:	66	points

Owner / location: John Pennecamp Coral Reef State Park / Key Largo, Monroe Co. [sec 23, T61S, R39E]

Nominator(s) / date: Jeanne M. Parks / 1989

Comments: Acknowledged by American Forests (1996 listing).

Conocarpus erectus L.
Buttonwood, Button Mangrove

(1)

★ National Champion.

Size:	Circumference:	174	inches
	Height:	51	feet
	Crown spread:	68	feet
	Total points:	242	points

Owner / location: Michael S. Poklepovic / 1161 N. Ocean Way, Palm Beach, Palm Beach Co. [sec 3, T43S, R43E]

Nominator(s) / date: Kenneth Van der Hulse, Donald L. Lockhart / 1974

Update: Michael Zimmerman / 1988

Update: Michael J. Greenstein / 1993

Comments: Earlier measurements: circ. = 127 in., ht. = 52 ft., spread = 67 ft. (Van der Hulse & Lockhart, 1974); circ. = 136 in., ht. = 41 ft., spread = 65 ft. (Zimmerman, 1988). Exceptional increase in circumference between 1988 and 1993 has been confirmed by M. Zimmerman (Jan 1995).

Acknowledged by American Forests (1996 listing).

(2)

Florida Challenger.

Size:	Circumference:	89	inches
	Height:	48	feet
	Crown spread:	31	feet
	Total points:	145	points

Owner / location: Sunset Cove Condominiums / Chokoloskee Island, Collier Co. [n.e. 1/4 of sec 36, T53S, R29E]

Nominator(s) / date: Elbert A. Schory / 1970

Update: Chris J. Anderson / 1994

Comments: Earlier measurements: circ. = 63 in., ht. = 34 ft., spread = 27 ft. (Schory, 1970, as *Laguncularia racemosa*).

(3)

Honorable Mention.

Size:	Circumference:	48	inches
	Height:	36	feet
	Crown spread:	31.5	feet
	Total points:	92	points

Owner / location: Key Largo Hammocks State Botanical Site / n. end of Key Largo, Monroe Co. [sec 24, T59S, R40E]

Nominator(s) / date: Jeanne M. Parks / 1989

Cornus alternifolia L.f.
Pagoda Dogwood

Title vacant.

Size:	Circumference:		
	Height:		
	Crown spread:		
	Total points:		

Owner / location:

Nominator(s) / date:

Comments: Native in central panhandle Florida.

National champion: Michigan (71 points).

Cornus asperifolia Michx.
= *Cornus microcarpa* Nash
Rough-leaf Cornel

(1)

☆ **Florida Champion.**

Size:	Circumference:	7	inches
	Height:	20	feet
	Crown spread:	16	feet
	Total points:	31	points

Owner / location: Prairie View Trust / Sugarfoot Hammock, n.e. of jct. S.W. 20th Ave. & S.W. 62nd St., Gainesville, Alachua Co. [n.e. 1/4 of sec 10, T10S, R19E]

Nominator(s) / date: Robert W. Simons, Daniel B. Ward / 1993

Comments: This is the rough-leaved upland species, tree-like in form although usually not big enough to qualify, not to be confused with the smooth-leaved, several-stemmed swamp *Cornus foemina* with which it is sometimes combined.

This species is not recognized as a tree by Little (1979), nor by American Forests (1996 listing).

(2)

Florida Challenger.

Size:	Circumference:	7	inches
	Height:	17	feet
	Crown spread:	16.5	feet
	Total points:	28	points

Owner / location: Jean F. De St. Croix / e. side of Santa Fe River, 3 mi. w. of Ft. White, Columbia Co. [s.w. 1/4 of sec 36, T6S, R15E]

Nominator(s) / date: Robert T. Ing, Daniel B. Ward / 1993

Cornus florida L.
Flowering Dogwood

(1)

☆ **Florida Champion.**

Size:	Circumference:	65	inches
	Height:	49	feet
	Crown spread:	51.5	feet
	Total points:	127	points

Owner / location: Mary Anderson / 616 Talaflo St., Tallahassee, Leon Co. [n.w. 1/4 of sec 31, T1N, R1E]

Nominator(s) / date: William O. Hardy / 1983

Update: Robert T. Ing, Daniel B. Ward, Charles E. Salter / 1993

Comments: Earlier measurements: circ. = 59 in., ht. = 41 ft., spread = 57 ft. (Hardy, 1983).

National champions: North Carolina (157 points); Virginia (154 points).

(2)

Florida Challenger.

Size:	Circumference:	57	inches
	Height:	36	feet
	Crown spread:	53	feet
	Total points:	106	points

Owner / location: Eartha Thompson / 3026 S.W. 13th
St., Ocala, Marion Co. [sec 23, T15S, R21E]

Nominator(s) / date: Joe Cunard, Duane R. Durgee /
1989

Update: Jeff Overby / 1993

Comments: Earlier measurements: circ. = 83.5 in., ht. =
40 ft., spread = 52 ft. (Cunard & Durgee, 1989).

(3)

Honorable Mention.

Size:	Circumference:	59	inches
	Height:	36	feet
	Crown spread:	40	feet
	Total points:	105	points

Owner / location: Alfred B. Maclay State Gardens / 3540
N. Thomasville Rd., Tallahassee, Leon Co. [sec 5,
T1N, R1E]

Nominator(s) / date: Thomas D. Beitzel, Beth Weidner /
1985

Cornus foemina Mill.
= *Cornus stricta* Lam.
Smooth-leaf Cornel, Swamp Dogwood

(1)

★ National Co-Champion.

Size:	Circumference:	10	inches
	Height:	23	feet
	Crown spread:	23.5	feet
	Total points:	39	points

Owner / location: Georgia Pacific Corp. / Rice Creek
Swamp, s. of Fla. 100, 6 mi. w. of Palatka, Putnam
Co. [e. 1/4 of sec 37, T9S, R25E]

Nominator(s) / date: Robert W. Simons, Buford C. Pruitt
/ 1981

Update: Robert W. Simons, Daniel B. Ward / 1993

Comments: Same tree as measured in 1981, but circumference taken on new, smaller trunk (original
trunk having died and disintegrated). Earlier measurements: circ. = 15 in., ht. = 23 ft., spread = 24 ft.
(Simons & Pruitt, 1981).

Acknowledged (as *Cornus stricta*) by American
Forests (1996 listing), with National co-champions:
Virginia, two trees (41 points, 39 points).

Most often a large shrub with wide-arching

branches. Not included in the Checklist of Trees Native to Florida (Ward, 1991).

(2)

Florida Challenger.

Size:	Circumference:	10.5	inches
	Height:	21	feet
	Crown spread:	13	feet
	Total points:	35	points

Owner / location: Lake Jem County Park / 3.5 mi. n.e. of
Astatula, Lake Co. [n.w. 1/4 of sec 14, T20S, R26E]

Nominator(s) / date: Robert W. Simons, Daniel B. Ward /
1993

(3)

Honorable Mention.

Size:	Circumference:	11	inches
	Height:	20	feet
	Crown spread:	13	feet
	Total points:	34	points

Owner / location: Robert W. Simons / s. end of Gad's Bay,
1 mi. w. of jct. U.S. 19 & Fla. 24 (Otter Creek), Levy
Co. [n.w. 1/4 of sec 26, T13S, R15E]

Nominator(s) / date: Robert W. Simons, Daniel B. Ward /
1993

Crataegus aestivalis (Walt.) Torr. & Gray
May Haw

(1)

☆ Florida Champion.

Size:	Circumference:	26	inches
	Height:	28	feet
	Crown spread:	26	feet
	Total points:	61	points

Owner / location: Jess Wilson / n. side of Fla. 268, 2 mi.
e. of Gretna, Gadsden Co. [n.w. 1/4 of sec 34, T3N,
R4W]

Nominator(s) / date: Robert T. Ing, Daniel B. Ward /
1995

Comments: National champion: Texas (79 points).

Crataegus crus-galli L.
= *Crataegus pyracanthoides* Beadle
Cockspur Haw

(1)

☆ Florida Champion.

Size:	Circumference:	28	inches
	Height:	35	feet
	Crown spread:	27.5	feet
	Total points:	70	points

Owner / location: Robert W. Simons / s. end of Gad's Bay, 1 mi. w. of jct. U.S. 19 & Fla. 24 (Otter Creek), Levy Co. [n.w. 1/4 of sec 26, T13S, R15E]

Nominator(s) / date: Robert W. Simon, Daniel B. Ward / 1993

Comments: National champions: Kentucky (112 points); Virginia (112 points).

Crataegus marshallii Egglest.
Parsley Haw

Title vacant.

Size:			
	Circumference:		
	Height:		
	Crown spread:		
	Total points:		

Owner / location:

Nominator(s) / date:

Comments: Native in north and central peninsular Florida.

A tree, now dead, in Gainesville, Alachua County, was measured in 1973 by Robert W. Simons as having circ. = 16 in., ht. = 33 ft., and spread = 23 ft.

National champion: Texas (54 points).

Crataegus michauxii Pers.
= *Crataegus flava*, misapplied
Summer Haw, Yellow Haw

(1)

★ **National Champion.**

Size:			
	Circumference:	41	inches
	Height:	25	feet
	Crown spread:	26	feet
	Total points:	73	points

Owner / location: Univ. of Florida / s. edge of University Ave., just e. of Buckman Dr., campus, Gainesville, Alachua Co. [s.e. 1/4 of sec 6, T10S, R20E]

Nominator(s) / date: Robert W. Simons / 1980

Update: Robert W. Simons, Daniel B. Ward / 1994

Comments: Earlier measurements: circ. = 37 in., ht. = 25 ft., spread = 25 ft. (Simons, 1980). When nominated, this tree was designated National champion, but was soon superceded by a larger tree (Pruitt & Simons, 1983). With the recent death of the larger tree, this tree has regained its status as National champion.

Acknowledged (as *Crataegus flava*) by American Forests (1996 listing).

(2)

Florida Challenger.

Size:			
	Circumference:	31	inches
	Height:	25	feet

	Crown spread:	38	feet
	Total points:	66	points

Owner / location: W. Lamar Upshaw / 2003 S.W. 44th Ave., Gainesville, Alachua Co. [sec 19, T10S, R20E]

Nominator(s) / date: Daniel B. Ward / 1994

Crataegus opaca Hook. & Arn.
Western May Haw, Apple Haw

(1)

☆ **Florida Champion.**

Size:			
	Circumference:	11	inches
	Height:	20	feet
	Crown spread:	16.5	feet
	Total points:	35	points

Owner / location: James Campbell / w. bank of Escambia River, n. of Fla. 4, 1 mi. s.e. of Century, Escambia Co. [n.w. 1/4 of sec 10, T5N, R30W]

Nominator(s) / date: James R. Burkhalter / 1994

Comments: Not included in the Checklist of Trees Native to Florida (Ward, 1991).

National champion: Mississippi (83 points).

Crataegus phaenopyrum (L.f.) Medic.
Washington Haw

Title vacant.

Size:			
	Circumference:		
	Height:		
	Crown spread:		
	Total points:		

Owner / location:

Nominator(s) / date:

Comments: Native in central panhandle Florida.

Herbarium records (FLAS, July 1995; FSU, Nov 1996) indicate this species, along Sister River, Walton County, to reach a height of 3 meters, and along the Ochlockonee River, Wakulla County, to reach 40 ft., with trunks to 10 centimeters dbh.

National champions: Virginia, two trees (100 points, 100 points); Tennessee (97 points).

Crataegus pulcherrima Ashe
Smooth Haw, Beautiful Haw

(1)

★ **National Champion.**

Size:			
	Circumference:	25	inches
	Height:	46	feet
	Crown spread:	31	feet
	Total points:	79	points

Owner / location: Mrs. Malcolm B. Johnson / 2933
  Meridian Rd., Tallahassee, Leon Co. [w. edge of sec
  18, T1N, R1E]

Nominator(s) / date: Malcolm B. Johnson, Charles E.
  Salter / 1968

Update: Robert T. Ing, Daniel B. Ward, Charles E.
  Salter / 1993

Comments: Earlier measurements: circ. = 23 in., ht. =
  43 ft., spread = 27 ft. (Johnson & Salter, 1968).

  Acknowledged by American Forests (1996 listing).

Crataegus rufula Sarg.
Rufous May Haw

Title vacant.

Size:			
	Circumference:		
	Height:		
	Crown spread:		
	Total points:		

Owner / location:

Nominator(s) / date:

Comments: Native in central panhandle Florida.

  This rare tree has been described as attaining a
  height of 5 meters (Phipps, 1988). Since this species
  was not recognized as a tree by Little (1979), it is
  not acknowledged by American Forests (1996
  listing).

Crataegus spathulata Michx.
Red Haw, Littlehip Haw

(1)

☆ **Florida Champion.**

Size:			
	Circumference:	23	inches
	Height:	29	feet
	Crown spread:	25	feet
	Total points:	58	points

Owner / location: Three Rivers State Recreation Area /
  e. edge of campground, 2 mi. n. of Sneads, Jackson
  Co. [s.e. 1/4 of sec 15, T4N, R7W]

Nominator(s) / date: Robert T. Ing, Daniel B. Ward /
  1995

Comments: National champions: Georgia (67 points);
  Texas (64 points).

(2)

Florida Challenger.

Size:			
	Circumference:	13	inches
	Height:	32	feet
	Crown spread:	25	feet
	Total points:	51	points

Owner / location: Three Rivers State Recreation Area /

s. of campground, 2 mi. n. of Sneads, Jackson Co.
  [s.e. 1/4 of sec 15, T4N, R7W]

Nominator(s) / date: Robert T. Ing, Daniel B. Ward / 1995

Crataegus uniflora Muench.
One-flowered Haw

(1)

★ **National Champion.**

Size:			
	Circumference:	13.5	inches
	Height:	18	feet
	Crown spread:	16	feet
	Total points:	36	points

Owner / location: Univ. of Florida / s. edge of McCarty
  Woods, across Museum Rd. from Florida State Museum, campus, Gainesville, Alachua Co. [s.e. 1/4 of
  sec 6, T10S, R20E]

Nominator(s) / date: Robert T. Ing, Daniel B. Ward /
  1991

Comments: This species is usually a several-stemmed
  shrub, but occasional individuals form a single
  trunk large enough to justify its treatment as a tree.
  Not included in the Checklist of Trees Native to
  Florida (Ward, 1991).

  Acknowledged by American Forests (1996 listing).

  A Leon County nomination of a larger tree (Simons, 1983), reported in the Florida listing (1986),
  was based upon a misidentification (R. W. Simons,
  Aug 1991).

Crataegus viridis L.
Green Haw

(1)

☆ **Florida Champion.**

Size:			
	Circumference:	48	inches
	Height:	32	feet
	Crown spread:	37.5	feet
	Total points:	89	points

Owner / location: O'Leno State Park / 0.5 mi. n. of River
  Rise, Alachua Co. [w. 1/2 of sec 14, T7S, R18E]

Nominator(s) / date: Michael J. Bordyn, Robert W. Simons / 1981

Update: Robert W. Simons, Daniel B. Ward / 1993

Comments: Tree was originally reported as *Crataegus
  aestivalis* (Bordyn & Simons, 1981), and acknowledged as National champion for that species by
  American Forests (1992 listing). But fruits are
  small, in many-flowered panicles; clearly *C. viridis*
  (R. W. Simons & D. B. Ward, May 1993).

  Earlier measurements: circ. = 48 in., ht. = 36 ft.,
  spread = 32.5 ft. (Bordyn & Simons, 1981).

  National champion: West Virginia (112 points).

Crossopetalum rhacoma Crantz
Rhacoma

Title vacant.

Size: Circumference:
             Height:
             Crown spread:
             Total points:

Owner / location:

Nominator(s) / date:

Comments: Native in south peninsular Florida and the Florida Keys.

   This species is most commonly a shrub, often quite low. However, herbarium records (FLAS, July 1995) indicate, on No Name Key, Monroe County, it reaches a height of 4 meters. This species is recognized as a tree by American Forests (1996 listing), but as a "species without a champion."

Cupania glabra Sw.
Florida Cupania

(1)

★ National Champion.

Size:			
	Circumference:	25	inches
	Height:	31	feet
	Crown spread:	22	feet
	Total points:	62	points

Owner / location: National Key Deer Refuge / Watson Hammock, w. side of Big Pine Key, Monroe Co. [s. 1/2 of sec 9, T66S, R29E]

Nominator(s) / date: Clifford Shaw, George Avery / 1976

Update: Jeanne M. Parks, Jon Andrew, Daniel B. Ward / 1993

Comments: Earlier measurements: circ. = 19 in., ht. = 27 ft., spread = 17 ft. (Shaw & Avery, 1976).

   Acknowledged by American Forests (1996 listing).

Cyrilla racemiflora L.
Titi, Swamp Cyrilla

(1)

★ National Champion.

Size:			
	Circumference:	51	inches
	Height:	44	feet
	Crown spread:	30	feet
	Total points:	103	points

Owner / location: Bert Mason / 1 mi. w. of old county landfill, 5 mi. e. of Vernon, Washington Co. [sec 3, T2N, R14W]

Nominator(s) / date: Charles R. Reeves / 1980

Update: Charles R. Reeves / 1993

Comments: Earlier measurements: circ. = 46 in., ht. = 52 ft., spread = 28 ft. (Reeves, 1980).

   Acknowledged by American Forests (1996 listing).

Diospyros virginiana L.
Persimmon

(1)

☆ Florida Champion.

Size:			
	Circumference:	59	inches
	Height:	118	feet
	Crown spread:	25	feet
	Total points:	183	points

Owner / location: Torreya State Park / on trail s.w. of Gregory house, w. edge of park, Liberty Co. [center of sec 17, T2N, R7W]

Nominator(s) / date: Robert W. Simons / 1993

Comments: National champions: South Carolina, two trees (226 points, 225 points); Arkansas (223 points); Georgia (223 points); Missouri (222 points); Mississippi (221 points).

(2)

Florida Challenger.

Size:			
	Circumference:	66	inches
	Height:	95	feet
	Crown spread:	44	feet
	Total points:	172	points

Owner / location: Prairie View Trust / Sugarfoot Hammock, n.e. of jct. S.W. 20th Ave. & S.W. 62nd St., Gainesville, Alachua Co. [n.e. 1/4 of sec 10, T10S, R19E]

Nominator(s) / date: Michael J. Bordyn, Robert W. Simons / 1981

Update: Robert W. Simons, Daniel B. Ward / 1993

Comments: Earlier measurements: circ. = 59 in., ht. = 88 ft., spread = 35.5 ft. (Bordyn & Simons, 1981).

(3)

Florida Challenger.

Size:			
	Circumference:	63	inches
	Height:	97	feet
	Crown spread:	42	feet
	Total points:	171	points

Owner / location: Andrews Wildlife Management Area / 3 mi. s. of Fanning Springs, Levy Co. [n.w. 1/4 of sec 8, T11S, R14E]

Nominator(s) / date: Dennis Andrews, Robert W. Simons / 1983

Update: Archie W. Gaylard, Daniel B. Ward / 1994

Comments: Earlier measurements: circ. = 60 in., ht. = 95 ft., spread = 39 ft. (Andrews & Simons, 1983).

Dipholis salicifolia (L.) A. DC.
= *Bumelia salicifolia* (L.) Sw.
Bustic, Willow Bustic

(1)

★ National Champion.

Size:	Circumference:	72	inches
	Height:	57	feet
	Crown spread:	29	feet
	Total points:	136	points

Owner / location: Barnacle State Historic Site / 3485 Main Hwy., Coconut Grove, Dade Co. [sec 21, T54S, R41E]

Nominator(s) / date: John T. Valenta, Roger L. Hammer / 1994

Comments: Same location, but different tree from former National champion (Newburne & Madsen, 1981), now dead.

 Acknowledged by American Forests (1996 listing).

(2)

Emeritus National Champion.

Size:	Circumference:	53	inches
	Height:	49	feet
	Crown spread:	16.5	feet
	Total points:	106	points

Owner / location: Simpson Park / jct. S. Miami Ave. & S.E. 15th Rd., Miami, Dade Co. [sec 12, T54S, R41E]

Nominator(s) / date: Clifford Shaw, Ralph Beaudry / 1975

Update: John T. Valenta, Ralph Beaudry / 1994

Comments: Earlier measurements: circ. = 48 in., ht. = 44 ft., spread = 23 ft. (Shaw & Beaudry, 1975).

Dodonaea viscosa (L.) Jacq.
Varnish-leaf, Florida Hop-bush

Title vacant.

Size:	Circumference:		
	Height:		
	Crown spread:		
	Total points:		

Owner / location:

Nominator(s) / date:

Comments: Native in south peninsular Florida and the Florida Keys.

 A native tree not included in the Checklist of Trees Native to Florida (Ward, 1991). Herbarium records (FLAS, Jan 1995) indicate this species, on Sanibel Island, Lee County, and Big Pine Key, Monroe County, to reach a height of 5 meters. It is recognized as a tree by American Forests (1996 listing), but as a "species without a champion."

Drypetes diversifolia Krug & Urban
Milk-bark

(1)

★ National Champion.

Size:	Circumference:	39	inches
	Height:	46	feet
	Crown spread:	18	feet
	Total points:	90	points

Owner / location: Lamar Louise Curry / Lot 14, Coral Coast Subdiv., Key Largo, Monroe Co. [sec 6, T62S, R39E]

Nominator(s) / date: Vincent P. Condon, William G. Miller / 1994

Comments: Acknowledged by American Forests (1996 listing).

(2)

Emeritus National Champion.

Size:	Circumference:	38	inches
	Height:	41	feet
	Crown spread:	19.5	feet
	Total points:	84	points

Owner / location: Key Largo Hammocks State Botanical Site / n. end of Key Largo, Monroe Co. [sec 26, T59S, R40E]

Nominator(s) / date: Jeanne M. Parks / 1989

Update: Jeanne M. Parks / 1993

Comments: Tree is still standing; not remeasured (J. M. Parks, Aug 1993).

Drypetes lateriflora (Sw.) Krug & Urban
Guiana Plum

(1)

★ National Champion.

Size:	Circumference:	22	inches
	Height:	31	feet
	Crown spread:	12	feet
	Total points:	56	points

Owner / location: Key Largo Hammocks State Botanical Site / n. end of Key Largo, Monroe Co. [sec 26, T59S, R40E]

Nominator(s) / date: Jeanne M. Parks / 1989

Comments: Acknowledged by American Forests (1996 listing).

Erythrina herbacea L.
Cherokee Bean, Coral Bean

(1)

★ National Champion.

Size:	Circumference:	40	inches
	Height:	32	feet

Crown spread:	30	feet
Total points:	80	points

Owner / location: Ding Darling National Wildlife Refuge / outside Shell Mound Trail loop, n. side of Sanibel-Captiva Rd., Sanibel Id., Lee Co. [n.w. 1/4 of sec 18, T46S, R22E]

Nominator(s) / date: Richard W. Workman / 1995

Comments: Acknowledged by American Forests (1996 listing).

(2)

Emeritus National Champion.

Size:	Circumference:	39	inches
	Height:	23	feet
	Crown spread:	27.5	feet
	Total points:	69	points

Owner / location: (unknown) / Sanibel Bayou subdivision, Wulfert Rd., w. end of Sanibel Id., Lee Co. [sec 12, T46S, R21E]

Nominator(s) / date: Eric H. Hoyer, Richard W. Workman / 1980

Update: Richard W. Workman / 1992

Comments: Earlier measurements: circ. = 38 in., ht. = 22 ft., spread = 25 ft. (Hoyer & Workman, 1980).

(3)

Honorable Mention.

Size:	Circumference:	25	inches
	Height:	15	feet
	Crown spread:	17	feet
	Total points:	44	points

Owner / location: Ding Darling National Wildlife Refuge / inside Shell Mound Trail loop, n. side of Sanibel-Captiva Rd., Sanibel Id., Lee Co. [n.w. 1/4 of sec 18, T46S, R22E]

Nominator(s) / date: Robert W. Simons / 1980

Update: Robert T. Ing, Daniel B. Ward, Layne Hamilton / 1994

Comments: Earlier measurements: circ. = 22 in., ht. = 18 ft., spread = 15 ft. (Simons, 1980).

(4)

Honorable Mention.

Size:	Circumference:	16	inches
	Height:	20	feet
	Crown spread:	8.5	feet
	Total points:	38	points

Owner / location: Key Largo Hammocks State Botanical Site / n. end of Key Largo, Monroe Co. [sec 25, T59S, R40E]

Nominator(s) / date: Jeanne M. Parks / 1989

Eugenia axillaris (Sw.) Willd.
White Stopper

(1)

★ **National Co-Champion**.

Size:	Circumference:	15	inches
	Height:	28	feet
	Crown spread:	9	feet
	Total points:	45	points

Owner / location: Barnacle State Historic Site / 3485 Main Hwy., Coconut Grove, Dade Co. [sec 21, T54S, R41E]

Nominator(s) / date: John T. Valenta, Roger L. Hammer / 1994

Comments: Acknowledged by American Forests (1996 listing).

(2)

★ **National Co-Champion**.

Size:	Circumference:	15	inches
	Height:	25	feet
	Crown spread:	11	feet
	Total points:	43	points

Owner / location: Sanctuary Golf Course / Wulfert Point, w. end of Sanibel Id., Lee Co. [sec 12, T46S, R21E]

Nominator(s) / date: Richard W. Workman / 1993

Comments: Tree is in old Wulfert Cemetery adjacent to golf course (R. W. Workman, Jan 1993).

Acknowledged by American Forests (1996 listing).

Eugenia confusa DC.
Redberry Stopper, Redberry Eugenia

(1)

★ **National Champion**.

Size:	Circumference:	60	inches
	Height:	46	feet
	Crown spread:	26	feet
	Total points:	113	points

Owner / location: Viscaya Museum & Gardens / Miami, Dade Co. [sec 14, T54S, R41E]

Nominator(s) / date: Albert H. Hetzell, Ron Smith / 1973

Update: American Forests, source unstated / 1991

Update: Carol L. Lippincott / 1993

Comments: Earlier measurements: circ. = 55 in., ht. = 43 ft., spread = 21 ft. (Hetzell & Smith, 1973); circ. = 58 in., ht. = 45 ft., spread = 25 ft. (A.F., 1992 listing). Tree is "simply magnificent" (C. L. Lippincott, July 1993).

Acknowledged by American Forests (1996 listing).

(2)

Florida Challenger.

Size:	Circumference:	14	inches
	Height:	22	feet
	Crown spread:	5	feet
	Total points:	37	points

Owner / location: Biscayne National Park / s. end of Totten Key, Dade Co. [s.w. 1/4 of sec 21, T58S, R41E]

Nominator(s) / date: Diane Riggs / 1995

Eugenia foetida Pers.
Spanish Stopper

Title vacant.

Size:	Circumference:		
	Height:		
	Crown spread:		
	Total points:		

Owner / location:

Nominator(s) / date:

Comments: Native in south peninsular Florida and the Florida Keys.

Several trees 20 ft. tall and 4 in. dbh. have been observed at Long Beach, Big Pine Key, Monroe County (G. Avery notes, Sept 1963). This species is recognized as a tree by American Forests (1996 listing), but as a "species without a champion."

Eugenia rhombea (Berg) Krug & Urban
Red Stopper

Title vacant.

Size:	Circumference:		
	Height:		
	Crown spread:		
	Total points:		

Owner / location:

Nominator(s) / date:

Comments: Native in the Florida Keys.

Trees to 15 ft. tall have been observed on Lower Sugarloaf Key, Monroe County; a larger one was seen at 1730 Flagler, Key West (G. Avery notes, Aug 1964).

This species is recognized as a tree by American Forests (1996 listing), but as a "species without a champion."

Euonymus atropurpureus Jacq.
Wahoo

Title vacant.

Size:	Circumference:		
	Height:		

Crown spread:

Total points:

Owner / location:

Nominator(s) / date:

Comments: Native in central panhandle Florida (Gadsden County).

Herbarium records (FLAS, July 1995) indicate this species, along Flat Creek, Gadsden County, reaches a height of 6 meters, with trees at Aspalaga Landing, Gadsden County, having trunks 19 centimeters dbh.

National champion: Michigan (61 points).

Exostema caribaeum (Jacq.) Roem. & Schult.
Princewood

Title vacant.

Size:	Circumference:		
	Height:		
	Crown spread:		
	Total points:		

Owner / location:

Nominator(s) / date:

Comments: Native in the Florida Keys.

"Small trees" have been observed in Cactus Hammock, Big Pine Key, Monroe County (G. Avery notes, Apr 1962). Herbarium records (FLAS, July 1995) indicate this species, on North Key Largo, Monroe County, to reach a height of 25 ft. with trunks 4.5 in. dbh. This species is recognized as a tree by American Forests (1996 listing), but as a "species without a champion."

Exothea paniculata (Juss.) Radlk.
Butterbough, Inkwood

(1)

★ National Champion.

Size:	Circumference:	49	inches
	Height:	38	feet
	Crown spread:	28	feet
	Total points:	94	points

Owner / location: Key Largo Hammocks State Botanical Site / n. end of Key Largo, Monroe Co. [sec 26, T59S, R40E]

Nominator(s) / date: Jeanne M. Parks / 1989

Comments: The larger of two similar sized trees at this location.

Acknowledged by American Forests (1996 listing).

(2)

Florida Challenger.

Size:	Circumference:	40	inches
	Height:	44	feet

Crown spread:	21	feet
Total points:	89	points

Owner / location: Key Largo Hammocks State Botanical Site / n. end of Key Largo, Monroe Co. [sec 26, T59S, R40E]

Nominator(s) / date: Jeanne M. Parks / 1989

Comments: The smaller of two similar sized trees at this location.

Fagus grandifolia Ehrh.
Beech
(1)

☆ **Florida Champion**.

Size:	Circumference:	134	inches
	Height:	121	feet
	Crown spread:	79	feet
	Total points:	275	points

Owner / location: Wakulla Springs State Park / Wakulla Springs, Wakulla Co. [n.w. 1/4 of sec 13, T3S, R1W]

Nominator(s) / date: Dana C. Bryan / 1988

Comments: National champion: Maryland (429 points).

(2)

Florida Challenger.

Size:	Circumference:	119	inches
	Height:	115	feet
	Crown spread:	81	feet
	Total points:	254	points

Owner / location: Martin Marietta Materials, Inc. / w. end of Satsuma Rd., Chattahoochee, Gadsden Co. [n.e. 1/4 of sec 5, T3N, R6W]

Nominator(s) / date: Angus K. Gholson, Robert T. Ing, Daniel B. Ward / 1995

(3)

Florida Challenger.

Size:	Circumference:	129	inches
	Height:	105	feet
	Crown spread:	70	feet
	Total points:	252	points

Owner / location: Wakulla Springs State Park / Wakulla Springs, Wakulla Co. [n.w. 1/4 of sec 13, T3S, R1W]

Nominator(s) / date: Dana C. Bryan, James R. Karels / 1987

Comments: This is a somewhat smaller tree at the same location as the Florida champion nominated in 1988 (D. C. Bryan, Jan 1994).

(4)

Emeritus Florida Champion.

Size:	Circumference:	126	inches
	Height:	106	feet
	Crown spread:	81	feet
	Total points:	252	points

Owner / location: Torreya State Park / w. of Gregory house, Liberty Co. [sec 8, T2N, R7W]

Nominator(s) / date: Joey T. Brady, Jerome Bracewell / 1986

(5)

Emeritus Florida Champion.

Size:	Circumference:	100	inches
	Height:	118	feet
	Crown spread:	68.5	feet
	Total points:	235	points

Owner / location: Anne Wright / Woodswell Farm, 7537 Proctor Rd., 0.3 mi. s. of s. of Centerville Rd. (Fla. 151), 12 mi. n.e. of Tallahassee, Leon Co. [s.w. 1/4 of sec 16, T2N, R2E]

Nominator(s) / date: Ralph Roberts / 1983

   Update: Robert T. Ing, Daniel B. Ward, Charles E. Salter / 1993

Comments: Earlier measurements: circ. = 95 in., ht. = 120 ft., spread = 59 ft. (Roberts, 1983).

(6)

Honorable Mention.

Size:	Circumference:	99	inches
	Height:	109	feet
	Crown spread:	66.5	feet
	Total points:	225	points

Owner / location: Anne Wright / Woodswell Farm, 7537 Proctor Rd., 0.3 mi. s. of s. of Centerville Rd. (Fla. 151), 12 mi. n.e. of Tallahassee, Leon Co. [s.w. 1/4 of sec 16, T2N, R2E]

Nominator(s) / date: Robert T. Ing, Daniel B. Ward, Charles E. Salter / 1993

Comments: The second largest tree at this location.

Ficus aurea Nutt.
Strangler Fig
(1)

★ **National Champion**.

Size:	Circumference:	360	inches
	Height:	63	feet
	Crown spread:	72	feet
	Total points:	441	points

Owner / location: Bill Sadowski Park / Old Cutler Hammock, s. of jct. of C-100 Canal & Cutler Canal, Dade Co. [n.e. 1/4 of sec 34, T55S, R40E]

Nominator(s) / date: Albert H. Hetzell, Ron Smith / 1973

   Update: William G. Miller, Roger L. Hammer / 1993

Comments: Earlier measurements: circ. = 288 in., ht. = 80 ft., spread = 76 ft. (Hetzell & Smith, 1973).

   Acknowledged by American Forests (1996 listing).

(2)

Florida Challenger.

Size:	Circumference:	148	inches
	Height:	76	feet
	Crown spread:	60	feet
	Total points:	239	points

Owner / location: Collier-Seminole State Park / 20200 E. Tamiami Trail, Monroe Co. [n.e. 1/4 of sec 34, T51S, R27E]

Nominator(s) / date: Daniel F. Austin, Richard Moyroud / 1995

Ficus citrifolia Mill.
Wild Banyan, Shortleaf Fig

(1)

★ National Champion.

Size:	Circumference:	248	inches
	Height:	41	feet
	Crown spread:	57	feet
	Total points:	303	points

Owner / location: Lignumvitae Key State Botanical Site / Lignumvitae Key, Monroe Co. [n.w. 1/4 of sec 2, T64S, R36E]

Nominator(s) / date: David M. Sinclair, Frank L. Zickar / 1986

Update: Robert Rose, Pat Wells / 1993

Comments: Earlier measurements: circ. = 245 in., ht. = 41 ft., spread = 57 ft. (Sinclair & Zickar, 1986); height & spread were not remeasured (R. Rose & P. Wells, Jan 1993).

Acknowledged by American Forests (1996 listing).

(2)

Emeritus National Champion.

Size:	Circumference:	214	inches
	Height:	71	feet
	Crown spread:	48	feet
	Total points:	297	points

Owner / location: Ron J. Pavlik / 1301 E. Broward Blvd., Ft. Lauderdale, Broward Co. [s.w. 1/4 of sec 2, T50S, R42E]

Nominator(s) / date: Thomas D. Williams / 1982

Update: Frank L. Zickar / 1994

Comments: Earlier measurements: circ. = 200 in., ht. = 52 ft., spread = 85 ft. (Williams, 1982).

Forestiera acuminata (Michx.)
Poir. in Lam.
Swamp Privet

(1)

☆ Florida Champion.

Size:	Circumference:	18	inches
	Height:	25	feet

	Crown spread:	28.5	feet
	Total points:	50	points

Owner / location: Jean F. De St. Croix / e. side of Santa Fe River, 3 mi. w. of Ft. White, Columbia Co. [s.w. 1/4 of sec 36, T6S, R15E]

Nominator(s) / date: Robert T. Ing, Daniel B. Ward / 1993

Comments: National champion: South Carolina (79 points).

Forestiera segregata (Jacq.)
Krug & Urban
Florida Privet

(1)

★ National Champion.

Size:	Circumference:	25	inches
	Height:	17.5	feet
	Crown spread:	21	feet
	Total points:	48	points

Owner / location: Humiston Beach Park / Ocean Drive, Vero Beach, Indian River Co. [sec 32, T32S, R40E]

Nominator(s) / date: Janice Broda / 1993

Comments: Acknowledged by American Forests (1996 listing).

Fraxinus americana L.
White Ash

(1)

☆ Florida Champion.

Size:	Circumference:	169	inches
	Height:	77	feet
	Crown spread:	61	feet
	Total points:	261	points

Owner / location: Carl Ivey Carter / 2 mi. s.e. of Alapaha River, 6 mi. s.w. of Jasper, Hamilton Co. [s.w. 1/4 of sec 20, T1N, R13E]

Nominator(s) / date: Norman Nichols / 1983

Update: Robert W. Simons, Daniel B. Ward / 1993

Comments: Earlier measurements: circ. = 154 in., ht. = 82 ft., spread = 63 ft. (Nichols, 1983).

National champion: New York (420 points).

(2)

Emeritus Florida Champion.

Size:	Circumference:	135	inches
	Height:	82	feet
	Crown spread:	50	feet
	Total points:	230	points

Owner / location: Univ. of Florida / e. edge of McCarty Woods, campus, Gainesville, Alachua Co. [s.e. 1/4 of sec 6, T10S, R20E]

Nominator(s) / date: Michael J. Bordyn / 1980

Update: Robert T. Ing, Daniel B. Ward / 1991

Comments: Earlier measurements: circ. = 128 in., ht. = 84 ft., spread = 80 ft. (Bordyn, 1980). Crown spread has been much reduced by recent limb fall (R. T. Ing & D. B. Ward, Oct 1991).

(3)

Honorable Mention.

Size:			
	Circumference:	114	inches
	Height:	95	feet
	Crown spread:	58	feet
	Total points:	224	points

Owner / location: Prairie View Trust / Sugarfoot Hammock, e. of Int. 75, 250 yds s. of S.W. 20th Ave. overpass, Gainesville, Alachua Co. [sec 10, T10S, R19E]

Nominator(s) / date: Robert W. Simons, Daniel B. Ward / 1994

Fraxinus caroliniana Mill.
Pop Ash, Carolina Ash

(1)

★ National Co-Champion.

Size:			
	Circumference:	56	inches
	Height:	58	feet
	Crown spread:	24	feet
	Total points:	120	points

Owner / location: O'Leno State Park / 0.5 mi. n.n.e. of River Rise, Alachua Co. [w. 1/2 of sec 14, T7S, R17E]

Nominator(s) / date: Robert W. Simons, Daniel B. Ward / 1993

Comments: Acknowledged by American Forests (1996 listing). National co-champion: Virginia (115 points).

Fraxinus pennsylvanica Marsh.
Green Ash

(1)

☆ Florida Champion.

Size:			
	Circumference:	123	inches
	Height:	93	feet
	Crown spread:	31	feet
	Total points:	224	points

Owner / location: H. E. Barr / floodplain of Santa Fe River, 2 mi. e. of Ginnie Springs, n.e. corner of Gilchrist Co. [s.e. 1/4 of sec 35, T7S, R16E]

Nominator(s) / date: Robert W. Simons, Daniel B. Ward / 1995

Comments: National champion: Michigan (403 points).

Fraxinus profunda (Bush) Bush
Pumpkin Ash

(1)

☆ Florida Champion.

Size:			
	Circumference:	119	inches
	Height:	100	feet
	Crown spread:	46	feet
	Total points:	231	points

Owner / location: Silver River State Park / n. edge of Silver River floodplain, 3 mi. below Silver Springs, 1.5 mi. above Fla. 40 bridge, Marion Co. [n.e. 1/4 of sec 9, T15S, R23E]

Nominator(s) / date: Robert W. Simons / 1988

Comments: National champion: Missouri (336 points).

Gleditsia aquatica Marsh.
Water Locust

(1)

☆ Florida Champion.

Size:			
	Circumference:	108	inches
	Height:	55	feet
	Crown spread:	52	feet
	Total points:	176	points

Owner / location: Catherine Avirett Dees / 3 mi. s.e. of Jennings, Hamilton Co. [sec 18, T2N, R13E]

Nominator(s) / date: Brian J. Wittwer / 1986

Comments: National champion: Pennsylvania (202 points).

(2)

Emeritus Florida Champion.

Size:			
	Circumference:	94	inches
	Height:	63	feet
	Crown spread:	43	feet
	Total points:	168	points

Owner / location: O'Leno State Park / 0.7 mi. s.e. of River Rise, Alachua Co. [s.w. 1/4 of sec 23, T7S, R17E]

Nominator(s) / date: Michael J. Bordyn, Robert W. Simons / 1981

Update: Robert T. Ing, Daniel B. Ward / 1993

Comments: Earlier measurements: circ. = 90 in., ht. = 60 ft., spread = 34.5 ft. (Bordyn & Simons, 1981).

(3)

Honorable Mention.

Size:			
	Circumference:	65	inches
	Height:	75	feet
	Crown spread:	31	feet
	Total points:	148	points

Owner / location: P. & G. Cellulose, Inc. / w. of Regular
Creek, 7 mi. s. of U.S. 98, 14 mi. w.s.w. of Perry,
Taylor Co. [s.w. 1/4 of sec 14, T5S, R5E]

Nominator(s) / date: Robert W. Simons, Daniel B. Ward /
1993

(4)

Honorable Mention.

Size:	Circumference:	61	inches
	Height:	78	feet
	Crown spread:	26.5	feet
	Total points:	146	points

Owner / location: Welaka State Forest / e. side St. Johns
River, 2 mi. s. of Welaka, Putnam Co. [n.e. 1/4 of sec
21, T12S, R26E]

Nominator(s) / date: Ned D. Neenan / 1992

(5)

Honorable Mention.

Size:	Circumference:	56	inches
	Height:	60	feet
	Crown spread:	35	feet
	Total points:	125	points

Owner / location: P. & G. Cellulose, Inc. / w. of Regular
Creek, 14 mi. s.w. of Perry, Taylor Co. [n.e. 1/4 of sec
23, T5S, R5E]

Nominator(s) / date: Robert Saults, Jerry N. Livingston /
1981

Update: Robert W. Simons, Daniel B. Ward / 1993

Comments: Earlier measurements: circ. = 55 in., ht. =
64 ft., spread = 41 ft. (Saults & Livingston, 1981; as
Gleditsia triacanthos).

Gleditsia triacanthos L.
Honey Locust

(1)

☆ Florida Champion.

Size:	Circumference:	49	inches
	Height:	76	feet
	Crown spread:	38	feet
	Total points:	135	points

Owner / location: (unknown) / w. edge of Old Bainbridge
Rd. (Fla. 157), 0.6 mi. n.w. of Fred George Rd., n.w.
Tallahassee, Leon Co. [n.w. 1/4 of sec 9, T1N, R1W]

Nominator(s) / date: Robert T. Ing, Daniel B. Ward,
Charles E. Salter / 1993

Comments: National champion: Michigan (320 points).

(2)

Emeritus Florida Champion.

Size:	Circumference:	52	inches
	Height:	67	feet

	Crown spread:	31	feet
	Total points:	127	points

Owner / location: Hattie Bell Love / near Suwannee
River, 1 mi. n.e. of U.S. 27, 11 mi. e.s.e. of Mayo,
Lafayette Co. [n.w. 1/4 of sec 34, T5S, R13E]

Nominator(s) / date: Jerry N. Livingston / 1990

Gordonia lasianthus (L.) Ellis
Loblolly Bay

(1)

★ National Champion.

Size:	Circumference:	164	inches
	Height:	95	feet
	Crown spread:	60	feet
	Total points:	274	points

Owner / location: Ocala National Forest / Hughes Island, 6.5 mi. w. of Silver Glen Spring, Marion Co.
[s.e. 1/4 of sec 24, T14S, R25E]

Nominator(s) / date: Robert W. Simons, Daniel B. Ward /
1963

Update: Robert W. Simons / 1972

Update: Robert W. Simons / 1983

Update: Robert W. Simons, Daniel B. Ward / 1993

Comments: Earlier measurements: circ. = 142 in., ht. =
94 ft., spread = 54 ft. (Simons & Ward, 1963); circ. =
153 in., ht. = 84 ft., spread = 57 ft. (Simons, 1972);
circ. = 161 in., ht. = 94 ft., spread = 52 ft. (Simons,
1983).

Acknowledged by American Forests (1996 listing).

Gossypium hirsutum L.
Wild Cotton

Title vacant.

Size:	Circumference:		
	Height:		
	Crown spread:		
	Total points:		

Owner / location:

Nominator(s) / date:

Comments: Wild cotton was once a frequent shrub or
small tree in the coastal hammocks of south peninsular Florida. Its wide distribution and lack of commercial value clearly indicates it to be native. However, because Little (1979) believed it to be a shrub,
and "apparently naturalized," it is not acknowledged
by American Forests (1996 listing).

Most plants of wild cotton have been destroyed by
a government program intended to eliminate an al-
ternate host for the pink boll worm, a potential

insect pest of commercial cotton. A "large tree-like plant" survived on Big Pine Key, Monroe County (G. Avery notes, May 1964). Herbarium records (FTG, Dec 1995) indicate this species, on Big Pine, still reaches a height of 3 meters.

Guaiacum sanctum L.
Holywood Lignum-vitae, Roughbark Lignum-vitae

(1)

★ **National Champion** (nominee).

Size:			
	Circumference:	37	inches
	Height:	31	feet
	Crown spread:	38.5	feet
	Total points:	78	points

Owner / location: Gerald Morgan, Samuel Senia / 1311 Truman Ave., Key West, Monroe Co. [n.w. 1/4 of sec 5, T68S, R25E]

Nominator(s) / date: Vincent P. Condon, Michael B. Miller / 1995

Comments: This tree, because of its size and slow rate of growth, is unquestionably a relic of pre-settlement vegetation.

(2)

★ **National Champion**.

Size:			
	Circumference:	26	inches
	Height:	28	feet
	Crown spread:	36	feet
	Total points:	63	points

Owner / location: Biscayne National Park / s. end of Totten Key, Dade Co. [s.w. 1/4 of sec 21, T58S, R41E]

Nominator(s) / date: Diane Riggs / 1995

Comments: A smaller tree at location of previous national champion, now deceased.

Acknowledged by American Forests (1996 listing).

(3)

Florida Challenger.

Size:			
	Circumference:	34	inches
	Height:	19	feet
	Crown spread:	22	feet
	Total points:	59	points

Owner / location: Lignumvitae Key State Botanical Site / at water hole, Lignumvitae Key, Monroe Co. [n.w. 1/4 of sec 2, T64S, R36E]

Nominator(s) / date: Elbert A. Schory, R. H. Niedhauk / 1970

Update: Robert Rose, Vincent P. Condon / 1995

Comments: Earlier measurements: circ. = 39 in., ht. = 16 ft., spread = 26 ft. (Schory & Niedhauk, 1970).

Tree was estimated by nominators to have an age of 1600 years.

Guettarda elliptica Sw.
Velvet-seed

(1)

★ **National Champion**.

Size:			
	Circumference:	36	inches
	Height:	23	feet
	Crown spread:	23.5	feet
	Total points:	65	points

Owner / location: Simpson Park / jct. S. Miami Ave. & S.E. 15th Rd., Miami, Dade Co. [sec 12, T54S, R41E]

Nominator(s) / date: William G. Miller, John T. Valenta / 1993

Comments: Acknowledged by American Forests (1996 listing).

Guettarda scabra (L.) Vent.
Rough Velvet-seed

(1)

★ **National Champion**.

Size:			
	Circumference:	13	inches
	Height:	8	feet
	Crown spread:	3	feet
	Total points:	22	points

Owner / location: Biscayne National Park / s. end of Totten Key, Dade Co. [s.w. 1/4 of sec 21, T58S, R41E]

Nominator(s) / date: Diane Riggs / 1995

Comments: Acknowledged by American Forests (1996 listing).

Gyminda latifolia (Sw.) Urban
False Boxwood

(1)

★ **National Champion** (nominee).

Size:			
	Circumference:	10	inches
	Height:	19	feet
	Crown spread:	13	feet
	Total points:	32	points

Owner / location: National Key Deer Refuge / s. of road, 1 mi. e. of bridge, No Name Key, Monroe Co. [s.w. 1/4 of sec 18, T66S, R30E]

Nominator(s) / date: Niko Reisinger, Dianna L. Stevenson / 1995

Comments: This species is recognized as a tree by American Forests (1996 listing), but as a "species without a champion."

Halesia carolina L.
= *Halesia parviflora* Michx.
Little Silver-bell

(1)

☆ **Florida Champion**.

Size:			
	Circumference:	10.5	inches
	Height:	23	feet
	Crown spread:	15	feet
	Total points:	38	points

Owner / location: Georgia Pacific Corp. / Rice Creek Swamp, s. of Fla 100, 6 mi. w. of Palatka, Putnam Co. [e. 1/4 of sec 37, T9S, R25E]

Nominator(s) / date: Robert W. Simon, Daniel B. Ward / 1993

Comments: National champions: Tennessee, three trees (266 points, 265 points, 261 points).

Halesia diptera Ellis
Two-wing Silver-bell

(1)

☆ **Florida Champion**.

Size:			
	Circumference:	60	inches
	Height:	51	feet
	Crown spread:	38	feet
	Total points:	121	points

Owner / location: Alfred B. Maclay State Gardens / 3540 N. Thomasville Rd., Tallahassee, Leon Co. [sec 5, T1N, R1E]

Nominator(s) / date: Thomas D. Beitzel, Beth Weidner / 1985

Comments: National champion: Ohio (166 points).

Hamelia patens Jacq.
Fire-bush

(1)

★ **National Champion** (nominee).

Size:			
	Circumference:	15	inches
	Height:	13	feet
	Crown spread:	15.5	feet
	Total points:	32	points

Owner / location: Adolf Grimal / 600 Cunningham Lane, Big Pine Key, Monroe Co. [n.e. 1/4 of sec 26, T66S, R29E]

Nominator(s) / date: Jean F. St. De Croix / 1996

Comments: Circumference measured at 1 ft. elevation; branched above (J. F. De St. Croix, July 1996).

Commonly a shrub, but occasionally attains tree size. Recognized as a tree by Little (1979), and by American Forests (1996 listing), but as a "species without a champion."

Hippomane mancinella L.
Manchineel

(1)

★ **National Champion**.

Size:			
	Circumference:	56	inches
	Height:	46	feet
	Crown spread:	51	feet
	Total points:	114	points

Owner / location: National Key Deer Refuge / Watson Hammock, w. side of Big Pine Key, Monroe Co. [s. 1/2 of sec 9, T66S, R29E]

Nominator(s) / date: Clifford Shaw, George Avery / 1976

Update: Robert W. Simons, Mary Lee Eletz / 1979

Update: Jeanne M. Parks, Jon Andrew, Daniel B. Ward / 1993

Comments: Earlier measurements: circ. = 48 in., ht. = 30 ft., spread = 41 ft. (Shaw & Avery, 1976); circ. = 47 in., ht. = 39 ft., spread = 34 ft. (Simons & Eletz, 1979).

Acknowledged by American Forests (1996 listing).

(2)

Florida Challenger.

Size:			
	Circumference:	22	inches
	Height:	23	feet
	Crown spread:	18	feet
	Total points:	50	points

Owner / location: Key Largo Hammocks State Botanical Site / n. end of Key Largo, Monroe Co. [sec 25, T59S, R40E]

Nominator(s) / date: Jeanne M. Parks / 1989

Hypelate trifoliata Sw.
White Ironwood

(1)

★ **National Champion**.

Size:			
	Circumference:	46	inches
	Height:	39	feet
	Crown spread:	24.5	feet
	Total points:	91	points

Owner / location: Lamar Louise Curry / Lot 4, Coral Coast Subdiv., Key Largo, Monroe Co. [sec 6, T62S, R39E]

Nominator(s) / date: Vincent P. Condon, William G. Miller / 1994

Comments: Acknowledged by American Forests (1996 listing).

Hypericum chapmanii Adams
Sponge-bark Hypericum

Title vacant.

Size:	Circumference:	
	Height:	
	Crown spread:	
	Total points:	

Owner / location:

Nominator(s) / date:

Comments: Native in central panhandle Florida.
Adams (1962), at the time this species was
named, commented, "Individuals often attain a
height of 3 or 4 m and a thickness of 10-15 cm."
Herbarium records (FLAS, July 1995) indicate this
species, near Wewahitchka, Calhoun County, to
reach a height of 3.5 meters. But not listed by Little
(1979) and thus not recognized as a tree by American Forests (1996 listing).

Ilex ambigua (Michx.) Torr.
Sand Holly, Carolina Holly

(1)

★ **National Champion** (nominee).

Size:	Circumference:	18	inches
	Height:	27	feet
	Crown spread:	30	feet
	Total points:	53	points

Owner / location: County of Pasco / s.e. of Moon Lake
Estates, 8 mi. e. of New Port Richey, Pasco Co. [n.e.
1/4 of sec 34, T25S, R17E]

Nominator(s) / date: Donald Robinson, Michael W.
Kenton / 1995

Comments: National champion: Florida (44 points).

(2)

★ **National Champion**.

Size:	Circumference:	14	inches
	Height:	25	feet
	Crown spread:	18	feet
	Total points:	44	points

Owner / location: (unknown) / s. end of Ft. George Island, Duval Co. [sec 37, T1S, R29E]

Nominator(s) / date: Buford C. Pruitt, Robert W. Simons
/ 1984

Comments: Acknowledged by American Forests (1996
listing).

(3)

Florida Challenger.

Size:	Circumference:	13	inches
	Height:	22	feet
	Crown spread:	21	feet
	Total points:	40	points

Owner / location: Prairie View Trust / n. of S.W. 20th
Ave., e. of S.W. 62nd St., Gainesville, Alachua Co.
[n.e. 1/4 of sec 10, T10S, R19E]

Nominator(s) / date: Robert W. Simons, Daniel B. Ward /
1993

Ilex cassine L.
Dahoon Holly

(1)

★ **National Co-Champion**.

Size:	Circumference:	32	inches
	Height:	68	feet
	Crown spread:	31	feet
	Total points:	108	points

Owner / location: Robert Fernandez / 8177 S. Cypress
Dr., San Carlos Park, 2 mi. n. of Estero, Lee Co.
[n.w. 1/4 of sec 16, T46S, R25E]

Nominator(s) / date: Chris J. Anderson / 1995

Comments: The tallest (and largest in point size) of
three similar-sized trees at this location.
Acknowledged by American Forests (1996 listing).

(2)

★ **National Co-Champion**.

Size:	Circumference:	54	inches
	Height:	42	feet
	Crown spread:	35.5	feet
	Total points:	105	points

Owner / location: Mike Ramsey / 3301 S.R. 29,
Immokalee, Collier Co. [s.e. 1/4 of sec 23, T47S,
R28E]

Nominator(s) / date: Chris J. Anderson / 1995

Comments: Acknowledged by American Forests (1996
listing).

(3)

★ **National Co-Champion**.

Size:	Circumference:	55	inches
	Height:	40	feet
	Crown spread:	36	feet
	Total points:	104	points

Owner / location: H. B. Moore / 3315 N. Indian River
Dr., 3 mi. n. of Fort Pierce, St. Lucie Co. [sec 28,
T34S, R40E]

Nominator(s) / date: Paul G. Williams / 1984

Comments: Acknowledged by American Forests (1996
listing).

(4)

★ **National Co-Champion** (nominee).

Size:	Circumference:	34	inches
	Height:	61	feet
	Crown spread:	34	feet
	Total points:	104	points

Owner / location: Robert Fernandez / 8177 S. Cypress Drive, San Carlos Park, 2 mi. n. of Estero, Lee Co. [n.w. 1/4 of sec 16, T46S, R25E]

Nominator(s) / date: Sam Allison, Chris J. Anderson / 1994

Comments: Three other similar-sized trees are also at this location (S. Allison, July 1994).

National co-champions: Florida (108 points, 105 points, 104 points).

(5)

Florida Challenger.

Size:			
	Circumference:	36	inches
	Height:	33	feet
	Crown spread:	18	feet
	Total points:	74	points

Owner / location: Continental Country Club / Orange Home, 3 mi. s.e. of Wildwood, Sumter Co. [s.e. 1/4 of sec 22, T19S, R23E]

Nominator(s) / date: F. C. Hester / 1971

Update: Jeff Overby / 1993

Comments: Tree was originally reported as *Ilex verticillata* (Hester, 1971), and until recently was assumed to be the Florida champion for that species (Florida listing, 1990). But winterberry is a northern species, occurring in Florida only in the central panhandle. Trees at the indicated site are *Ilex cassine* (J. Overby, Oct 1993).

Earlier measurements: circ. = 28 in., ht. = 40 ft., spread = 16 ft. (Hester, 1971).

Ilex decidua Walt.
Possum Haw

(1)

★ National Co-Champion.

Size:			
	Circumference:	39	inches
	Height:	47	feet
	Crown spread:	31	feet
	Total points:	94	points

Owner / location: Soterra, Inc. / e. bank of Apalachicola River, 0.5 mi. s. of Int. 10, 6 mi. s.w. of Chattahoochee, Gadsden Co. [s.e. 1/4 of sec 26, T3N, R7W]

Nominator(s) / date: Robert W. Simons, Angus K. Gholson, Robert K. Godfrey / 1993

Comments: Acknowledged by American Forests (1996 listing), with National co-champion: South Carolina (90 points).

Ilex krugiana Loesn.
Krug's Holly, Tawnyberry Holly

Title vacant.

Size:		
	Circumference:	
	Height:	

Crown spread:		
Total points:		

Owner / location:

Nominator(s) / date:

Comments: Native in south peninsular Florida (Dade County).

A tree, now dead, at Camp Owaissa Bauer, Dade County, was measured in 1968 by Francis Young and Elbert A. Schory as having circ. = 40 in., ht. = 55 ft., and spread = 22 ft. It was formerly the National champion (101 points).

This species is recognized as a tree by American Forests (1996 listing), but as a "species without a champion."

Ilex longipes Chapm. ex Trel.
Georgia Holly

Title vacant.

Size:		
	Circumference:	
	Height:	
	Crown spread:	
	Total points:	

Owner / location:

Nominator(s) / date:

Comments: Native in panhandle Florida.

This species is recognized as a tree by American Forests (1996 listing), but as a "species without a champion."

Ilex myrtifolia Walt.
Myrtle Holly, Myrtle Dahoon Holly

(1)

★ National Champion.

Size:			
	Circumference:	74	inches
	Height:	40	feet
	Crown spread:	35	feet
	Total points:	123	points

Owner / location: ITT Rayonier, Inc. / 3 mi. n. of Lawtey, Bradford Co. [n.e. 1/4 of sec 2, T5S, R22E]

Nominator(s) / date: Nelson B. Blocker / 1972

Update: Robert T. Ing, Daniel B. Ward / 1993

Comments: Earlier measurements: circ. = 67 in., ht. = 46 ft., spread = 35 ft. (Blocker, 1972). The largest of a small grove of remarkable trees.

(2)

Florida Challenger.

Size:			
	Circumference:	52	inches
	Height:	54	feet
	Crown spread:	42	feet
	Total points:	117	points

Owner / location: John J. Ayres / n. of Fla. 20, 4 mi. w. of Blountstown, Calhoun Co. [sec 36, T1N, R9W]

Nominator(s) / date: Chris Linton / 1981

Update: Stephen Oswalt / 1994

Comments: Earlier measurements: circ. = 48 in., ht. = 36 ft., spread = 23 ft. (Linton, 1981).

(3)

Honorable Mention.

Size:			
	Circumference:	51	inches
	Height:	45	feet
	Crown spread:	25.5	feet
	Total points:	102	points

Owner / location: ITT Rayonier, Inc. / 3 mi. n. of Lawtey, Bradford Co. [n.e. 1/4 of sec 2, T5S, R22E]

Nominator(s) / date: Robert T. Ing, Daniel B. Ward / 1993

Comments: The second largest of a small grove of remarkable trees.

(4)

Honorable Mention.

Size:			
	Circumference:	59	inches
	Height:	28	feet
	Crown spread:	21.5	feet
	Total points:	92	points

Owner / location: ITT Rayonier, Inc. / 3 mi. n. of Lawtey, Bradford Co. [n.e. 1/4 of sec 2, T5S, R22E]

Nominator(s) / date: Robert T. Ing, Daniel B. Ward / 1993

Comments: The third largest of a small grove of remarkable trees.

(5)

Honorable Mention.

Size:			
	Circumference:	42	inches
	Height:	42	feet
	Crown spread:	23	feet
	Total points:	90	points

Owner / location: Container Corp. / s. side of Fla. 100, 1.4 mi. e. of Fla. 235, 7 mi. w.n.w. of Starke, Bradford Co. [n.e. 1/4 of sec 17, T6S, R21E]

Nominator(s) / date: Mark G. Fries / 1980

Update: Robert T. Ing, Daniel B. Ward / 1993

Comments: Earlier measurements: circ. = 30 in., ht. = 44 ft., spread = 20 ft. (Fries, 1980).

Ilex opaca Ait.
American Holly

(1)

☆ Florida Champion.

Size:			
	Circumference:	95	inches
	Height:	69	feet
	Crown spread:	61.5	feet
	Total points:	179	points

Owner / location: Robert Head / 1329 Kingsley Ave., Hibernia subdivision, 5 mi. n. of Green Cove Springs, Clay Co. [sec 38, T5S, R26E]

Nominator(s) / date: William L. Rutherford / 1984

Update: Robert W. Ray / 1994

Comments: Earlier measurements: circ. = 108 in. (measured below low fork), ht. = 71 ft., spread = 52 ft. (Rutherford, 1984).

National champions: Alabama (205 points); Virginia (203 points).

(2)

Florida Challenger.

Size:			
	Circumference:	69	inches
	Height:	65	feet
	Crown spread:	37	feet
	Total points:	143	points

Owner / location: Bivens Arm Nature Park / w. side Main St. (Fla. 329), n. of jct. Fla. 331, s. Gainesville, Alachua Co. [s.w. 1/4 of sec 17, T10S, R20E]

Nominator(s) / date: Robert W. Simons / 1984

Update: Robert W. Simons, Daniel B. Ward / 1993

Comments: Earlier measurements: circ. = 60 in., ht. = 65 ft., spread = 42 ft. (Simons, 1984).

Ilex verticillata (L.) Gray
Winterberry

Title vacant.

Size:		
	Circumference:	
	Height:	
	Crown spread:	
	Total points:	

Owner / location:

Nominator(s) / date:

Comments: Native in west and central panhandle Florida. In Florida, infrequently of tree stature. A tree, now dead, at Aspalaga Landing, Gadsden County, was measured in 1967 by M. B. Johnson and C. E. Salter as having circ. = 18 in., ht. = 26 ft., and spread = 16 ft.

National champions: Virginia, two trees (41 points, 38 points).

The former 74-point Florida champion of this species (Wildwood, Sumter County—Hester, 1971) has been identified as Ilex cassine (J. Overby, Oct 1993).

Ilex vomitoria Ait.
Yaupon

(1)

☆ Florida Champion.

Size:			
	Circumference:	19	inches
	Height:	32	feet
	Crown spread:	21	feet
	Total points:	56	points

Owner / location: Ravine State Gardens / Twigg St., Palatka, Putnam Co. [s.e. 1/4 of sec 12, T10S, R26E]

Nominator(s) / date: Ned D. Neenan / 1993

Comments: This tree is a smaller replacement for the previous Florida champion (Dale, 1989—96 points) also at this location, and now deceased.

National champion: Texas (104 points).

Illicium floridanum Ellis
Florida Anise-tree

Title vacant.

Size:	Circumference:		
	Height:		
	Crown spread:		
	Total points:		

Owner / location:

Nominator(s) / date:

Comments: Native in west and central panhandle Florida. Herbarium records (FSU, Nov 1996) indicate this species, s.w of Crestview, Okaloosa County, to reach a height of 30 ft., with trunks to 5.5 centimeters dbh.

National champion: Alabama (49 points).

Illicium parviflorum Michx. ex Vent.
Florida Banana-shrub, Yellow Anise

(1)

★ National Champion.

Size:	Circumference:	7	inches
	Height:	18	feet
	Crown spread:	13	feet
	Total points:	28	points

Owner / location: Ocala National Forest / Morman Branch, tributary of Juniper Creek, at F. S. Rd. 71, Marion Co. [sec 37, T15S, R26E]

Nominator(s) / date: Jeff Overby, Ilke Toklu / 1993

Comments: This species is most commonly a large many-stemmed shrub, only rarely with stems persisting and becoming tree-like. Not included in the Checklist of Trees Native to Florida (Ward, 1991).

Acknowledged by American Forests (1996 listing).

Jacquinia keyensis Mez
Joe-wood

(1)

★ National Champion (nominee).

Size:	Circumference:	23	inches
	Height:	13	feet
	Crown spread:	13	feet
	Total points:	39	points

Owner / location: Diego Toiran / E. Fifth Ave., Key West, Monroe Co. [n.w. 1/4 of sec 32, T66S, R28E]

Nominator(s) / date: Dianna L. Stevenson, Vincent P. Condon / 1995

Comments: National champion: Florida (31 points).

(2)

Florida Challenger.

Size:	Circumference:	18	inches
	Height:	14	feet
	Crown spread:	11.5	feet
	Total points:	35	points

Owner / location: Fred Guarnieri / 14 Colson Dr., Cudjoe Key, Monroe Co. [s.w. 1/4 of sec 29, T66S, R28E]

Nominator(s) / date: Patricia L. McNeese / 1995

(3)

★ National Champion.

Size:	Circumference:	16	inches
	Height:	11	feet
	Crown spread:	15.5	feet
	Total points:	31	points

Owner / location: Marsha Van Duren / w. of Egret Lane, w. side of Big Torch Key, Monroe Co. [n.e. 1/4 of sec 13, T66S, R29E]

Nominator(s) / date: Vincent P. Condon / 1995

Comments: Acknowledged by American Forests (1996 listing).

Juglans nigra L.
Black Walnut

(1)

☆ Florida Co-Champion.

Size:	Circumference:	124	inches
	Height:	66	feet
	Crown spread:	67	feet
	Total points:	207	points

Owner / location: Mrs. Allen B. Tyree / 1.5 mi. s. of Fla. 6, w. of Alapaha River, 9 mi. s. of Jennings, Hamilton Co. [s.e. 1/4 of sec 23, T1N, R12E]

Nominator(s) / date: Allen B. Tyree / 1986

Comments: American Forests (1996 listing) records a National champion from Oregon, with a height of 130 ft. and circumference of 278 in. (443 points). This is appreciably beyond the size reached by virgin trees in areas where it is native.

(2)

☆ Florida Co-Champion.

Size:	Circumference:	84	inches
	Height:	108	feet
	Crown spread:	57	feet
	Total points:	206	points

Owner / location: Torreya State Park / s.e. of Gregory house, Liberty Co. [sec 17, T2N, R7W]

Nominator(s) / date: Joey T. Brady, Jerome Bracewell / 1986

(3)
Emeritus Florida Champion.

Size:			
	Circumference:	95	inches
	Height:	92	feet
	Crown spread:	57.5	feet
	Total points:	201	points

Owner / location: City of High Springs / S.W. 5th Ave, just e. of S. Main St., High Springs, Alachua Co. [sec 3, T8S, R17E]

Nominator(s) / date: Michael J. Bordyn / 1981

Update: Robert T. Ing, Daniel B. Ward / 1991

Comments: Earlier measurements: circ. = 88 in., ht. = 75 ft., spread = 55.5 ft. (Bordyn, 1981).

(4)
Honorable Mention.

Size:			
	Circumference:	115	inches
	Height:	55	feet
	Crown spread:	60	feet
	Total points:	185	points

Owner / location: Paul McDowell / w. side of Union Ave., n.w. side of Crescent City, Putnam Co. [n.e. 1/4 of sec 14, T12S, R27E]

Nominator(s) / date: Ned D. Neenan / 1993

(5)
Honorable Mention.

Size:			
	Circumference:	98	inches
	Height:	52	feet
	Crown spread:	30	feet
	Total points:	158	points

Owner / location: Emory Osteen / s. of U.S. 27, 7 mi. e.s.e. of Mayo, Lafayette Co. [s.e. 1/2 of sec 30, T5S, R13E]

Nominator(s) / date: Jerry N. Livingston / 1991

Juniperus silicicola (Small) Bailey
Southern Red Cedar

(1)
★ **National Champion**.

Size:			
	Circumference:	195	inches
	Height:	75	feet
	Crown spread:	51.5	feet
	Total points:	283	points

Owner / location: Donald Grubbs / Moss Oak Lane (S.W. 162nd St.), 1.5 mi. s. of Archer, Alachua Co. [sec 21, T11S, R18E]

Nominator(s) / date: Robert W. Simons / 1976

Update: Robert W. Simons, William Russell / 1987

Update: Robert T. Ing, Daniel B. Ward / 1991

Comments: Earlier measurements: circ. = 178 in., ht. = 70 ft., spread = 57 ft. (Simons, 1976); circ. = 193 in., ht. = 80 ft., spread = 59 ft.

Local lore (as told to Simons, 1976) maintains this tree marks a buried treasure. The survivors of a ship that had been driven aground and sunk at Cedar Key attempted to cross the peninsula to settlements along the St. Johns River, but stopped to bury their valuables atop a prominent hill and marked the site by planting this tree. They never returned.

Acknowledged by American Forests (1996 listing).

(2)
Florida Challenger.

Size:			
	Circumference:	208	inches
	Height:	36	feet
	Crown spread:	37.5	feet
	Total points:	253	points

Owner / location: David P. Etherington / e. side of Fla. 234, 3 mi. n. of Micanopy, Alachua Co. [n.e. 1/4 of sec 10, T11S, R20E]

Nominator(s) / date: Robert W. Simons / 1986

Update: Robert W. Simons, Daniel B. Ward / 1993

Comments: Earlier measurements: circ. = 196 in., ht. = 47 ft., spread = 38 ft. (Simons, 1986).

As reported by the property owner: The tree is near a house built in the 1870s by the captain of the "Micanopy" (the paddle-wheel boat that crossed Payne's Prairie when it was a lake), and recent tenants have repeatedly claimed seeing a "nautical figure" walking near the tree.

(3)
Florida Challenger.

Size:			
	Circumference:	186	inches
	Height:	48	feet
	Crown spread:	67.5	feet
	Total points:	251	points

Owner / location: Mark W. Hollmann / 310 W. Minnesota Ave., DeLand, Volusia Co. [sec 9, T17S, R30E]

Nominator(s) / date: Brad D. Johnson / 1993

Update: Robert W. Simons, Daniel B. Ward / 1993

Comments: Tree is known as the "Livingston Cedar" in commemoration of the builder of the home on whose grounds it stands.

This tree was originally reported to have circ. = 337 in., yielding 402 points. Tree was examined and remeasured (R. W. Simons & D. B. Ward, June 1993). Original data noted circumference to have been measured at 0.5 ft. But tree was found to be of two trunks, perhaps initially of two trees, with fork at 3 ft. By American Forests measurement rules, the larger of the two trunks should have been selected for measurement at 4.5 ft.

(4)

Florida Challenger.

Size:	Circumference:	176	inches
	Height:	55	feet
	Crown spread:	65.5	feet
	Total points:	247	points

Owner / location: Robby R. Terry / 2112 Morgan Johnson Rd., e. side of Braden River, Bradenton, Manatee Co. [sec 34, T34S, R18E]

Nominator(s) / date: William J. Schilling / 1970

Update: Jeff Deatherage / 1986

Update: William J. Schilling / 1993

Comments: Earlier measurements: circ. = 163 in., ht. = 48 ft., spread = 65 ft. (Schilling, 1970); circ. = 175 in., ht. = 55 ft., spread = 58.5 ft. (Deatherage, 1986).

(5)

Honorable Mention.

Size:	Circumference:	119	inches
	Height:	76	feet
	Crown spread:	47	feet
	Total points:	207	points

Owner / location: John Dunn / Indian River Park subdivision, Aurantia, 9 mi. n.n.w. of Titusville, Brevard Co. [sec 26, T20S, R34E]

Nominator(s) / date: Rudy Smith / 1990

(6)

Honorable Mention.

Size:	Circumference:	120	inches
	Height:	51	feet
	Crown spread:	48	feet
	Total points:	183	points

Owner / location: Kingsley Plantation / 11676 Palmetto Ave., n. end of Ft. George Id., Duval Co. [sec 37, T1S, R29E]

Nominator(s) / date: Jim Bryan / 1984

Juniperus virginiana L.
Eastern Red Cedar

Title vacant.

Size:	Circumference:		
	Height:		

	Crown spread:		
	Total points:		

Owner / location:

Nominator(s) / date:

Comments: Native in north Florida.

National champions: Texas (284 points); Georgia (283 points).

Kalmia latifolia L.
Mountain Laurel

(1)

☆ **Florida Champion.**

Size:	Circumference:	10	inches
	Height:	11	feet
	Crown spread:	10.5	feet
	Total points:	24	points

Owner / location: John L. Dean / 821 E. 7th Ave., Tallahassee, Leon Co. [center of sec 30, T1N, R1E]

Nominator(s) / date: Robert T. Ing, Daniel B. Ward, Charles E. Salter / 1993

Comments: National champion: North Carolina (90 points).

Krugiodendron ferreum (Vahl) Urban
Black Ironwood, Leadwood

(1)

★ **National Champion.**

Size:	Circumference:	70	inches
	Height:	33	feet
	Crown spread:	25.5	feet
	Total points:	109	points

Owner / location: Lignumvitae Key State Botanical Site / Lignumvitae Key, Monroe Co. [n.w. 1/4 of sec 2, T64S, R36E]

Nominator(s) / date: David M. Sinclair, Frank L. Zickar / 1986

Update: Robert Rose, Vincent P. Condon / 1995

Comments: Earlier measurements: circ. = 67 in., ht. = 37 ft., spread = 27 ft. (Sinclair & Zickar, 1986)

Acknowledged by American Forests (1996 listing).

Laguncularia racemosa (L.) Gaertn. f.
White Mangrove

Title vacant.

Size:	Circumference:		
	Height:		
	Crown spread:		
	Total points:		

Owner / location:

Nominator(s) / date:

Comments: Native in coastal central and south peninsular Florida.

Although this species is often a shrub, it has been
described as having a height of 30 ft. or more, with a
trunk diameter of 12 in. (West & Arnold, 1956).
Herbarium records (FLAS, July 1995) indicate this
species, on both Sanibel and Captiva Islands, Lee
County, to reach a height of 7 meters.

A tree that for many years was assumed to be of
this species (Schory, 1970) and was ranked as its
National champion (American Forests, 1994 listing),
has now been identified as *Conocarpus erectus* (C. J.
Anderson, Apr 1994).

Leitneria floridana Chapm.
Corkwood

(1)

★ **National Champion** (nominee).

Size:			
	Circumference:	8	inches
	Height:	16	feet
	Crown spread:	7	feet
	Total points:	26	points

Owner / location: Waccasassa Bay State Preserve / near
n. fork of Ramsey Creek, 10 mi. n. of Yankeetown,
Levy Co. [s.e. 1/4 of sec 27, T15S, R15E]

Nominator(s) / date: Robert W. Simons, Thomas M.
Rooks / 1989

Comments: This specimen appears marginally qualified for national standing on the basis of trunk circumference. It is nevertheless of tree form, and
larger ones are believed to be nearby (R. W. Simons,
Dec 1990).

This species has been recognized as a tree by
American Forests (1996 listing), as a "species
without a champion."

Licaria triandra (Sw.) Kostermans
Florida Licaria

Title vacant.

Size:			
	Circumference:		
	Height:		
	Crown spread:		
	Total points:		

Owner / location:

Nominator(s) / date:

Comments: Native in south peninsular Florida (Dade
County).

A "large tree" has been observed in Simpson Park,
Miami, Dade County (G. Avery notes, Nov 1965).

This species is recognized as a tree by American
Forests (1996 listing), but as a "species without a
champion."

Liquidambar styraciflua L.
Sweet Gum

(1)

☆ **Florida Champion**.

Size:			
	Circumference:	160	inches
	Height:	128	feet
	Crown spread:	68	feet
	Total points:	305	points

Owner / location: Torreya State Park / on trail s.w. from
Gregory house, w. edge of park, Liberty Co. [center
of sec 17, T2N, R7W]

Nominator(s) / date: Robert W. Simons, Jim Buckner /
1993

Comments: National champion: North Carolina (430
points).

(2)

Emeritus Florida Champion.

Size:			
	Circumference:	158	inches
	Height:	116	feet
	Crown spread:	49	feet
	Total points:	286	points

Owner / location: Gold Head Branch State Park / nature
trail, Clay Co. [sec 36, T7S, R23E]

Nominator(s) / date: William L. Rutherford / 1983
Update: Robert W. Ray / 1994

Comments: Earlier measurements: circ. = 162 in. (measured lower on slope), ht. = 102 ft., spread = 71 ft.
(Rutherford, 1983).

(3)

Emeritus Florida Champion.

Size:			
	Circumference:	149	inches
	Height:	98	feet
	Crown spread:	68	feet
	Total points:	264	points

Owner / location: J. M. McLellan / 2 mi. s. of state line,
15 mi. e. of Jay, Santa Rosa Co. [s.e. 1/4 of sec 2,
T5N, R27W]

Nominator(s) / date: Radford M. Locklin / 1981
Update: Kenneth L. Oser / 1994

Comments: Earlier measurements: circ. = 139 in., ht. =
106 ft., spread = 75 ft. (Locklin, 1981).

(4)

Honorable Mention.

Size:			
	Circumference:	117	inches
	Height:	118	feet

Crown spread:	63	feet
Total points:	251	points

Owner / location: Leland C. Thomas / 5 mi. w. of Marianna, Jackson Co. [s.w. 1/4 of sec 3, T4N, R11W]

Nominator(s) / date: R. Bruce Turnbull / 1994

Liriodendron tulipifera L.
Tulip-tree, Yellow Poplar

(1)

☆ **Florida Champion**.

Size:	Circumference:	196	inches
	Height:	109	feet
	Crown spread:	67	feet
	Total points:	322	points

Owner / location: Larry Barnett / e. of Fla. 21, between Johnson and Orange Springs, Putnam Co. [n.e. 1/4 of sec 12, T11S, R23E]

Nominator(s) / date: Ned D. Neenan / 1988

Comments: National champion: Virginia (551 points).

(2)

Florida Challenger.

Size:	Circumference:	159	inches
	Height:	130	feet
	Crown spread:	58	feet
	Total points:	304	points

Owner / location: Torreya State Park / n.w. corner of park, Liberty Co. [n.e. 1/4 of sec 17, T2N, R7W]

Nominator(s) / date: Robert W. Simons, Jim Buckner / 1993

(3)

Honorable Mention.

Size:	Circumference:	142	inches
	Height:	93	feet
	Crown spread:	59	feet
	Total points:	250	points

Owner / location: Maude A. Nixon / 1112 N.W. 9th Ave., Gainesville, Alachua Co. [s.w. corner of sec 32, T9S, R20E]

Nominator(s) / date: Robert T. Ing, Daniel B. Ward / 1991

Comments: Tree is of a small stand native at this location.

(4)

Emeritus Florida Champion.

Size:	Circumference:	140	inches
	Height:	90	feet
	Crown spread:	51	feet
	Total points:	243	points

Owner / location: Estella Barthle / 2 mi. s.e. of Alapaha River, 6 mi. s.w. of Jasper, Hamilton Co. [sec 20, T1N, R13E]

Nominator(s) / date: Charles R. Marcus / 1983

Update: Doug Longshore / 1993

Comments: Earlier measurements: circ. = 139 in., ht. = 118 ft., spread = 44 ft. (Marcus, 1983).

(5)

Honorable Mention.

Size:	Circumference:	99	inches
	Height:	118	feet
	Crown spread:	64	feet
	Total points:	233	points

Owner / location: Martin Marietta Materials, Inc. / w. end of Satsuma Rd., Chattahoochee, Gadsden Co. [n.e. 1/4 of sec 5, T3N, R6W]

Nominator(s) / date: Angus K. Gholson, Robert T. Ing, Daniel B. Ward / 1995

(6)

Emeritus Florida Champion.

Size:	Circumference:	84	inches
	Height:	90	feet
	Crown spread:	54	feet
	Total points:	188	points

Owner / location: Medical Gardens, Inc. / 1110 N.W. 8th Ave., Gainesville, Alachua Co. [s.w. 1/4 of sec 32, T9S, R20E]

Nominator(s) / date: Michael J. Bordyn / 1980

Update: Robert T. Ing, Daniel B. Ward / 1991

Comments: Earlier measurements: circ. (measured at 1 ft., below low fork) = 128 in.; now 140 in., ht. = 90 ft., spread = 54 ft. (Bordyn, 1980).

Lyonia ferruginea (Walt.) Nutt.
Rusty Lyonia, Staggerbush, Tree Lyonia

(1)

★ **National Co-Champion**.

Size:	Circumference:	29	inches
	Height:	35	feet
	Crown spread:	27	feet
	Total points:	71	points

Owner / location: Ocala National Forest / 2 mi. s.w. of Mud Lake, w. side of forest, Marion Co. [n.w. of sec 15, T14S, R24E]

Nominator(s) / date: Jeff Overby / 1993

Comments: Acknowledged by American Forests (1996 listing).

(2)

★ **National Co-Champion**.

Size:	Circumference:	28	inches
	Height:	36	feet
	Crown spread:	15	feet
	Total points:	68	points

Owner / location: Ocala National Forest / Kerr Key Rd., n. side of Lake Kerr, 2 mi. n.w. of Salt Springs, Marion Co. [sec 13, T13S, R25E]

Nominator(s) / date: Jeff Overby, Frank Brandt / 1993

Comments: Acknowledged by American Forests (1996 listing).

(3)

Honorable Mention.

Size:	Circumference:	27	inches
	Height:	32	feet
	Crown spread:	22	feet
	Total points:	64	points

Owner / location: (unknown) / n. end of Ft. George Id., Duval Co. [sec 37, T1S, R29E]

Nominator(s) / date: Buford C. Pruitt / 1984

(4)

Honorable Mention.

Size:	Circumference:	22	inches
	Height:	30	feet
	Crown spread:	17	feet
	Total points:	56	points

Owner / location: Marion Holder / w. end of Fowlers Lake, 1 mi. w. of Fla. 21, 5 mi. s. of Melrose, Putnam Co. [sec 18, T10S, R23E]

Nominator(s) / date: Ned D. Neenan / 1990

Lysiloma latisiliquum (L.) Benth.
Wild Tamarind, Bahama Lysiloma

(1)

★ **National Champion**.

Size:	Circumference:	72	inches
	Height:	40	feet
	Crown spread:	50.5	feet
	Total points:	125	points

Owner / location: Key Largo Hammocks State Botanical Site / n. end of Key Largo, Monroe Co. [sec 26, T59S, R40E]

Nominator(s) / date: Jeanne M. Parks / 1989

Comments: The report of a much larger (263 points) tree from Key West, formerly designated National champion for this species (American Forests, 1994), was based upon a misidentification of a well-known tree of *Tamarindus indica*, the National champion for that species.

Acknowledged by American Forests (1996 listing).

(2)

Florida Challenger.

Size:	Circumference:	69	inches
	Height:	42	feet
	Crown spread:	42.5	feet
	Total points:	122	points

Owner / location: Biscayne National Park / s. end of Totten Key, Dade Co. [s.w. 1/4 of sec 21, T58S, R41E]

Nominator(s) / date: Diane Riggs / 1995

Magnolia acuminata (L.) L.
Yellow Cucumber-tree

Title vacant.

Size:	Circumference:		
	Height:		
	Crown spread:		
	Total points:		

Owner / location:

Nominator(s) / date:

Comments: Native in west peninsular Florida.

Herbarium records (FLAS, July 1995) indicate this species, near DeFuniak Springs, Walton County, to reach a height of 50 ft.

National champion: Iowa (389 points).

Magnolia ashei Weatherby
Ashe Magnolia

Title vacant.

Size:	Circumference:		
	Height:		
	Crown spread:		
	Total points:		

Owner / location:

Nominator(s) / date:

Comments: Native in central peninsular Florida.

A tree, now dead, at Torreya State Park, Liberty County, was measured in 1991 by Jerome Bracewell, Angus K. Gholson and Joey T. Brady as having circ. = 35 in., ht. = 53 ft., and spread = 36 ft.

National champion: Pennsylvania (116 points), a cultivated tree. The species is endemic to Florida.

Magnolia grandiflora L.
Southern Magnolia, Bull Bay

(1)

☆ **Florida Co-Champion**.

Size:	Circumference:	198	inches
	Height:	94	feet
	Crown spread:	62.5	feet
	Total points:	308	points

Owner / location: C. H. Donovan / 1110 N.W. 36th Rd., Gainesville, Alachua Co. [n.w. 1/4 of sec 29, T9S, R20E]

Nominator(s) / date: Robert W. Simons, Michael J. Bordyn / 1981

Update: Robert T. Ing, Daniel B. Ward / 1991

Comments: Earlier measurements: circ. = 196 in., ht. = 88 ft., spread = 63 ft. (Simons & Bordyn, 1981). National champion: Mississippi (389 points).

(2)

☆ **Florida Co-Champion**.

Size:	Circumference:	202	inches
	Height:	84	feet
	Crown spread:	88	feet
	Total points:	308	points

Owner / location: J. C. Horton / 1775 Kingsley Ave. (Fla. 224), Orange Park, Clay Co. [s.e. 1/4 of sec 7, T4S, R26E]

Nominator(s) / date: William L. Rutherford / 1980

Update: Robert W. Ray / 1994

Comments: Earlier measurements: circ. = 187 in., ht. = 69 ft., spread = 83 ft. (Rutherford, 1980).

(3)

Florida Challenger.

Size:	Circumference:	183	inches
	Height:	93	feet
	Crown spread:	80	feet
	Total points:	296	points

Owner / location: David E. Halstead / between Fla. 13 & St. Johns River, 1.5 mi. s.e. of Riverdale, 15 mi. s.w. of St. Augustine, St. Johns Co. [sec 38, T8S, R27E]

Nominator(s) / date: David E. Halstead / 1980

Update: John L. Accardi / 1993

Comments: Earlier measurements: circ. = 177 in., ht. = 92 ft., spread = 77.5 ft. (Halstead, 1980).

(4)

Emeritus Florida Champion.

Size:	Circumference:	205	inches
	Height:	62	feet
	Crown spread:	95	feet
	Total points:	291	points

Owner / location: Billy Hill / 5 mi. n.w. of Jasper, Hamilton Co. [s.e. 1/4 of sec 14, T2N, R13E]

Nominator(s) / date: George Webb / 1980

Update: Doug Longshore / 1993

Comments: Earlier measurements: circ. = 200 in., ht. = 75 ft., spread = 99.5 ft. (Webb, 1980). Tree is reported to have been planted in 1868 (G. Webb, Sept 1980).

(5)

Honorable Mention.

Size:	Circumference:	193	inches
	Height:	68	feet

	Crown spread:	74	feet
	Total points:	280	points

Owner / location: Harry Walsh / 6872 Henderson St., Bagdad, Santa Rosa Co. [sec 14, T1N, R28W]

Nominator(s) / date: John D. Crawford / 1980

Update: Daniel Walsh / 1991

Comments: Earlier measurements: circ. = 188 in., ht. = 72 ft., spread = 76 ft. (Crawford, 1980).

Magnolia pyramidata Bartr.
Pyramid Magnolia

(1)

★ **National Co-Champion**.

Size:	Circumference:	62	inches
	Height:	65	feet
	Crown spread:	32	feet
	Total points:	135	points

Owner / location: Apalachicola Bluffs and Ravines Preserve / Abel's Hollow, Alum Bluff, 2 mi. n. of Bristol, Liberty Co. [sec 24, T1N, R8W]

Nominator(s) / date: Robert W. Simons, Mark W. Schwartz / 1988

Comments: Location is apparently not as clear as text implies (R. W. Simons, Aug 1991). Acknowledged by American Forests (1996 listing). National co-champion: Texas (132 points).

(2)

Not ranked; possibly still alive, but not verified for many years.

Size:	Circumference:	37	inches
	Height:	55	feet
	Crown spread:	22	feet
	Total points:	98	points

Owner / location: A. S. Harris / 7 mi. s.e. of Chattahoochee, Gadsden Co. [n.e. 1/4 of sec 31, T3N, R5W]

Nominator(s) / date: Charles E. Salter / 1967

Comments: This tree was designated the Florida champion (1986 listing), but was never ranked as National champion because that title was held by a larger tree in Texas.

(3)

Not ranked; possibly still alive, but not verified for many years.

Size:	Circumference:	27	inches
	Height:	61	feet
	Crown spread:	19	feet
	Total points:	93	points

Owner / location: Apalachicola Bluffs and Ravines Preserve / head of Kelley Branch, 2 mi. n. of Bristol, Liberty Co. [sec 20, T1N, R8W]

Nominator(s) / date: Charles E. Salter / 1967

Magnolia tripetala (L.) L.
Umbrella Magnolia

Title vacant.

Size: Circumference:
          Height:
          Crown spread:
          Total points:

Owner / location:

Nominator(s) / date:

Comments: Very rare: native in west peninsular
   Florida (Okaloosa County).
        National champion: Pennsylvania (185 points).

Magnolia virginiana L.
Sweetbay

(1)

☆ **Florida Champion**.

Size:			
	Circumference:	113	inches
	Height:	90	feet
	Crown spread:	52	feet
	Total points:	216	points

Owner / location: Ventura Ranch / 6 mi. n. of Rutland,
   11 mi. w.n.w. of Wildwood, Sumter Co. [n.e. 1/4 of sec
   9, T18S, R21E]
Nominator(s) / date: David L. Fogler / 1994
Comments: National champion: Arkansas (278 points).

(2)

Florida Challenger.

Size:			
	Circumference:	47	inches
	Height:	72	feet
	Crown spread:	21	feet
	Total points:	124	points

Owner / location: Aycock Trust Co. / 8 mi. s. of Mayo,
   Lafayette Co. [n.e. 1/4 of sec 23, T6S, R11E]
Nominator(s) / date: Jerry N. Livingston / 1987

Malus angustifolia (Ait.) Michx.
Wild Crab Apple

(1)

☆ **Florida Champion**.

Size:			
	Circumference:	20	inches
	Height:	29	feet
	Crown spread:	17	feet
	Total points:	53	points

Owner / location: Robert W. Simons / 1122 S.W. 11th
   Ave., Gainesville, Alachua Co. [n.w. 1/4 of sec 8,
   T11S, R20E]
Nominator(s) / date: Robert W. Simons, Daniel B. Ward /
   1993
Comments: Cultivated tree, planted about 1963 (R. W.
   Simons, May 1993).
        National champion: Maryland (153 points).

(2)

Florida Challenger.

Size:			
	Circumference:	10	inches
	Height:	26	feet
	Crown spread:	17	feet
	Total points:	40	points

Owner / location: Three Rivers State Recreation Area /
   nature trail, s. end of park, 2 mi. n. of Sneads,
   Jackson Co. [s.e. 1/4 of sec 15, T4N, R7W]
Nominator(s) / date: Robert T. Ing, Daniel B. Ward /
   1995

Manilkara bahamensis (Baker)
H. J. Lam & Meeuse
= *Achras emarginata* (L.) Little
Wild Dilly

(1)

★ **National Champion**.

Size:			
	Circumference:	22	inches
	Height:	21	feet
	Crown spread:	32.5	feet
	Total points:	51	points

Owner / location: Key West Botanical Garden Society /
   Botanical Garden, Stock Island, Monroe Co. [n.e. 1/4
   of sec 34, T67S, R25E]
Nominator(s) / date: Michael B. Miller, Vincent P.
   Condon / 1995
Comments: Acknowledged by American Forests (1996
   listing).

(2)

Florida Challenger.

Size:			
	Circumference:	11	inches
	Height:	10	feet
	Crown spread:	21	feet
	Total points:	26	points

Owner / location: Biscayne National Park / s. end of
   Totten Key, Dade Co. [s.w. 1/4 of sec 21, T58S, R41E]
Nominator(s) / date: Diane Riggs / 1995

Mastichodendron foetidissimum
(Jacq.) H. J. Lam
= *Sideroxylon foetidissimum* Jacq.
False Mastic

(1)

★ **National Champion** (nominee).

Size:			
	Circumference:	105	inches
	Height:	118	feet
	Crown spread:	94	feet
	Total points:	247	points

Owner / location: Castellow Hammock Park / 22430 S.W. 153rd St., Homestead, Dade Co. [n.e. 1/4 of sec 17, T56S, R39E]

Nominator(s) / date: Albert H. Hetzell, Ron Smith / 1973

Update: Jerry Cordy / 1982

Update: Roger Hammer / 1995

Comments: Earlier measurements: circ. = 100 in., ht. = 105 ft., spread = 36 ft. (Hetzell & Smith, 1973). Tree was thought to have been destroyed by Hurricane Andrew, August 1992, and was dropped as National champion; but when debris was cleared, tree was found with some of the crown lost but still in good health (R. Hammer, Oct 1995).

(2)

★ National Champion.

Size:			
	Circumference:	104	inches
	Height:	59	feet
	Crown spread:	65	feet
	Total points:	179	points

Owner / location: City of Ft. Lauderdale / 100 N.E. Victoria Park Rd., Ft. Lauderdale, Broward Co. [s.e. 1/4 of sec 2, T50S, R42E]

Nominator(s) / date: John W. Kern / 1988

Comments: Acknowledged by American Forests (1996 listing).

(3)

Florida Challenger.

Size:			
	Circumference:	76	inches
	Height:	44	feet
	Crown spread:	45.5	feet
	Total points:	131	points

Owner / location: Lignumvitae Key State Botanical Site / off Matheson Trail, Lignumvitae Key, Monroe Co. [n.w. 1/4 of sec 2, T64S, R36E]

Nominator(s) / date: Robert Rose, Vincent P. Condon / 1995

Comments: The larger of two similar-sized trees at this location.

(4)

Honorable Mention.

Size:			
	Circumference:	74	inches
	Height:	37	feet
	Crown spread:	44.5	feet
	Total points:	122	points

Owner / location: Lignumvitae Key State Botanical Site / off Matheson Trail, Lignumvitae Key, Monroe Co. [n.w. 1/4 of sec 2, T64S, R36E]

Nominator(s) / date: Robert Rose, Vincent P. Condon / 1995

Comments: The smaller of two similar-sized trees at this location.

(5)

Emeritus National Champion.

Size:			
	Circumference:	54	inches
	Height:	30	feet
	Crown spread:	31.5	feet
	Total points:	92	points

Owner / location: Ted Watrous / s. end of Buck Key, just e. of Captiva Id., Lee Co. [sec 2, T46S, R21E]

Nominator(s) / date: David Fox, Dee Slinkard / 1984

(6)

Not ranked; possibly still alive, but not verified for many years.

Size:			
	Circumference:	76	inches
	Height:	42	feet
	Crown spread:	32	feet
	Total points:	126	points

Owner / location: Lignumvitae Key State Botanical Site / Lignumvitae Key, Monroe Co. [n.w. 1/4 of sec 2, T64S, R36E]

Nominator(s) / date: Robert W. Simons / 1978

Comments: When measured (Simons, 1978), this tree was presumed to be the National champion (Niedhauk, 1975: 163 points), now deceased. Its dimensions, however, are appreciably less and its location does not correspond to the map of Roundtree & Zickar (1986).

Maytenus phyllanthoides Benth.
Florida Mayten

(1)

★ National Co-Champion.

Size:			
	Circumference:	17	inches
	Height:	18	feet
	Crown spread:	36	feet
	Total points:	40	points

Owner / location: Sanibel-Captiva Conservation Foundation / Bay Drive, just w. of bridge, near e. end of Sanibel Id., Lee Co. [s.e. 1/4 of sec 18, T46S, R23E]

Nominator(s) / date: Richard W. Workman / 1995

Comments: The larger of two similar-sized trees of this species at this location.

Acknowledged by American Forests (1996 listing).

(2)

★ National Co-Champion.

Size:			
	Circumference:	15	inches
	Height:	17	feet

Crown spread: 21.5   feet

         Total points: 38   points

Owner / location: Sanibel-Captiva Conservation Foundation / Bay Drive, just w. of bridge, near e. end of Sanibel Id., Lee Co. [s.e. 1/4 of sec 18, T46S, R23E]

Nominator(s) / date: Richard W. Workman / 1995

Comments: The second largest tree of this species at this location.

Metopium toxiferum (L.) Krug & Urban
Poisonwood, Florida Poisontree

(1)

★ **National Champion**.

Size:	Circumference:	79	inches
	Height:	38	feet
	Crown spread:	29	feet
	Total points:	124	points

Owner / location: Lignumvitae Key State Botanical Site / Lignumvitae Key, Monroe Co. [n.w. 1/4 of sec 2, T64S, R36E]

Nominator(s) / date: Ken Roundtree, David M. Sinclair / 1986

Update: Robert Rose, Vincent P. Condon / 1995

Comments: Earlier measurements: circ. = 81 in., ht. = 39 ft., spread = 32 ft. (Roundtree & Sinclair, 1986)

    Acknowledged by American Forests (1996 listing), with 1986 measurements.

Morus rubra L.
Red Mulberry

(1)

☆ **Florida Champion**.

Size:	Circumference:	204	inches
	Height:	51	feet
	Crown spread:	58.5	feet
	Total points:	270	points

Owner / location: Moses W. Braxton / 2 mi. w. of Cottondale, Jackson Co. [sec 35, T6N, R12W]

Nominator(s) / date: Stan Humphries, David L. Fogler / 1989

Comments: National champion: Oklahoma (343 points).

(2)

Florida Challenger.

Size:	Circumference:	210	inches
	Height:	40	feet
	Crown spread:	62	feet
	Total points:	266	points

Owner / location: James Brown / 16021 N. U.S. 441, Reddick, Marion Co. [s.w. 1/4 of sec 2, T13S, R21E]

Nominator(s) / date: Robert W. Simons / 1994

(3)

Honorable Mention.

Size:	Circumference:	111	inches
	Height:	58	feet
	Crown spread:	73	feet
	Total points:	187	points

Owner / location: U.S.D.A. Entomology Research Laboratory / 1600 S.W. 23rd Drive, Gainesville, Alachua Co. [s.w. 1/4 of sec 12, T10S, R19E]

Nominator(s) / date: Robert W. Simons, Daniel B. Ward / 1993

(4)

Honorable Mention.

Size:	Circumference:	60	inches
	Height:	58	feet
	Crown spread:	38	feet
	Total points:	128	points

Owner / location: Ruth Hayworth / 2812 Tallevast Rd., Tallevast, Manatee Co. [n.w. 1/4 of sec 32, T35S, R18E]

Nominator(s) / date: Mark Bakeman / 1981

Update: Robert T. Ing, Daniel B. Ward / 1994

Comments: Earlier measurements: circ. = 51 in., ht. = 45 ft., spread = 45 ft. (Bakeman, 1981).

Myrcianthes fragrans (Sw.) McVaugh
Twinberry Stopper

Title vacant.

Size:	Circumference:		
	Height:		
	Crown spread:		
	Total points:		

Owner / location:

Nominator(s) / date:

Comments: Native in coastal central and south peninsular Florida.

    Trees to 25 centimeters dbh. have been observed in Collier-Seminole Park, Collier County (G. Avery notes, June 1967). This species (as var. *fragrans*) is recognized as a tree by American Forests (1996 listing), but as a "species without a champion."

Myrcianthes simpsonii (Small) K. A. Wils.
= *Myrcianthes fragrans* (Sw.) McVaugh
var. *simpsonii* (Small) R. W. Long
Simpson's Twinberry, Simpson Stopper

(1)

★ **National Champion**.

Size:	Circumference:	34	inches
	Height:	51	feet

Crown spread:	40	feet	
Total points:	95	points	

Owner / location: County of Broward / Fern Forest Nature Preserve, 201 Lyons Rd., Pompano Beach, Broward Co. [n.e. 1/4 of sec 6, T49S, R42E]

Nominator(s) / date: Jim Higgins / 1995

Comments: Acknowledged (as *Myrcianthes fragrans* var. *simpsonii*) by American Forests (1996 listing).

(2)

Emeritus National Champion.

Size:	Circumference:	37	inches
	Height:	37	feet
	Crown spread:	32	feet
	Total points:	82	points

Owner / location: Ely Walker / n. of Fla. 60, w. of Kings Hwy. (Fla. 613), Vero Beach, Indian River Co. [n. 1/2 of sec 5, T33S, R39E]

Nominator(s) / date: William K. DeBraal / 1986

Comments: This tree was previously the National champion, but was incorrectly displaced from that status by a multi-stemmed tree (Spicer, 1991) on the basis of a circumference measurement taken below the point of branching.

(3)

Emeritus National Champion.

Size:	Circumference:	33	inches
	Height:	33	feet
	Crown spread:	38	feet
	Total points:	76	points

Owner / location: Alandco, Inc. / 2900 block of S.W. 36th St., Ft. Lauderdale, Broward Co. [n.w. 1/4 of sec 29, T50S, R42E]

Nominator(s) / date: David A. Spicer / 1991

Update: Frank L. Zickar / 1994

Update: Jim Higgins / 1995

Comments: Earlier measurements: circ. = 53 in. (measured at 2.5 ft.), ht. = 32 ft., spread = 34 ft. (Spicer, 1991); circ. = 31 in., ht. = 32 ft., spread = 34 ft. (Zickar, 1994).

Myrica cerifera L.
Wax Myrtle, Bayberry

(1)

☆ **Florida Champion.**

Size:	Circumference:	41	inches
	Height:	36	feet
	Crown spread:	29.5	feet
	Total points:	84	points

Owner / location: Charles Garrison / end of West Harbor Drive, off River Road (Fla. 15), 1 mi. s. of Bridge-

port, 7 mi. n.e. of Palatka, Putnam Co. [n.e. 1/4 of sec 3, T9S, R27E]

Nominator(s) / date: Ned D. Neenan / 1993

Comments: National champions: North Carolina (104 points); Virginia, three trees (106 points, 106 points, 102 points).

(2)

Florida Challenger.

Size:	Circumference:	29	inches
	Height:	31	feet
	Crown spread:	27	feet
	Total points:	67	points

Owner / location: (unknown) / n. end of Ft. George Id., Duval Co. [sec 37, T1S, R29E]

Nominator(s) / date: Buford C. Pruitt, David L. Evans, Kirk M. Stage / 1984

Comments: Circ. at 6 in. = 49 in. (B. C. Pruitt, Mar 1992).

Myrica inodora Bartr.
Odorless Bayberry

Title vacant.

Size:	Circumference:	
	Height:	
	Crown spread:	
	Total points:	

Owner / location:

Nominator(s) / date:

Comments: Native in panhandle Florida.

Although usually a shrub, herbarium records (FLAS, July 1995) indicate this species near Wetumpka, Gadsden County, and Shalimar, Okaloosa County, to reach a height of 6 meters.

National champion: Alabama (57 points).

Myrsine floridana A. DC.
= *Rapanea punctata* (Lam.) Lundell;
Rapanea guianensis, misapplied
Myrsine, Florida Rapanea

(1)

★ **National Champion.**

Size:	Circumference:	29	inches
	Height:	30	feet
	Crown spread:	17	feet
	Total points:	63	points

Owner / location: Ding Darling National Wildlife Refuge / n. side of Sanibel-Captiva Rd., Sanibel Id., Lee Co. [s.w. 1/4 of sec 21, T46S, R22E]

Nominator(s) / date: Ferrell Johns / 1992

Comments: Acknowledged (as *Rapanea punctata*) by American Forests (1996 listing).

Nectandra coriacea (Sw.) Griseb.
Lancewood, Florida Nectandra

Title vacant.

Size: Circumference:
           Height:
           Crown spread:
           Total points:

Owner / location:

Nominator(s) / date:

Comments: Native in coastal central and south peninsular Florida.

Trees of this species have been observed as "common" on Lignumvitae Key, Monroe County (G. Avery notes, Apr 1962). Herbarium records (FLAS, July 1995) indicate in Fuchs Hammock, Dade County, it reaches a height of 20 meters. It is recognized as a tree by American Forests (1996 listing), but as a "species without a champion."

Nyssa biflora Walt.
= *Nyssa sylvatica* Marsh. var. *biflora* (Walt.) Sarg.
Swamp Tupelo

(1)

☆ **Florida Champion**.

Size:			
	Circumference:	158	inches
	Height:	94	feet
	Crown spread:	34	feet
	Total points:	261	points

Owner / location: Ocala National Forest / just e. of Fla. 314, 2 mi. n. of Fla. 40, 20 mi. s. of Orange Springs, Marion Co. [s.e. 1/4 of sec 2, T15S, R24E]

Nominator(s) / date: Jerry Clutts, Robert W. Simons, Jim Buckner / 1994

Comments: National champion: Virginia (354 points).

(2)

Florida Challenger.

Size:			
	Circumference:	131	inches
	Height:	100	feet
	Crown spread:	53	feet
	Total points:	244	points

Owner / location: Ocala National Forest / Hughes Island, 6.5 mi. w. of Silver Glen Spring, Marion Co. [s.e. 1/4 of sec 24, T14S, R25E]

Nominator(s) / date: Robert W. Simons, Daniel B. Ward / 1993

(3)

Honorable Mention.

Size:			
	Circumference:	110	inches
	Height:	108	feet
	Crown spread:	58	feet
	Total points:	233	points

Owner / location: Ravine State Gardens / Twigg St., Palatka, Putnam Co. [s.e. 1/4 of sec 12, T10S, R26E]

Nominator(s) / date: Steven Dale / 1989

Update: Ned D. Neenan / 1993

Comments: Earlier measurements: circ. = 109 in., ht. = 101 ft., spread = 67 ft. (Dale, 1989).

First identified as *Nyssa sylvatica* and recorded as Florida champion for that species; trunk scarcely enlarged at base, but small untoothed leaves and stream-margin habitat indicate *N. biflora* (D. B. Ward, June 1995).

Nyssa ogeche Bartr. ex Marsh.
Ogeechee Lime, Ogeechee Tupelo

(1)

★ **National Co-Champion**.

Size:			
	Circumference:	166	inches
	Height:	93	feet
	Crown spread:	41	feet
	Total points:	269	points

Owner / location: Apalachicola National Forest / n. of Florida Trail, Bradwell Bay Wilderness, 8 mi. n.w. of Sopchoppy, Wakulla Co. [s. 1/2 of sec 7, T4S, R3W]

Nominator(s) / date: Robert W. Simons, Dale Allen / 1981

Update: Robert W. Simons, Daniel B. Ward, Dale Allen, Gary Hegg / 1993

Comments: Largest of many similar-sized *Nyssa ogeche* in stand. Earlier measurements: circ. = 162 in., ht. = 95 ft., spread = 40 ft. (Simons & Allen, 1981).

Acknowledged by American Forests (1996 listing).

(2)

★ **National Co-Champion**.

Size:			
	Circumference:	174	inches
	Height:	81	feet
	Crown spread:	48	feet
	Total points:	267	points

Owner / location: Apalachicola National Forest / n. of Florida Trail, Bradwell Bay Wilderness, 8 mi. n.w. of Sopchoppy, Wakulla Co. [s. 1/2 of sec 7, T4S, R3W]

Nominator(s) / date: Robert W. Simons, Daniel B. Ward, Dale Allen, Gary Hegg / 1993

Comments: Second largest of many similar-sized *Nyssa ogeche* in stand.

Acknowledged by American Forests (1996 listing).

(3)

Florida Challenger.

Size:			
	Circumference:	171	inches
	Height:	83	feet
	Crown spread:	33	feet
	Total points:	262	points

Owner / location: Apalachicola National Forest / n. of Florida Trail, Bradwell Bay Wilderness, 8 mi. n.w. of

Sopchoppy, Wakulla Co. [s. 1/2 of sec 7, T4S, R3W]

Nominator(s) / date: Robert W. Simons, Daniel B. Ward, Dale Allen, Gary Hegg / 1993

Comments: Third largest of many similar-sized *Nyssa ogeche* in stand.

(4)

Emeritus National Champion.

Size:	Circumference:	200	inches
	Height:	45	feet
	Crown spread:	54	feet
	Total points:	259	points

Owner / location: (unknown) / Cone Bridge boat ramp, e. bank of Suwannee River, 20 mi. n. of Lake City, Columbia Co. [s.w. 1/4 of sec 36, T1N, R16E]

Nominator(s) / date: Dodie Pedlow / 1982

Update: Robert T. Ing, Daniel B. Ward / 1993

Comments: Earlier measurements: circ. = 201 in., ht. = 60 ft., spread = 61 ft. (Pedlow, 1982).

At medium water levels, tree appears free-standing in stream channel of Suwannee River (D. B. Ward, May 1993); with low water, tree can be seen to be on peninsula protruding from east bank, formed by its own roots (R. T. Ing & D. B. Ward, Aug 1993).

Nyssa sylvatica Marsh.
Black Tupelo, Black Gum

Size:	Circumference:		
	Height:		
	Crown spread:		
	Total points:		

Owner / location:

Nominator(s) / date:

Comments: Native in north Florida.

In Florida this species is usually smaller than *Nyssa biflora* from which it is tenuously distinguished. Herbarium records (FLAS, July 1995) of indisputable *N. sylvatica* indicate it to reach a height, at Aspalaga Landing, Gadsden County, of 25 ft., at DeFuniak Springs, Walton County, of 35 ft., and near Tallahassee, Leon County, of 50 ft.

National champion: Louisiana (358 points).

Nyssa uniflora Wangenh.
= *Nyssa aquatica*, misapplied
Water Tupelo

(1)

☆ Florida Champion.

Size:	Circumference:	149	inches
	Height:	104	feet
	Crown spread:	40	feet
	Total points:	263	points

Owner / location: Neal Land & Timber, Inc. / just w. of

Torreya State Park, Liberty Co. [center of sec 17, T2N, R7W]

Nominator(s) / date: Robert W. Simons, Jim Buckner / 1993

Comments: National champion: Virginia (455 points).

Osmanthus americanus (L.) Benth.
& Hook. f. ex Gray
Wild Olive, Devilwood

(1)

★ National Champion.

Size:	Circumference:	36	inches
	Height:	46	feet
	Crown spread:	27	feet
	Total points:	89	points

Owner / location: Marshall Flournoy / s. of Fla. 308, 5 mi. w. of Crescent City, Putnam Co. [sec 30, T12S, R27E]

Nominator(s) / date: Ned D. Neenan / 1990

Comments: Acknowledged by American Forests (1996 listing).

(2)

Florida Challenger.

Size:	Circumference:	37	inches
	Height:	23	feet
	Crown spread:	30	feet
	Total points:	68	points

Owner / location: Florida Div. of Forestry / O'Leno fire tower, 6 mi. n. of High Springs, Columbia Co. [s.w. 1/4 of sec 34, T6S, R17E]

Nominator(s) / date: Robert W. Simons, Daniel B. Ward / 1993

(3)

Emeritus National Champion.

Size:	Circumference:	10	inches
	Height:	36	feet
	Crown spread:	15	feet
	Total points:	50	points

Owner / location: P. & G. Cellulose, Inc. / along Steinhatchee River, 3 mi. s.e. of Cooks Hammock, 12 mi. s.w. of Mayo, Lafayette Co. [s.w. 1/4 of sec 7, T7S, R11E]

Nominator(s) / date: Jerry N. Livingston / 1988

Osmanthus megacarpus (Small) Little
Scrub Wild Olive

(1)

★ National Champion (nominee).

Size:	Circumference:	19	inches
	Height:	40	feet
	Crown spread:	33	· feet
	Total points:	67	points

Owner / location: Florida Dept. of Transportation / s.e. of Moon Lake Estates, 8 mi. e. of New Port Richey, Pasco Co. [n.e. 1/4 of sec 34, T25S, R17E]

Nominator(s) / date: Donald Robinson, William J. Schilling / 1996

Comments: Growing in scrub soil; a male tree, but nearby smaller trees have distinctive large fruits (D. Robinson, Nov 1996).

Treated by Little (1979) as synonymous with *Osmanthus americanus* and thus not recognized by American Forests (1996 listing).

Ostrya virginiana (Mill.) K. Koch
Ironwood, Hop Hornbeam

(1)

☆ **Florida Co-Champion**.

Size:			
	Circumference:	49	inches
	Height:	57	feet
	Crown spread:	20	feet
	Total points:	111	points

Owner / location: Richard Ohmes / just n. of Int. 10, e. of U.S. 19, 3 mi. s. of Monticello, Jefferson Co. [s.e. 1/4 of sec 18, T1N, R25E]

Nominator(s) / date: Michael Humphrey / 1987

Comments: National champion: Michigan (217 points).

(2)

☆ **Florida Co-Champion**.

Size:			
	Circumference:	50	inches
	Height:	48	feet
	Crown spread:	50	feet
	Total points:	111	points

Owner / location: Bradley Co., Inc. / 3921 S.W. 34th St., Gainesville, Alachua Co. [s.e. 1/4 of sec 13, T10S, R19E]

Nominator(s) / date: Duane R. Durgee / 1995

(3)

Florida Challenger.

Size:			
	Circumference:	56	inches
	Height:	39	feet
	Crown spread:	49	feet
	Total points:	107	points

Owner / location: Roy Davis / jct. U.S. 19 & Fla. 14, Eridu, 16 mi. n.w. of Perry, Taylor Co. [n.e. 1/4 of sec 20, T2S, R6E]

Nominator(s) / date: John K. Fish, Jerry N. Livingston / 1994

(4)

Emeritus Florida Champion.

Size:			
	Circumference:	39	inches
	Height:	54	feet
	Crown spread:	30	feet
	Total points:	101	points

Owner / location: Jack E. Greene / 8 mi. s. of Chipley, Washington Co. [n.e. 1/4 of sec 5, T3N, R12W]

Nominator(s) / date: Charles R. Reeves / 1986

(5)

Honorable Mention.

Size:			
	Circumference:	19	inches
	Height:	38	feet
	Crown spread:	26	feet
	Total points:	63	points

Owner / location: Aycock Trust Co. / 8 mi. s. of Mayo, Lafayette Co. [n.e. 1/4 of sec 23, T6S, R11E]

Nominator(s) / date: Jerry N. Livingston / 1989

Oxydendrum arboreum (L.) DC.
Sourwood

(1)

☆ **Florida Champion**.

Size:			
	Circumference:	67	inches
	Height:	68	feet
	Crown spread:	26	feet
	Total points:	142	points

Owner / location: Eugene H. Syfrett / 1/4 mi. s. of house, Sunny Hills Rd., 5 mi. s.e. of Wausau, Washington Co. [s.e. 1/4 of sec 10, T2N, R13W]

Nominator(s) / date: Charles R. Reeves / 1990

Comments: National champion: Tennessee (209 points).

Persea borbonia (L.) Spreng.
Red Bay

(1)

★ **National Co-Champion**.

Size:			
	Circumference:	152	inches
	Height:	77	feet
	Crown spread:	52	feet
	Total points:	242	points

Owner / location: Estella Barthle / 2 mi. s.e. of Alapaha River, 6 mi. s.w. of Jasper, Hamilton Co. [sec 20, T1N, R13E]

Nominator(s) / date: Norman Nichols / 1983

Update: Doug Longshore / 1993

Comments: Earlier measurements: circ. = 135 in., ht. = 87 ft., spread = 45 ft. (Nichols, 1983).

    Acknowledged by American Forests (1996 listing), with National co-champion: Georgia (239 points).

(2)

Florida Challenger.

Size:			
	Circumference:	130	inches
	Height:	77	feet
	Crown spread:	66	feet
	Total points:	224	points

Owner / location: Prairie View Trust / Sugarfoot Hammock, e. side of Int. 75, 200 yds. s. of S.W. 20th Ave. overpass, Gainesville, Alachua Co. [sec 10, T10S, R19E]

Nominator(s) / date: Robert W. Simons / 1986

Update: Robert W. Simons, Daniel B. Ward / 1994

Comments: Earlier measurements: circ. = 127 in., ht. = 75 ft., spread = 67 ft. (Simons, 1986).

(3)

Honorable Mention.

Size:			
	Circumference:	128	inches
	Height:	72	feet
	Crown spread:	61.5	feet
	Total points:	215	points

Owner / location: Rosemarie Permenter / 2 mi. e. of Fla. 475, 1.5 mi. n. of county line, 6 mi. s.w. of Belleview, Marion Co. [s.e. 1/4 of sec 34, T17S, R22E]

Nominator(s) / date: Jeff Overby / 1993

(4)

Honorable Mention.

Size:			
	Circumference:	95	inches
	Height:	63	feet
	Crown spread:	57	feet
	Total points:	172	points

Owner / location: Evergreen Cemetery Ass'n / 4535 N. Main St., Jacksonville, Duval Co. [sec 50, T1S, R26E]

Nominator(s) / date: Joseph E. Dunbar, Richard W. Gorden / 1985

(5)

Emeritus Florida Champion.

Size:			
	Circumference:	108	inches
	Height:	55	feet
	Crown spread:	21	feet
	Total points:	168	points

Owner / location: Arlene Blander / 21340 N.E. 23rd Court, 1/2 mi. e. of Int. 95, just s. of county line, North Miami Beach, Dade Co. [n. 1/2 of sec 33, T51S, R42E]

Nominator(s) / date: Robert Newburne / 1981

Update: Roger L. Hammer, Daniel B. Ward / 1994

Comments: Earlier measurements: circ. = 95 in., ht. = 57 ft., spread = 57 ft. (Newburne, 1981).

Persea humilis Nash
= *Persea borbonia* (L.) Spreng.
var. *humilis* (Nash) Kopp
Silk Bay

(1)

★ National Champion.

Size:			
	Circumference:	55	inches
	Height:	38	feet
	Crown spread:	46	feet
	Total points:	105	points

Owner / location: Ocala National Forest / Eureka Tower site, 2 mi. w. of w. edge of Lake Kerr, Marion Co. [s. 1/2 of sec 13, T13S, R24E]

Nominator(s) / date: Robert W. Simons / 1991

Comments: Acknowledged (as *P. borbonia* var. *humilis*) by American Forests (1996 listing).

Persea palustris (Raf.) Sarg.
= *Persea borbonia* (L.) Spreng.
var. *pubescens* (Pursh) Little
Swamp Bay

Title vacant.

Size:			
	Circumference:		
	Height:		
	Crown spread:		
	Total points:		

Owner / location:

Nominator(s) / date:

Comments: Native throughout Florida.

    Herbarium records (FLAS, July 1995) indicate this species, near Lake Placid, Highlands County, to reach a height of 10 meters.

    National champion: North Carolina (251 points).

Picramnia pentandra Sw.
Bitterbush

Title vacant.

Size:			
	Circumference:		
	Height:		
	Crown spread:		
	Total points:		

Owner / location:

Nominator(s) / date:

Comments: Native in south peninsular Florida (Dade County).

This species has been observed to be a "common tree" in Brickell Hammock, Dade County (G. Avery notes, Jan 1965), where herbarium records (FLAS, July 1995) indicate it to reach a height of 12 ft. It is recognized as a tree by American Forests (1996 listing), but as a "species without a champion."

Pinckneya bracteata (Bartr.) Raf.
= *Pinckneya pubens* Michx.
Fever-tree

(1)

★ National Champion.

Size:			
	Circumference:	10	inches
	Height:	21	feet
	Crown spread:	7	feet
	Total points:	33	points

Owner / location: C. G. Money / between Orange Springs Country Inn and Orange Creek, Orange Springs, Marion Co. [n.w. 1/4 of sec 30, T11S, R24E]

Nominator(s) / date: Robert T. Ing, Daniel B. Ward / 1991

Comments: This tree is a smaller replacement for the previous Florida champion (Simons & Morris, 1980 - 48 points) also at this location, and now deceased.

Acknowledged by American Forests (1996 listing).

Pinus clausa (Chapm. ex Engelm.)
Vasey ex Sarg.
Sand Pine

(1)

★ National Co-Champion.

Size:			
	Circumference:	86	inches
	Height:	95	feet
	Crown spread:	41	feet
	Total points:	191	points

Owner / location: Starkey Wilderness Park / 6 mi. e. of New Port Richey, 6 mi. s. of Fla. 52, Pasco Co. [n.w. 1/4 of sec 8, T26S, R17E]

Nominator(s) / date: Garry A. Flood / 1990

Update: Ken L. Stay, Jeff Overby / 1993

Comments: Earlier measurements: circ. = 86 in., ht. = 93 ft., spread = 38 ft. (Flood, 1990).

This tree is one of several of almost identical size from the same location, measured on the same date but nominated by different individuals. The largest (Garcia, 1990 - 198 points) is now deceased.

This tree and all others nominated from peninsular Florida are of the Ocala sand pine, *Pinus clausa* var. *clausa*, whose cones remain tightly closed until the seed are released by fire. Trees in the Florida panhandle are of the Choctawhatchee sand pine, *P. clausa* var. *immuginata* D. B. Ward, with cones that open promptly at maturity.

Acknowledged by American Forests (1996 listing).

(2)

★ National Co-Champion.

Size:			
	Circumference:	77	inches
	Height:	100	feet
	Crown spread:	42	feet
	Total points:	188	points

Owner / location: Starkey Wilderness Park / 6 mi. e. of New Port Richey, 6 mi. s. of Fla. 52, Pasco Co. [n.w. 1/4 of sec 8, T26S, R17E]

Nominator(s) / date: Kevin W. Love / 1990

Comments: This tree is the second of several of almost identical size from the same location.

Acknowledged by American Forests (1996 listing).

(3)

★ National Co-Champion.

Size:			
	Circumference:	84	inches
	Height:	94	feet
	Crown spread:	39	feet
	Total points:	188	points

Owner / location: Starkey Wilderness Park / 6 mi. e. of New Port Richey, 6 mi. s. of Fla. 52, Pasco Co. [n.w. 1/4 of sec 8, T26S, R17E]

Nominator(s) / date: Kerry Tully / 1990

Comments: This tree is the third of several of almost identical size from the same location.

Acknowledged by American Forests (1996 listing).

(4)

Honorable Mention.

Size:			
	Circumference:	85	inches
	Height:	81	feet
	Crown spread:	46	feet
	Total points:	178	points

Owner / location: Lower Wekiva State Preserve / e. side of Wekiva River, n. side of Fla 29, Seminole Co. [sec 39, T19S, R29E]

Nominator(s) / date: Walter Thompson, John T. Koehler / 1987

Pinus echinata Mill.
Shortleaf Pine

(1)

☆ **Florida Champion.**

Size:			
	Circumference:	124	inches
	Height:	122	feet
	Crown spread:	52	feet
	Total points:	259	points

Owner / location: Alfred B. Maclay State Gardens / 3540 N. Thomasville Rd., Tallahassee, Leon Co. [sec 5, T1N, R1E]

Nominator(s) / date: Thomas D. Beitzel, Beth Weidner / 1985

Comments: National champion: Mississippi (290 points).

(2)

Florida Challenger.

Size:			
	Circumference:	89	inches
	Height:	108	feet
	Crown spread:	44.5	feet
	Total points:	208	points

Owner / location: Sam E. Hand / 712 North Ride, Tallahassee, Leon Co. [n.e. 1/4 of sec 19, T1N, R1E]

Nominator(s) / date: Charles E. Salter, Daniel B. Ward / 1995

Comments: Larger of two trees at this location.

(3)

Honorable Mention.

Size:			
	Circumference:	96	inches
	Height:	85	feet
	Crown spread:	55.5	feet
	Total points:	195	points

Owner / location: Sam E. Hand / 712 North Ride, Tallahassee, Leon Co. [n.e. 1/4 of sec 19, T1N, R1E]

Nominator(s) / date: Charles E. Salter, Daniel B. Ward / 1995

Comments: Second larger of two trees at this location.

Pinus elliottii Engelm.
Slash Pine

(1)

★ **National Champion.**

Size:			
	Circumference:	130	inches
	Height:	138	feet
	Crown spread:	55	feet
	Total points:	282	points

Owner / location: Laetitia Rogers / 7800 Miller Oaks Dr., Jacksonville, Duval Co. [w. 1/4 of sec 44, T3S, R27E]

Nominator(s) / date: James R. Karels / 1985

Update: Scott A. Crosby / 1992

Comments: Earlier measurements: circ. = 129 in., ht. = 126 ft., spread = 72 ft. (Karels, 1985; as *Pinus taeda*). This tree is the typical variety (var. *elliottii*), and is north of the known range of *Pinus elliottii* var. *densa* (South Florida slash pine); not remeasured (R. T. Ing & D. B. Ward, Oct 1993).

Acknowledged by American Forests (1996 listing).

(2)

Emeritus National Champion.

Size:			
	Circumference:	128	inches
	Height:	129	feet
	Crown spread:	29	feet
	Total points:	264	points

Owner / location: Apalachicola National Forest / s.e. of Florida Trail, Bradwell Bay Wilderness, 8 mi. n.w. of Sopchoppy, Wakulla Co. [s. 1/2 of sec 7, T4S, R3W]

Nominator(s) / date: John H. Courtenay / 1962

Update: Robert W. Simons, Daniel B. Ward, Dale Allen, Gary Hegg / 1993

Comments: Earlier measurements: circ. = 125 in., ht. = 119 ft., spread = 41 ft. (Courtenay, 1962). The largest of several similar-sized trees in stand. This tree is *Pinus elliottii* var. *elliottii*.

(3)

Honorable Mention.

Size:			
	Circumference:	118	inches
	Height:	123	feet
	Crown spread:	68	feet
	Total points:	258	points

Owner / location: William S. Rosasco / 4 mi. s.s.e. of Milton, Santa Rosa Co. [sec 25, T1N, R28W]

Nominator(s) / date: William S. Rosasco / 1990

Update: Kenneth L. Oser / 1994

Comments: Tree has recently been struck by lightning, foliage is now discolored, and tree may be dying; not remeasured (Oser, Jan 1994). This tree is *Pinus elliottii* var. *elliottii*.

(4)

Honorable Mention.

Size:			
	Circumference:	139	inches
	Height:	87	feet
	Crown spread:	63	feet
	Total points:	242	points

Owner / location: U.S. Army / w. end of Lowry Lake, s. portion of Camp Blanding, 4 mi. n. of Keystone Heights, Clay Co. [n.e. 1/4 of sec 32, T7S, R23E]

Nominator(s) / date: Dave Loper / 1980

Update: Robert W. Ray / 1994

Comments: Earlier measurements: circ. = 135 in., ht. = 73 ft., spread = 60.5 ft. (Loper, 1980). This tree is *Pinus elliottii* var. *elliottii*.

(5)

Florida Challenger.

Size:			
	Circumference:	101	inches
	Height:	130	feet
	Crown spread:	38	feet
	Total points:	241	points

Owner / location: Apalachicola National Forest / s. of Florida Trail, Bradwell Bay Wilderness, 8 mi. n.w. of Sopchoppy, Wakulla Co. [s. 1/2 of sec 7, T4S, R3W]

Nominator(s) / date: Robert W. Simons, Daniel B. Ward, Dale Allen, Gary Hegg / 1993

Comments: The second largest of several similar-sized trees in stand. This tree is *Pinus elliottii* var. *elliottii*.

Pinus elliottii Engelm. var. densa Little & Dorman
South Florida Slash Pine

(1)

★ National Champion.

Size:			
	Circumference:	130	inches
	Height:	67	feet
	Crown spread:	75	feet
	Total points:	216	points

Owner / location: Univ. of South Florida / 5700 N. Tamiami Trail (U.S. 41), n. Sarasota, Sarasota Co. [n.e. 1/4 of sec 2, T36S, R17E]

Nominator(s) / date: William J. Schilling / 1984

Update: William J. Schilling / 1993

Comments: Earlier measurements: circ. = 130 in., ht. = 60 ft., spread = 65.5 ft. (Schilling, 1984).

This tree is *Pinus elliottii* var. *densa* (South Florida slash pine).

Acknowledged by American Forests (1996 listing).

(2)

Emeritus National Champion.

Size:			
	Circumference:	122	inches
	Height:	69	feet
	Crown spread:	56	feet
	Total points:	205	points

Owner / location: Marie Selby Botanical Gardens / 800 S. Palm Ave., Sarasota, Sarasota Co. [n.w. 1/4 of sec 30, T36S, R18E]

Nominator(s) / date: William J. Schilling / 1980

Update: William J. Schilling, Lee Barnwell / 1990

Update: William J. Schilling / 1993

Comments: Earlier measurements: circ. = 112 in., ht. = 64 ft., spread = 49 ft. (Schilling, 1980); circ. = 120 in., ht. = 69 ft., spread = 56 ft. (Schilling & Barnwell, 1990).

This tree is *Pinus elliottii* var. *densa* (South Florida slash pine).

(3)

Honorable Mention.

Size:			
	Circumference:	101	inches
	Height:	58	feet
	Crown spread:	60	feet
	Total points:	174	points

Owner / location: Ron Bell / 2606 Este Ave., Naples, Collier Co. [s.e. 1/4 of sec 2, T50S, R25E]

Nominator(s) / date: Chris J. Anderson / 1994

Comments: This tree is *Pinus elliottii* var. *densa* (South Florida slash pine).

(4)

Honorable Mention.

Size:			
	Circumference:	104	inches
	Height:	42	feet
	Crown spread:	60	feet
	Total points:	161	points

Owner / location: (unknown) / just e. of Int. 75, n. edge of Charlotte Co. [n. 1/2 of sec 6, T40S, R23E]

Nominator(s) / date: Sandy Christopher / 1991

Comments: This tree is *Pinus elliottii* var. *densa* (South Florida slash pine).

Pinus glabra Walt.
Spruce Pine

(1)

☆ Florida Champion.

Size:			
	Circumference:	165	inches
	Height:	81	feet
	Crown spread:	63.5	feet
	Total points:	262	points

Owner / location: John Matheny / 0.2 mi. e. of U.S. 301, 1 mi. n. of Waldo, Alachua Co. [n.e. 1/4 of sec 14, T8S, R21E]

Nominator(s) / date: Michael J. Bordyn / 1980

Update: Robert T. Ing, Daniel B. Ward / 1991

Comments: Earlier measurements: circ. = 160 in., ht. = 78 ft., spread = 76 ft. (Bordyn, 1980).

National champion: Louisiana (292 points).

(2)

Florida Challenger.

Size:	Circumference:	97	inches
	Height:	118	feet
	Crown spread:	45	feet
	Total points:	226	points

Owner / location: Martin Marietta Materials, Inc. / w. end of Satsuma Rd., Chattahoochee, Gadsden Co. [n.e. 1/4 of sec 5, T3N, R6W]

Nominator(s) / date: Angus K. Gholson, Robert T. Ing, Daniel B. Ward / 1995

(3)

Honorable Mention.

Size:	Circumference:	87	inches
	Height:	102	feet
	Crown spread:	53	feet
	Total points:	202	points

Owner / location: Anne Wright / Woodswell Farm, 7537 Proctor Rd., 0.3 mi. s. of s. of Centerville Rd. (Fla. 151), 12 mi. n.e. of Tallahassee, Leon Co. [s.w. 1/4 of sec 16, T2N, R2E]

Nominator(s) / date: Ralph Roberts / 1983

Update: Robert T. Ing, Daniel B. Ward, Charles E. Salter / 1993

Comments: Earlier measurements: circ. = 75 in., ht. = 85 ft., spread = 37.5 ft. (Roberts, 1983).

Pinus palustris Mill.
Longleaf Pine

(1)

☆ Florida Champion.

Size:	Circumference:	116	inches
	Height:	83	feet
	Crown spread:	63	feet
	Total points:	215	points

Owner / location: Dixie M. Hollins / Hollinswood Ranch, s. of Power Line Rd., 6 mi. n.w. of Crystal River, Citrus Co. [sec 3, T18S, R16E]

Nominator(s) / date: Wilbur C. Priest / 1990

Comments: National champions: Mississippi, two trees (238 points, 235 points).

(2)

Florida Challenger.

Size:	Circumference:	98	inches
	Height:	101	feet
	Crown spread:	50	feet
	Total points:	212	points

Owner / location: Arthur Brennan / n. edge of Lake Kerr, 4 mi. n.w. of Salt Springs, Marion Co. [sec 10, T13S, R25E]

Nominator(s) / date: Jeff Overby / 1993

(3)

Honorable Mention.

Size:	Circumference:	114	inches
	Height:	81	feet
	Crown spread:	58	feet
	Total points:	209	points

Owner / location: Fred Thomas / 5820 Cherry Laurel Drive, Jacksonville, Duval Co. [sec 31, T2S, R26E]

Nominator(s) / date: Scott A. Crosby / 1992

(4)

Honorable Mention.

Size:	Circumference:	85	inches
	Height:	105	feet
	Crown spread:	41	feet
	Total points:	200	points

Owner / location: Univ. of Florida / s. side of Flint Hall, campus, Gainesville, Alachua Co. [s.e. 1/4 of sec 6, T10S, R20E]

Nominator(s) / date: Lynn C. Badger, Daniel B. Ward / 1994

Comments: Carved stone at base: "University of Florida Bicentennial Tree. Age 227 years. January 16, 1976." The age, though reasonable for a tree of this size, was obtained "out of the air" for the purpose of the dedication ceremony (N. R. Lake, Feb 1994).

(5)

Emeritus Florida Champion.

Size:	Circumference:	88	inches
	Height:	97	feet
	Crown spread:	53	feet
	Total points:	198	points

Owner / location: Blackwater River State Forest / 15 mi. n.n.e. of Milton, Santa Rosa Co. [s.w. 1/4 of sec 17, T4N, R27W]

Nominator(s) / date: Wilbur K. Howell / 1981

Update: Kenneth L. Oser / 1994

Comments: Earlier measurements: circ. = 80 in., ht. = 90 ft., spread = 47.5 ft. (Howell, 1981).

(6)

Honorable Mention.

Size:	Circumference:	100	inches
	Height:	72	feet
	Crown spread:	59	feet
	Total points:	187	points

Owner / location: Univ. of Florida / Agricultural Research Center, 5336 University Ave., Leesburg, Lake Co. [sec 25, T20S, R24E]

Nominator(s) / date: Catherine M. Benton / 1996

Pinus serotina Michx.
Pond Pine

(1)

☆ Florida Co-Champion.

Size:	Circumference:	109	inches
	Height:	100	feet
	Crown spread:	53	feet
	Total points:	222	points

Owner / location: Lake Griffin State Recreation Area / Fruitland Park, Lake Co. [n.w. 1/4 of sec 10, T19S, R24E]

Nominator(s) / date: Brian Underwood / 1994

Comments: National champion: Georgia (231 points).

(2)

☆ Florida Co-Champion.

Size:	Circumference:	110	inches
	Height:	99	feet
	Crown spread:	44	feet
	Total points:	220	points

Owner / location: Ocala National Forest / near spring at head of Juniper Creek, Marion Co. [n.e. 1/4 of sec 20, T15S, R26E]

Nominator(s) / date: Jeff Overby, Jerry Clutts / 1993

Pinus taeda L.
Loblolly Pine

(1)

☆ Florida Champion.

Size:	Circumference:	139	inches
	Height:	145	feet
	Crown spread:	65	feet
	Total points:	300	points

Owner / location: Buddy Paterson / n.w. side of Kingsley Lake, e. of Fla. 230, Clay Co. [s.w. 1/4 of sec 21, T6S, R23E]

Nominator(s) / date: Mark G. Fries / 1980

Update: David W. Norton / 1987

Comments: Earlier measurements: circ. = 128 in., ht. = 126 ft., spread = 57 ft. (Fries, 1980).

National champion: Arkansas (357 points).

(2)

Florida Challenger.

Size:	Circumference:	144	inches
	Height:	127	feet
	Crown spread:	54.5	feet
	Total points:	285	points

Owner / location: Roy Stockstill / 412 St. Dunston Ct., just e. of Meridian Rd., Tallahassee, Leon Co. [s.w. 1/4 of sec 18, T1N, R1E]

Nominator(s) / date: Thomas D. Beitzel, Michael Humphrey / 1985

Update: Robert T. Ing, Daniel B. Ward, Charles E. Salter / 1993

Comments: Earlier measurements: circ. = 137 in., ht. = 112 ft., spread = 57 ft. (Beitzel & Humphrey, 1985).

(3)

Florida Challenger.

Size:	Circumference:	164	inches
	Height:	98	feet
	Crown spread:	82	feet
	Total points:	283	points

Owner / location: Tony Lopez / s. side of airport, 5 mi. s. of Fernandina Beach, Nassau Co. [n.w. 1/4 of sec 12, T2N, R28E]

Nominator(s) / date: Scott Zobel / 1986

(4)

Honorable Mention.

Size:	Circumference:	146	inches
	Height:	103	feet
	Crown spread:	69	feet
	Total points:	266	points

Owner / location: Ocala National Forest / just e. of Fla. 314, 2 mi. n. of Fla. 40, 20 mi. s. of Orange Springs, Marion Co. [s.e. 1/4 of sec 2, T15S, R24E]

Nominator(s) / date: Glenn D. Cunningham / 1982

Update: Jeff Overby / 1993

Comments: Earlier measurements: circ. = 142 in., ht. = 112 ft., spread = 68 ft. (Cunningham, 1982).

(5)

Honorable Mention.

Size:	Circumference:	118	inches
	Height:	130	feet
	Crown spread:	50	feet
	Total points:	260	points

Owner / location: Ravine State Gardens / Twigg St., Palatka, Putnam Co. [s.e. 1/4 of sec 12, T10S, R26E]

Nominator(s) / date: Steven Dale / 1989

(6)

Honorable Mention.

Size:	Circumference:	111	inches
	Height:	117	feet
	Crown spread:	70	feet
	Total points:	246	points

Owner / location: Florida Power Corp. / Hollinswood Ranch, s. of Power Line Rd., 5 mi. n.w. of Crystal River, Citrus Co. [sec 11, T18S, R16E]

Nominator(s) / date: Wilbur C. Priest / 1990

(7)

Honorable Mention.

Size:			
	Circumference:	127	inches
	Height:	102	feet
	Crown spread:	62	feet
	Total points:	245	points

Owner / location: Florida Caverns State Park / fish-hatchery area, s. of Blue Hole, 2 mi. n. of Marianna, Jackson Co. [s.w. 1/4 of sec 21, T5N, R10W]

Nominator(s) / date: Robert T. Ing, Daniel B. Ward / 1995

Piscidia piscipula (L.) Sarg.
Fish-fuddle, Jamaica Dogwood, Fishpoison-tree

(1)

★ National Champion.

Size:			
	Circumference:	101	inches
	Height:	41	feet
	Crown spread:	48	feet
	Total points:	154	points

Owner / location: Ted Watrous / s. end of Buck Key, just e. of Captiva Id., Lee Co. [sec 2, T46S, R21E]

Nominator(s) / date: David Fox, Dee Slinkard / 1984

Comments: Acknowledged by American Forests (1996 listing).

Pisonia discolor Spreng.
= *Guapira discolor* (Spreng.) Little
Blolly, Longleaf Blolly

(1)

★ National Champion.

Size:			
	Circumference:	64	inches
	Height:	34	feet
	Crown spread:	21.5	feet
	Total points:	103	points

Owner / location: Key Largo Hammocks State Botanical Site / n. end of Key Largo, Monroe Co. [sec 26, T59S, R40E]

Nominator(s) / date: Jeanne M. Parks / 1989

Update: Jeanne M. Parks / 1993

Comments: Tree is still standing; not remeasured (J. M. Parks, Aug 1993).

Acknowledged by American Forests (1996 listing).

(2)

Emeritus National Champion.

Size:			
	Circumference:	55	inches
	Height:	21	feet
	Crown spread:	10.5	feet
	Total points:	79	points

Owner / location: Lignumvitae Key State Botanical Site / Lignumvitae Key, Monroe Co. [n.w. 1/4 of sec 2, T64S, R36E]

Nominator(s) / date: Charlotte Niedhauk / 1975

Update: David M. Sinclair, Frank L. Zickar / 1986

Update: Robert Rose / 1993

Comments: Earlier measurements: circ. = 55 in., ht. = 48 ft., spread = 14 ft. (Niedhauk, 1975). Alive, but in decline; not remeasured (R. Rose, Jan 1993); degree of decline clearly indicated by diminished size since 1975 (as measured by Sinclair & Zickar, 1986).

(3)

Florida Challenger.

Size:			
	Circumference:	35	inches
	Height:	34	feet
	Crown spread:	17	feet
	Total points:	73	points

Owner / location: National Key Deer Refuge / s. of road, 1 mi. e. of bridge, No Name Key, Monroe Co. [s.w. 1/4 of sec 18, T66S, R30E]

Nominator(s) / date: T. Ann Williams, Vincente Lopez / 1995

(4)

Honorable Mention.

Size:			
	Circumference:	24	inches
	Height:	30	feet
	Crown spread:	7	feet
	Total points:	56	points

Owner / location: Biscayne National Park / s. end of Totten Key, Dade Co. [s.w. 1/4 of sec 21, T58S, R41E]

Nominator(s) / date: Diane Riggs / 1995

Pisonia rotundata Griseb.
Pisonia

(1)

★ National Champion.

Size:			
	Circumference:	38	inches
	Height:	28	feet
	Crown spread:	13.5	feet
	Total points:	69	points

Owner / location: National Key Deer Refuge / e. side of No Name Key, Monroe Co. [s.e. 1/4 of sec 18, T66S, R30E]

Nominator(s) / date: Robert W. Ehrig / 1994

Comments: Acknowledged by American Forests (1996 listing).

(2)

Florida Challenger.

Size:	Circumference:	31	inches
	Height:	19	feet
	Crown spread:	14.5	feet
	Total points:	54	points

Owner / location: John Vincent / s. side of U.S. 1, 1 mi. e. of Fla. 940 jct., Big Pine Key, Monroe Co. [s.w. 1/4 of sec 25, T66S, R29E]

Nominator(s) / date: Chad Bryant / 1993

Pithecellobium keyense Britt. & Rose
= *Pithecellobium guadalupense* (Pers.) Chapm.
Black-bead

(1)

★ National Champion (nominee).

Size:	Circumference:	9	inches
	Height:	19	feet
	Crown spread:	15.5	feet
	Total points:	32	points

Owner / location: National Key Deer Refuge / s. of road, 1 mi. e. of bridge, No Name Key, Monroe Co. [s.w. 1/4 of sec. 18, T66S, R30E]

Nominator(s) / date: T. Ann Williams, Vincent P. Condon / 1995

Comments: Most commonly a shrub. "Large, sprawling shrub-like trees" have been observed on Boot Key, Monroe County (G. Avery notes, July 1964).

National champion: Florida (31 points), perhaps now deceased.

(2)

Not ranked; possibly still alive, but not verified for many years.

Size:	Circumference:	11	inches
	Height:	16	feet
	Crown spread:	16	feet
	Total points:	31	points

Owner / location: National Key Deer Refuge / Cactus Hammock, s. end of Big Pine Key, Monroe Co. [n.e. 1/4 of sec 1, T67S, R29E]

Nominator(s) / date: Robert W. Simons, Mary Lee Eletz / 1978

Comments: Tree apparently has not been seen since the original nomination. Still acknowledged (as National champion) by American Forests (1996 listing).

Pithecellobium unguis-cati (L.) Benth.
Cat's-claw

(1)

★ National Champion.

Size:	Circumference:	150	inches
	Height:	72	feet
	Crown spread:	48.5	feet
	Total points:	234	points

Owner / location: Frederic Rabeler / 3630 Camino Real, Sarasota, Sarasota Co. [sec 6, T37S, R18E]

Nominator(s) / date: Steven Spezia / 1976

Update: William J. Schilling / 1994

Comments: Earlier measurements: circ. = 122 in., ht. = 88 ft., spread = 63 ft. (Spezia, 1976).

Acknowledged by American Forests (1996 listing).

(2)

Florida Challenger.

Size:	Circumference:	132	inches
	Height:	24	feet
	Crown spread:	28.5	feet
	Total points:	163	points

Owner / location: Village of Key Biscayne / 400 block, Fernwood Dr., Key Biscayne, Dade Co. [s.e. 1/4 of sec 32, T54S, R42E]

Nominator(s) / date: Joan Gill Blank / 1995

Planera aquatica Walt. ex Gmel.
Water Elm

(1)

☆ Florida Champion.

Size:	Circumference:	135	inches
	Height:	41	feet
	Crown spread:	60	feet
	Total points:	191	points

Owner / location: San Felasco Hammock State Preserve / Bromeliad Pond, n. of Fla. 232, 8 mi. n.w. of Gainesville, Alachua Co. [sec 12, T9S, R19E]

Nominator(s) / date: Robert W. Simons, Erika H. Simons / 1994

Comments: The tree recognized by American Forests (1996 listing) as National champion (New Bern, North Carolina—313 points) is north of the natural range of *Planera aquatica*. Because of its habitat requirements it is unlikely to be a cultivated tree. Its height—106 ft.—is well beyond that observed elsewhere for this species. The probability is high that the report is based upon a misidentification. Should this prove to be the case, the present Florida champion is next in size for designation as National Champion.

(2)

Florida Challenger.

Size:	Circumference:	78	inches
	Height:	36	feet
	Crown spread:	47	feet
	Total points:	126	points

Owner / location: City of Gainesville / Hogtown Prairie, w. of Int 75, n. end of Lake Kanapaha, s.w. Gainesville, Alachua Co. [n.e. 1/4 of sec 16, T10S, R19E]

Nominator(s) / date: Robert T. Ing, Daniel B. Ward / 1991

Platanus occidentalis L.
Sycamore

(1)

☆ Florida Champion.

Size:	Circumference:	186	inches
	Height:	97	feet
	Crown spread:	92.5	feet
	Total points:	306	points

Owner / location: City of Apopka / City Hall, downtown Apopka, Orange Co. [sec 10, T21S, R28E]

Nominator(s) / date: W. W. Smith, Russell Fatic / 1981

Update: David P. Wentzel / 1993

Comments: Earlier measurements: circ. = 177 in., ht. = 92 ft., spread = 90 ft. (Smith & Fatic, 1981).

The tree designated as the Florida champion is a cultivated specimen outside of its natural range. A champion tree from within its natural range in the Florida panhandle would be welcome.

National champion: Ohio (737 points).

(2)

Florida Challenger.

Size:	Circumference:	168	inches
	Height:	93	feet
	Crown spread:	80	feet
	Total points:	281	points

Owner / location: Church of God by Faith / 1601 N.W. 1st Ave., High Springs, Alachua Co. [sec 33, T7S, R17E]

Nominator(s) / date: Robert T. Ing, Daniel B. Ward / 1993

(3)

Honorable Mention.

Size:	Circumference:	124	inches
	Height:	106	feet
	Crown spread:	64	feet
	Total points:	246	points

Owner / location: A. C. Reynolds / 2 mi. e. of Fla. 277, 6 mi. n.e. of Vernon, Washington Co. [sec 14, T3N, R14W]

Nominator(s) / date: Charles R. Reeves / 1980

Update: Charles R. Reeves / 1993

Comments: Earlier measurements: circ. = 106 in., ht. = 101 ft., spread = 64 ft. (Reeves, 1980).

Populus deltoides Bartr. ex Marsh.
Eastern Cottonwood

(1)

☆ Florida Champion.

Size:	Circumference:	109	inches
	Height:	75	feet
	Crown spread:	79	feet
	Total points:	204	points

Owner / location: Florida Div. of Forestry / Andrews Nursery, s. of Fla. 345 (U.S. 27 Alt.), 1 mi. e. of Chiefland, Levy Co. [n.e. 1/4 of sec 6, T12S, R15E]

Nominator(s) / date: Michael J. Bordyn / 1985

Update: Robert T. Ing, Daniel B. Ward / 1993

Comments: Earlier measurements: circ. = 99 in., ht. = 76 ft., spread = 65.5 ft. (Bordyn, 1985).

National champions: Idaho (548 points); Nebraska (546 points).

The tree designated as the Florida champion is a cultivated specimen outside of its natural range. A champion tree from within its natural range in the Florida panhandle would be welcome.

Populus heterophylla L.
Swamp Cottonwood

Title vacant.

Size:	Circumference:		
	Height:		
	Crown spread:		
	Total points:		

Owner / location:

Nominator(s) / date:

Comments: Native in central panhandle Florida. Herbarium records (FSU, Nov 1996) indicate this species, near Wewahitchka, Gulf County, to reach a height of 14 meters, with trunks 3 decimeters dbh.

This species is recognized as a tree by American Forests (1996 listing), but as a "species without a champion."

Prunus alabamensis Mohr
= *Prunus serotina* Ehrh.
var. *alabamensis* (Mohr) Little
Alabama Cherry

(1)

★ National Champion (nominee).

Size:			
	Circumference:	40	inches
	Height:	35	feet
	Crown spread:	27	feet
	Total points:	82	points

Owner / location: St. Joseph Land & Development Co. / just e. of Fla. 270, 5 mi. n. of Bristol, Liberty Co. [n.w. 1/4 of sec 8, T1N, R7W]

Nominator(s) / date: Robert T. Ing, Daniel B. Ward / 1995

Comments: This species was not included in the Checklist of Trees Native to Florida (Ward, 1991). It is recognized as a tree (as *Prunus serotina* var. *alabamensis*) by American Forests (1996 listing), but as a "species without a champion."

Prunus americana Marsh.
Wild Plum

(1)

★ National Champion.

Size:			
	Circumference:	39	inches
	Height:	48	feet
	Crown spread:	36	feet
	Total points:	96	points

Owner / location: Soterra, Inc. / e. bank of Apalachicola River, 0.5 mi. s. of Int. 10, 6 mi. s.w. of Chattahoochee, Gadsden Co. [s.e. 1/4 of sec 26, T3N, R7W]

Nominator(s) / date: Robert W. Simons, Angus K. Gholson, Robert K. Godfrey / 1993

Comments: Acknowledged by American Forests (1996 listing).

(2)

Emeritus National Champion.

Size:			
	Circumference:	39	inches
	Height:	35	feet
	Crown spread:	27	feet
	Total points:	81	points

Owner / location: Univ. of Florida / n.e. corner of Wilmot Gardens, campus, Gainesville, Alachua Co. [n.w. 1/4 of sec 7, T10S, R20E]

Nominator(s) / date: Robert W. Simons / 1986

Update: Robert T. Ing, Daniel B. Ward / 1991

Comments: Earlier measurements: circ. = 38 in., ht. = 30 ft., spread = 36.5 ft. (Simons, 1986).

This tree was probably part of the Wilmot plantings since the species is otherwise not known in the immediate area.

Prunus angustifolia Marsh.
Chickasaw Plum

(1)

☆ Florida Champion.

Size:			
	Circumference:	12	inches
	Height:	15	feet
	Crown spread:	12	feet
	Total points:	30	points

Owner / location: Tall Timbers Research, Inc. / Fla. 12, 15 mi. n.n.e. of Tallahassee, Leon Co. [n.w. 1/4 of sec 22, T3N, R1E]

Nominator(s) / date: W. Wilson Baker, Charles E. Salter, Daniel B. Ward / 1995

Comments: This small tree is apparently indigenous to areas west of Florida. It was found to be widespread in northern Florida by the 1770s, usually in association with sites of Indian settlement. Beause of its early, surely pre-Columbian introduction into the state, it is justifiably classified as "native." It rarely reaches tree stature; many individuals so identified are *Prunus umbellata*.

National champion: North Carolina (91 points).

Prunus caroliniana (Mill.) Ait.
Cherry Laurel, Laurel Cherry

(1)

★ National Champion.

Size:			
	Circumference:	127	inches
	Height:	47	feet
	Crown spread:	55	feet
	Total points:	188	points

Owner / location: Ernest Jones / 724 Sagamore St., Lakeland, Polk Co. [sec 31, T28S, R24E]

Nominator(s) / date: Nick Sykes / 1987

Update: Cherry W. Platt / 1993

Comments: Tree is still alive; not remeasured (C. W. Platt, Dec 1993).

Acknowledged by American Forests (1996 listing).

(2)

Florida Challenger.

Size:			
	Circumference:	100	inches
	Height:	62	feet
	Crown spread:	10	feet
	Total points:	165	points

Owner / location: Tim Honderick / 1246 S.W. 9th Rd., Gainesville, Alachua Co. [n.w. 1/4 of sec 8, T10S, R20E]

Nominator(s) / date: Robert W. Simons, Daniel B. Ward / 1993

Prunus myrtifolia (L.) Urban
West Indian Cherry Laurel

(1)

★ National Champion.

Size:	Circumference:	65	inches
	Height:	53	feet
	Crown spread:	50	feet
	Total points:	131	points

Owner / location: Lutheran Church / 11295 S.W. 57th Ave., Miami, Dade Co. [s.w. 1/4 of sec 7, T55S, R41E]

Nominator(s) / date: Carol L. Lippincott / 1989

Comments: Acknowledged by American Forests (1996 listing).

Prunus serotina Ehrh.
Black Cherry

(1)

☆ Florida Champion.

Size:	Circumference:	177	inches
	Height:	54	feet
	Crown spread:	30	feet
	Total points:	239	points

Owner / location: W. D. Parrish / n.w. of jct. Fla. 235 & Fla. 239, n.e. edge of Alachua, Alachua Co. [sec 11, T8S, R18E]

Nominator(s) / date: Michael J. Bordyn / 1980
Update: Robert T. Ing, Daniel B. Ward / 1991

Comments: Earlier measurements: circ. = 175 in., ht. = 50 ft., spread = 37 ft. (Bordyn, 1980).
National champion: Michigan (361 points).

(2)

Florida Challenger.

Size:	Circumference:	105	inches
	Height:	110	feet
	Crown spread:	47	feet
	Total points:	227	points

Owner / location: Prairie View Trust / Sugarfoot Hammock, e. of Int. 75, 300 yds. s. of S.W. 20th Ave. overpass, Gainesville, Alachua Co. [sec 10, T10S, R19E]

Nominator(s) / date: Robert W. Simons, Daniel B. Ward / 1994

(3)

Florida Challenger.

Size:	Circumference:	122	inches
	Height:	88	feet
	Crown spread:	55	feet
	Total points:	224	points

Owner / location: San Felasco Hammock State Preserve / s. of Fla. 232, 8 mi. n.w. of Gainesville, Alachua Co. [sec 13, T9S, R18E]

Nominator(s) / date: Robert W. Simons / 1991

(4)

Honorable Mention.

Size:	Circumference:	111	inches
	Height:	78	feet
	Crown spread:	27.5	feet
	Total points:	196	points

Owner / location: Deer Lake School / s.e. corner of school, e. of Bull Headley Rd., s. side of Lake Iamonia, n. Tallahassee, Leon Co. [n.e. 1/4 of sec 4, T2N, R1E]

Nominator(s) / date: Robert T. Ing, Daniel B. Ward, Charles E. Salter / 1993

Prunus umbellata Ell.
Hog Plum, Flatwoods Plum

(1)

★ National Champion.

Size:	Circumference:	18	inches
	Height:	34	feet
	Crown spread:	24	feet
	Total points:	58	points

Owner / location: Paynes Prairie State Preserve / e. of headquarters, 2 mi. s.s.e. of Gainesville, Alachua Co. [sec 22, T10S, R20E]

Nominator(s) / date: Robert T. Ing, Daniel B. Ward, Robert W. Simons / 1991

Comments: Acknowledged by American Forests (1996 listing).

Pseudophoenix sargentii Wendl. ex Sarg.
Buccaneer Palm, Sargent's Cherry Palm

(1)

★ National Champion.

Size:	Circumfrece:	26	inches
	Height:	25	feet
	Crown spread:	7.5	feet
	Total points:	53	points

Owner / location: Biscayne National Monument / n. end of Elliott Key, Dade Co. [s.w. 1/4 of sec 18, T57S, R42E]

Nominator(s) / date: Carol L. Lippincott / 1994

Comments: Acknowledged by American Forests (1996 listing).

Psidium longipes (Berg) McVaugh
= *Mosiera bahamensis* (Kiaersk.) Small
Bahama Stopper

Title vacant.

Size:	Circumference:		
	Height:		
	Crown spread:		
	Total points:		

Owner / location:

Nominator(s) / date:

Comments: Native in south peninsular Florida (Everglade Keys, Dade County) and the Florida Keys (Monroe County).

Herbarium records (FLAS, July 1995) indicate this species, on Big Pine Key, Monroe County, to attain a height of 10 ft. It is most often a shrub but rarely becomes a small tree; not included in the Checklist of Trees Native to Florida (Ward, 1991). It is recognized as a tree by American Forests (1996 listing), but as a "species without a champion."

Ptelea trifoliata L.
Wafer Ash, Hop-tree

(1)

☆ **Florida Champion.**

Size:			
	Circumference:	11	inches
	Height:	21	feet
	Crown spread:	13	feet
	Total points:	35	points

Owner / location: Robert W. Simons / 1122 S.W. 11th Ave., Gainesville, Alachua Co. [n.w. 1/4 of sec 8, T10S, R20E]

Nominator(s) / date: Robert W. Simons / 1991

Comments: Cultivated tree, from native local stand (R. W. Simons, Oct 1991).

National champion: Michigan (78 points).

Quercus alba L.
White Oak

(1)

☆ **Florida Champion.**

Size:			
	Circumference:	139	inches
	Height:	112	feet
	Crown spread:	96	feet
	Total points:	275	points

Owner / location: J. O. Hannaford / 1 mi. w. of Boulougne, Nassau Co. [sec 47, T4N, R23E]

Nominator(s) / date: Scott Zobel / 1986

Comments: National champion: Maryland (479 points).

(2)

Florida Challenger.

Size:			
	Circumference:	153	inches
	Height:	89	feet
	Crown spread:	99	feet
	Total points:	267	points

Owner / location: Jessie M. McNeil / w. side of Fla. 85,

just below Alabama line, n.w. corner of Walton Co. [n.w. 1/4 of sec 27, T6N, R21W]

Nominator(s) / date: Alto Smith / 1994

(3)

Honorable Mention.

Size:			
	Circumference:	116	inches
	Height:	116	feet
	Crown spread:	63	feet
	Total points:	248	points

Owner / location: Torreya State Park / main campground, Liberty Co. [n.e. 1/4 of sec 17, T2N, R7W]

Nominator(s) / date: Robert W. Simons / 1988

(4)

Honorable Mention.

Size:			
	Circumference:	136	inches
	Height:	85	feet
	Crown spread:	48	feet
	Total points:	233	points

Owner / location: Artie McCall / s. of Fla. 53, w. of Fla. 251, 5 mi. w.n.w. of Mayo, Lafayette Co. [n.e. 1/4 of sec 6, T5S, R11E]

Nominator(s) / date: Owen McCall, Jerry N. Livingston / 1986

(5)

Honorable Mention.

Size:			
	Circumference:	122	inches
	Height:	90	feet
	Crown spread:	70	feet
	Total points:	229	points

Owner / location: Torreya State Park / between Gregory house and Apalachicola River, Liberty Co. [s.w. 1/4 of sec 9, T2N, R7W]

Nominator(s) / date: Joey T. Brady, Jerome Bracewell / 1986

(6)

Emeritus Florida Champion.

Size:			
	Circumference:	58	inches
	Height:	55	feet
	Crown spread:	39	feet
	Total points:	123	points

Owner / location: Univ. of Florida / e. of Weimer Hall, campus, Gainesville, Alachua Co. [s.w. 1/4 of sec 6, T10S, R20E]

Nominator(s) / date: Duane R. Durgee, Donald West / 1984

Update: Robert T. Ing, Daniel B. Ward / 1991

Comments: Earlier measurements: circ. = 51 in., ht. =

52 ft., spread =33 ft. (Durgee & West, 1984). A modest tree, but once Florida champion since when it was nominated there were no others on record. This tree is cultivated, somewhat south of its native range.

Quercus arkansana Sarg.
Arkansas Oak

(1)

★ National Champion (nominee).

Size:			
	Circumference:	39	inches
	Height:	49	feet
	Crown spread:	18.5	feet
	Total points:	93	points

Owner / location: Eglin Air Force Base / w. slope of upper Little Rocky Creek, 2/3 mi. n.w. of Fla. 285, 12 mi. s.e. of Crestview, Okaloosa Co. [s.e. 1/4 of sec 34, T2N, R22W]

Nominator(s) / date: Brenda Herring / 1996

Comments: Several other trees at this site are nearly as large (B. Herring, Nov 1996).

National champion: Alabama (87 points).

Quercus austrina Small
= *Quercus durandii*, misapplied
Bluff Oak

(1)

☆ Florida Champion.

Size:			
	Circumference:	127	inches
	Height:	104	feet
	Crown spread:	70	feet
	Total points:	249	points

Owner / location: Kanapaha Botanical Gardens / n. of Fla. 24, s.w. Gainesville, Alachua Co. [n.e. 1/4 of sec 21, T10S, R19E]

Nominator(s) / date: Robert C. Wilkinson, Clifton Cullenberg, Don Goodman / 1989

Comments: National champion: Georgia (314 points).

(2)

Emeritus Florida Champion.

Size:			
	Circumference:	105	inches
	Height:	110	feet
	Crown spread:	68.5	feet
	Total points:	232	points

Owner / location: Andrews Wildlife Management Area / 3 mi. s. of Fanning Springs, Levy Co. [s.w. 1/4 of sec 7, T11S, R14E]

Nominator(s) / date: Dennis Andrews, Robert W. Simons / 1983

Update: Archie W. Gaylard, Daniel B. Ward / 1994

Comments: Earlier measurements: circ. = 101 in., ht. = 105 ft., spread = 78 ft. (Andrews & Simons, 1983).

(3)

Honorable Mention.

Size:			
	Circumference:	108	inches
	Height:	98	feet
	Crown spread:	55.5	feet
	Total points:	220	points

Owner / location: O'Leno State Park / w. of River Rise, Columbia Co. [s.w. 1/4 of sec 14, T7S, R17E]

Nominator(s) / date: Robert W. Simons, Robert T. Ing, Daniel B. Ward / 1991

(4)

Emeritus Florida Champion.

Size:			
	Circumference:	104	inches
	Height:	87	feet
	Crown spread:	36	feet
	Total points:	200	points

Owner / location: Prairie View Trust / Sugarfoot Hammock, n.e. of jct. S.W. 20th Ave. & S.W. 62nd St., Gainesville, Alachua Co. [n.e. 1/4 of sec 10, T10S, R19E]

Nominator(s) / date: Michael J. Bordyn, Robert W. Simons / 1981

Update: Robert W. Simons, Daniel B. Ward / 1993

Comments: Earlier measurements: circ. = 103 in., ht. = 106 ft., spread = 43 ft. (Bordyn & Simons, 1981). Top has been blown off, appreciably shortening an impressive tree (R. W. Simons & D. B. Ward, Oct 1993).

Quercus chapmanii Sarg.
Chapman Oak

(1)

★ National Champion.

Size:			
	Circumference:	81	inches
	Height:	45	feet
	Crown spread:	50	feet
	Total points:	139	points

Owner / location: Ocala National Forest / along roadway to Sweetwater Cabin, n. of Juniper Creek bridge, Marion Co. [sec 37, T15S, R26E]

Nominator(s) / date: Robert W. Simons / 1989

Update: Robert W. Simons / 1993

Comments: Recently seen; still alive, but not remeasured (R. W. Simons, Aug 1993).

Acknowledged by American Forests (1996 listing).

Quercus falcata Michx.
Southern Red Oak

(1)

☆ **Florida Champion.**

Size:

	Circumference:	288	inches
	Height:	123	feet
	Crown spread:	124.5	feet
	Total points:	442	points

Owner / location: Mark Chauncey / n. side of District Line Rd., 2.5 mi. w. of Fla. 51, 5 mi. s.w. of Live Oak, Suwannee Co. [s.w. 1/4 of sec 36, T2S, R12E]

Nominator(s) / date: Mark Chauncey / 1981

Update: Robert T. Ing, Daniel B. Ward / 1993

Comments: Earlier measurements: circ. = 279 in., ht. = 96 ft., spread = 145 ft. (Chauncey, 1981).

National champion: Maryland (469 points).

(2)

Florida Challenger.

Size:

	Circumference:	198	inches
	Height:	98	feet
	Crown spread:	97.5	feet
	Total points:	320	points

Owner / location: Jervey Gantt Park / w. side of S.E. 36th Ave., s.e. Ocala, Marion Co. [n. 1/2 of sec 15, T15S, R22E]

Nominator(s) / date: Jeff Overby / 1993

(3)

Honorable Mention.

Size:

	Circumference:	176	inches
	Height:	76	feet
	Crown spread:	89	feet
	Total points:	274	points

Owner / location: Suzie Folsom Wisehart / e. of Fla. 53, 2 mi. s. of jct. U.S. 27, 7 mi. n.w. of Mayo, Lafayette Co. [s.e. 1/4 of sec 26, T4S, R10E]

Nominator(s) / date: Jerry N. Livingston / 1994

(4)

Honorable Mention.

Size:

	Circumference:	147	inches
	Height:	88	feet
	Crown spread:	96	feet
	Total points:	259	points

Owner / location: Ottis Townsend / 305 N.W. 3rd Ave., e. of 10th St., High Springs, Alachua Co. [s.w. 1/4 of sec 34, T7S, R17E]

Nominator(s) / date: Michael J. Bordyn / 1981

Update: Robert T. Ing, Daniel B. Ward / 1993

Comments: Earlier measurements: circ. = 141 in., ht. = 85 ft., spread = 87.5 ft. (Bordyn, 1981).

(5)

Honorable Mention.

Size:

	Circumference:	117	inches
	Height:	91	feet
	Crown spread:	91	feet
	Total points:	231	points

Owner / location: John Lloyd / n. of Fla. 251, 2.5 mi. s.e. of Mayo, Lafayette Co. [n.e. 1/4 of sec 20, T5S, R12E]

Nominator(s) / date: Jerry N. Livingston / 1991

Quercus geminata Small
= Quercus virginiana Mill.
var. geminata (Small) Sarg.
Sand Live Oak

(1)

★ **National Co-Champion.**

Size:

	Circumference:	181	inches
	Height:	94	feet
	Crown spread:	100	feet
	Total points:	300	points

Owner / location: Lorine Wesley / 526 N.W. 3rd Ave., Gainesville, Alachua Co. [n.e. 1/4 of sec 5, T10S, R20E]

Nominator(s) / date: Daniel B. Ward / 1995

Comments: This tree is located in a residential area, as is another sand live oak (Simons, 1985) one-half mile to the west. By its streetside location, this tree appears to be appropriately placed for a planted specimen. However, houses in the neighborhood do not exceed seventy-five years in age, surely less than the age of a sand live oak of this dimension. Most probably it is a survivor of the now-vanished longleaf pine–turkey oak association once prevalent in this area.

Acknowledged (as *Q. virginiana* var. *geminata*) by American Forests (1996 listing).

(2)

★ **National Co-Champion.**

Size:

	Circumference:	184	inches
	Height:	82	feet
	Crown spread:	88	feet
	Total points:	288	points

Owner / location: Susie Mae White / 1004 N.W. 5th Ave., Gainesville, Alachua Co. [n.w. 1/4 of sec 5, T10S, R20E]

Nominator(s) / date: Robert W. Simons / 1985

Update: Robert W. Simons, Daniel B. Ward / 1995

Comments: Earlier measurements: circ. = 184 in., ht. = 82 ft., spread = 88 ft. (Simons, 1985).

Acknowledged (as *Q. virginiana* var. *geminata*) by American Forests (1996 listing).

(3)

Emeritus Florida Champion.

Size:	Circumference:	114	inches
	Height:	70	feet
	Crown spread:	75.5	feet
	Total points:	203	points

Owner / location: City of High Springs / jct. S.W. 7th Ave. & S.W. 2nd St., High Springs, Alachua Co. [sec 3, T8S, R17E]

Nominator(s) / date: Michael J. Bordyn / 1980

Update: Robert T. Ing, Daniel B. Ward / 1991

Comments: Earlier measurements: circ. = 107 in., ht. = 58 ft., spread = 72.5 ft. (Bordyn, 1980).

(4)

Honorable Mention.

Size:	Circumference:	104	inches
	Height:	52	feet
	Crown spread:	68	feet
	Total points:	173	points

Owner / location: Joe McNeil / 18 S.W. First St., High Springs, Alachua Co. [n.e. 1/4 of sec 3, T8S, R17E]

Nominator(s) / date: Michael J. Bordyn / 1980

Update: Robert T. Ing, Daniel B. Ward / 1993

Comments: Earlier measurements: circ. = 101 in., ht. = 52 ft., spread = 61.5 ft. (Bordyn, 1980).

Quercus hemisphaerica Willd.
= *Quercus laurifolia*, misapplied
Laurel Oak

(1)

★ National Champion (nominee).

Size:	Circumference:	258	inches
	Height:	80	feet
	Crown spread:	113.5	feet
	Total points:	366	points

Owner / location: James R. Griffith / Fla. 4, 0.75 mi. w. of Baker, Okaloosa Co. [n.e. 1/4 of sec 1, T3N, R25W]

Nominator(s) / date: Geoffrey A. Cummings / 1987

Comments: This tree was reported as "*Quercus laurifolia*." That name is now restricted to a swamp species. The tree of drier upland sites, the habitat of the present tree, is more correctly known as *Q. hemisphaerica*.

National champion: Georgia (354 points).

(2)

Florida Challenger.

Size:	Circumference:	226	inches
	Height:	99	feet
	Crown spread:	134	feet
	Total points:	359	points

Owner / location: Terry M. Freiberg / 14003 N.W. 150th Ave., Alachua, Alachua Co. [n.e. 1/4 of sec 15, T8S, R18E]

Nominator(s) / date: Gordon C. Ward, Daniel B. Ward / 1996

(3)

Honorable Mention.

Size:	Circumference:	233	inches
	Height:	74	feet
	Crown spread:	114.5	feet
	Total points:	336	points

Owner / location: City of Ocala / 1900 S.E. 7th St., Ocala, Marion Co. [s.e. 1/4 of sec 16, T15S, R22E]

Nominator(s) / date: Gibson T. Kiley / 1994

(4)

Honorable Mention.

Size:	Circumference:	228	inches
	Height:	76	feet
	Crown spread:	73	feet
	Total points:	322	points

Owner / location: Harold Crevasse / Cottonwood Plantation, e. of U.S. 27, n. edge of Archer, Alachua Co. [s.w. 1/4 of sec 9, T11S, R18E]

Nominator(s) / date: Dave Conser / 1988

Update: Robert T. Ing, Daniel B. Ward / 1991

Comments: Earlier measurements: circ. = 231 in., ht. = 74 ft., spread = 97 ft. (Conser, 1988). A large limb has recently fallen and several other limbs are dead (R. T. Ing & D. B. Ward, Oct 1991).

(5)

Honorable Mention.

Size:	Circumference:	186	inches
	Height:	105	feet
	Crown spread:	90	feet
	Total points:	314	points

Owner / location: Prairie View Trust / Sugarfoot Hammock, n.e. of jct. S.W. 20th Ave. & S.W. 62nd St., Gainesville, Alachua Co. [n.e. 1/4 of sec 10, T10S, R19E]

Nominator(s) / date: Robert W. Simons, Daniel B. Ward / 1993

(6)

Emeritus Florida Champion.

Size:	Circumference:	171	inches
	Height:	90	feet
	Crown spread:	110	feet
	Total points:	289	points

Owner / location: Joe Fortner / w. side of Fla. 73, w. edge of Chipola Park, 18 mi. s.w. of Blountstown, Calhoun Co. [n.w. 1/4 of sec 11, T3S, R10W]

Nominator(s) / date: G. Owen House / 1980

   Update: Stephen Oswalt / 1994

Comments: This tree was reported as *Quercus lauri-folia.*

   Earlier measurements: circ. = 167 in., ht. = 86 ft., spread = 108 ft. (House, 1980).

Quercus incana Bartr.
Bluejack Oak

(1)

★ **National Champion.**

Size:	Circumference:	119	inches
	Height:	54	feet
	Crown spread:	54	feet
	Total points:	187	points

Owner / location: Jerry Leach / s. side, jct. of Rosery Rd. & Peaceful Lane, just e. of Highlands Ave., 1 mi. n.e. of Largo, Pinellas Co. [s.w. 1/4 of sec 26, T29S, R15E]

Nominator(s) / date: Gregory P. Barton / 1992

Comments: Acknowledged by American Forests (1996 listing).

(2)

Florida Challenger.

Size:	Circumference:	80	inches
	Height:	64	feet
	Crown spread:	69	feet
	Total points:	161	points

Owner / location: Florida Div. of Forestry / Bushnell firetower, w. side of U.S. 301, 2 mi. n. of Bushnell, Sumter Co. [n.e. 1/4 of sec 4, T21S, R22E]

Nominator(s) / date: David L. Fogler, Wayne Jones / 1993

(3)

Florida Challenger.

Size:	Circumference:	88	inches
	Height:	56	feet
	Crown spread:	65	feet
	Total points:	160	points

Owner / location: Michaeline I. Little / n. side of Pithlachascotee river, 3 mi. e. of New Port Richey, Pasco Co. [n.e. 1/4 of sec 2, T26S, R16E]

Nominator(s) / date: Michael W. Kenton / 1992

Quercus inopina Ashe
Archbold Oak

Title vacant.

Size:	Circumference:		
	Height:		
	Crown spread:		
	Total points:		

Owner / location:

Nominator(s) / date:

Comments: Native in central peninsular Florida Herbarium records (FTG, Dec 1995) indicate this species, at the Archbold Biological Station, Highlands County, to reach a height of 5 meters.

   This species was not recognized by Little (1979) and is thus not acknowledged as a tree by American Forests (1996 listing).

Quercus laevis Walt.
Turkey Oak

(1)

☆ **Florida Champion.**

Size:	Circumference:	127	inches
	Height:	72	feet
	Crown spread:	75	feet
	Total points:	218	points

Owner / location: Southwest Florida Water Management District / n. of Withlacoochee River, 7 mi. s.e. of Dade City, Pasco Co. [s.e. 1/4 of sec 22, T25S, R22E]

Nominator(s) / date: David Brown, Tony Richards, Kenneth B. Weber / 1994

Comments: National champion: Maryland (276 points).

(2)

Florida Challenger.

Size:	Circumference:	84	inches
	Height:	80	feet
	Crown spread:	48.5	feet
	Total points:	176	points

Owner / location: Grady Smith / 1101 N.W. 44th Ave., Gainesville, Alachua Co. [s.w. 1/4 of sec 20, T9S, R20E]

Nominator(s) / date: Robert T. Ing, Daniel B. Ward / 1991

(3)

Florida Challenger.

Size:	Circumference:	86	inches
	Height:	73	feet
	Crown spread:	62.5	feet
	Total points:	175	points

Owner / location: Jim Padgett / n. side of Fla. 308, 5 mi. w. of Crescent City, Putnam Co. [n.e. 1/4 of sec 20, T12S, R27E]

Nominator(s) / date: Ned D. Neenan / 1993

(4)

Florida Challenger.

Size:	Circumference:	92	inches
	Height:	67	feet

Crown spread: 57 feet

Total points: 173 points

Owner / location: Mrs. H. M. Coachman / n. of Coachman Rd., w. of U.S. 19, n.e. Clearwater, Pinellas Co. [sec 7, T29S, R16E]

Nominator(s) / date: Scott Bates / 1991

(5)

Honorable Mention.

Size:	Circumference:	77	inches
	Height:	68	feet
	Crown spread:	53.5	feet
	Total points:	158	points

Owner / location: Dale Byrd / e. side of U.S. 27, 4 mi. n.w. of Branford, Lafayette Co. [s.e. 1/4 of sec 11, T6S, R13E]

Nominator(s) / date: Jerry N. Livingston / 1987

(6)

Honorable Mention.

Size:	Circumference:	83	inches
	Height:	54	feet
	Crown spread:	48	feet
	Total points:	149	points

Owner / location: K. M. Harper / 1234 Grove Park Blvd., e. side Pottsburg Creek, just n. of Beach Blvd., Jacksonville, Duval Co. [sec 26, T2S, R27E]

Nominator(s) / date: Richard W. Gorden / 1986

(7)

Honorable Mention.

Size:	Circumference:	48	inches
	Height:	65	feet
	Crown spread:	40	feet
	Total points:	123	points

Owner / location: Artie McCall / s. of Fla. 251, w. of Fla. 53, 5 mi. w. of Mayo, Lafayette Co. [sec 7, T5S, R11E]

Nominator(s) / date: Owen McCall, Jerry N. Livingston / 1986

Quercus laurifolia Michx.
Swamp Laurel Oak

(1)

☆ Florida Champion.

Size:	Circumference:	165	inches
	Height:	102	feet
	Crown spread:	89	feet
	Total points:	289	points

Owner / location: O'Leno State Park / 0.7 mi. s.e. of River Rise, Alachua Co. [s.w. 1/4 of sec 23. T7S, Rl7E]

Nominator(s) / date: Robert T. Ing, Daniel B. Ward / 1993

Comments: Trees identified as "*Quercus laurifolia*" have been nominated as Florida champions. Previously, however, all appear to be the upland *Quercus hemisphaerica*. True *Quercus laurifolia*, although common, is a swamp tree and is often not recognized as a distinct species.

National champions (reported as "*Quercus laurifolia*"): Mississippi (396 points); Alabama (391 points).

Quercus lyrata Walt.
Overcup Oak

(1)

☆ Florida Champion.

Size:	Circumference:	123	inches
	Height:	89	feet
	Crown spread:	58	feet
	Total points:	227	points

Owner / location: Suwannee River Water Management District / w. bank of Suwannee River, 1.5 mi. n.e. of U.S. 27, 10 mi. e.s.e. of Mayo, Lafayette Co. [s.w. 1/4 of sec 27, T5S, R13E]

Nominator(s) / date: Jerry N. Livingston / 1990

Comments: National champion: North Carolina (444 points).

(2)

Emeritus Florida Champion.

Size:	Circumference:	102	inches
	Height:	88	feet
	Crown spread:	46	feet
	Total points:	202	points

Owner / location: Jewell Springer / e. of Fla. 51, n. of Fla. 357, 11 mi. s.w. of Mayo, Lafayette Co. [sec 30, T6S, R11E]

Nominator(s) / date: Jerry N. Livingston, Owen Cannon / 1986

Quercus margaretta (Ashe) Small
= *Quercus stellata* Wangenh.
var. *margaretta* (Ashe) Sarg.
Sand Post Oak

(1)

★ National Champion (nominee).

Size:	Circumference:	157	inches
	Height:	87	feet
	Crown spread:	92	feet
	Total points:	267	points

Owner / location: Florida Caverns State Park / e. of group campground, 2 mi. n. of Marianna, Jackson Co. [s.w. 1/4 of sec 22, T5N, R10W]

Nominator(s) / date: Robert T. Ing, Daniel B. Ward / 1995

Comments: National champion: Georgia (220 points).

(2)

Florida Challenger.

Size:	Circumference:	77	inches
	Height:	62	feet
	Crown spread:	44	feet
	Total points:	150	points

Owner / location: Elbert Hughes / w. side of Fla. 135, 0.3 mi. s. of Fla. 6, 15 mi. e. of Jasper, Hamilton Co. [s.e. 1/4 of sec 16, T1N, R16E]

Nominator(s) / date: Robert T. Ing, Daniel B. Ward / 1993

Comments: Closely spaced clump of three trees, the others 74 in. and 66 in. circ. (R. T. Ing & D. B. Ward, Aug 1993).

Quercus marilandica Muench.
Blackjack Oak

(1)

☆ **Florida Champion.**

Size:	Circumference:	92	inches
	Height:	64	feet
	Crown spread:	63	feet
	Total points:	172	points

Owner / location: Three Rivers State Recreation Area / along road e. of park entrance, 2 mi. n. of Sneads, Jackson Co. [s.e. 1/4 of sec 16, T4N, R7W]

Nominator(s) / date: Robert T. Ing, Daniel B. Ward / 1995

Comments: National champions: Virginia (214 points); Missouri (213 points); South Carolina (213 points).

(2)

Florida Challenger.

Size:	Circumference:	54	inches
	Height:	47	feet
	Crown spread:	29	feet
	Total points:	108	points

Owner / location: Three Rivers State Recreation Area / slope s. of campground, 2 mi. n. of Sneads, Jackson Co. [s.e. 1/4 of sec 15, T4N, R7W]

Nominator(s) / date: Robert T. Ing, Daniel B. Ward / 1995

Quercus michauxii Nutt.
= Quercus prinus, misapplied
Swamp Chestnut Oak, Basket Oak, Cow Oak

(1)

☆ **Florida Co-Champion.**

Size:	Circumference:	154	inches
	Height:	91	feet

	Crown spread:	86.5	feet
	Total points:	267	points

Owner / location: Lenvil H. Dicks / s. of U.S. 90, w. of Fla. 137, 10 mi. s.e. of Live Oak, Suwannee Co. [s.e. 1/4 of sec 20, T3S, R15E]

Nominator(s) / date: Stuart Moore / 1980

Update: J. Brad Ellis / 1993

Comments: Earlier measurements: circ. = 152 in., ht. = 92 ft., spread = 86 ft. (Moore, 1980).

National champion: Alabama (434 points).

(2)

☆ **Florida Co-Champion.**

Size:	Circumference:	140	inches
	Height:	105	feet
	Crown spread:	85	feet
	Total points:	266	points

Owner / location: Silver River State Park / w. bank of Silver River, 1 mi. s.w. of Fla. 40 bridge, Marion Co. [n.e. 1/4 of sec 9, T15S, R23E]

Nominator(s) / date: Robert W. Simons, Jim Thorsen, Ellison Hardee / 1994

(3)

Florida Challenger.

Size:	Circumference:	131	inches
	Height:	109	feet
	Crown spread:	73	feet
	Total points:	258	points

Owner / location: San Felasco Hammock State Preserve / Bromeliad Pond, n. of Fla. 232, 8 mi. n.w. of Gainesville, Alachua Co. [sec 12, T9S, R19E]

Nominator(s) / date: Robert W. Simons / 1993

(4)

Honorable Mention.

Size:	Circumference:	126	inches
	Height:	106	feet
	Crown spread:	64	feet
	Total points:	248	points

Owner / location: San Felasco Hammock State Preserve / Big Otter Ravine, n. of Fla. 232, 8 mi. n.w. of Gainesville, Alachua Co. [sec 8, T9S, R19E]

Nominator(s) / date: Robert W. Simons, Daniel B. Ward / 1991

(5)

Honorable Mention.

Size:	Circumference:	84	inches
	Height:	75	feet
	Crown spread:	65.5	feet
	Total points:	173	points

Owner / location: James A. Corbett / 1 mi. n. of Suwannee River, l.5 mi. w. of U.S. 129, 6 mi. s. of Jasper, Hamilton Co. [center of sec 6, T1S, R14E]

Nominator(s) / date: Robert W. Simons, Daniel B. Ward / 1991

Quercus muehlenbergii Engelm.
Chinquapin Oak

(1)

☆ Florida Champion.

Size:			
	Circumference:	57	inches
	Height:	55	feet
	Crown spread:	43	feet
	Total points:	123	points

Owner / location: Soterra, Inc. / e. bank of Apalachicola River, 0.5 mi. s. of Int. 10, 6 mi. s.w. of Chatta-hoochee, Gadsden Co. [s.e. 1/4 of sec 26, T3N, R7W]

Nominator(s) / date: Angus K. Gholson, Robert T. Ing, Daniel B. Ward / 1995

Comments: National champion: Kentucky (391 points).

Quercus myrtifolia Willd.
Myrtle Oak

(1)

★ National Champion.

Size:			
	Circumference:	69	inches
	Height:	36	feet
	Crown spread:	35	feet
	Total points:	114	points

Owner / location: Ft. Clinch State Park / near the fort, Fernandina Beach, Nassau Co. [n.w. 1/4 of sec 10, T3N, R28E]

Nominator(s) / date: Carol Beck / 1967

Update: Carol Beck / 1976

Update: Robert Rahberg, Scott Zobel / 1986

Comments: Earlier measurements: circ. = 44 in., ht. = 21 ft., spread = 36 ft. (Beck, 1967); circ. = 51 in., ht. = 26 ft., spread = 33 ft. (Beck, 1976).

Acknowledged by American Forests (1996 listing).

Quercus nigra L.
Water Oak

(1)

★ National Champion.

Size:			
	Circumference:	266	inches
	Height:	128	feet
	Crown spread:	79	feet
	Total points:	414	points

Owner / location: Louis Atkins / 0.5 mi. w. of Apalachicola River, 7 mi. n.n.e. of Blountstown, Calhoun Co. [s.w. 1/4 of sec 25, T2N, R8W]

Nominator(s) / date: Jake Almond / 1990

Comments: Acknowledged by American Forests (1996 listing).

(2)

Florida Challenger.

Size:			
	Circumference:	217	inches
	Height:	84	feet
	Crown spread:	120	feet
	Total points:	331	points

Owner / location: Radford M. Locklin / w. side of Fla. 191, n. of McLellan, just s. of state line, Santa Rosa Co. [s.e. 1/4 of sec 25, T6N, R27W]

Nominator(s) / date: Radford M. Locklin / 1981

Update: Kenneth L. Oser / 1994

Comments: Earlier measurements: circ. = 207 in., ht. = 100 ft., spread = 127 ft. (Locklin, 1981).

(3)

Honorable Mention.

Size:			
	Circumference:	195	inches
	Height:	92	feet
	Crown spread:	118.5	feet
	Total points:	317	points

Owner / location: Daniel F. Roberts / e. side of Fla. 278A, 5 mi. n.e. of Vernon, Washington Co. [s.w. 1/4 of sec 15, T3N, R14W]

Nominator(s) / date: Charles R. Reeves / 1980

Update: Charles R. Reeves / 1993

Comments: Earlier measurements: circ. = 180 in., ht. = 83 ft., spread = 96 ft. (Reeves, 1980).

Quercus pagoda Raf.
= *Quercus falcata* Michx. var. *pagodifolia* Ell.
Cherrybark Oak

(1)

☆ Florida Champion.

Size:			
	Circumference:	127	inches
	Height:	81	feet
	Crown spread:	94	feet
	Total points:	232	points

Owner / location: Martin R. Butler / 554 Satsuma St., Chattahoochee, Gadsden Co. [n.w. 1/4 of sec 33, T4N, R6W]

Nominator(s) / date: Angus K. Gholson, Robert T. Ing, Daniel B. Ward / 1995

Comments: National champions: Virginia, two trees (482 points, 479 points).

Quercus phellos L.
Willow Oak

(1)

☆ **Florida Champion.**

Size:			
	Circumference:	57	inches
	Height:	65	feet
	Crown spread:	45	feet
	Total points:	133	points

Owner / location: Univ. of Florida / s.e. corner of Jennings Hall, campus, Gainesville, Alachua Co. [n.e. 1/4 of sec 7, T10S, R20E]

Nominator(s) / date: Robert T. Ing, Daniel B. Ward / 1991

Comments: Tree was planted soon after building was constructed, probably in the early 1960s. Rare in Florida; common, and much larger, in Georgia and the Carolinas.

National champions: Mississippi (424 points); Tennesee (422 points); Maryland (420 points).

Quercus shumardii Buckl.
Shumard Oak

(1)

☆ **Florida Champion.**

Size:			
	Circumference:	149	inches
	Height:	116	feet
	Crown spread:	77	feet
	Total points:	284	points

Owner / location: Silver River State Park / n. side of Silver River, 1.5 mi. below Silver Springs, 3 mi. above Fla. 40 bridge, Marion Co. [s.w. 1/4 of sec 5, T15S, R23E]

Nominator(s) / date: Robert W. Simons / 1986

Comments: National champions: Tennessee (461 points); Louisiana (384 points); Mississippi (384 points); Kentucky (379 points).

Quercus stellata Wangenh.
Post Oak

(1)

☆ **Florida Champion.**

Size:			
	Circumference:	194	inches
	Height:	88	feet
	Crown spread:	96.5	feet
	Total points:	306	points

Owner / location: Jennings Thomas / n.e. corner of Marion St. & Saint Johns St., Marianna, Jackson Co. [s. 1/2 of sec 3, T4N, R10W]

Nominator(s) / date: James A. Potts, Robert C. Williams / 1983

Update: R. Bruce Turnbull / 1994

Comments: Earlier measurements: circ. = 181 in., ht. = 80 ft., spread = 96 ft. (Potts & Williams, 1983). National champion: Virginia (343 points).

(2)

Florida Challenger.

Size:			
	Circumference:	180	inches
	Height:	78	feet
	Crown spread:	97	feet
	Total points:	282	points

Owner / location: J. R. Keene / 0.5 mi. w. of Int. 75, 2 mi. s. of Santa Fe River, Alachua Co. [sec 37, T7S, R18E]

Nominator(s) / date: Robert W. Simons / 1987

(3)

Emeritus Florida Champion.

Size:			
	Circumference:	159	inches
	Height:	87	feet
	Crown spread:	93	feet
	Total points:	269	points

Owner / location: Farrell Nelson / s. of Fla. 280, 5 mi. s.e. of Chipley, Washington Co. [s.w. 1/4 of sec 30, T4N, R12W]

Nominator(s) / date: Charles R. Reeves / 1981

Update: Charles R. Reeves / 1993

Comments: Earlier measurements: circ. = 155 in., ht. = 75 ft., spread = 90 ft. (Reeves, 1981).

(4)

Emeritus Florida Champion.

Size:			
	Circumference:	150	inches
	Height:	76	feet
	Crown spread:	88	feet
	Total points:	248	points

Owner / location: R. D. Justice / n. side of Fla. 280, 6 mi. s.e. of Chipley, Washington Co. [s.w. 1/4 of sec 20, T4N, R12W]

Nominator(s) / date: Charles R. Reeves / 1980

Update: Charles R. Reeves / 1993

Comments: Earlier measurements: circ. = 140 in., ht. = 72 ft., spread = 76 ft. (Reeves, 1980).

(5)

Honorable Mention.

Size:			
	Circumference:	120	inches
	Height:	60	feet
	Crown spread:	60.5	feet
	Total points:	195	points

Owner / location: Albert Boston / s.e. corner, N.W. 71st St. & N.W. 25th Lane, Gainesville, Alachua Co. [s.w. 1/4 of sec 28, T9S, R19E]

Nominator(s) / date: Robert T. Ing, Daniel B. Ward / 1991

Quercus velutina Lam.
Black Oak

(1)

☆ Florida Champion.

Size:			
	Circumference:	89	inches
	Height:	95	feet
	Crown spread:	50	feet
	Total points:	197	points

Owner / location: Jewell Springer / e. of Fla. 51, n. of Fla. 357, 12 mi. s.w. of Mayo, Lafayette Co. [sec 30, T6S, R11E]

Nominator(s) / date: Jerry N. Livingston, Owen Cannon / 1986

Comments: National champions: Connecticut (416 points); Michigan (412 points).

Quercus virginiana Mill.
Live Oak

(1)

☆ Florida Co-Champion.

Size:			
	Circumference:	360	inches
	Height:	85	feet
	Crown spread:	160	feet
	Total points:	485	points

Owner / location: County of Alachua / Cellon Oak Park, 0.2 mi. w. of Fla. 121, 3 mi. s. of LaCrosse, Alachua Co. [n.w. 1/4 of sec 11, T8S, R19E]

Nominator(s) / date: Robert W. Simons / 1976

Update: Michael J. Bordyn, Robert W. Simons / 1981

Update: Duane R. Durgee / 1985

Update: Robert T. Ing, Daniel B. Ward / 1993

Comments: Earlier measurements: circ. = 324 in., ht. = 83 ft., spread = 146 ft. (Simons, 1976); circ. = 340 in., ht. = 83 ft., spread = 150.5 ft. (Bordyn & Simons, 1981); circ. = 344 in., ht. = 79 ft., spread = 154 ft. (Durgee, 1985).

Limb, broken in storm and smoothly cut 8 ft. above ground, showed ring count of 134 years (D. R. Durgee, July 1993). Implication is that tree is very probably less than 200 years of age.

Known as the "Cellon Oak" (former owner Ralph W. Cellon).

National champion: Louisiana (527 points).

(2)

☆ Florida Co-Champion.

Size:			
	Circumference:	345	inches
	Height:	78	feet
	Crown spread:	153.5	feet
	Total points:	461	points

Owner / location: Jacksonville Naval Air Station / Mul-

berry Grove Park, Mustin Rd., 8 mi. s. of Jacksonville, Duval Co. [s.e. 1/4 of sec 44, T3S, R26E]

Nominator(s) / date: Henry Rogers / 1980

Update: Joseph E. Dunbar / 1985

Update: Robert T. Ing, Daniel B. Ward / 1993

Comments: Earlier measurements: circ. = 330 in., ht. = 90 ft., spread = 151 ft. (Rogers, 1980); circ. = 340 in., ht. = 88 ft., spread = 153 ft. (Dunbar, 1985).

This tree is known as the "Timucua Oak." The Timucua Indians, however, had largely been destroyed by disease and by warfare with invading Creeks by about 1750. At that date this tree would have been of very modest size, and it is unlikely there was any historic connection.

(3)

Florida Challenger.

Size:			
	Circumference:	329	inches
	Height:	103	feet
	Crown spread:	99.5	feet
	Total points:	457	points

Owner / location: Rosemarie Permenter / 2 mi. e. of Fla. 475, 1.5 mi. n. of county line, 6 mi. s.w. of Belleview, Marion Co. [s.e. 1/4 of sec 34, T17S, R22E]

Nominator(s) / date: Jeff Overby / 1993

(4)

Florida Challenger.

Size:			
	Circumference:	355	inches
	Height:	67	feet
	Crown spread:	137	feet
	Total points:	456	points

Owner / location: Jimmy Davis Enterprises, Inc. / 0.5 mi. n. of Int. 10, w. of Captain Brown Rd., 5 mi. w.s.w. of Madison, Madison Co. [sec 34, T1N, R8E]

Nominator(s) / date: Herb Platt, Robert W. Simons / 1991

(5)

Honorable Mention.

Size:			
	Circumference:	322	inches
	Height:	86	feet
	Crown spread:	141	feet
	Total points:	443	points

Owner / location: Brian Thorpe / 0.3 mi. s. of Fla. 270, 0.7 mi. w. of Scotland, 3 mi. s. of Havana, Gadsden Co. [n.w. 1/4 of sec 16, T2N, R2W]

Nominator(s) / date: J. B. Snowden / 1967

Update: John David Core / 1995

Comments: Earlier measurements: circ. = 272 in., ht. = 86 ft., spread = 117 ft. (Snowden, 1967).

Tree is known as the "Bert Brothers Oak" in honor of its previous owners.

(6)

Honorable Mention.

Size:			
	Circumference:	336	inches
	Height:	70	feet
	Crown spread:	137	feet
	Total points:	440	points

Owner / location: Lake Griffin State Recreation Area / Fruitland Park, Lake Co. [n.w. 1/4 of sec 10, T19S, R24E]

Nominator(s) / date: Debi Richards / 1980

Update: Brett J. States, Keith Westlake / 1986

Update: Robert W. Simons, Daniel B. Ward / 1993

Comments: Earlier measurements: circ. = 380 in., ht. = 73 ft., spread = 64 ft. (Richards, 1980); circ. = 354 in., ht. = 72 ft., spread = 138 ft. (States & Westlake, 1986). Trunk has not grown progressively smaller, as implied by sequential measurements; rather, earlier measurements were taken either above or below 2 ft., the minimum circumference.

(7)

Honorable Mention.

Size:			
	Circumference:	306	inches
	Height:	97.5	feet
	Crown spread:	98	feet
	Total points:	428	points

Owner / location: San Felasco Hammock State Preserve / n. of Fla. 232, 8 mi. n.w. of Gainesville, Alachua Co. [sec 37, T9S, R19E]

Nominator(s) / date: Robert T. Ing, Daniel B. Ward / 1991

Comments: The "Helen Hood Oak," named for the woman who was primarily responsible for acquisition of the Hammock by the State.

(8)

Honorable Mention.

Size:			
	Circumference:	306	inches
	Height:	95	feet
	Crown spread:	88.5	feet
	Total points:	423	points

Owner / location: Gerald L. Rogers / between Santa Fe Road & Santa Fe River, s. end of Three Rivers Estates, 3 mi. w. of Ft. White, Columbia Co. [n.w. 1/4 of sec 36, T6S, R15E]

Nominator(s) / date: Robert T. Ing, Daniel B. Ward / 1993

(9)

Honorable Mention.

Size:			
	Circumference:	309	inches
	Height:	74	feet
	Crown spread:	138	feet
	Total points:	416	points

Owner / location: R. J. Huffman / 2850 Wilde Lake Blvd., s.w. of jct. Int. 10 & Fla. 297, n.w. Pensacola, Escambia Co. [s.e. 1/4 of sec 11, T1S, R31W]

Nominator(s) / date: Thomas H. Serviss / 1980

Update: Thomas H. Serviss / 1994

Comments: Earlier measurements: circ. = 288 in., ht. = 74 ft., spread = 125 ft. (Serviss, 1980).

(10)

Honorable Mention.

Size:			
	Circumference:	314	inches
	Height:	70	feet
	Crown spread:	96	feet
	Total points:	408	points

Owner / location: Neal Land and Timber Co. / Ocheesee Landing, w. bank of Apalachicola River, 10 mi. n.n.e. of Blountstown, Calhoun Co. [s.e. 1/4 of sec 7, T2N, R7W]

Nominator(s) / date: G. Owen House / 1980

Update: Stephen Oswalt / 1994

Comments: Earlier measurements: circ. = 312 in., ht. = 81 ft., spread = 88 ft. (House, 1980).

(11)

Honorable Mention.

Size:			
	Circumference:	270	inches
	Height:	86	feet
	Crown spread:	93	feet
	Total points:	389	points

Owner / location: Ocala National Forest / 1 mi. n.w. of Mud Lake, Marion Co. [sec 34, T13S, R24E]

Nominator(s) / date: Jeff Overby / 1993

(12)

Honorable Mention.

Size:			
	Circumference:	287	inches
	Height:	68	feet
	Crown spread:	133	feet
	Total points:	388	points

Owner / location: Bulow Creek State Park / 8 mi. n.n.w. of Ormond Beach, Volusia Co. [sec 37, T12S, R31E]

Nominator(s) / date: Robert W. Simons, Daniel B. Ward / 1993

Comments: Tree is known as the "Fairchild Oak" in honor of Dr. David Fairchild.

(13)

Honorable Mention.

Size:			
	Circumference:	256	inches
	Height:	91	feet
	Crown spread:	96	feet
	Total points:	371	points

Owner / location: C. H. Ratliff / n. bank of Suwannee River, 2 mi. w. of Fla. 51, 6 mi. s. of Jasper, Hamilton Co. [sec 12, T1S, R13E]

Nominator(s) / date: Doug Longshore / 1980

Update: Doug Longshore / 1993

Comments: Earlier measurements: circ. = 252 in., ht. = 115 ft., spread = 93 ft. (Longshore, 1980).

(14)

Honorable Mention.

Size:			
	Circumference:	260	inches
	Height:	78	feet
	Crown spread:	128.5	feet
	Total points:	370	points

Owner / location: Allen R. Bush / Silver Lake Dr., e. of Fla. 19, 4 mi. s.w. of Palatka, Putnam Co. [n.e. 1/4 of sec 21, T10S, R26E]

Nominator(s) / date: Roy A. Lima / 1980

Update: Ned D. Neenan / 1993

Comments: Earlier measurements: circ. = 235 in., ht. = 70 ft., spread = 128.5 ft. (Lima, 1980).

(15)

Honorable Mention.

Size:			
	Circumference:	252	inches
	Height:	81	feet
	Crown spread:	128.5	feet
	Total points:	365	points

Owner / location: Gladys Johnson / 2 mi. n. of Fla. 2, 7 mi. n.e. of Campbellton, Jackson Co. [s.w. 1/4 of sec 25, T7N, R11W]

Nominator(s) / date: Diane Johnson / 1989

Update: R. Bruce Turnbull / 1994

Comments: Earlier measurements: circ. = 248 in., ht. = 89 ft., spread = 131 ft. (Johnson, 1989).

(16)

Honorable Mention.

Size:			
	Circumference:	262	inches
	Height:	70	feet
	Crown spread:	130	feet
	Total points:	365	points

Owner / location: DeLeon Springs State Recreation Area / DeLeon Springs, Volusia Co. [sec 38, T16S, R29E]

Nominator(s) / date: Robert W. Simons, Daniel B. Ward / 1993

(17)

Honorable Mention.

Size:			
	Circumference:	250	inches
	Height:	85	feet
	Crown spread:	109	feet
	Total points:	362	points

Owner / location: First Presbyterian Church / s. of jct. Lee St. & Second St., Ft. Myers, Lee Co. [s.w. 1/4 of sec 13, T44S, R24E]

Nominator(s) / date: Jeffrey S. Mangun, Michael Curtis / 1991

(18)

Honorable Mention.

Size:			
	Circumference:	270	inches
	Height:	62	feet
	Crown spread:	120.5	feet
	Total points:	362	points

Owner / location: Linda J. Peterson / 870 Indian Beach Dr., Sarasota, Sarasota Co. [s.e. 1/4 of sec 12, T36S, R17E]

Nominator(s) / date: Lee Barnwell / 1994

(19)

Honorable Mention.

Size:			
	Circumference:	234	inches
	Height:	95	feet
	Crown spread:	125	feet
	Total points:	360	points

Owner / location: Gene Yearty / 8060 Hammond Blvd., just n.e. of Devoe St., Jacksonville, Duval Co. [sec 22, T2S, R25E]

Nominator(s) / date: Scott A. Crosby / 1991

(20)

Honorable Mention.

Size:			
	Circumference:	238	inches
	Height:	75	feet
	Crown spread:	117	feet
	Total points:	342	points

Owner / location: John DeSandro / 1 mi. n.e. of Grand Ridge, Jackson Co. [n.w. 1/4 of sec 23, T4N, R8W]

Nominator(s) / date: R. Bruce Turnbull / 1993

(21)

Honorable Mention.

Size:			
	Circumference:	245	inches
	Height:	60	feet
	Crown spread:	144	feet
	Total points:	341	points

Owner / location: City of Jacksonville / 815 S. Main St., between Alvarez St. & Prudential Dr., Jacksonville, Duval Co. [n.w. 1/4 of sec 44, T2S, R26E]

Nominator(s) / date: Albert P. Simmons / 1981

Update: Bruce Hill / 1987

Comments: Earlier measurements: circ. = 234 in., ht. = 66 ft., spread = 180 ft. (Simmons, 1981).

This tree is known as the "Treaty Oak." Although

legend has long attributed this tree to be the site of the first conference between Indians and whites in the vicinity of present-day Jacksonville, the size of the tree suggests an age of perhaps no more than 150 years. Healthy; part of a profuse crop of acorns is collected annually by a local nurseryman, for sale of seedlings from the famous tree; not remeasured (R. T. Ing & D. B. Ward, Oct 1993).

(22)
Honorable Mention.

Size:			
	Circumference:	219	inches
	Height:	90	feet
	Crown spread:	118	feet
	Total points:	339	points

Owner / location: Mrs. Jim Cassin Corbett Camp / 406 S.W. Central Ave., Jasper, Hamilton Co. [s.e. 1/4 of sec 6, T1N, R14E]

Nominator(s) / date: Robert T. Ing, Daniel B. Ward / 1993

(23)
Honorable Mention.

Size:			
	Circumference:	218	inches
	Height:	80	feet
	Crown spread:	108	feet
	Total points:	325	points

Owner / location: Frank Sears / 506 Ravine St., s.w. side of Milton, Santa Rosa Co. [sec 4, T1N, R28W]

Nominator(s) / date: Kenneth L. Oser / 1986

Reynosia septentrionalis Urban
Darling Plum

(1)
★ National Champion.

Size:			
	Circumference:	20.5	inches
	Height:	28	feet
	Crown spread:	13	feet
	Total points:	52	points

Owner / location: Lignumvitae Key State Botanical Site / Lignumvitae Key, Monroe Co. [n.w. 1/4 of sec 2, T64S, R36E]

Nominator(s) / date: Charlotte Niedhauk / 1975

Update: Ken Roundtree, David M. Sinclair / 1986

Update: Robert Rose / 1993

Comments: Earlier measurements: circ. = 17 in., ht. = 40 ft., spread = 10.5 ft. (Niedhauk, 1975); circ. = 19 in., ht. = 28 ft., spread = 13 ft. (Roundtree & Sinclair, 1986); height & spread were not remeasured (R. Rose, Jan 1993).

Acknowledged by American Forests (1996 listing).

(2)
Florida Challenger.

Size:			
	Circumference:	22	inches
	Height:	19	feet
	Crown spread:	25	feet
	Total points:	47	points

Owner / location: Fred Guarnieri / 14 Colson Dr., Cudjoe Key, Monroe Co. [s.w. 1/4 of sec 29, T66S, R28E]

Nominator(s) / date: Patricia L. McNeese / 1995

Rhamnus caroliniana Walt.
Carolina Buckthorn

(1)
☆ Florida Champion.

Size:			
	Circumference:	19	inches
	Height:	44	feet
	Crown spread:	15	feet
	Total points:	67	points

Owner / location: Florida Caverns State Park / e. of group campground, 2 mi. n. of Marianna, Jackson Co. [s.w. 1/4 of sec 22, T5N, R10W]

Nominator(s) / date: Robert T. Ing, Daniel B. Ward / 1995

Comments: National champions: Virginia (74 points); Tennessee (71 points).

Rhizophora mangle L.
Red Mangrove

(1)
★ National Champion.

Size:			
	Circumference:	47	inches
	Height:	58	feet
	Crown spread:	42	feet
	Total points:	116	points

Owner / location: Ding Darling National Wildlife Refuge / n. side of Sanibel-Captiva Rd., Sanibel Id., Lee Co. [n.w. 1/4 of sec 18, T46S, R22E]

Nominator(s) / date: Amy Bennett, Richard W. Workman / 1995

Comments: Acknowledged by American Forests (1996 listing).

Rhus copallinum L.
Winged Sumac, Shining Sumac

(1)
☆ Florida Champion.

Size:			
	Circumference:	18	inches
	Height:	18	feet
	Crown spread:	18	feet
	Total points:	41	points

Owner / location: Dennis Durant / Hardee's Restaurant, 651 W. Washington St., Chattahoochee, Gadsden Co. [n.e. 1/4 of sec 32, T4N, R6W]

Nominator(s) / date: Robert T. Ing, Daniel B. Ward / 1995

Comments: National champion: Texas (89 points).

The epithet of this species is often spelled "*copallina*," an incorrect "correction" of the original spelling.

Rhus glabra L.
Smooth Sumac

Title vacant.

Size: Circumference:

         Height:

         Crown spread:

         Total points:

Owner / location:

Nominator(s) / date:

Comments: Native in central panhandle Florida.

Herbarium records (FLAS, July 1995) indicate this species, near Chattahoochee, Gadsden County, to reach a height of 3 meters.

National champions: Washington, two trees (71 points, 69 points).

Rhus vernix L.
= *Toxicodendron vernix* (L.) Kuntze
Poison Sumac

(1)

☆ **Florida Champion.**

Size:			
	Circumference:	11	inches
	Height:	16	feet
	Crown spread:	15	feet
	Total points:	31	points

Owner / location: Ravine State Gardens / Twigg St., Palatka, Putnam Co. [s.e. 1/4 of sec 12, T10S, R26E]

Nominator(s) / date: Ned D. Neenan / 1993

Comments: This tree is a smaller replacement for the previous Florida champion (Dale, 1989 - 44 points) also at this location, and now deceased.

National champions: New York (54 points); Virginia (51 points).

Roystonea elata (Bartr.) F. Harper
Florida Royal Palm

(1)

★ **National Champion** (nominee).

Size:			
	Circumference:	50	inches
	Height:	99	feet
	Crown spread:	18	feet
	Total points:	154	points

Owner / location: Fakahatchee Strand State Preserve / 5 mi. n.w. of Copeland, Collier Co. [n.e. 1/4 of sec 28, T51S, R29E]

Nominator(s) / date: Daniel B. Ward / 1995

Comments: National champion: Florida (143 points).

(2)

★ **National Champion.**

Size:			
	Circumference:	70	inches
	Height:	66	feet
	Crown spread:	26	feet
	Total points:	143	points

Owner / location: Ken Sargent / Ft. Denaud Rd. (Fla. 78A), s. bank of Caloosahatchee River, 1.5 mi. e. of Ft. Denaud bridge, 3 mi. w.s.w. of LaBelle, Hendry Co. [s.e. 1/4 of sec 11, T43S, R28E]

Nominator(s) / date: Chris J. Anderson / 1994

Comments: Acknowledged by American Forests (1996 listing).

(3)

Honorable Mention.

Size:			
	Circumference:	71	inches
	Height:	49	feet
	Crown spread:	24	feet
	Total points:	126	points

Owner / location: (unknown) / 703 N. 100th Ave., s. of Fla. 846, w. of U.S. 41, North Naples, Collier Co. [sec 28, T48S, R25E]

Nominator(s) / date: Chris J. Anderson / 1980

Update: Chris J. Anderson / 1994

Comments: Earlier measurements: circ. = 72 in., ht. = 34 ft., spread = 21 ft. (Anderson, 1980).

Sabal palmetto (Walt.) Lodd.
ex Schult. & Schult.
Cabbage Palm

(1)

☆ **Florida Champion.**

Size:			
	Circumference:	69	inches
	Height:	60	feet
	Crown spread:	14	feet
	Total points:	133	points

Owner / location: R. M. Meares / Hatchbend, e. of Fla. 342, s.e. corner of Lafayette Co. [s.w. 1/4 of sec 23, T7S, R14E]

Nominator(s) / date: Jerry N. Livingston / 1994

Comments: National champion: Georgia (140 points).

Salix caroliniana Michx.
Carolina Willow, Coastal Plain Willow

(1)

☆ **Florida Champion.**

Size:	Circumference:	41	inches
	Height:	43	feet
	Crown spread:	26	feet
	Total points:	91	points

Owner / location: City of Gainesville / Hogtown Prairie, w. of Int 75, n. end of Lake Kanapaha, s.w. Gainesville, Alachua Co. [n.e. 1/4 of sec 16, T10S, R19E]

Nominator(s) / date: Daniel B. Ward / 1995

Comments: National champions: Virginia (177 points); North Carolina (172 points).

Salix floridana Chapm.
Florida Willow

(1)

★ **National Champion.**

Size:	Circumference:	11	inches
	Height:	20	feet
	Crown spread:	23	feet
	Total points:	37	points

Owner / location: Ocala National Forest / channel of Morman Branch, tributary of Juniper Creek, s. of F. S. Rd. 71, Marion Co. [sec 37, T15S, R26E]

Nominator(s) / date: Jeff Overby, Ilke Toklu / 1993

Comments: Acknowledged by American Forests (1996 listing).

Salix nigra Marsh.
Black Willow

(1)

☆ **Florida Champion.**

Size:	Circumference:	47	inches
	Height:	68	feet
	Crown spread:	24	feet
	Total points:	121	points

Owner / location: St. Joseph Land & Development Co. / bank of Crooked Creek, 7 mi. s.s.w. of Chattahoochee, Gadsden Co. [s.e. 1/4 of sec 36, T3N, R7W]

Nominator(s) / date: Robert T. Ing, Daniel B. Ward / 1995

Comments: National champion: Michigan (499 points).

Florida Challenger.

(2)

Size:	Circumference:	41	inches
	Height:	59	feet
	Crown spread:	32	feet
	Total points:	108	points

Owner / location: City of Chattahoochee / Apalachicola River bottom, w. edge of Chattahoochee, Gadsden Co. [n.e. 1/4 of sec 32, T4N, R6W]

Nominator(s) / date: Robert T. Ing, Daniel B. Ward / 1995

Sambucus canadensis L.
= *Sambucus simpsonii* Rehder
Elderberry

(1)

★ **National Champion.**

Size:	Circumference:	26	inches
	Height:	18	feet
	Crown spread:	12	feet
	Total points:	47	points

Owner / location: Jeri Baldwin / 1 mi. w. of Fla. 318, 6 mi. n.e of Citra, Marion Co. [n.w. 1/4 of sec 7, T12S, R23E]

Nominator(s) / date: Robert W. Simons / 1994

Comments: The Florida record is based on the southern var. *laciniata* Gray, and is the largest registered for that variety. However, a larger tree in Virginia (circ. = 38 in., ht. = 16 ft., spread = 22 ft., 60 points), though reported as the usually smaller northern var. *canadensis*, may also be var. *laciniata*.

Acknowledged by American Forests (1996 listing).

Florida Challenger.

(2)

Size:	Circumference:	16	inches
	Height:	13	feet
	Crown spread:	6.5	feet
	Total points:	31	points

Owner / location: Lake Jem County Park / 3.5 mi. n.e. of Astatula, Lake Co. [n.w. 1/4 of sec 14, T20S, R26E]

Nominator(s) / date: Robert W. Simons, Daniel B. Ward / 1993

Comments: This is the southern var. *laciniata* Gray.

Sapindus marginatus Willd.
Florida Soapberry

(1)

★ National Champion.

Size:	Circumference:	88	inches
	Height:	72	feet
	Crown spread:	36	feet
	Total points:	169	points

Owner / location: Paynes Prairie State Preserve / e. of
   headquarters, 2 mi. s.s.e. of Gainesville, Alachua Co.
   [sec 22, T10S, R20E]

Nominator(s) / date: Robert W. Simons / 1977

   Update: Robert W. Simons / 1991

Comments: Earlier measurements: circ. = 85 in., ht. =
   70 ft., spread = 39 ft. (Simons, 1977).

   Acknowledged (as *Sapindus saponaria*, as an
inclusive listing) by American Forests (1996 listing).
Trees of *Sapindus* in the more northern portion of its
eastern U.S. range have been segregated as *S. marginatus*, a useful if tenuous distinction.

(2)

Florida Challenger.

Size:	Circumference:	61	inches
	Height:	68	feet
	Crown spread:	36.5	feet
	Total points:	138	points

Owner / location: U.S.D.A. Plant Materials Center / w.
   side of U.S. 41, s. of Fla. 476, 6 mi. n.e. of
   Brooksville, Hernando Co. [sec 30, T21S, R20E]

Nominator(s) / date: Robert Dudley, Wilbur C. Priest /
   1990

Sapindus saponaria L.
Tropical Soapberry, Winged Soapberry

(1)

★ National Champion (nominee).

Size:	Circumference:	25	inches
	Height:	33	feet
	Crown spread:	17.5	feet
	Total points:	62	points

Owner / location: Key Largo Hammocks State Botanical
   Site / n. end of Key Largo, Monroe Co. [sec 25, T59S,
   R40E]

Nominator(s) / date: Jeanne M. Parks / 1989

Comments: If *Sapindus* in the eastern U.S. is recognized to consist of two species, this tree merits
   championship rank as the largest within the range
   of *S. saponaria*, in the narrow sense.

Sassafras albidum (Nutt.) Nees
Sassafras

(1)

☆ Florida Champion.

Size:	Circumference:	60	inches
	Height:	75	feet
	Crown spread:	31	feet
	Total points:	143	points

Owner / location: Wakulla Springs State Park / Wakulla
   Springs, Wakulla Co. [sec 18, T3S, R1E]

Nominator(s) / date: Steve L. Brown / 1988

Comments: National champion: Kentucky (357 points).

(2)

Emeritus Florida Champion.

Size:	Circumference:	81	inches
	Height:	41	feet
	Crown spread:	36.5	feet
	Total points:	131	points

Owner / location: Apalachee Correctional Institution /
   Sneads, Jackson Co. [s.w. 1/4 of sec 25, T4N, R7W]

Nominator(s) / date: Jack Clarkson / 1983

   Update: Robert T. Ing, Daniel B. Ward / 1995

Comments: Earlier measurements: circ. = 62 in., ht. =
   40 ft., spread = 30 ft. (Clarkson, 1983). This tree was
   Florida champion between 1983 and 1988, when it
   was deposed by a larger tree (Brown—Wakulla
   County).

(3)

Florida Challenger.

Size:	Circumference:	64	inches
	Height:	40	feet
	Crown spread:	25	feet
	Total points:	110	points

Owner / location: Ernie Medley / 2047 Gorrie Ave.,
   Sneads, Jackson Co. [s.w. 1/4 of sec 27, T4N, R7W]

Nominator(s) / date: Robert T. Ing, Daniel B. Ward / 1995

Savia bahamensis Britt.
Maidenbush

Title vacant.

Size:	Circumference:		
	Height:		
	Crown spread:		
	Total points:		

Owner / location:

Nominator(s) / date:

Comments: Native in the Florida Keys.

Herbarium records (FLAS, July 1995) indicate this species, on Big Pine Key, Monroe County, to reach a height of 4.5 meters. It is recognized as a tree by American Forests (1996 listing), but as a "species without a champion."

Schaefferia frutescens Jacq.
Florida Boxwood

(1)

★ **National Champion.**

Size:	Circumference:	24	inches
	Height:	27	feet
	Crown spread:	16	feet
	Total points:	55	points

Owner / location: Lignumvitae Key State Botanical Site / Lignumvitae Key, Monroe Co. [n.w. 1/4 of sec 2, T64S, R36E]

Nominator(s) / date: Ken Roundtree, David M. Sinclair / 1986

Update: Robert Rose / 1993

Comments: Earlier measurements: circ. = 24 in., ht. = 27 ft., spread = 16 ft. (Roundtree & Sinclair, 1986); circ. unchanged, height & spread not remeasured (R. Rose, Jan 1993).

Acknowledged by American Forests (1996 listing).

Schoepfia chrysophylloides
(A. Rich.) Planch.
Whitewood, Graytwig

(1)

★ **National Champion.**

Size:	Circumference:	7	inches
	Height:	18	feet
	Crown spread:	18	feet
	Total points:	30	points

Owner / location: Dennis McIltrot / 3960 Ellis Rd., Ft. Myers, Lee Co. [s.w. 1/4 of sec 35, T43S, R25E]

Nominator(s) / date: Jeffrey S. Mangun / 1994

Comments: Acknowledged by American Forests (1996 listing).

Serenoa repens (Bartr.) Small
Saw Palmetto

(1)

★ **National Co-Champion.**

Size:	Circumference:	27	inches
	Height:	21	feet
	Crown spread:	8	feet
	Total points:	50	points

Owner / location: Agricultural Research Center / Picos Rd., 3 mi. w. of Ft. Pierce, St. Lucie Co. [n.w. 1/4 of sec 14, T35S, R39E]

Nominator(s) / date: Steven J. Fousek, Paul G. Williams / 1986

Comments: Acknowledged by American Forests (1996 listing).

(2)

★ **National Co-Champion.**

Size:	Circumference:	22	inches
	Height:	20	feet
	Crown spread:	13	feet
	Total points:	45	points

Owner / location: Withlacoochee State Forest / 8 mi. s.w. of Bushnell, Sumter Co. [s.e. 1/4 of sec 4, T22S, R21E]

Nominator(s) / date: Buford C. Pruitt, David L. Evans / 1982

Update: David L. Fogler / 1994

Comments: Earlier measurements: circ. = 26 in., ht. = 17 ft., spread = 11 ft. (Pruitt & Evans, 1982). Acknowledged by American Forests (1996 listing).

Simarouba glauca L.
Paradise-tree

(1)

★ **National Champion.**

Size:	Circumference:	109	inches
	Height:	63	feet
	Crown spread:	59	feet
	Total points:	187	points

Owner / location: Florida Trust for Historic Preservation, Inc. / Bonnett House, 900 N. Birch Rd., Fort Lauderdale, Broward Co. [n.e. 1/4 of sec 1, T50S, R42E]

Nominator(s) / date: Ann Buckley, Ted Hendrickson, Robert Trickel / 1984

Update: Jim Higgins, Frank L. Zickar / 1994

Comments: Earlier measurements: circ. = 78 in., ht. = 62 ft., spread = 47 ft. (Buckley, Hendrickson & Trickel, 1984). Acknowledged by American Forests (1996 listing).

(2)

Florida Challenger.

Size:	Circumference:	60	inches
	Height:	45	feet
	Crown spread:	10.5	feet
	Total points:	108	points

Owner / location: Simpson Park / jct. S. Miami Ave. &

S.E. 15th Rd., Miami, Dade Co. [sec 12, T54S, R41E]

Nominator(s) / date: William G. Miller, John T. Valenta / 1993

(3)

Honorable Mention.

Size:			
	Circumference:	39	inches
	Height:	39	feet
	Crown spread:	14.5	feet
	Total points:	82	points

Owner / location: Key Largo Hammocks State Botanical Site / n. end of Key Largo, Monroe Co. [sec 26, T59S, R40E]

Nominator(s) / date: Jeanne M. Parks / 1989

Solanum erianthum D. Don
= *Solanum verbascifolium* L.
Potato-tree

Title vacant.

Size:			
	Circumference:		
	Height:		
	Crown spread:		
	Total points:		

Owner / location:

Nominator(s) / date:

Comments: Native in south peninsular Florida and the Florida Keys.

This species is usually a shrub, with occasional individuals forming trees. Herbarium records (FTG, Dec 1995) indicate this species, on north Key Largo, Monroe Co., reaches a height of 3 meters with trunk diameters of 6 centimeters. It was recognized as a tree by American Forests (1996 listing), but as a "species without a champion."

Staphylea trifolia L.
Bladdernut

Title vacant.

Size:			
	Circumference:		
	Height:		
	Crown spread:		
	Total points:		

Owner / location:

Nominator(s) / date:

Comments: Native in central panhandle Florida (Liberty County)

Often a shrub. Herbarium records (FLAS, July 1995) indicate this species, in Torreya State Park, Liberty County, to reach a height of 4 meters.

National champion: Michigan (64 points).

Stewartia malacodendron L.
Silky Camellia

(1)

★ **National Co-Champion.**

Size:			
	Circumference:	10	inches
	Height:	19	feet
	Crown spread:	28	feet
	Total points:	36	points

Owner / location: C. J. Laird / s. side of Fla. 183, 8 mi. s.e. of DeFuniak Springs, Walton Co. [s.w. 1/4 of sec 24, T2N, R18W]

Nominator(s) / date: Murdock R. Gillis / 1994

Comments: The largest of three trees at this location.

Acknowledged by American Forests (1996 listing), with National co-champion: Virginia (31 points).

(2)

Florida Challenger.

Size:			
	Circumference:	7	inches
	Height:	13	feet
	Crown spread:	21.5	feet
	Total points:	25	points

Owner / location: C. J. Laird / s. side of Fla. 183, 8 mi. s.e. of DeFuniak Springs, Walton Co. [s.w. 1/4 of sec 24, T2N, R18W]

Nominator(s) / date: Murdock R. Gillis / 1994

Comments: The second largest of three trees at this location.

(3)

Florida Challenger.

Size:			
	Circumference:	6	inches
	Height:	14	feet
	Crown spread:	20.5	feet
	Total points:	25	points

Owner / location: C. J. Laird / s. side of Fla. 183, 8 mi. s.e. of DeFuniak Springs, Walton Co. [s.w. 1/4 of sec 24, T2N, R18W]

Nominator(s) / date: Murdock R. Gillis / 1994

Comments: The third largest of three trees at this location.

Styrax americanum Lam.
American Snow-bell

Title vacant.

Size:			
	Circumference:		
	Height:		
	Crown spread:		
	Total points:		

Owner / location:

Nominator(s) / date:

Comments: Native in northern and central Florida.

Most often a shrub, with occasional individuals becoming trees. Herbarium records (FLAS, July 1995) indicate this species, near Holt, Okaloosa County, and in the Myakka River State Park, Sarasota County, to reach a height of 5 meters. Not included in the Checklist of Trees Native to Florida (Ward, 1991).

National champions: South Carolina (26 points); Texas (25 points).

Styrax grandifolium Ait.
Bigleaf Snow-bell

Title vacant.

Size:	Circumference:		
	Height:		
	Crown spread:		
	Total points:		

Owner / location:

Nominator(s) / date:

Comments: Native in panhandle Florida.

Usually a shrub, infrequently tall enough to be called a tree. Herbarium records (FLAS, July 1995) indicate this species, near DeFuniak Springs, Walton County, to reach a height of 5 meters. Not included in the Checklist of Trees Native to Florida (Ward, 1991).

National champion: North Carolina (33 points).

Suriana maritima L.
Bay Cedar

(1)
★ National Champion.

Size:	Circumference:	10	inches
	Height:	12	feet
	Crown spread:	22.5	feet
	Total points:	28	points

Owner / location: William R. Redman / Long Beach Rd., s. end of Big Pine Key, Monroe Co. [s.e. 1/4 of sec 2, T67S, R29E]

Nominator(s) / date: Vincent P. Condon, William G. Miller / 1995

Comments: Acknowledged by American Forests (1996 listing).

Swietenia mahagoni Jacq.
West Indian Mahogany

(1)
★ National Champion.

Size:	Circumference:	175	inches
	Height:	79	feet
	Crown spread:	96	feet
	Total points:	278	points

Owner / location: St. Mary's Catholic Church / 1010 Windsor Lane, Key West, Monroe Co. [s.w. 1/4 of sec 1, T68S, R25E]

Nominator(s) / date: William S. Hubard, Beverlee Wang / 1992

Comments: Acknowledged by American Forests (1996 listing).

(2)
Florida Challenger.

Size:	Circumference:	160	inches
	Height:	67	feet
	Crown spread:	69	feet
	Total points:	244	points

Owner / location: Ron J. Pavlik / 1301 E. Broward Blvd., Ft. Lauderdale, Broward Co. [s.w. 1/4 of sec 2, T50S, R42E]

Nominator(s) / date: Frank L. Zickar, Gene Dempsey / 1994

(3)
Honorable Mention.

Size:	Circumference:	128	inches
	Height:	71	feet
	Crown spread:	60	feet
	Total points:	214	points

Owner / location: Jim Hanlon / 2416 Bay St., Ft. Myers, Lee Co. [s.w. 1/4 of sec 13, T44S, R24E]

Nominator(s) / date: Eric H. Hoyer, Tim Eckert / 1980

Update: Robert T. Ing, Daniel B. Ward / 1994

Comments: Earlier measurements: circ. = 130 in. (measured at 4.5 ft., where 132 in. in 1994), spread = 59 ft., height = 70 ft. (Hoyer & Eckert, 1980).

(4)
Honorable Mention.

Size:	Circumference:	93	inches
	Height:	58	feet
	Crown spread:	48	feet
	Total points:	163	points

Owner / location: Key Largo Hammocks State Botanical Site / n. end of Key Largo, Monroe Co. [sec 24, T59S, R40E]

Nominator(s) / date: Joseph Nemec, Jeanne M. Parks / 1989

Symplocos tinctoria (L.) L'Her.
Sweetleaf

(1)
☆ Florida Champion.

Size:	Circumference:	30	inches
	Height:	67	feet
	Crown spread:	21	feet
	Total points:	102	points

Owner / location: City of Tallahassee / Brinkley Glen Park, e. side of Meridian Rd., 0.5 mi. s. of Int 10, Tallahassee, Leon Co. [w. edge of sec 18, T1N, R1E]

Nominator(s) / date: Robert T. Ing, Daniel B. Ward, Charles E. Salter / 1993

Comments: This tree is a smaller replacement for the previous Florida champion (Johnson, 1967 - 109 points) also at this location, and now deceased.

National champions: Virginia, two trees (118 points, 114 points).

(2)

Florida Challenger.

Size:			
	Circumference:	24	inches
	Height:	21	feet
	Crown spread:	19.5	feet
	Total points:	50	points

Owner / location: Robert T. Ing / 1400 N.W. 35th Way, Gainesville, Alachua Co. [s.e. 1/4 of sec 35, T9S, R19E]

Nominator(s) / date: Robert T. Ing, Daniel B. Ward / 1991

Taxodium ascendens Brongn.
= *Taxodium distichum* (L.) L. Rich.
var. *nutans* (Ait.) Sweet
Pond Cypress

(1)

☆ Florida Champion.

Size:			
	Circumference:	127	inches
	Height:	64	feet
	Crown spread:	21	feet
	Total points:	196	points

Owner / location: Museum of History and Natural Science / 3945 Museum Dr., n. side of Lake Bradford, s.w. Tallahassee, Leon Co. [s.w. 1/4 of sec 9, T1S, R1W]

Nominator(s) / date: Malcomb B. Johnson / 1967

Update: Doug Alderson, Claude Stephens / 1994

Comments: Earlier measurements: circ. = 125 in., ht. = 70 ft., spread = 35 ft. (Johnson, 1967).

Remeasurement of tree was delayed since it is now within the Museum's "problem alligator" enclosure (R. T. Ing, D. B. Ward & C. E. Salter, Sept 1993).

National champion: Georgia (439 points).

(2)

Not ranked; possibly still alive, but not verified for many years.

Size:			
	Circumference:	230	inches
	Height:	115	feet
	Crown spread:	50	feet
	Total points:	376	points

Owner / location: Apalachicola National Forest / Florida Trail, Bradwell Bay, 6 mi. n.n.w. of Sopchoppy, Wakulla Co. [sec 7?, T4S, R3W]

Nominator(s) / date: Dale Allen, Robert W. Simons / 1981

Comments: Although a day-long effort by the original nominators to relocate this tree was unsuccessful, much of the area remained unvisited and the tree may still survive (R. W. Simons, D. B. Ward, D. Allen & G. Hegg, Sept 1993).

National champion: Georgia (439 points).

Taxodium distichum (L.) L. Rich.
Bald Cypress

(1)

☆ Florida Champion.

Size:			
	Circumference:	425	inches
	Height:	118	feet
	Crown spread:	57	feet
	Total points:	557	points
	Volume:	3731	cubic feet

Owner / location: County of Seminole / Big Tree Park, n. of Fla. 434, 1 mi. n.e. of Longwood, Seminole Co. [n.e. 1/4 of sec 29, T20S, R30E]

Nominator(s) / date: Michael J. Martin / 1981

Update: Robert W. Simons, Daniel B. Ward / 1993

Comments: Ranked on basis of volume.

This tree is known as "The Senator." It has a massive, tall, nearly cylindrical trunk, with little butt swell, and was long assumed to be the largest cypress in Florida. However, in 1981 a tree with a greatly swollen base was discovered in Hamilton County (J. C. Mathis) that exceeded the Senator in total points, as measured by the standard American Forests formula which emphasizes lower trunk circumference and does not take into account upper trunk circumference. The Senator was thus displaced from its championship status.

More recently American Forests (1992) has revised its guidelines. The standard formula is to be used in all cases *except* where accurate volume figures are available for all contending trees. Where volume figures are available and yield rankings that differ from those produced by the standard formula, volume will be the deciding factor.

Volume of the larger bald cypresses have now been measured. The Senator was found to have a volume of 3731 cubic feet (measured by R. W. Simons, 19 July 1993), a figure nearly twice as great as that of any challenger. The Senator is thus restored to its former rank as Florida Champion.

Earlier measurements: circ. = 408 in., ht. = 108 ft., spread = 62 ft. (Martin, 1981).

National champion: Louisiana (748 points).

(2)

Florida Challenger.

Size:	Circumference:	486	inches
	Height:	90	feet
	Crown spread:	45	feet
	Total points:	587	points
	Volume:	2068	cubic feet

Owner / location: Suwannee River Water Management District / channel of Holton Creek, 1/4 mi. n. of Suwannee River, 3 mi. e. of Noble's Ferry bridge, 10 mi. s.w. of Jasper, Hamilton Co. [s.w. 1/4 of sec 31, T1N, R13E]

Nominator(s) / date: Robert W. Simons, Daniel B. Ward / 1993

Comments: Ranked on basis of volume. Volume of tree = 2068 cu. ft. (measured by R. W. Simons, 15 Aug 1993). Base of tree is greatly enlarged, the upper trunk much smaller.

    Although the American Forests standard formula would place this tree at lower rank than the former Florida champion from Hamilton County (Mathis, 1981), the volume of this tree is appreciable larger.

(3)

Emeritus Florida Champion.

Size:	Circumference:	550	inches
	Height:	89	feet
	Crown spread:	46	feet
	Total points:	651	points
	Volume:	1872	cubic feet

Owner / location: Suwannee River Water Management District / Karst depression, 1/4 mi. n. of Suwannee River, 4 mi. e. of Noble's Ferry bridge, 9 mi. s.w. of Jasper, Hamilton Co. [n.e. 1/4 of sec 5, T1S, R13E]

Nominator(s) / date: Joe Corbett Mathis / 1981

Update: Robert W. Simons, Daniel B. Ward / 1993

Comments: Ranked on basis of volume. Volume of tree = 1872 cu. ft. (measured by R. W. Simons, 6 Aug 1993). Base of tree is very enlarged, reduced above 20 ft. to relatively slender trunk.

    Earlier measurements: circ. = 548 in., ht. = 85 ft., spread = 44 ft. (Mathis, 1981).

(4)

Honorable Mention.

Size:	Circumference:	394	inches
	Height:	88	feet
	Crown spread:	60.5	feet
	Total points:	497	points

Owner / location: Florida Power and Light, Inc. / Barley Barber Swamp, n.e. of Port Mayaca, n.w. of Indiantown, Martin Co. [sec 35, T39S, R37E]

Nominator(s) / date: Mrs. William Martin / 1986

(5)

Honorable Mention.

Size:	Circumference:	376	inches
	Height:	105	feet
	Crown spread:	48	feet
	Total points:	493	points

Owner / location: Florida Conference of Seventh Day Adventists / Camp Kulaqua, head of Hornsby Run, 2 mi. n. of High Springs, Alachua Co. [n.e. 1/4 of sec 27, T7S, R17E]

Nominator(s) / date: Robert W. Simons, Daniel B. Ward / 1993

Comments: This tree is known as "Big Dan."

(6)

Honorable Mention.

Size:	Circumference:	389	inches
	Height:	89	feet
	Crown spread:	52.5	feet
	Total points:	491	points

Owner / location: County of Seminole / Big Tree Park, n. of Fla. 434, 1 mi. n.e. of Longwood, Seminole Co. [n.e. 1/4 of sec 29, T20S, R30E]

Nominator(s) / date: Robert W. Simons, Daniel B. Ward / 1993

Comments: This tree is known as "The Senator's Brother," and is located just west of the larger tree.

(7)

Honorable Mention.

Size:	Circumference:	289	inches
	Height:	115	feet
	Crown spread:	69	feet
	Total points:	421	points

Owner / location: Apalachicola National Forest / Rock Bluff, 3 mi. s.w. of Bloxham, Leon Co. [s.w. 1/4 of sec 30, T1S, R4W]

Nominator(s) / date: Robert W. Simons, Daniel B. Ward / 1993

(8)

Honorable Mention.

Size:	Circumference:	267	inches
	Height:	104	feet
	Crown spread:	51	feet
	Total points:	384	points

Owner / location: DeLeon Springs State Recreation Area / DeLeon Springs, Volusia Co. [sec 38, T16S, R29E]

Nominator(s) / date: Robert W. Simons, Daniel B. Ward / 1993

Comments: This tree is known as "Old Methuselah."

    Volume of tree = 1155 cu. ft. (measured by R. W. Simons, 20 Aug 1993).

(9)

Honorable Mention.

Size:			
	Circumference:	229	inches
	Height:	115	feet
	Crown spread:	76	feet
	Total points:	363	points

Owner / location: Floyd Crews / e. of Fla. 135, 2 mi. s. of Fla. 6, 15 mi. e. of Jasper, Hamilton Co. [s.e. 1/4 of sec 16, T1N, R16E]

Nominator(s) / date: Charles R. Marcus / 1981

Update: Doug Longshore / 1993

Comments: Earlier measurements: circ. = 214 in., ht. = 108 ft., spread = 45 ft. (Marcus, 1981).

(10)

Honorable Mention.

Size:			
	Circumference:	228	inches
	Height:	118	feet
	Crown spread:	58.5	feet
	Total points:	361	points

Owner / location: Bayard Raceways, Inc. / along Durbin Creek, w. of U.S. 1, 0.5 mi. from n. edge of St. Johns Co. [sec 3, T5S, R28E]

Nominator(s) / date: Joseph E. Dunbar, Richard W. Gorden / 1985

(11)

Honorable Mention.

Size:			
	Circumference:	176	inches
	Height:	104	feet
	Crown spread:	58.5	feet
	Total points:	295	points

Owner / location: Jack Scott / 4231 Ortega Blvd., w. side of St. Johns River, Duval Co. [n. 1/4 of sec 42, T3S, R26E]

Nominator(s) / date: Mrs. Wallace Allen / 1981

Update: Robert T. Ing, Daniel B. Ward / 1993

Comments: Earlier measurements: circ. = 168 in., ht. = 92 ft., spread = 57.5 ft. (Allen, 1981).

Taxus floridana Nutt. ex Chapm.
Florida Yew

(1)

★ National Champion.

Size:			
	Circumference:	25	inches
	Height:	20	feet
	Crown spread:	26	feet
	Total points:	52	points

Owner / location: Torreya State Park / near stone bridge, e. side of park, Liberty Co. [center of sec 16, T2N, R7W]

Nominator(s) / date: Joey T. Brady, Jerome Bracewell / 1986

Comments: Acknowledged by American Forests (1996 listing).

Tetrazygia bicolor (Mill.) Cogn.
Florida Tetrazygia

Title vacant.

Size:			
	Circumference:		
	Height:		
	Crown spread:		
	Total points:		

Owner / location:

Nominator(s) / date:

Comments: Native in south peninsular Florida (Dade County) and the Florida Keys.

A tree, now dead, in Castellow Hammock Park, Dade County, was measured by John G. Cordy and Roger L. Hammer as having circ. = 16 in., ht. = 41 ft., and spread = 19 ft. It was formerly the National champion (62 points).

This species is recognized as a tree by American Forests (1996 listing), but as a "species without a champion."

Thrinax morrisii Wendl.
Brittle Thatch Palm

(1)

★ National Champion (nominee).

Size:			
	Circumference:	19	inches
	Height:	19	feet
	Crown spread:	9	feet
	Total points:	40	points

Owner / location: Fairchild Tropical Garden / 10901 Old Cutler Rd., Miami, Dade Co. [n.e. 1/4 of sec 7, T55S, R41E]

Nominator(s) / date: Don Evans, Daniel B. Ward / 1995

Comments: This species is recognized as a tree by American Forests (1996 listing), but as a "species without a champion."

Thrinax radiata Lodd. ex Schult. & Schult.
Florida Thatch Palm

(1)

★ National Champion.

Size:			
	Circumference:	17	inches
	Height:	28	feet
	Crown spread:	6.5	feet
	Total points:	47	points

Owner / location: R. A. Morcroft / 1055 N. South Lake
Dr., Hollywood, Broward Co. [n.w. 1/4 of sec 14,
T51S, R42E]

Nominator(s) / date: David A. Spicer / 1991

Update: Frank L. Zickar, Gene Dempsey / 1994

Comments: Tree is still present; not remeasured (F. L.
Zickar & G. Dempsey, Feb 1994).

Acknowledged by American Forests (1996 listing).

Tilia caroliniana Mill.
Carolina Basswood

(1)

☆ **Florida Champion.**

Size:			
	Circumference:	74	inches
	Height:	84	feet
	Crown spread:	46	feet
	Total points:	170	points

Owner / location: Wakulla Springs State Park / Wakulla
Springs, Wakulla Co. [sec 11, T3S, R1W]

Nominator(s) / date: John A. Wallace, Thomas D. Beitzel
/ 1986

Comments: National champion: Missouri (279 points).

Tilia heterophylla Vent.
White Basswood

Title vacant.

Size:		
	Circumference:	
	Height:	
	Crown spread:	
	Total points:	

Owner / location:

Nominator(s) / date:

Comments: Native in central and east panhandle
Florida.

Herbarium records (FLAS, July 1995) indicate
this species, near Quincy, Gadsden County, to reach
a height of 30 ft. with a trunk diameter of 8 in.

National champion: Maryland (295 points).

Torreya taxifolia Arn.
Gopherwood, Florida Torreya

(1)

☆ **Florida Champion.**

Size:			
	Circumference:	45	inches
	Height:	39	feet
	Crown spread:	36	feet
	Total points:	93	points

Owner / location: S. L. Brothers / jct. Sumter St. & Washington St., Madison, Madison Co. [sec 22, T1N, R9E]

Nominator(s) / date: Michael A. Neal / 1983

Update: Frank A. Rathburn / 1994

Comments: Earlier measurements: circ. = 40 in., ht. =
40 ft., spread = 29 ft. (Neal, 1983). A cultivated tree,
outside the natural range of the species.

Following the fungal disease that afflicted Torreya
in the 1960s, few if any tree-size specimens remain
within the natural range. Just south of Chattahoochee, Gadsden County, where this species was
once a forest component, a Torreya log, although
reduced in size by decay of the sapwood, was measured to have a circumference of 50 inches (A. K.
Gholson, D. B. Ward, Oct 1995).

National champion: North Carolina (164 points), a
cultivated tree.

Trema lamarckiana (R. & S.) Blume
West Indian Trema

Title vacant.

Size:		
	Circumference:	
	Height:	
	Crown spread:	
	Total points:	

Owner / location:

Nominator(s) / date:

Comments: Native in south peninsular Florida (Dade
County) and the Florida Keys.

Herbarium records (FTG, Dec 1995) indicate this
species, on upper Key Largo, Monroe Co., to reach a
height of 15 ft. with trunks 4 in. diameter. It is
recognized as a tree by American Forests (1996
listing), but as a "species without a champion."

Trema micrantha (L.) Blume
Florida Trema

(1)

★ **National Champion.**

Size:			
	Circumference:	18	inches
	Height:	39	feet
	Crown spread:	30	feet
	Total points:	65	points

Owner / location: Southern Gulf West Construction Co.,
Inc. / 4227 Exchange Ave, Naples, Collier Co. [s.e.
1/4 of sec 36, T49S, R25E]

Nominator(s) / date: Chris J. Anderson, Lisa Moore /
1995

Comments: Acknowledged by American Forests (1996
listing).

(2)

Florida Challenger.

Size:			
	Circumference:	17	inches
	Height:	18	feet
	Crown spread:	16.5	feet
	Total points:	39	points

Owner / location: Augusta Woods Condominiums / 5857 Rattlesnake Hammock Rd. (Fla. 864), 1.7 mi. e. of jct. with U.S. 41, s.e. Naples, Collier Co. [n.e. 1/4 of sec 20, T50S, R26E]

Nominator(s) / date: Chris J. Anderson / 1994

Ulmus alata Michx.
Winged Elm

(1)

☆ Florida Champion.

Size:			
	Circumference:	135	inches
	Height:	126	feet
	Crown spread:	59	feet
	Total points:	276	points

Owner / location: Torreya State Park / on trail s.w. from Gregory house, w. edge of park, Liberty Co. [center of sec 17, T2N, R7W]

Nominator(s) / date: Robert W. Simons / 1977
    Update: Robert W. Simons / 1988
    Update: Robert W. Simons / 1993
Comments: Earlier measurements: circ. = 133 in., ht. = 116 ft., spread = 56 ft. (Simons, 1977); circ. = 135 in., ht. = 118 ft., spread = 63 ft. (Simons, 1988).
    National champion: North Carolina (302 points).

(2)

Florida Challenger.

Size:			
	Circumference:	98	inches
	Height:	73	feet
	Crown spread:	44	feet
	Total points:	182	points

Owner / location: O'Leno State Park / just n. of River Rise, Alachua Co. [s.w. 1/4 of sec 14, T7S, R17E]

Nominator(s) / date: Robert T. Ing, Daniel B. Ward / 1993

Ulmus americana L.
var. **floridana** (Chapm.) Little
Florida Elm

(1)

★ National Champion (nominee).

Size:			
	Circumference:	120	inches
	Height:	102	feet
	Crown spread:	70	feet
	Total points:	240	points

Owner / location: Florida Caverns State Park / 400 ft. n. of visitor's center, 2 mi. n. of Marianna, Jackson Co. [s.w. 1/4 of sec 22, T5N, R10W]

Nominator(s) / date: Robert T. Ing, Daniel B. Ward / 1995

Comments: National champions for *Ulmus americana* var. *floridana*: Florida (188 points, 184 points). For *Ulmus americana* var. *americana*: Kansas (435 points).

(2)

★ National Co-Champion.

Size:			
	Circumference:	117	inches
	Height:	57	feet
	Crown spread:	71	feet
	Total points:	192	points

Owner / location: Olustee Battlefield State Historical Site / n. side U.S. 90, 2 mi. e. of Olustee, Baker Co. [s.w. 1/4 of sec 23, T3S, R19E]

Nominator(s) / date: Frank Loughran / 1985
    Update: Frank Loughran / 1995
Comments: Earlier measurements: circ. = 117 in., ht. = 56 ft., spread = 60 ft. (Loughran, 1985).
    Acknowledged by American Forests (1996 listing).

(3)

★ National Co-Champion.

Size:			
	Circumference:	95	inches
	Height:	70	feet
	Crown spread:	77	feet
	Total points:	184	points

Owner / location: Daniel L. Hewett / e. side Fla. 51, n. of U.S. 27, Mayo, Lafayette Co. [sec 13, T5S, R11E]

Nominator(s) / date: Jerry N. Livingston / 1989

Comments: Acknowledged by American Forests (1996 listing).

Ulmus crassifolia Nutt.
Cedar Elm

(1)

★ National Co-Champion.

Size:			
	Circumference:	112	inches
	Height:	107	feet
	Crown spread:	69	feet
	Total points:	236	points

Owner / location: Silver River State Park / w. bank of Silver River, 1 mi. s.w. of Fla. 40 bridge, Marion Co. [n.e. 1/4 of sec 9, T15S, R23E]

Nominator(s) / date: Robert W. Simons, Jim Buckner, Jerry Clutts / 1994

Comments: Located near previous National co-champion (Simons & Buckner, 1984), now dead (R. W. Simons, May 1994).
    National co-champion: Mississippi (238 points).

Ulmus rubra Muhl.
Slippery Elm

☆ Florida Champion.

(1)

Size:

	Circumference:	34	inches
	Height:	67	feet
	Crown spread:	38	feet
	Total points:	111	points

Owner / location: Soterra, Inc. / e. bank of Apalachicola River, 0.5 mi. s. of Int. 10, 6 mi. s.w. of Chattahoochee, Gadsden Co. [s.e. 1/4 of sec 26, T3N, R7W]

Nominator(s) / date: Angus K. Gholson, Robert T. Ing, Daniel B. Ward / 1995

Comments: National champions: Ohio, two trees (375 points, 370 points).

Vaccinium arboreum Marsh.
Farkleberry, Sparkleberry,
Tree Huckleberry

☆ Florida Champion.

(1)

Size:

	Circumference:	34	inches
	Height:	39	feet
	Crown spread:	30.5	feet
	Total points:	81	points

Owner / location: Univ. of West Florida / n.n.w. of Bldg. 58, campus, Pensacola, Escambia Co. [e. 1/2 of sec 25, T1N, R30W]

Nominator(s) / date: Mark Scheller / 1977

Update: James R. Burkhalter / 1993

Comments: Earlier measurements: circ. = 43 in. (at 1 ft. above base), ht. = 30 ft., spread = 30 ft. (Scheller, 1977). This tree was National champion until 1986, when superceded by a South Carolina tree.

National champions: Alabama (92 points); South Carolina (90 points).

Florida Challenger.

(2)

Size:

	Circumference:	41	inches
	Height:	24	feet
	Crown spread:	24	feet
	Total points:	71	points

Owner / location: Northwest Florida Water Management District / e. side of Econfina Creek, 1/4 mi. s.s.w. of Blue Springs, s.e. corner of Washington Co. [n.w. 1/4 of sec 34, T1N, R13W]

Nominator(s) / date: Charles R. Reeves, Thomas Francis / 1994

Honorable Mention.

(3)

Size:

	Circumference:	31	inches
	Height:	32	feet
	Crown spread:	24	feet
	Total points:	69	points

Owner / location: W. M. Craven / just s. of Crews Lake, 2 mi. s.w. of Ebro, Washington Co. [s.e. 1/4 of sec 2, T1N, R17W]

Nominator(s) / date: Charles R. Reeves, Bill Craven / 1992

Emeritus Florida Champion.

(4)

Size:

	Circumference:	25	inches
	Height:	33	feet
	Crown spread:	24	feet
	Total points:	64	points

Owner / location: D. J. Culbreth / 0.5 mi. e. of Fla. 278A, 10 mi. s.w. of Chipley, Washington Co. [s.w. 1/4 of sec 10. T3N, R14W]

Nominator(s) / date: Charles R. Reeves / 1980

Update: Charles R. Reeves / 1993

Comments: Earlier measurements: circ. = 24 in., ht. = 36 ft., spread = 22 ft. (Reeves, 1980).

Honorable Mention.

(5)

Size:

	Circumference:	23	inches
	Height:	24	feet
	Crown spread:	25	feet
	Total points:	53	points

Owner / location: City of Gainesville / city park, 400 block, S. Main St., Gainesville, Alachua Co. [s.e. 1/4 of sec 5, T10S, R20E]

Nominator(s) / date: Michael J. Bordyn / 1982

Update: Robert T. Ing, Daniel B. Ward / 1991

Comments: Earlier measurements: circ. = 32 in. (at 0.5 ft. above base), ht. = 22 ft., spread = 21 ft. (Bordyn, 1982).

Vallesia antillana Woodson
Pearl-berry

Title vacant.

Size:

	Circumference:		
	Height:		
	Crown spread:		
	Total points:		

Owner / location:

Nominator(s) / date:

Comments: Native in the Florida Keys.

Commonly a shrub. Sprawling trees to 12 ft. tall have been observed on Big Pine Key and Boot Key, Monroe County (G. Avery notes). Not included in the Checklist of Trees Native to Florida (Ward, 1991). Not recognized as a tree by Little (1979), and thus no champion is acknowledged by American Forests (1996 listing).

Viburnum nudum L.
Possum Blackhaw

Title vacant.

Size: Circumference:
              Height:
              Crown spread:
              Total points:

Owner / location:

Nominator(s) / date:

Comments: Native in north Florida, south to central Peninsula.

Usually a large shrub. Herbarium records (FLAS, July 1995) indicate this species, near Lake Wales, Polk County, to reach a height of 5 meters.

A previous record for this species (Bielling, 1972 - Marion County) was misidentified; corrected to *Viburnum obovatum* (P. E. Bielling, Sept 1991).

Viburnum obovatum Walt.
Blackhaw, Walter's Viburnum

(1)

★ National Champion.

Size:	Circumference:	17	inches
	Height:	23	feet
	Crown spread:	23	feet
	Total points:	46	points

Owner / location: San Felasco Hammock State Preserve / n. side of Fla. 232, 8 mi. n.w. of Gainesville, Alachua Co. [sec 37, T8S, R19E]

Nominator(s) / date: Robert W. Simons, Daniel B. Ward / 1991

Comments: This tree is a smaller replacement for the previous National champion (Simons, 1976 - 58 points) also at this location, and now deceased. Acknowledged by American Forests (1996 listing).

Viburnum rufidulum Raf.
Rusty Blackhaw

(1)

☆ Florida Champion.

Size:	Circumference:	11	inches
	Height:	21	feet
	Crown spread:	11	feet
	Total points:	35	points

Owner / location: Univ. of Florida / wooded slope, n. side

of Museum Rd., just w. of Fraternity Dr., campus, Gainesville, Alachua Co. [s.e. 1/4 of sec 1, T10S, R19E]

Nominator(s) / date: Lynn C. Badger, Daniel B. Ward / 1994

Comments: National champion: Arkansas (80 points).

Viburnum scabrellum (Torr. & Gray) Chapm.
Southern Arrow-wood

(1)

★ National Champion (nominee).

Size:	Circumference:	8	inches
	Height:	26	feet
	Crown spread:	13	feet
	Total points:	38	points

Owner / location: Three Rivers State Recreation Area / nature trail, s. end of park, 2 mi. n. of Sneads, Jackson Co. [s.e. 1/4 of sec 15, T4N, R7W]

Nominator(s) / date: Robert T. Ing, Daniel B. Ward / 1995

Comments: This species is often confused with the northern *Viburnum dentatum*, which is consistently a shrub. The southern species is also often shrubby, but may frequently be found with a single trunk and of a size that justifies its treatment as a tree. Not recognized as a tree by Little (1979) nor by American Forests (1996 listing). Not included in the Checklist of Trees Native to Florida (Ward, 1991).

Ximenia americana L.
Tallow-wood

Title vacant.

Size: Circumference:
              Height:
              Crown spread:
              Total points:

Owner / location:

Nominator(s) / date:

Comments: Native in central and south peninsular Florida.

Most often a shrub; only rarely, in southernmost Florida, does this species become a tree. Herbarium records (FLAS, July 1995) indicate this species, on Big Pine Key, Monroe County, to reach a height of 15 ft. A tree, now dead, on Totten Key, Dade County, was measured in 1975 by Clifford Shaw and Jim Tilmant as having circ. = 16 in., ht. = 25 ft., and spread = 20.5 ft.

This species is recognized as a tree by American Forests (1996 listing), but as a "species without a champion."

Yucca aloifolia L.
Spanish-dagger, Aloe Yucca
Title vacant.

Size:	Circumference:		
	Height:		
	Crown spread:		
	Total points:		

Owner / location:

Nominator(s) / date:

Comments: Native in north and central Florida, mostly coastal.

A tree-like plant, now dead, near Lakeland, Polk County, was measured in 1967 by Eldredge T. Carnes as having circ. = 18 ft., ht. = 15 ft., and spread = 4 ft. This species is included by Little (1979) and is recognized as a tree by American Forests (1996 listing) as a "species without a champion".

Zanthoxylum clava-herculis L.
Hercules-club, Toothache-tree

(1)

★ **National Co-Champion.**

Size:	Circumference:	33	inches
	Height:	65	feet
	Crown spread:	20	feet
	Total points:	103	points

Owner / location: Prairie View Trust / Sugarfoot Hammock, n.e. of jct. S.W. 20th Ave. & S.W. 62nd St., Gainesville, Alachua Co. [n.e. 1/4 of sec 10, T10S, R19E]

Nominator(s) / date: Robert W. Simons, Daniel B. Ward / 1993

Comments: Exceptionally tall for this species.
Acknowledged by American Forests (1996 listing).
National co-champion: Texas (108 points).

(2)

Florida Challenger.

Size:	Circumference:	37	inches
	Height:	55	feet
	Crown spread:	29	feet
	Total points:	99	points

Owner / location: Johnny Walker / 12191 S. Old Jones Rd. (Fla. 39), 5 mi. s. of Floral City, Citrus Co. [s.e. 1/4 of sec 2, T21S, R19E]

Nominator(s) / date: Wilbur C. Priest, Robbie Lovestrand / 1994

(3)

Honorable Mention.

Size:	Circumference:	29	inches
	Height:	61	feet
	Crown spread:	12	feet
	Total points:	93	points

Owner / location: Paynes Prairie State Preserve / e. of headquarters, 2 mi. s.s.e. of Gainesville, Alachua Co. [sec 22, T10S, R20E]

Nominator(s) / date: Robert T. Ing, Daniel B. Ward, Robert W. Simons / 1991

(4)

Emeritus Florida Champion.

Size:	Circumference:	45	inches
	Height:	31	feet
	Crown spread:	33	feet
	Total points:	84	points

Owner / location: Riverside Day Care Center / 484 Riverside Ave., Jacksonville, Duval Co. [sec 56, T2S, R26E]

Nominator(s) / date: James Karels / 1985

Zanthoxylum coriaceum A. Rich. in Sagra
Biscayne Prickly Ash
Title vacant.

Size:	Circumference:		
	Height:		
	Crown spread:		
	Total points:		

Owner / location:

Nominator(s) / date:

Comments: Native in coastal south Florida.

This species is recognized as a tree by American Forests (1996 listing), but as a "species without a champion."

Zanthoxylum fagara (L.) Sarg.
Wild Lime, Lime Prickly Ash

(1)

★ **National Champion.**

Size:	Circumference:	21	inches
	Height:	26	feet

Crown spread:	38	feet
Total points:	57	points

Owner / location: Sanibel-Captiva Conservation Foundation / office, s. side Sanibel-Captive Rd., w. of jct. Tarpon Bay Rd., Sanibel Id., Lee Co. [n.w. 1/4 of sec 26, T46S, R22E]

Nominator(s) / date: Eric H. Hoyer, Norma Jean Byrd / 1980

Update: Richard W. Workman, Dee Serage / 1993

Comments: Earlier measurements: circ. = 16 in., ht. = 25 ft., spread = 31 ft. (Hoyer & Byrd, 1980).

Acknowledged by American Forests (1996 listing).

Zanthoxylum flavum Vahl
Yellowheart, West Indies Satinwood

(1)

★ **National Champion.**

Size:	Circumference:	33	inches
	Height:	20	feet
	Crown spread:	28	feet
	Total points:	60	points

Owner / location: Bahia Honda State Park / Bahia Honda Key, Monroe Co. [n.w. 1/4 of sec 35, T66S, R30E]

Nominator(s) / date: John A. Baust / 1979

Update: Monay Markey / 1993

Comments: Earlier measurements: circ. = 43 in. (measured near base, below low fork), ht. = 20 ft., spread = 30 ft. (Baust, 1979).

Acknowledged by American Forests (1996 listing).

Part II.—SIGNIFICANT NON-NATIVE TREES

Acacia smallii Isely
Small's Acacia

Title vacant.

Size:	Circumference:
	Height:
	Crown spread:
	Total points:

Owner / location:

Nominator(s) / date:

Comments: Widespread in northeast Mexico and eastern Texas, now naturalized on disturbed sites in the western coastal panhandle of Florida. Herbarium records (FLAS, July 1995) indicate this species, near Pensacola, Escambia County, to reach a height of 7 ft. Recent efforts to locate tree-sized specimens along the Pensacola waterfront have been unsuccessful; a few shrubby plants are still present, but all arborescent individuals have fallen prey to construction and development activities (J. R. Burkhalter, Oct 1994).

  Champion trees of this species are not recorded by American Forests (1996 listing).

Adansonia digitata L.
Baobab

☆ **Florida Champion.** (1)

Size:	Circumference:	331	inches
	Height:	45	feet
	Crown spread:	66	feet
	Total points:	393	points

Owner / location: City of Hollywood / Young Circle, U.S. 1, Hollywood, Broward Co. [center of sec 15, T51S, R42E]

Nominator(s) / date: Gene Dempsey, Greg Turek / 1987

Comments: Champion trees of this species are not recorded by American Forests (1996 listing).

Florida Challenger. (2)

Size:	Circumference:	247	inches
	Height:	69	feet
	Crown spread:	49	feet
	Total points:	328	points

Owner / location: Fairchild Tropical Garden / 10901 Old Cutler Rd., Miami, Dade Co. [n.e. 1/4 of sec 7, T55S, R41E]

Nominator(s) / date: Don Evans, Daniel B. Ward / 1995

Comments: Crown spread of this tree was much reduced by Hurricane Andrew (Aug 1992).

Honorable Mention. (3)

Size:	Circumference:	180	inches
	Height:	37	feet
	Crown spread:	36	feet
	Total points:	226	points

Owner / location: Alberto Fernandez / 412 Fernwood Dr., Key Biscayne, Dade Co. [s.e. 1/4 of sec 32, T54S, R42E]

Nominator(s) / date: Joan Gill Blank / 1995

Ailanthus altissima (Mill.) Swingle
Tree-of-heaven

☆ **Florida Champion.** (1)

Size:	Circumference:	106	inches
	Height:	71	feet
	Crown spread:	48	feet
	Total points:	189	points

Owner / location: Univ. of Florida / Dauer Hall, campus, Gainesville, Alachua Co. [s.e. 1/4 of sec 6, T10S, R20E]

Nominator(s) / date: Robert T. Ing, Michele W. Ing / 1991

Comments: National champion: New York (321 points).

(2)

Emeritus Florida Champion.

Size:	Circumference:	102	inches
	Height:	47	feet
	Crown spread:	43	feet
	Total points:	160	points

Owner / location: (unknown) / 1000 Jefferson St., Jacksonville, Duval Co. [sec 39, T2S, R26E]

Nominator(s) / date: Richard W. Gorden, Joe Dunbar / 1987

(3)

Emeritus Florida Champion.

Size:	Circumference:	79	inches
	Height:	58	feet
	Crown spread:	42	feet
	Total points:	148	points

Owner / location: (unknown) / jct. N.W. 2nd Ave. & N.W. 9th St., High Springs, Alachua Co. [sec 34, T7S, R17E]

Nominator(s) / date: Michael J. Bordyn / 1981

Update: Robert. T. Ing, Daniel B. Ward / 1991

Comments: Earlier measurements: circ. = 72 in., ht. = 54 ft., spread = 47 ft. (Bordyn, 1981).

Albizia caribaea (Urban) Britt. & Rose
Tantacayo

(1)

☆ Florida Champion.

Size:	Circumference:	151	inches
	Height:	95	feet
	Crown spread:	78	feet
	Total points:	266	points

Owner / location: Fairchild Tropical Garden / 10901 Old Cutler Rd., Miami, Dade Co. [n.e. 1/4 of sec 7, T55S, R41E]

Nominator(s) / date: Don Evans, Daniel B. Ward / 1995

Comments: Champion trees of this species are not recorded by American Forests (1996 listing).

Albizia lebbek (L.) Benth.
Woman's-tongue

(1)

☆ Florida Champion.

Size:	Circumference:	127	inches
	Height:	51	feet
	Crown spread:	85	feet
	Total points:	199	points

Owner / location: (unknown) / 116 S. Seacrest Blvd., Boynton Beach, Palm Beach Co. [sec 28, T45S, R43E]

Nominator(s) / date: Kevin Hallahan, Ed Isenhour / 1981

Update: Michael J. Greenstein / 1993

Comments: Earlier measurements: circ. = 109 in., ht. = 52 ft., spread = 70 ft. (Hallahan & Isenhour, 1981). National champion: Hawaii (346 points).

Aleurites fordii Hemsl.
Tung-tree

(1)

☆ Florida Champion.

Size:	Circumference:	53	inches
	Height:	43	feet
	Crown spread:	42.5	feet
	Total points:	106	points

Owner / location: Forrest F. Lisle / 1920 N.W. 8th Ave., Gainesville, Alachua Co. [s.w. 1/4 of sec 31, T9S, R20E]

Nominator(s) / date: Robert T. Ing, Daniel B. Ward / 1991

Comments: Champion trees of this species are not recorded by American Forests (1996 listing).

(2)

Florida Challenger.

Size:	Circumference:	44	inches
	Height:	46	feet
	Crown spread:	33	feet
	Total points:	98	points

Owner / location: Univ. of Florida / e. end of Newins-Ziegler Hall, campus, Gainesville, Alachua Co. [s.e. 1/4 of sec 6, T10S, R20E]

Nominator(s) / date: Robert W. Simons / 1991

Aleurites moluccana (L.) Willd.
Candlenut-tree

(1)

☆ Florida Champion.

Size:	Circumference:	57	inches
	Height:	72	feet
	Crown spread:	34	feet
	Total points:	138	points

Owner / location: Indian River Land Trust, Inc. / 4871 North A1A, Vero Beach, Indian River Co. [sec 18, T33S, R40E]

Nominator(s) / date: James Haeger, Daniel F. Culbert / 1996

Comments: Champion trees of this species are not
recorded by American Forests (1996 listing).

Alstonia scholaris (L.) R. Br.
Devil-tree

(1)

☆ **Florida Champion.**

Size:			
	Circumference:	116	inches
	Height:	58	feet
	Crown spread:	39	feet
	Total points:	184	points

Owner / location: Fairchild Tropical Garden / 10901 Old
Cutler Rd., Miami, Dade Co. [n.e. 1/4 of sec 7, T55S,
R41E]

Nominator(s) / date: Don Evans, Daniel B. Ward / 1995

Comments: Champion trees of this species are not
recorded by American Forests (1996 listing).

Araucaria araucana (Mol.) K. Koch
Monkey-puzzle

(1)

☆ **Florida Champion.**

Size:			
	Circumference:	100	inches
	Height:	91	feet
	Crown spread:	38	feet
	Total points:	201	points

Owner / location: Doris Vaughan / Ft. Denaud Rd. (Fla.
78A), 1.7 mi. e. of Ft. Denaud bridge, 3 mi. w.s.w. of
LaBelle, Hendry Co. [s.w. 1/4 of sec 12, T43S, R28E]

Nominator(s) / date: Chris J. Anderson, Eric H. Hoyer /
1981

Update: Jeffrey S. Mangun, Chris J. Anderson / 1994

Comments: Earlier measurements: circ. = 84 in., ht. =
82 ft., spread = 30 ft. (Anderson & Hoyer, 1981).

Champion trees of this species are not recorded by
American Forests (1996 listing).

(2)

Florida Challenger.

Size:			
	Circumference:	107	inches
	Height:	64	feet
	Crown spread:	38	feet
	Total points:	181	points

Owner / location: Martha McClellan / s. of Fla. 20,
Blountstown, Calhoun Co. [sec 33, T1N, R8W]

Nominator(s) / date: Joey T. Brady, J. L. McCroan / 1986

(3)

Honorable Mention.

Size:			
	Circumference:	88	inches
	Height:	77	feet
	Crown spread:	39.5	feet
	Total points:	175	points

Owner / location: Koreshan State Historic Park / Estero,
Lee Co. [s.w. 1/4 of sec 28, T46S, R25E]

Nominator(s) / date: Eric H. Hoyer, Chris J. Anderson /
1980

Update: Chris J. Anderson / 1994

Comments: The larger of two trees at this location.
Earlier measurements: circ. = 76 in., ht. = 66 ft.,
spread = 33 ft. (Hoyer & Anderson, 1980).

(4)

Honorable Mention.

Size:			
	Circumference:	90	inches
	Height:	73	feet
	Crown spread:	31.5	feet
	Total points:	171	points

Owner / location: Koreshan State Historic Park / Estero,
Lee Co. [s.w. 1/4 of sec 28, T46S, R25E]

Nominator(s) / date: Chris J. Anderson / 1994

Comments: The smaller of two trees at this location.

(5)

Honorable Mention.

Size:			
	Circumference:	46	inches
	Height:	65	feet
	Crown spread:	30	feet
	Total points:	119	points

Owner / location: West Jacksonville Christian Center /
7800 Ramona Blvd., w. Jacksonville, Duval Co. [sec
23, T2S, R25E]

Nominator(s) / date: Richard W. Gorden / 1987

Comments: Trunk forked; circ. 95 in. at 3 ft.

Araucaria bidwillii Hook.
Bunya-bunya

(1)

☆ **Florida Champion.**

Size:			
	Circumference:	116	inches
	Height:	79	feet
	Crown spread:	50	feet
	Total points:	208	points

Owner / location: Marie Selby Botanical Gardens / 800 S. Palm Ave., Sarasota, Sarasota Co. [n.w. 1/4 of sec 30, T36S, R18E]

Nominator(s) / date: William J. Schilling / 1980

Update: William J. Schilling / 1993

Comments: Earlier measurements: circ. = 110 in., ht. = 75 ft., spread = 40 ft. (Schilling, 1980).

Champion trees of this species are not recorded by American Forests (1996 listing).

Araucaria heterophylla (Salisb.) Franco
= *Araucaria excelsa* Hort.
Norfolk Island Pine

(1)

☆ Florida Champion.

Size:			
	Circumference:	90	inches
	Height:	87	feet
	Crown spread:	23	feet
	Total points:	183	points

Owner / location: Uri Bergbaum / 745 N. Crescent Dr., Hollywood, Broward Co. [n.w. 1/4 of sec 17, T51S, R42E]

Nominator(s) / date: David A. Spicer / 1991

Comments: Champion trees of this species are not recorded by American Forests (1996 listing).

(2)

Emeritus Florida Champion.

Size:			
	Circumference:	85	inches
	Height:	81	feet
	Crown spread:	38	feet
	Total points:	176	points

Owner / location: Charles Sanford / 706 N.W. 15th Ave., Largo, Pinellas Co. [s.w. 1/4 of sec 27, T29S, R15E]

Nominator(s) / date: Sandy S. Semple / 1989

Averrhoa carambola L.
Carambola

(1)

☆ Florida Champion.

Size:			
	Circumference:	44	inches
	Height:	57	feet
	Crown spread:	43.5	feet
	Total points:	112	points

Owner / location: Flamingo Tropical Gardens / 3750 Flamingo Rd. (Fla. 823), Ft. Lauderdale, Broward Co. [sec 25, T50S, R40E]

Nominator(s) / date: Lillian Millman, Jonathan Iles / 1983

Update: Frank L. Zickar, David Bar-Zvi / 1993

Comments: Earlier measurements: circ. = 41 in., ht. = 56 ft., spread = 38 ft. (Millman & Iles, 1983).

Champion trees of this species are not recorded by American Forests (1996 listing).

Bischofia javanica Blume
Toog

(1)

☆ Florida Champion.

Size:			
	Circumference:	138	inches
	Height:	64	feet
	Crown spread:	32	feet
	Total points:	210	points

Owner / location: Indian River Land Trust, Inc. / McKee Jungle Gardens, Vero Beach, Indian River Co. [n.w. 1/4 of sec 18, T33S, R40E]

Nominator(s) / date: Daniel F. Culbert / 1994

Comments: Champion trees of this species are not recorded by American Forests (1996 listing).

(2)

Florida Challenger.

Size:			
	Circumference:	129	inches
	Height:	57	feet
	Crown spread:	53.5	feet
	Total points:	199	points

Owner / location: Susan Dobson / 712 Anderson Dr., Naples, Collier Co. [n.e. 1/4 of sec 16, T49S, R25E]

Nominator(s) / date: Chris J. Anderson / 1994

(3)

Honorable Mention.

Size:			
	Circumference:	112	inches
	Height:	51	feet
	Crown spread:	61	feet
	Total points:	178	points

Owner / location: Gregory Hanny / Cortez Blvd. & Hanson St., Ft. Myers, Lee Co. [n. 1/2 of sec 26, T44S, R24E]

Nominator(s) / date: Eric H. Hoyer, Patrick T. Fennimore / 1981

Update: Robert T. Ing, Daniel B. Ward / 1994

Comments: Earlier measurements: circ. = 92 in., ht. = 50 ft., spread = 50.5 ft. (Hoyer & Fennimore, 1981).

(4)

Honorable Mention.

Size:			
	Circumference:	92	inches
	Height:	50	feet
	Crown spread:	50.5	feet
	Total points:	155	points

Owner / location: Arthur Gravengood / 5317 Majestic Ct., off Del Prado Blvd., Cape Coral, Lee Co. [sec 24, T45S, R23E]

Nominator(s) / date: Jeffrey S. Mangun / 1992

Bombax ceiba L.
= *Bombax malabaricum* DC.
Red Silk-cotton

(1)

☆ **Florida Champion.**

Size:			
	Circumference:	417	inches
	Height:	62	feet
	Crown spread:	109	feet
	Total points:	506	points

Owner / location: Thoroughbred Music, Inc. / 923 Mc-Mullen Booth Rd., Clearwater, Pinellas Co. [sec 9, T29S, R16E]

Nominator(s) / date: James A. Brewer / 1980

Update: Gregory P. Barton / 1993

Comments: Earlier measurements: circ. = 403 in., ht. = 93 ft., spread = 115 ft. (Brewer, 1980).

Champion trees of this species are not recorded by American Forests (1996 listing).

(2)

Florida Challenger.

Size:			
	Circumference:	197	inches
	Height:	130	feet
	Crown spread:	77	feet
	Total points:	346	points

Owner / location: Doris Vaughan / Ft. Denaud Rd. (Fla. 78A), 1.7 mi. e. of Ft. Denaud bridge, 3 mi. w.s.w. of LaBelle, Hendry Co. [s.w. 1/4 of sec 12, T43S, R28E]

Nominator(s) / date: Eric H. Hoyer, Chris J. Anderson / 1981

Update: Jeffrey S. Mangun, Chris J. Anderson / 1994

Comments: Earlier measurements: circ. = 167 in., ht. = 99 ft., spread = 70 ft. (Hoyer & Anderson, 1981).

(3)

Honorable Mention.

Size:			
	Circumference:	211	inches
	Height:	105	feet
	Crown spread:	86	feet
	Total points:	338	points

Owner / location: Mrs. Keith Sullivan / 1121 S.E. 9th St., Ft. Lauderdale, Broward Co. [s.w. 1/4 of sec 11, T50S, R42E]

Nominator(s) / date: Frank L. Zickar, Richard Moyroud / 1995

Comments: Tree was planted in 1940.

Borassus aethiopum Mart.
Wine Palm, Toddy Palm

(1)

☆ **Florida Champion.**

Size:			
	Circumference:	112	inches
	Height:	61	feet
	Crown spread:	20	feet
	Total points:	178	points

Owner / location: Fairchild Tropical Garden / 10901 Old Cutler Rd., Miami, Dade Co. [n.e. 1/4 of sec 7, T55S, R41E]

Nominator(s) / date: Don Evans, Daniel B. Ward / 1995

Comments: Champion trees of this species are not recorded by American Forests (1996 listing).

Brachychiton discolor F. Muell.
Pink Bottle-tree

(1)

☆ **Florida Champion.**

Size:			
	Circumference:	62	inches
	Height:	41	feet
	Crown spread:	30.5	feet
	Total points:	111	points

Owner / location: Marie Selby Botanical Gardens / 800 S. Palm Ave., Sarasota, Sarasota Co. [n.w. 1/4 of sec 30, T36S, R18E]

Nominator(s) / date: William J. Schilling / 1980

Update: William J. Schilling / 1993

Comments: Earlier measurements: circ. = 61 in., ht. = 41 ft., spread = 30.5 ft. (Schilling, 1980).

Champion trees of this species are not recorded by American Forests (1996 listing).

Brosimum alicastrum Swartz
Breadnut

(1)

☆ **Florida Champion.**

Size:			
	Circumference:	99	inches
	Height:	84	feet
	Crown spread:	61	feet
	Total points:	198	points

Owner / location: Flamingo Tropical Gardens / 3750
Flamingo Rd. (Fla. 823), Ft. Lauderdale, Broward
Co. [sec 25, T50S, R40E]

Nominator(s) / date: Terry Wolfe / 1982

Update: Frank L. Zickar, David Bar-Zvi / 1993

Comments: Earlier measurements: circ. = 79 in., ht. =
67 ft., spread = 62 ft. (Wolfe, 1982).

Champion trees of this species are not recorded by
American Forests (1996 listing).

Broussonetia papyrifera (L.) Vent.
Paper Mulberry

(1)

★ **National Champion**.

Size:			
	Circumference:	157	inches
	Height:	75	feet
	Crown spread:	55	feet
	Total points:	246	points

Owner / location: Flamingo Tropical Gardens / 3750
Flamingo Rd. (Fla. 823), Ft. Lauderdale, Broward
Co. [sec 25, T50S, R40E]

Nominator(s) / date: David Bar-Zvi / 1991

Comments: Acknowledged by American Forests (1996
listing).

(2)

Florida Challenger.

Size:			
	Circumference:	172	inches
	Height:	42	feet
	Crown spread:	40.5	feet
	Total points:	224	points

Owner / location: Dolores Standley / 1124 N.W. 40th
Ave., Gainesville, Alachua Co. [s.w. 1/4 of sec 20,
T9S, R20E]

Nominator(s) / date: Robert T. Ing, Daniel B. Ward / 1991

(3)

Honorable Mention.

Size:			
	Circumference:	73	inches
	Height:	46	feet
	Crown spread:	46	feet
	Total points:	131	points

Owner / location: Patricia Powers / 4103 N.W. 12th Terr.,
Gainesville, Alachua Co. [s.w. 1/4 of sec 20, T9S,
R20E]

Nominator(s) / date: Robert T. Ing, Daniel B. Ward / 1991

Bucida buceras L.
Black Olive

(1)

★ **National Champion** (nominee).

Size:			
	Circumference:	139	inches
	Height:	50	feet
	Crown spread:	48	feet
	Total points:	201	points

Owner / location: Charles Deering Estate / 16701 S.W.
72nd Ave., Miami, Dade Co. [s.e. 1/4 of sec 26, T55S,
R40E]

Nominator(s) / date: John T. Valenta, Adriana Lupas,
Roger L. Hammer / 1994

Comments: This species is recognized as a tree by
American Forests (1996 listing), but as a "species
without a champion."

Bucida buceras has often been considered a
Florida native on the basis of two late-nineteenth-
century collections from Elliott Key, Dade County.
The tree is widely planted for shade and ornament
in South Florida, and Little (1979), probably correctly, has concluded this species is neither native
nor naturalized. However, the very similar *Bucida
spinosa*, also in cultivation, does seem to be sparingly present in the wild, and is treated here as a
native species (q. v.).

(2)

Florida Challenger.

Size:			
	Circumference:	108	inches
	Height:	56	feet
	Crown spread:	67.5	feet
	Total points:	181	points

Owner / location: Key West Botanical Garden Society /
Botanical Garden, Stock Island, Monroe Co. [n.e. 1/4
of sec 34, T67S, R25E]

Nominator(s) / date: Michael B. Miller, Vincent P.
Condon / 1995

(3)

Honorable Mention.

Size:			
	Circumference:	114	inches
	Height:	26	feet
	Crown spread:	27	feet
	Total points:	147	points

Owner / location: U.S.D.A. Plant Introduction Station /
13601 Old Cutler Road, Miami, Dade Co. [n.w. 1/4 of
sec 24, T55S, R40E]

Nominator(s) / date: Elbert A. Schory / 1968

Update: John T. Valenta, Adriana Lupas, Roger L.
Hammer / 1994

Comments: Earlier measurements: circ. = 90 in., ht. = 47 ft., spread = 66 ft. (Schory, 1968). Tree was much broken by Hurricane Andrew (Aug 1992), but survived (J. Sharp, Oct 1993).

Bulnesia arborea (Jacq.) Engl.
Vera

(1)

☆ **Florida Champion.**

Size:			
	Circumference:	75	inches
	Height:	63	feet
	Crown spread:	47	feet
	Total points:	150	points

Owner / location: Fairchild Tropical Garden / 10901 Old Cutler Rd., Miami, Dade Co. [n.e. 1/4 of sec 7, T55S, R41E]

Nominator(s) / date: Don Evans, Daniel B. Ward / 1995

Comments: Badly broken by Hurricane Andrew (Aug 1992); cut limbs a striking "jade green" in color.

Champion trees of this species are not recorded by American Forests (1996 listing).

Butia capitata (Mart.) Becc.
Pindo Palm

(1)

☆ **Florida Champion.**

Size:			
	Circumference:	60	inches
	Height:	26	feet
	Crown spread:	21	feet
	Total points:	91	points

Owner / location: Howard H. Wilkowske / 1040 S.W. 11th St., Gainesville, Alachua Co. [n.w. 1/4 of sec 8, T10S, R20E]

Nominator(s) / date: Robert W. Simons / 1989
Update: Duane R. Durgee / 1991

Comments: Tree was planted by homeowner in 1960 (R. W. Simons, Aug 1989).

Champion trees of this species are not recorded by American Forests (1996 listing).

Caesalpinia pulcherrima (L.) Sw.
= *Poinciana pulcherrima* L.
Pride-of-Barbados, Barbados Flowerfence

(1)

★ **National Co-Champion.**

Size:			
	Circumference:	20	inches
	Height:	12	feet
	Crown spread:	15	feet
	Total points:	36	points

Owner / location: (unknown) / 1000 block of S.E. 13th Terr., Ft. Lauderdale, Broward Co. [s.w. 1/4 of sec 11, T50S, R42E]

Nominator(s) / date: John W. Kern / 1990

Comments: Acknowledged by American Forests (1996 listing).

(2)

★ **National Co-Champion.**

Size:			
	Circumference:	16	inches
	Height:	16	feet
	Crown spread:	14	feet
	Total points:	36	points

Owner / location: Uri Bergbaum / 745 N. Crescent Drive, Hollywood, Broward Co. [n.w. 1/4 of sec 17, T51S, R42E]

Nominator(s) / date: David A. Spicer / 1991

Comments: Acknowledged by American Forests (1996 listing).

Callistemon rigidus R. Br.
Stiff Bottlebrush

(1)

☆ **Florida Champion.**

Size:			
	Circumference:	92	inches
	Height:	62	feet
	Crown spread:	39.5	feet
	Total points:	164	points

Owner / location: Ruth Hayworth / 2812 Tallevast Rd., Tallevast, Manatee Co. [n.w. 1/4 of sec 32, T35S, R18E]

Nominator(s) / date: Mark Bakeman / 1981
Update: William J. Schilling / 1994

Comments: Earlier measurements: circ. = 79 in., ht. = 53 ft., spread = 41 ft. (Bakeman, 1981).

Champion trees of this species are not recorded by American Forests (1996 listing).

Callistemon viminalis (Gaertn.) Cheel
Weeping Bottlebrush

(1)

☆ **Florida Champion.**

Size:			
	Circumference:	77.5	inches
	Height:	26	feet
	Crown spread:	40.5 feet	
	Total points:	114	points

Owner / location: Robert Dent / 611 S. 6th St., Ft. Pierce, St. Lucie Co. [s.w. 1/4 of sec 10, T35S, R40E]

Nominator(s) / date: Steven J. Fousek / 1986

Comments: Champion trees of this species are not recorded by American Forests (1996 listing).

(2)

Florida Challenger.

Size:	Circumference:	34	inches
	Height:	35	feet
	Crown spread:	29.5 feet	
	Total points:	76	points

Owner / location: Laurel Willard / 123 McKinley Ave., Lehigh Acres, Lee Co. [s.w. 1/4 of sec 33, T44S, R27E]

Nominator(s) / date: Jeffrey S. Mangun / 1994

Callitris columellaris F. Muell.
= *Callitris glauca* R. Br.;
Callitris hugelii, misapplied
Cypress Pine

(1)

★ National Champion.

Size:	Circumference:	180	inches
	Height:	60	feet
	Crown spread:	50	feet
	Total points:	253	points

Owner / location: Ronald Friedel / W. 24th St. & W. 12th Ave., Bradenton, Manatee Co. [n.e. 1/4 of sec 34, T34S, R17E]

Nominator(s) / date: Steven Spezia / 1975

Update: William J. Schilling / 1994

Comments: Earlier measurements: circ. = 186 in., ht. = 57 ft., spread = 58 ft. (Spezia, 1975).

Acknowledged (as *C. hugelii*) by American Forests (1996 listing).

(2)

Florida Challenger.

Size:	Circumference:	92	inches
	Height:	57	feet
	Crown spread:	19	feet
	Total points:	154	points

Owner / location: Wayne C. Rickert / 2309 W. Manatee Ave., Bradenton, Manatee Co. [s.e. 1/4 of sec 27, T34S, R17E]

Nominator(s) / date: Robert T. Ing, Daniel B. Ward / 1994

Comments: Three similar-sized trees at this location.

Calophyllum inophyllum L.
Alexandrian Laurel

(1)

☆ Florida Champion.

Size:	Circumference:	61	inches
	Height:	36	feet
	Crown spread:	46	feet
	Total points:	109	points

Owner / location: County of Monroe / Public Service Bldg., Stock Island, Monroe Co. [n.e. 1/4 of sec 34, T67S, R25E]

Nominator(s) / date: Lois Kitching, Janet Bunch / 1986

Comments: Champion trees of this species are not recorded by American Forests (1996 listing).

Carya illinoinensis (Wangenh.) K. Koch
Pecan

(1)

☆ Florida Champion.

Size:	Circumference:	217	inches
	Height:	114	feet
	Crown spread:	117	feet
	Total points:	360	points

Owner / location: Mrs. O. V. Walker / n. side of U.S. 27, 2 mi. w. of Suwannee River bridge, 15 mi. s.e. of Mayo, Lafayette Co. [s.e. 1/4 of sec 13, T6S, R13E]

Nominator(s) / date: Jerry N. Livingston, Jason P. Livingston / 1993

Comments: The name is frequently misspelled *Carya "illinoensis."*

National champion: Texas (409 points).

(2)

Florida Challenger.

Size:	Circumference:	170	inches
	Height:	117	feet
	Crown spread:	103	feet
	Total points:	313	points

Owner / location: Florida Div. of Forestry / Andrews Nursery, s. of Fla. 345 (U.S. 27 Alt.), 1 mi. e. of Chiefland, Levy Co. [n.e. 1/4 of sec 6, T12S, R15E]

Nominator(s) / date: Michael J. Bordyn / 1985

Update: Robert T. Ing, Daniel B. Ward / 1993

Comments: The largest of five survivors of an old grove. Earlier measurements: circ. = 164 in., ht. = 96 ft., spread = 94 ft. (Bordyn, 1985).

(3)

Florida Challenger.

Size:	Circumference:	168	inches
	Height:	121	feet
	Crown spread:	89	feet
	Total points:	311	points

Owner / location: Allen Bell / 9 mi. n. of Crestview, Okaloosa Co. [s.e. 1/4 of sec 36, T5N, R23W]

Nominator(s) / date: John McMahon / 1981

Update: Geoffrey A. Cummings / 1993

Comments: Earlier measurements: circ. = 159 in., ht. = 105 ft., spread = 125 ft. (McMahon, 1981).

Honorable Mention. (4)

Size:	Circumference:	166	inches
	Height:	116	feet
	Crown spread:	89	feet
	Total points:	304	points

Owner / location: Florida Div. of Forestry / Andrews Nursery, s. of Fla. 345 (U.S. 27 Alt.), 1 mi. e. of Chiefland, Levy Co. [n.e. 1/4 of sec 6, T12S, R15E]

Nominator(s) / date: Robert T. Ing, Daniel B. Ward / 1993

Comments: The second largest of five survivors of an old grove.

Emeritus Florida Champion. (5)

Size:	Circumference:	155	inches
	Height:	100	feet
	Crown spread:	108	feet
	Total points:	282	points

Owner / location: Mrs. Allen B. Tyree / 1.5 mi. s. of Fla. 6, w. of Alapaha River, 9 mi. s. of Jennings, Hamilton Co. [s.e. 1/4 of sec 23, T1N, R12E]

Nominator(s) / date: Charles R. Marcus / 1980

Update: Robert W. Simons, Daniel B. Ward / 1993

Comments: Earlier measurements: circ. = 156 in., ht. = 99 ft., spread = 137 ft. (Marcus, 1980).

Honorable Mention. (6)

Size:	Circumference:	149	inches
	Height:	86	feet
	Crown spread:	95	feet
	Total points:	259	points

Owner / location: Roy Sewell / n. side of Fla. 280, 6 mi. s.e. of Chipley, Washington Co. [n.w. 1/4 of sec 20, T4N, R12W]

Nominator(s) / date: Charles R. Reeves / 1980

Update: Charles R. Reeves / 1993

Comments: Earlier measurements: circ. = 138 in., ht. = 80 ft., spread = 91 ft. (Reeves, 1980). Tree was planted in 1895, according to owner.

Castanea mollissima Blume
Chinese Chestnut

☆ **Florida Champion.** (1)

Size:	Circumference:	164	inches
	Height:	30	feet
	Crown spread:	68	feet
	Total points:	211	points

Owner / location: E. Hugh Howell / 6490 Jesse Allen Rd., 8 mi. n. of Milton, Santa Rosa Co. [s.e. 1/4 of sec 21, T3N, R28W]

Nominator(s) / date: James R. Burkhalter / 1993

Comments: Champion trees of this species are not recorded by American Forests (1996 listing).

Casuarina equisetifolia L.
Australian Pine, She-oak, Beefwood

☆ **Florida Champion.** (1)

Size:	Circumference:	159	inches
	Height:	82	feet
	Crown spread:	83	feet
	Total points:	262	points

Owner / location: City of Ft. Myers / Thomas Edison home, 2350 McGregor Blvd., Ft. Myers, Lee Co. [center of sec 23, T44S, R24E]

Nominator(s) / date: Eric H. Hoyer / 1978

Update: Deborah K. Brooker / 1987

Update: Jeffrey S. Mangun, Chris J. Anderson / 1994

Comments: Earlier measurements: circ. = 140 in., ht. = 99 ft., spread = 72 ft. (Hoyer, 1978); circ. = 153 in., ht. = 92 ft., spread = 73 ft. (Brooker, 1987).

National champion: Hawaii (310 points).

Catalpa longissima (Jacq.) Dum.-Cours.
Haiti Catalpa

☆ **Florida Champion.** (1)

Size:	Circumference:	96	inches
	Height:	77	feet
	Crown spread:	51	feet
	Total points:	186	points

Owner / location: Flamingo Tropical Gardens / 3750 Flamingo Rd. (Fla. 823), Ft. Lauderdale, Broward Co. [sec 25, T50S, R40E]

Nominator(s) / date: Terry Wolfe / 1983

Update: Frank L. Zickar, David Bar-Zvi / 1993

Comments: Earlier measurements: circ. = 91 in., ht. = 66 ft., spread = 39 ft. (Wolfe, 1983).

Champion trees of this species are not recorded by American Forests (1996 listing).

Cavanillesia platanifolia (Humb. & Bonpl.) HBK.
Cuipo

☆ **Florida Champion.** (1)

Size:	Circumference:	91	inches
	Height:	68	feet
	Crown spread:	20	feet
	Total points:	164	points

Owner / location: Flamingo Tropical Gardens / 3750 Flamingo Rd. (Fla. 823), Ft. Lauderdale, Broward Co. [sec 25, T50S, R40E]

Nominator(s) / date: David Bar-Zvi / 1991

Comments: Champion trees of this species are not recorded by American Forests (1996 listing).

Cedrus deodara (D. Don) G. Don
Deodar Cedar

(1)

☆ **Florida Champion.**

Size:			
	Circumference:	73	inches
	Height:	46	feet
	Crown spread:	44	feet
	Total points:	130	points

Owner / location: Southwest Forest Industries / just n. of Falling Waters State Park, 3 mi. s. of Chipley, Washington Co. [s.w. 1/4 of sec 22, T4N, R13W]

Nominator(s) / date: Charles R. Reeves / 1986

Comments: When nominated in 1986 this tree was Florida Champion. It was then superceded by a Duval County tree (Gorden, 139 points). But with the death of the larger tree, the Washington County tree again merits championship status.

Champion trees of this species are not recorded by American Forests (1996 listing).

Ceiba pentandra (L.) Gaertn.
Kapok, Silk-cotton

(1)

☆ **Florida Champion.**

Size:			
	Circumference:	204	inches
	Height:	61	feet
	Crown spread:	73	feet
	Total points:	283	points

Owner / location: Village of Key Biscayne / 400 block, Fernwood Dr., Key Biscayne, Dade Co. [s.e. 1/4 of sec 32, T54S, R42E]

Nominator(s) / date: Joan Gill Blank / 1995

Comments: Champion trees of this species are not recorded by American Forests (1996 listing).

Chorisia insignis HBK.
Yellow-flowered Chorisia

(1)

☆ **Florida Champion.**

Size:			
	Circumference:	120	inches
	Height:	55	feet
	Crown spread:	47.5	feet
	Total points:	187	points

Owner / location: Flamingo Tropical Gardens / 3750 Flamingo Rd. (Fla. 823), Ft. Lauderdale, Broward Co. [sec 25, T50S, R40E]

Nominator(s) / date: James Brenner / 1983

Update: Frank L. Zickar, David Bar-Zvi / 1993

Comments: Earlier measurements: circ. = 113 in., ht. = 69 ft., spread = 45 ft. (Brenner, 1983).

Champion trees of this species are not recorded by American Forests (1996 listing).

Chorisia speciosa St. Hil.
Floss-silk-tree

(1)

☆ **Florida Champion.**

Size:			
	Circumference:	168	inches
	Height:	46	feet
	Crown spread:	61.5	feet
	Total points:	229	points

Owner / location: Jay Shartzer / 1346 Almeria Ave., Ft. Myers, Lee Co. [n.w. 1/4 of sec 26, T44S, R24E]

Nominator(s) / date: Jeffrey S. Mangun / 1992

Comments: Champion trees of this species are not recorded by American Forests (1996 listing).

(2)

Florida Challenger.

Size:			
	Circumference:	151	inches
	Height:	50	feet
	Crown spread:	71.5	feet
	Total points:	219	points

Owner / location: Virginia Woodward / 1375 Alcazar Ave., Ft. Myers, Lee Co. [n.w. 1/4 of sec 26, T44S, R24E]

Nominator(s) / date: Jeffrey S. Mangun / 1992

Comments: Champion trees of this species are not recorded by American Forests (1996 listing).

(3)

Florida Challenger.

Size:			
	Circumference:	160	inches
	Height:	44	feet
	Crown spread:	56.5	feet
	Total points:	218	points

Owner / location: Barbara Elliott / 2865 Bentley St., Sarasota, Sarasota Co. [n.w. 1/4 of sec 33, T36S, R18E]

Nominator(s) / date: William J. Schilling / 1980

Update: William J. Schilling / 1993

Comments: Earlier measurements: circ. = 112 in., ht. = 36 ft., spread = 45 ft. (Schilling, 1980).

(4)

Emeritus Florida Champion.

Size:	Circumference:	136	inches
	Height:	47	feet
	Crown spread:	73	feet
	Total points:	201	points

Owner / location: County of Lee / Court House, Second St. & Monroe St., Ft. Myers, Lee Co. [s.w. 1/4 of sec 13, T44S, R24E]

Nominator(s) / date: Eric H. Hoyer, Tim Eckert / 1980

Update: Chris J. Anderson / 1994

Comments: Earlier measurements: circ. = 132 in., ht. = 55 ft., spread = 66.5 ft. (Hoyer & Eckert, 1980).

Cinnamomum camphora (L.) J. Presl
Camphor-tree

(1)

★ National Champion.

Size:	Circumference:	422	inches
	Height:	67	feet
	Crown spread:	103	feet
	Total points:	515	points

Owner / location: Thomas J. Hanlon / Darby community, w. end of Bellamy Rd. (Fla. 578A), 6 mi. w.n.w. of St. Leo, Pasco Co. [s.w. 1/4 of sec 25, T24S, R19E]

Nominator(s) / date: Sylvia Young / 1992

Comments: Acknowledged by American Forests (1996 listing).

(2)

Emeritus National Champion.

Size:	Circumference:	369	inches
	Height:	67	feet
	Crown spread:	135	feet
	Total points:	470	points

Owner / location: Richard J. Kinney / 40455 Otis Allen Rd. (Fla. 530), 3 mi. n.e. of Zephyrhills, Pasco Co. [s.w. 1/4 of sec 30, T25S, R22E]

Nominator(s) / date: Perna M. Stine / 1971

Update: Edward L. Flowers / 1980

Update: Thomas S. Haxby / 1989

Update: Daniel B. Ward / 1994

Comments: Tree is reported to have been planted by the Capt. J. P. Renfroe family in 1890 (P. M. Stine, July 1971).

Earlier measurements: circ. = 329 in., ht. = 65 ft., spread = 116 ft. (Stine, 1971); circ. = 349 in., ht. = 62 ft., spread = 109 ft. (Flowers, 1980); circ. = 366 in., ht. = 68 ft., spread = 131 ft. (Haxby, 1989).

(3)

Honorable Mention.

Size:	Circumference:	390	inches
	Height:	60	feet
	Crown spread:	53	feet
	Total points:	463	points

Owner / location: Joy Trask / 6529 Farris Drive, n. of Shepherd Rd., s. Lakeland, Polk Co. [s.e. 1/4 of sec 20, T29S, R23E]

Nominator(s) / date: James Truitt, J. P. Greene / 1974

Update: Cherry W. Platt / 1993

Comments: Earlier measurements: circ. = 373 in., ht. = 65 ft., spread = 74 ft. (Truitt & Greene, 1974).

(4)

Emeritus National Champion.

Size:	Circumference:	384	inches
	Height:	53	feet
	Crown spread:	68	feet
	Total points:	454	points

Owner / location: Maurice Clavel / 311 Ohio Ave., Wauchula, Hardee Co. [s.w. 1/4 of sec 4, T34S, R25E]

Nominator(s) / date: Steven Spezia, William J. Schilling / 1976

Update: Robert T. Ing, Daniel B. Ward / 1994

Comments: Earlier measurements: circ. = 368 in., ht. = 72 ft., spread = 102 ft. (Spezia & Schilling, 1976). Height and spread are much reduced; outer branches were killed by cold winds in 1989 (H. Clavel, July 1994).

(5)

Emeritus National Champion.

Size:	Circumference:	375	inches
	Height:	50	feet
	Crown spread:	105	feet
	Total points:	451	points

Owner / location: El Rancho Village, Inc. / 508 E. 44th Ave., Bradenton, Manatee Co. [sec 1, T35S, R17E]

Nominator(s) / date: Eldredge T. Carnes / 1968

Update: William J. Schilling / 1987

Comments: Earlier measurements: circ. = 336 in., ht. = 46 ft., spread = 106 ft. (Carnes, 1968).

(6)

Honorable Mention.

Size:	Circumference:	307	inches
	Height:	52	feet
	Crown spread:	101.5	feet
	Total points:	384	points

Owner / location: Perkins Restaurant / n.e. of int. U.S. 19 and Fla. 60, Clearwater, Pinellas Co. [n.w. 1/4 of sec 17, T29S, R16E]

Nominator(s) / date: Michael W. Kettles / 1987

  Update: Chris J. Anderson / 1994

Comments: Earlier measurements: circ. = 292 in., ht. = 54 ft., spread = 97.5 ft. (Kettles, 1987).

(7)

Honorable Mention.

Size:			
	Circumference:	265	inches
	Height:	45	feet
	Crown spread:	79	feet
	Total points:	330	points

Owner / location: Barbara Garcia / 210 Palmetto Ave., Crescent City, Putnam Co. [s.e. 1/4 of sec 25, T12S, R28E]

Nominator(s) / date: John H. Holzaepfel / 1986

(8)

Honorable Mention.

Size:			
	Circumference:	238	inches
	Height:	60	feet
	Crown spread:	87	feet
	Total points:	320	points

Owner / location: Bennigan's Restaurant / n.e. of int. U.S. 19 and Fla. 60, Clearwater, Pinellas Co. [n.w. 1/4 of sec 17, T29S, R16E]

Nominator(s) / date: Chris J. Anderson / 1994

Comments: Earlier measurements: circ. = 217 in., ht. = 64 ft., spread = 88.5 ft. (Kettles, 1987).

(9)

Honorable Mention.

Size:			
	Circumference:	260	inches
	Height:	44	feet
	Crown spread:	44	feet
	Total points:	315	points

Owner / location: William Weber / 8560 E. Orange Ave., Floral City, Citrus Co. [n.e. 1/4 of sec 15, T20S, R20E]

Nominator(s) / date: Richard F. Degen / 1986

  Update: Duane R. Durgee, Daniel B. Ward / 1994

Comments: Earlier measurements: circ. = 256 in., ht. = 60 ft., spread = 75 ft. (Degen, 1986). Tree is now recovering from severe freeze damage, but spread is much reduced (D. R. Durgee & D. B. Ward, Apr 1994).

(10)

Honorable Mention.

Size:			
	Circumference:	213	inches
	Height:	62	feet
	Crown spread:	84.5	feet
	Total points:	296	points

Owner / location: Mr. Langley / s. end of Pretty Lake, 8 mi. s.s.e. of Groveland, Lake Co. [sec 28, T23S, R25E]

Nominator(s) / date: A. B. Shiver / 1985

Citrus paradisi Macf.
Grapefruit

Title vacant.

Size:		
	Circumference:	
	Height:	
	Crown spread:	
	Total points:	

Owner / location:

Nominator(s) / date:

Comments: A tree of this species, now dead, was measured at circ. = 75, ht. = 35, spread = 42, 120 points (Flowers, 1983—Land O'Lakes, Pasco County).

  Champion trees of this species are not recorded by American Forests (1996 listing).

Citrus sinensis (L.) Osbeck
Orange

Title vacant.

Size:		
	Circumference:	
	Height:	
	Crown spread:	
	Total points:	

Owner / location:

Nominator(s) / date:

Comments: It is inexplicable that no tree of this species, so important to Florida agriculture and so characteristic of the Florida mystique, has ever been nominated as a champion.

  Champion trees of this species are not recorded by American Forests (1996 listing).

Cocos nucifera L.
Coconut

(1)

☆ **Florida Champion.**

Size:			
	Circumference:	44	inches
	Height:	67	feet
	Crown spread:	27	feet
	Total points:	118	points

Owner / location: (unknown) / jct. Jackson St. & First St., Ft. Myers, Lee Co. [s.w. 1/4 of sec 13, T44S, R24E]

Nominator(s) / date: Eric H. Hoyer, Glen Atkinson / 1977

Update: Chris J. Anderson / 1994

Comments: Earlier measurements: circ. = 44 in., ht. = 67 ft., spread = 27 ft. (Hoyer & Atkinson, 1977). The tallest of 8 trees at this location; dimensions appear not to have changed in 17 years (C. J. Anderson, June 1994).

National champion: Hawaii (159 points).

Copernicia baileyana Leon
Bailey's Petticoat Palm

(1)

☆ **Florida Champion.**

Size:			
	Circumference:	73	inches
	Height:	34	feet
	Crown spread:	13	feet
	Total points:	110	points

Owner / location: Fairchild Tropical Garden / 10901 Old Cutler Rd., Miami, Dade Co. [n.e. 1/4 of sec 7, T55S, R41E]

Nominator(s) / date: Don Evans, Daniel B. Ward / 1995

Comments: Champion trees of this species are not recorded by American Forests (1996 listing).

Cordia sebestena L.
Geiger-tree

(1)

★ **National Champion.**

Size:			
	Circumference:	27	inches
	Height:	24	feet
	Crown spread:	18.5	feet
	Total points:	56	points

Owner / location: Tarpon Bay Marina / n. end Tarpon Bay Rd., Sanibel, Lee Co. [s.w. 1/4 of sec 23, T46S, R22E]

Nominator(s) / date: Eric H. Hoyer, Chris J. Anderson / 1980

Update: Robert T. Ing, Daniel B. Ward / 1994

Comments: Earlier measurements: circ. = 50 in. (mismeasured), ht. = 25 ft., spread = 23 ft. (Hoyer & Anderson, 1980). Tree was never as large as recorded in 1980; trunk in 1994 was 38 in. at 1 ft., forked at 2 ft., with branches of 27 in. and 26 in. at 4.5 ft.

This species, though long cultivated and now somewhat naturalized in the Keys, appears to have been introduced, possibly (according to J. J. Audubon, 1834) from Cuba.

Acknowledged by American Forests (1996 listing).

Couroupita guianensis Aubl.
Cannonball-tree

(1)

☆ **Florida Champion.**

Size:			
	Circumference:	127	inches
	Height:	44	feet
	Crown spread:	30	feet
	Total points:	179	points

Owner / location: Jim Hanlon / 2416 Bay St., Ft. Myers, Lee Co. [s.w. 1/4 of sec 13, T44S, R24E]

Nominator(s) / date: Eric H. Hoyer, Tim Eckert / 1980

Update: Robert T. Ing, Daniel B. Ward / 1994

Comments: Earlier measurements: circ. = 125 in., ht. = 56 ft., spread = 38 ft. (Hoyer & Eckert, 1980).

Champion trees of this species are not recorded by American Forests (1996 listing).

Cryptomeria japonica (L. f.) D. Don
Japanese Cedar

(1)

☆ **Florida Champion.**

Size:			
	Circumference:	58	inches
	Height:	60	feet
	Crown spread:	29.5	feet
	Total points:	125	points

Owner / location: J. H. Nelson / 6 mi. s.s.e. of Chipley, Washington Co. [n.w. 1/4 of sec 2, T3N, R13W]

Nominator(s) / date: Charles R. Reeves / 1983

Update: Charles R. Reeves / 1993

Comments: Earlier measurements: circ. = 43 in., ht. = 51 ft., spread = 22 ft. (Reeves, 1983).

Champion trees of this species are not recorded by American Forests (1996 listing).

Cunninghamia lanceolata (Lamb.) Hook.
China Fir

(1)

☆ **Florida Champion.**

Size:			
	Circumference:	49	inches
	Height:	64	feet
	Crown spread:	30	feet
	Total points:	121	points

Owner / location: Ricky Henderson / jct. Fla. 145 & Fraleigh Dr., Madison, Madison Co. [sec 23, T1N, R9E]

Nominator(s) / date: Mike Evans / 1991

Comments: Champion trees of this species are not recorded by American Forests (1996 listing).

(2)

Florida Challenger.

Size:			
	Circumference:	47	inches
	Height:	61	feet
	Crown spread:	30	feet
	Total points:	115	points

Owner / location: Hugh W. Cunningham / 229 N.W. 14th Ave., Gainesville, Alachua Co. [s.e. 1/4 of sec 32, T9S, R20E]

Nominator(s) / date: Robert T. Ing, Daniel B. Ward / 1991

Comments: Lower trunk forked, circ. measured (on larger branch) at 5 ft.; trunk 70 in. at 4.5 ft., 69 in. at 2 ft.

(3)

Emeritus Florida Champion.

Size:			
	Circumference:	39	inches
	Height:	44	feet
	Crown spread:	22	feet
	Total points:	88	points

Owner / location: Univ. of Florida / courtyard of Murphree Hall, campus, Gainesville, Alachua Co. [s.w. 1/4 of sec 6, T10S, R20E]

Nominator(s) / date: Michael J. Bordyn / 1980

Update: Robert T. Ing, Daniel B. Ward / 1991

Comments: Earlier measurements: circ. = 36 in., ht. = 49 ft., spread = 27 ft. (Bordyn, 1980).

Cupressocyparis leylandii (A. B. Jacks. & Dallim.) Dallim. & A. B. Jacks. Leyland Cypress

(1)

☆ Florida Champion.

Size:			
	Circumference:	53	inches
	Height:	34	feet
	Crown spread:	31	feet
	Total points:	95	points

Owner / location: Univ. of Florida / Corry Village, campus, Gainesville, Alachua Co. [s.e. 1/4 of sec 1, T10S, R19E]

Nominator(s) / date: Noel R. Lake, Daniel B. Ward / 1996

Comments: Tree was planted as a sapling in late 1960s (N. R. Lake, Oct 1996). It is an intergeneric hybrid between *Chamaecyparis nootkatensis* and *Cupressus macrocarpa*.

Champion trees of this species are not recorded by American Forests (1996 listing).

Cupressus sempervirens L. Italian Cypress

(1)

☆ Florida Champion.

Size:			
	Circumference:	38	inches
	Height:	74	feet
	Crown spread:	8	feet
	Total points:	114	points

Owner / location: O. G. Evans / N.W. 2nd Ave., High Springs, Alachua Co. [sec 3, T8S, R17E]

Nominator(s) / date: Michael J. Bordyn / 1981

Update: Robert T. Ing, Daniel B. Ward / 1991

Comments: Earlier measurements: circ. = 35 in., ht. = 72 ft., spread = 9 ft. (Bordyn, 1981).

Champion trees of this species are not recorded by American Forests (1996 listing).

Cycas circinalis L. Sago Palm, Queen Sago

(1)

☆ Florida Champion.

Size:			
	Circumference:	74	inches
	Height:	21	feet
	Crown spread:	16	feet
	Total points:	99	points

Owner / location: Indian River Land Trust, Inc. / McKee Jungle Gardens, Vero Beach, Indian River Co. [n.w. 1/4 of sec 18, T33S, R40E]

Nominator(s) / date: Daniel F. Culbert / 1994

Comments: Champion trees of this species are not recorded by American Forests (1996 listing).

Dalbergia sissoo DC. Indian Rosewood, Sissoo-tree

(1)

☆ Florida Champion.

Size:			
	Circumference:	117	inches
	Height:	62	feet
	Crown spread:	66	feet
	Total points:	196	points

Owner / location: City of St. Petersburg / n.w. corner of Central Ave. & N. 34th St. (U.S. 19), St. Petersburg, Pinellas Co. [n.e. 1/4 of sec 22, T31S, R16E]

Nominator(s) / date: Chris J. Anderson / 1994

Comments: Champion trees of this species are not recorded by American Forests (1996 listing).

Florida Challenger. (2)

Size:	Circumference:	100	inches
	Height:	64	feet
	Crown spread:	40	feet
	Total points:	174	points

Owner / location: City of St. Petersburg / s.w. corner of N. 3rd Ave. & N. 36th St., St. Petersburg, Pinellas Co. [n.e. 1/4 of sec 22, T31S, R16E]

Nominator(s) / date: Chris J. Anderson / 1994

Honorable Mention. (3)

Size:	Circumference:	82	inches
	Height:	68	feet
	Crown spread:	53	feet
	Total points:	163	points

Owner / location: Kenneth Curtis / 3785 Ft. Denaud Rd. (Fla. 78A), 4 mi. w.s.w of LaBelle, Hendry Co. [s.w. 1/4 of sec 11, T43S, R28E]

Nominator(s) / date: Chris J. Anderson / 1994

Comments: The larger of two trees at this location (C. J. Anderson, Apr 1994).

Honorable Mention. (4)

Size:	Circumference:	83	inches
	Height:	62	feet
	Crown spread:	55	feet
	Total points:	159	points

Owner / location: Kenneth Curtis / 3785 Ft. Denaud Rd. (fla. 78A), 4 mi. w.s.w of LaBelle, Hendry Co. [s.w. 1/4 of sec 11, T43S, R28E]

Nominator(s) / date: Chris J. Anderson / 1994

Comments: The smaller of two trees at this location (C. J. Anderson, Mar 1994).

Delonix regia (Bojer) Raf.
Royal Poinciana, Flamboyant

★ **National Champion**. (1)

Size:	Circumference:	102	inches
	Height:	61	feet
	Crown spread:	56.5	feet
	Total points:	177	points

Owner / location: Doris Vaughan / Ft. Denaud Rd. (Fla. 78A), 1.7 mi. e. of Ft. Denaud bridge, 3 mi. w.s.w. of LaBelle, Hendry Co. [s.w. 1/4 of sec 12, T43S, R28E]

Nominator(s) / date: Michael W. Kenton / 1972

Update: Chris J. Anderson, Eric H. Hoyer / 1981

Update: Chris J. Anderson, Jeffrey S. Mangun / 1994

Comments: Earlier measurements: circ. = 163 in. (incl. 2 trunks), ht. = 68 ft., spread = 69 ft. (Kenton, 1972); circ. = 175 in. (incl. 2 trunks), ht. = 53 ft., spread = 47.5 ft. (Anderson & Hoyer, 1981).

Reported as National champion by American Forests in 1973, and continued until 1978. Deleted by A.F. in 1980 after Little (1979) called it "omitted as apparently not naturalized." Reinstated by A.F. in 1996.

Florida Challenger. (2)

Size:	Circumference:	93	inches
	Height:	48	feet
	Crown spread:	83	feet
	Total points:	162	points

Owner / location: The Kampong / 4013 S.W. 37th Ave. (Douglas Rd.), Coconut Grove, Dade Co. [n.w. 1/4 of sec 28, T54S, R41E]

Nominator(s) / date: Adriana Lupas, John T. Valenta, Helen Eidson / 1994

Honorable Mention. (3)

Size:	Circumference:	41	inches
	Height:	50	feet
	Crown spread:	41	feet
	Total points:	101	points

Owner / location: Key West Botanical Garden Society / Botanical Garden, Stock Island, Monroe Co. [n.e. 1/4 of sec 34, T67S, R25E]

Nominator(s) / date: Janet Bunch, Michael D. Brady / 1986

Duranta repens L.
Golden-dewdrop

Title vacant.

Size:	Circumference:		
	Height:		
	Crown spread:		
	Total points:		

Owner / location:

Nominator(s) / date:

Comments: This shrub or small tree has occasionally been considered a native species, and was so treated in the Checklist of Trees Native to Florida (Ward, 1991). It, however, has no natural range within the state, and apparently occurs only as an infrequent escape. Champion trees of this species are not recorded by American Forests (1996 listing).

Enterolobium contortisiliquum
(Vell.) Morong
Pacara

(1)

☆ **Florida Champion.**

Size:	Circumference:	182	inches
	Height:	85	feet
	Crown spread:	122	feet
	Total points:	298	points

Owner / location: Flamingo Tropical Gardens / 3750 Flamingo Rd. (Fla. 823), Ft. Lauderdale, Broward Co. [sec 25, T50S, R40E]

Nominator(s) / date: Frank L. Zickar / 1985

Comments: Champion trees of this species are not recorded by American Forests (1996 listing).

(2)

Florida Challenger.

Size:	Circumference:	172	inches
	Height:	68	feet
	Crown spread:	87	feet
	Total points:	262	points

Owner / location: Fairchild Tropical Garden / 10901 Old Cutler Rd., Miami, Dade Co. [n.e. 1/4 of sec 7, T55S, R41E]

Nominator(s) / date: Don Evans, Daniel B. Ward / 1995

Enterolobium cyclocarpum Griseb.
Guanacaste, Ear-tree

(1)

☆ **Florida Champion.**

Size:	Circumference:	171	inches
	Height:	53	feet
	Crown spread:	69	feet
	Total points:	241	points

Owner / location: City of Ft. Myers / Thomas Edison home, 2350 McGregor Blvd., Ft. Myers, Lee Co. [center of sec 23, T44S, R24E]

Nominator(s) / date: Eric H. Hoyer / 1978

Update: Deborah K. Brooker / 1987

Update: Chris J. Anderson, Jeffrey S. Mangun / 1994

Comments: Earlier measurements: circ. = 159 in., ht. = 59 ft., spread = 79 ft. (Hoyer, 1978); circ. = 177 in. (measured at fork), ht. = 62 ft., spread = 86.5 ft. (Brooker, 1987). Damaged in 1987 freeze (R. W. Workman, June 1993).

Champion trees of this species are not recorded by American Forests (1996 listing).

(2)

Emeritus Florida Champion.

Size:	Circumference:	117	inches
	Height:	60	feet
	Crown spread:	83	feet
	Total points:	198	points

Owner / location: Betty Greely / 5340 Cypress Rd., Plantation, Broward Co. [s.e. 1/4 of sec 2, T50S, R41E]

Nominator(s) / date: David M. Sinclair / 1984

Comments: Tree believed to have been planted about 1958 (D. M. Sinclair, Feb 1984).

Erythrina crista-galli L.
Cockspur Coral-tree

(1)

☆ **Florida Champion.**

Size:	Circumference:	128	inches
	Height:	36	feet
	Crown spread:	51	feet
	Total points:	177	points

Owner / location: Florida Div. of Forestry / 4723 E. 53rd Ave., Bradenton, Manatee Co. [s.w. 1/4 of sec 9, T35S, R18E]

Nominator(s) / date: Mark B. Meador / 1981

Update: William J. Schilling / 1994

Comments: Earlier measurements: circ. = 109 in., ht. = 28 ft., spread = 41.5 ft. (Meador, 1981).

Champion trees of this species are not recorded by American Forests (1996 listing).

Erythrina variegata L.
= *Erythrina indica* Lam.
Indian Coral-tree

(1)

☆ **Florida Champion.**

Size:	Circumference:	188	inches
	Height:	41	feet
	Crown spread:	65	feet
	Total points:	245	points

Owner / location: City of Deerfield Beach / jct. S.E. 19th Ave. & S.E. 8th St., Deerfield Beach, Broward Co. [sec 5, T48S, R43E]

Nominator(s) / date: Peter Burke / 1988

Comments: Champion trees of this species are not recorded by American Forests (1996 listing).

(2)

Emeritus Florida Champion.

Size:			
	Circumference:	103	inches
	Height:	42	feet
	Crown spread:	52	feet
	Total points:	158	points

Owner / location: City of Ft. Myers / Thomas Edison home, 2350 McGregor Blvd., Ft. Myers, Lee Co. [center of sec 23, T44S, R24E]

Nominator(s) / date: Vicki King, George Krauss / 1974

Update: Chris J. Anderson, Jeffrey S. Mangun / 1994

Comments: Earlier measurements: circ. = 72 in., ht. = 41 ft., spread = 41 ft. (King & Krauss, 1974).

Eucalyptus cinerea Benth.
Silver-dollar Eucalyptus

(1)

☆ Florida Champion.

Size:			
	Circumference:	46	inches
	Height:	23	feet
	Crown spread:	15	feet
	Total points:	73	points

Owner / location: George W. Dekle / 3600 N.W. 12th St., Gainesville, Alachua Co. [n.w. 1/4 of sec 29, T9S, R20E]

Nominator(s) / date: Robert W. Simons, Michael J. Bordyn / 1981

Update: Robert T. Ing, Daniel B. Ward / 1991

Comments: Tree was planted in 1961 (G. W. Dekle, Oct 1991). Badly damaged by 1984 freeze; bark shed, upper branches killed, now resprouting from trunk. Earlier measurements: circ. = 48 in., ht. = 38 ft., spread = 27.5 ft. (Simons & Bordyn, 1981).

When nominated in 1981 this tree was Florida Champion. It was then superceded by two Duval County trees (Allen, 1983 - 124 points; Becker, 1982 - 121 points). But in following years both of these larger trees died, returning the Alachua County tree to championship status.

Champion trees of this species are not recorded by American Forests (1996 listing).

Eucalyptus citriodora Hook.
Lemon-scented Gum

(1)

☆ Florida Champion.

Size:			
	Circumference:	168	inches
	Height:	85	feet
	Crown spread:	77.5	feet
	Total points:	272	points

Owner / location: June Linzalone / Corkscrew Rd. (Fla. 850), 1 mi. e. of Koreshan State Historic Park, Lee Co. [n.w. 1/4 of sec 34, T46S, R25E]

Nominator(s) / date: Eric H. Hoyer, Tim Eckert / 1980

Update: Chris J. Anderson / 1994

Comments: Earlier measurements: circ. = 156 in., ht. = 104 ft., spread = 90.5 ft. (Hoyer & Eckert, 1980).

This tree was originally identified as *Eucalyptus camaldulensis* Dehnh. (river red gum). However this tree is erect, as is *E. citriodora* (vs. usually forked and crooked in *E. camaldulensis*), with a smooth, entirely light gray trunk (vs. smooth above and scaly toward base); the flowers are usually solitary, in panicles (vs. several-flowered umbels); and the leaves when crushed have a strong scent of lemon (D. B. Ward, Jan 1996).

Champion trees of this species are not recorded by American Forests (1996 listing).

Eucalyptus deglupta Blume
Rainbow Eucalyptus

(1)

☆ Florida Champion.

Size:			
	Circumference:	102	inches
	Height:	96	feet
	Crown spread:	57.5	feet
	Total points:	212	points

Owner / location: Mary Homan / 7755 S.W. 120th St., Miami, Dade Co. [s.e. 1/4 of sec 15, T55S, R40E]

Nominator(s) / date: Roger L. Hammer, Daniel B. Ward / 1994

Comments: Tree is spectacular in rate of growth (planted about 1974) and multicolored trunk (smooth, scaling in thin, elongate, blue-gray flakes to expose green, then salmon-orange underbark).

Champion trees of this species are not recorded by American Forests (1996 listing).

Eucalyptus robusta Sm.
Swamp Mahogany

(1)

☆ Florida Champion.

Size:			
	Circumference:	100	inches
	Height:	100	feet
	Crown spread:	68	feet
	Total points:	217	points

Owner / location: Koreshan Unity, Inc. / n.e. of jct. U.S. 41 & Corkscrew Rd. (Fla. 850), Estero, Lee Co. [n.e. 1/4 of sec 33, T46S, R25E]

Nominator(s) / date: Chris J. Anderson / 1994

Comments: Champion trees of this species are not recorded by American Forests (1996 listing).

(2)

Florida Challenger.

Size:	Circumference:	103	inches
	Height:	63	feet
	Crown spread:	39.5	feet
	Total points:	176	points

Owner / location: Koreshan State Historic Park / Estero, Lee Co. [s.w. 1/4 of sec 28, T46S, R25E]

Nominator(s) / date: Chris J. Anderson / 1994

(3)

Honorable Mention.

Size:	Circumference:	67	inches
	Height:	61	feet
	Crown spread:	38	feet
	Total points:	138	points

Owner / location: Kenneth Curtis / 3785 Ft. Denaud Rd. (fla. 78A), 4 mi. w.s.w. of LaBelle, Hendry Co. [s.w. 1/4 of sec 11, T43S, R28E]

Nominator(s) / date: Chris J. Anderson / 1994

Comments: Larger of two trees of this species at this location (C. J. Anderson, Apr 1994).

(4)

Honorable Mention.

Size:	Circumference:	65	inches
	Height:	65	feet
	Crown spread:	27.5	feet
	Total points:	137	points

Owner / location: Kenneth Curtis / 3785 Ft. Denaud Rd. (Fla. 78A), 4 mi. w.s.w. of LaBelle, Hendry Co. [s.w. 1/4 of sec 11, T43S, R28E]

Nominator(s) / date: Chris J. Anderson / 1994

Comments: The smaller of two trees of this species at this location (C. J. Anderson, Apr 1994).

Eucalyptus torelliana F. Muell.
Torelliana Gum

(1)

☆ Florida Champion.

Size:	Circumference:	56	inches
	Height:	61	feet
	Crown spread:	29	feet
	Total points:	124	points

Owner / location: Kenneth Curtis / 3785 Ft. Denaud Rd. (Fla. 78A), 4 mi. w.s.w. of LaBelle, Hendry Co. [s.w. 1/4 of sec 11, T43S, R28E]

Nominator(s) / date: Chris J. Anderson / 1994

Comments: Champion trees of this species are not recorded by American Forests (1996 listing).

Ficus altissima Blume
Lofty Fig

(1)

☆ Florida Champion.

Size:	Circumference:	356	inches
	Height:	92	feet
	Crown spread:	173	feet
	Total points:	492	points

Owner / location: Hugh Taylor Birch State Park / 3109 E. Sunrise Blvd., Ft. Lauderdale, Broward Co. [s.e. 1/4 of sec 36, T49S, R42E]

Nominator(s) / date: Jim Higgins / 1995

Comments: Champion trees of this species are not recorded by American Forests (1996 listing).

(2)

Emeritus Florida Champion.

Size:	Circumference:	408	inches
	Height:	50	feet
	Crown spread:	90	feet
	Total points:	481	points

Owner / location: Coral Gables Federal Savings, Inc. / 3050 N. Federal Hwy. (U.S. 1), Lighthouse Point, Broward Co. [center of sec 19, T48S, R43E]

Nominator(s) / date: Trygve Winther / 1982

Update: Frank L. Zickar / 1994

Comments: Earlier measurements: circ. = 464 in. (measured outside some separate root-trunks), ht. = 41 ft., spread = 105 ft. (Winther, 1982). Tree is in good health, very attractive, often photographed by visitors (M. Denny, July 1993).

(3)

Honorable Mention.

Size:	Circumference:	278	inches
	Height:	65	feet
	Crown spread:	133	feet
	Total points:	376	points

Owner / location: City of Ft. Myers / Thomas Edison home, 2350 McGregor Blvd., Ft. Myers, Lee Co. [center of sec 23, T44S, R24E]

Nominator(s) / date: Eric H. Hoyer / 1978

Update: Deborah K. Brooker, Mark Hooten / 1987

Update: Richard W. Workman / 1995

Comments: Earlier measurements: circ. = 616 in. (measured outside all free-standing root-trunks), ht. = 61 ft., spread = 119 ft. (Hoyer, 1978); circ. = 700 in. (measured outside root-trunks), ht. = 65 ft., spread = 133 ft. (Brooker & Hooten, 1987). Trunk measured at minimum circumference, inside root-trunks; height & spread were not remeasured (R. W. Workman, July 1995).

Ficus benghalensis L.
Banyan Fig

(1)

☆ **Florida Champion.**

Size:			
	Circumference:	376	inches
	Height:	62	feet
	Crown spread:	191	feet
	Total points:	486	points

Owner / location: City of Ft. Myers / Thomas Edison home, 2350 McGregor Blvd., Ft. Myers, Lee Co. [center of sec 23, T44S, R24E]

Nominator(s) / date: Eric H. Hoyer, Tim Eckert / 1980

Update: Jeffrey S. Mangun, Chris J. Anderson / 1994

Comments: Earlier measurements: circ. = 386 in. (above narrowest point), ht. = 64 ft., spread = 190 ft. (Hoyer & Eckert, 1980). Tree covers nearly an acre of ground, with many secondary trunks developed from aerial roots (R. W. Workman, June 1993).

Champion trees of this species are not recorded by American Forests (1996 listing).

(2)

Florida Challenger.

Size:			
	Circumference:	385	inches
	Height:	61	feet
	Crown spread:	119	feet
	Total points:	476	points

Owner / location: Holiday Inn, Inc. / 300 W. Retta Esplanade, Punta Gorda, Charlotte Co. [s.w. 1/4 of sec 6, T41S, R23E]

Nominator(s) / date: James L. Bernett / 1993

(3)

Honorable Mention.

Size:			
	Circumference:	101	inches
	Height:	62	feet
	Crown spread:	80	feet
	Total points:	183	points

Owner / location: Fairchild Tropical Garden / 10901 Old Cutler Rd., Miami, Dade Co. [n.e. 1/4 of sec 7, T55S, R41E]

Nominator(s) / date: Don Evans, Daniel B. Ward / 1995

Comments: A remarkable tree whose point score fails to represent its aspect of size. The original central trunk, however, is no longer present, and none of the fifty or so secondary trunks is of large circumference. The crown spread is also reduced in that what may once have been a single tree is presently composed of more than one independent group of trunks.

Ficus minahassea
(Teysm. & DeVr.) Miq.
Ayumit Fig

(1)

☆ **Florida Champion.**

Size:			
	Circumference:	68	inches
	Height:	36	feet
	Crown spread:	48	feet
	Total points:	116	points

Owner / location: Flamingo Tropical Gardens / 3750 Flamingo Rd. (Fla. 823), Ft. Lauderdale, Broward Co. [sec 25, T50S, R40E]

Nominator(s) / date: John G. Cordy / 1983

Update: Frank L. Zickar, David Bar-Zvi / 1993

Comments: Earlier measurements: circ. = 83 in., ht. = 39 ft., spread = 55 ft. (Cordy, 1983).

Champion trees of this species are not recorded by American Forests (1996 listing).

Ficus mysorensis Roth
Mysore Fig

(1)

☆ **Florida Champion.**

Size:			
	Circumference:	252	inches
	Height:	105	feet
	Crown spread:	116	feet
	Total points:	386	points

Owner / location: City of Ft. Myers / Thomas Edison home, 2350 McGregor Blvd., Ft. Myers, Lee Co. [center of sec 23, T44S, R24E]

Nominator(s) / date: Eric H. Hoyer / 1978

Update: Eric H. Hoyer, Tim Eckert / 1980

Update: Robert T. Ing, Daniel B. Ward / 1994

Comments: Earlier measurements: circ. = 157 in., ht. = 83 ft., spread = 71 ft. (Hoyer, 1978); circ. = 172 in., ht. = 84 ft., spread = 99 ft. (Hoyer & Eckert, 1980).

This tree has long been thought to be *Ficus nekbudu* Warb. (= *Ficus utilis* Sims), the Kaffir or Zulu fig. It appears to have been first correctly identified by A. P. Simmons (Feb 1987).

Champion trees of this species are not recorded by American Forests (1996 listing).

Ficus nitida Thunb.
= *Ficus retusa* L. var. *nitida* (Thunb.) Miq.
Cuban Laurel

(1)

☆ **Florida Champion.**

Size:	Circumference:	336	inches
	Height:	85	feet
	Crown spread:	116	feet
	Total points:	450	points

Owner / location: City of Ft. Myers / Thomas Edison home, 2350 McGregor Blvd., Ft. Myers, Lee Co. [center of sec 23, T44S, R24E]

Nominator(s) / date: Eric H. Hoyer, Glen Atkinson / 1977

Update: Eric H. Hoyer, Tim Eckert / 1980

Update: Robert T. Ing, Daniel B. Ward / 1994

Comments: Earlier measurements: circ. = (not measured; entire group of stems measured 810 in.), ht. = 82 ft., spread = 97 ft. (Hoyer & Atkinson, 1977); circ. = 311 in., ht. = 78 ft., spread = 103.5 ft. (Hoyer & Eckert, 1980).

Champion trees of this species are not recorded by American Forests (1996 listing).

(2)

Florida Challenger.

Size:	Circumference:	288	inches
	Height:	62	feet
	Crown spread:	85.5	feet
	Total points:	372	points

Owner / location: Thomas G. Finney / 1876 Oak St., Sarasota, Sarasota Co. [s.e. 1/4 of sec 19, T36S, R18E]

Nominator(s) / date: Lee Barnwell / 1994

Ficus racemosa L.
= *Ficus glomerata* Roxb.
Cluster Fig

(1)

☆ **Florida Champion.**

Size:	Circumference:	649	inches
	Height:	102	feet
	Crown spread:	95	feet
	Total points:	775	points

Owner / location: Flamingo Tropical Gardens / 3750 Flamingo Rd. (Fla. 823), Ft. Lauderdale, Broward Co. [sec 25, T50S, R40E]

Nominator(s) / date: Hank Graham / 1983

Update: Frank L. Zickar, David Bar-Zvi / 1993

Comments: Earlier measurements: circ. = 586 in., ht. = 108 ft., spread = 105 ft. (Graham, 1983).

Champion trees of this species are not recorded by American Forests (1996 listing).

Ficus religiosa L.
Bo-tree

(1)

☆ **Florida Champion.**

Size:	Circumference:	246	inches
	Height:	42	feet
	Crown spread:	63	feet
	Total points:	304	points

Owner / location: Marie Selby Botanical Gardens / 800 S. Palm Ave., Sarasota, Sarasota Co. [n.w. 1/4 of sec 30, T36S, R18E]

Nominator(s) / date: William J. Schilling / 1980

Update: William J. Schilling / 1993

Comments: Earlier measurements: circ. = 211 in., ht. = 26 ft., spread = 44.5 ft. (Schilling, 1980).

A species of great religious symbolism. It was beneath a bo-tree that the founder of Buddhism attained his spiritual enlightenment.

Champion trees of this species are not recorded by American Forests (1996 listing).

Ficus virens Ait.
Spotted Fig

(1)

☆ **Florida Champion.**

Size:	Circumference:	103	inches
	Height:	32	feet
	Crown spread:	45.5	feet
	Total points:	146	points

Owner / location: Marie Selby Botanical Gardens / 800 S. Palm Ave., Sarasota, Sarasota Co. [n.w. 1/4 of sec 30, T36S, R18E]

Nominator(s) / date: William J. Schilling / 1980

Update: William J. Schilling / 1993

Comments: Earlier measurements: circ. = 100 in., ht. = 32 ft., spread = 45.5 ft. (Schilling, 1980).

Champion trees of this species are not recorded by American Forests (1996 listing).

Ficus vogelii Miq.
West African Rubber-tree

(1)

☆ **Florida Champion.**

Size:			
	Circumference:	300	inches
	Height:	26	feet
	Crown spread:	53	feet
	Total points:	339	points

Owner / location: Marie Selby Botanical Gardens / 800 S. Palm Ave., Sarasota, Sarasota Co. [n.w. 1/4 of sec 30, T36S, R18E]

Nominator(s) / date: William J. Schilling / 1980

Update: William J. Schilling / 1993

Comments: Earlier measurements: circ. = 252 in., ht. = 19 ft., spread = 53 ft. (Schilling, 1980).

Champion trees of this species are not recorded by American Forests (1996 listing).

Firmiana simplex (L.) Wight
Chinese Parasol-tree

(1)

☆ **Florida Champion.**

Size:			
	Circumference:	40	inches
	Height:	28	feet
	Crown spread:	35	feet
	Total points:	77	points

Owner / location: Mr. DeYoung / w. side of Union Ave., 1.5 mi. s. of U.S. 17, Crescent City, Putnam Co. [n.e. 1/4 of sec 14, T12S, R27E]

Nominator(s) / date: Ned D. Neenan / 1993

Comments: National champion: Texas (148 points).

Gliricidia sepium (Jacq.) Walp.
Madre de Cacao

(1)

☆ **Florida Champion.**

Size:			
	Circumference:	109	inches
	Height:	30	feet
	Crown spread:	48.5	feet
	Total points:	151	points

Owner / location: Lignumvitae Key State Botanical Site / Lignumvitae Key, Monroe Co. [n.w. 1/4 of sec 2, T64S, R36E]

Nominator(s) / date: David M. Sinclair, Michael J. Cullen / 1986

Update: Robert Rose / 1993

Comments: Tree was uprooted by Hurricane Donna, 1960, but was tipped back up, and continues to grow (D. M. Sinclair, Apr 1986). Earlier measurements: circ. = 105 in., ht. = 30 ft., spread = 48.5 ft. (Sinclair & Cullen, 1986); height & spread were not remea-

sured (R. Rose, Jan 1993).

Champion trees of this species are not recorded by American Forests (1996 listing).

Grevillea robusta A. Cunn.
Silk Oak

(1)

☆ **Florida Champion.**

Size:			
	Circumference:	109	inches
	Height:	76	feet
	Crown spread:	40	feet
	Total points:	195	points

Owner / location: Doris Vaughan / 4155 Ft. Denaud Rd. (Fla. 78A), 0.5 mi. e. of Ft. Denaud bridge, 4 mi. w.s.w. of LaBelle, Hendry Co. [s.e. 1/4 of sec 10, T43S, R28E]

Nominator(s) / date: Chris J. Anderson / 1994

Comments: Champion trees of this species are not recorded by American Forests (1996 listing).

Hibiscus tiliaceus L.
Mahoe, Sea Hibiscus

(1)

★ **National Champion.**

Size:			
	Circumference:	102	inches
	Height:	50	feet
	Crown spread:	74	feet
	Total points:	171	points

Owner / location: Boca Raton Garden Club, Inc. / 4281 N.W. 3rd Ave., Boca Raton, Palm Beach Co. [n.e. 1/4 of sec 7, T47S, R43E]

Nominator(s) / date: Evelyn Somerville / 1991

Comments: Acknowledged by American Forests (1996 listing).

Although this species was apparently known in South Florida (Key West) prior to 1860, it is native to tropical Asia. A closely related species native to the West Indies (*H. pernambucensis* Arruda) is also probably native to Florida, but does not reach tree size.

Hura crepitans L.
Sandbox-tree

(1)

☆ **Florida Champion.**

Size:			
	Circumference:	156	inches
	Height:	107	feet
	Crown spread:	83.5	feet
	Total points:	284	points

Owner / location: Flamingo Tropical Gardens / 3750
Flamingo Rd. (Fla. 823), Ft. Lauderdale, Broward
Co. [sec 25, T50S, R40E]

Nominator(s) / date: Terry Wolfe / 1983

Update: Frank L. Zickar, David Bar-Zvi / 1993

Comments: Earlier measurements: circ. = 148 in., ht. =
80 ft., spread = 91 ft. (Wolfe, 1983).

Champion trees of this species are not recorded by
American Forests (1996 listing).

Ilex attenuata Ashe
= *Ilex opaca* Ait. x *Ilex cassine* L.
East Palatka Holly

(1)

☆ **Florida Champion.**

Size:	Circumference:	58	inches
	Height:	40	feet
	Crown spread:	28	feet
	Total points:	105	points

Owner / location: Myrtle Ripley / 3419 S. Crystal Lake
Dr., Orlando, Orange Co. [s.w. 1/4 of sec 8, T23S,
R30E]

Nominator(s) / date: Steve Ripley, Tom Donohoe / 1992

Comments: Tree was planted about 1965 (T. Donohoe,
Apr 1992).

Champion trees of this species are not recorded by
American Forests (1996 listing).

(2)

Florida Challenger.

Size:	Circumference:	48	inches
	Height:	46	feet
	Crown spread:	24	feet
	Total points:	100	points

Owner / location: Ravine State Gardens / Twigg St.,
Palatka, Putnam Co. [s.e. 1/4 of sec 12, T10S,
R26E]

Nominator(s) / date: Ned D. Neenan / 1993

(3)

Honorable Mention.

Size:	Circumference:	41	inches
	Height:	45	feet
	Crown spread:	31	feet
	Total points:	94	points

Owner / location: Mrs. William M. Hood / 12535 Hood
Landing Rd., Jacksonville, Duval Co. [sec 21, T4S,
R27E]

Nominator(s) / date: Richard W. Gorden / 1986

(4)

Honorable Mention.

Size:	Circumference:	46	inches
	Height:	31	feet
	Crown spread:	24.5	feet
	Total points:	83	points

Owner / location: Univ. of Florida / n.w. corner of Murphree Hall, campus, Gainesville, Alachua Co. [s.w.
1/4 of sec 6, T10S, R20E]

Nominator(s) / date: Michael J. Bordyn / 1980

Update: Robert T. Ing, Daniel B. Ward / 1993

Comments: Earlier measurements: circ. = 38 in., ht. =
32 ft., spread = 25 ft. (Bordyn, 1980).

Ilex rotunda Thunb.
Round Holly

(1)

☆ **Florida Champion.**

Size:	Circumference:	51	inches
	Height:	37	feet
	Crown spread:	31.5	feet
	Total points:	96	points

Owner / location: Univ. of Florida / n.e. corner of Mc-
Carty Hall, campus, Gainesville, Alachua Co. [s.e.
1/4 of sec 6, T10S, R20E]

Nominator(s) / date: Michael J. Bordyn / 1980

Update: Robert T. Ing, Daniel B. Ward / 1991

Comments: Tree was planted in 1954. Earlier measurements: circ. = 41 in., ht. = 33 ft., spread = 29.5 ft.
(Bordyn, 1980).

Champion trees of this species are not recorded by
American Forests (1996 listing).

Jacaranda cuspidifolia Mart.
= *Jacaranda acutifolia*, misapplied
Jacaranda

(1)

☆ **Florida Champion.**

Size:	Circumference:	97	inches
	Height:	66	feet
	Crown spread:	74	feet
	Total points:	182	points

Owner / location: Doris Vaughan / 4155 Ft. Denaud Rd.
(Fla. 78A), 0.5 mi. e. of Ft. Denaud bridge, 4 mi.
w.s.w. of LaBelle, Hendry Co. [s.e. 1/4 of sec 10,
T43S, R28E]

Nominator(s) / date: Chris J. Anderson / 1994

Comments: Champion trees of this species are not
recorded by American Forests (1996 listing).

Florida Challenger. (2)

Size:	Circumference:	74	inches
	Height:	58	feet
	Crown spread:	61.5	feet
	Total points:	147	points

Owner / location: Leonard Rosenthal / 16 N. Lincoln Ave., Lehigh Acres, Lee Co. [s.w. 1/4 of sec 33, T44S, R27E]

Nominator(s) / date: Jeffrey S. Mangun / 1992

Khaya nyasica Baker f.
Nyasaland Mahogany, African Mahogany

☆ **Florida Champion.** (1)

Size:	Circumference:	252	inches
	Height:	98	feet
	Crown spread:	112	feet
	Total points:	378	points

Owner / location: IFAS Experiment Station / U.S. 441, 3 mi. s.e. of Belle Glade, Palm Beach Co. [sec 3, T44S, R37E]

Nominator(s) / date: Joseph R. Orsenigo / 1973

Update: Joseph R. Orsenigo / 1981

Update: Michael J. Greenstein / 1993

Comments: Tree is reported to have been transplanted from a "wild site" in the Florida Keys in the early 1930s (J. R. Orsenigo, May 1973). Earlier measurements: circ. = 181 in., ht. = 75 ft., spread = 75 ft. (Orsenigo, 1973); circ. = 215 in., ht. = 94 ft., spread = 88 ft. (Orsenigo, 1981).

Champion trees of this species are not recorded by American Forests (1996 listing).

Khaya senegalensis (Desr.) A. Juss.
Senegal Mahogany, African Mahogany

☆ **Florida Champion.** (1)

Size:	Circumference:	120	inches
	Height:	70	feet
	Crown spread:	85	feet
	Total points:	211	points

Owner / location: Kevin High / 2300 North Rd., Naples, Collier Co. [n.e. 1/4 of sec 2, T50S, R25E]

Nominator(s) / date: Chris J. Anderson / 1994

Comments: Tree is reported to have been planted about 1950 (C. J. Anderson, June 1994).

The distinctions between this species and *K. nyasica* are not clearly understood in Florida. It is possible that only a single species of *Khaya* is in cultivation within the state.

Champion trees of this species are not recorded by American Forests (1996 listing).

Kigelia africana (Lam.) Benth.
= *Kigelia pinnata* (Jacq.) DC.
Sausage-tree

☆ **Florida Champion.** (1)

Size:	Circumference:	170	inches
	Height:	49	feet
	Crown spread:	62	feet
	Total points:	235	points

Owner / location: Ann Fields / 325 Palmetto Dr., Miami Springs, Dade Co. [s.e. 1/4 of sec 19, T53S, R41E]

Nominator(s) / date: Bruce Walton / 1981

Update: Roger L. Hammer, Daniel B. Ward / 1994

Comments: Earlier measurements: circ. = 168 in., ht. = 49 ft., spread = 63 ft. (Walton, 1981).

Champion trees of this species are not recorded by American Forests (1996 listing).

Emeritus Florida Champion. (2)

Size:	Circumference:	125	inches
	Height:	50	feet
	Crown spread:	74	feet
	Total points:	194	points

Owner / location: City of Ft. Myers / Thomas Edison home, 2350 McGregor Blvd., Ft. Myers, Lee Co. [center of sec 23, T44S, R24E]

Nominator(s) / date: Eric H. Hoyer, Tim Eckert / 1980

Update: Jeffrey S. Mangun, Chris J. Anderson / 1994

Comments: Earlier measurements: circ. = 106 in., ht. = 46 ft., spread = 53 ft. (Hoyer & Eckert, 1980). Tree suffered freeze damage in 1989, now largely recovered (R. W. Workman, June 1993).

Koelreuteria elegans (Seem.) A. C. Sm.
= *Koelreuteria formosana* Hayata
Golden-rain-tree

☆ **Florida Champion.** (1)

Size:	Circumference:	77	inches
	Height:	47	feet
	Crown spread:	44	feet
	Total points:	135	points

Owner / location: Forrest F. Lisle / 1920 N.W. 8th Ave., Gainesville, Alachua Co. [s.w. 1/4 of sec 31, T9S, R20E]

Nominator(s) / date: Robert T. Ing, Daniel B. Ward / 1991

Comments: Champion trees of this species are not recorded by American Forests (1996 listing).

(2)

Florida Challenger.

Size:	Circumference:	73	inches
	Height:	40	feet
	Crown spread:	53.5	feet
	Total points:	126	points

Owner / location: Robert Rice / 1214 Newmarket Rd., Immokalee, Collier Co. [n.w. 1/4 of sec 33, T46S, R29E]

Nominator(s) / date: Chris J. Anderson / 1994

(3)

Honorable Mention.

Size:	Circumference:	54	inches
	Height:	47	feet
	Crown spread:	41	feet
	Total points:	111	points

Owner / location: Marilyn Mesh / 1704 N.W. 10th Ave., Gainesville, Alachua Co. [s.e. 1/4 of sec 31, T9S, R20E]

Nominator(s) / date: Robert T. Ing, Daniel B. Ward / 1991

(4)

Emeritus Florida Champion.

Size:	Circumference:	54	inches
	Height:	32.5	feet
	Crown spread:	32.5	feet
	Total points:	95	points

Owner / location: Univ. of Florida / s.w. of McCarty Hall, campus, Gainesville, Alachua Co. [s.e. 1/4 of sec 6, T10S, R20E]

Nominator(s) / date: Michael J. Bordyn / 1980

Update: Robert T. Ing, Daniel B. Ward / 1991

Comments: Tree was originally reported (Bordyn, 1980) as circ. = 102 in., ht. = 31 ft., spread = 45.5 ft., and 144 points. The tree, however, forks repeatedly just above the base, and the original circumference was measured below the lowest fork (now 116 in. at 12 in. above ground), rather than on the largest branch (as was done above).

Tree is now in decline, with dead branches (not measured) extending beyond live ones (R. T. Ing & D. B. Ward, Sept 1992).

Lagerstroemia indica L.
Crape Myrtle

(1)

☆ Florida Champion.

Size:	Circumference:	64	inches
	Height:	45	feet
	Crown spread:	27	feet
	Total points:	116	points

Owner / location: Virginia C. Blinn / 5733 5th St., McIntosh, Marion Co. [s.w. 1/4 of sec 16, T12S, R21E]

Nominator(s) / date: Virginia C. Blinn / 1984

Update: Noel R. Lake, Daniel B. Ward / 1994

Comments: Earlier measurements: circ. = 61 in., ht. = 52 ft., spread = 40 ft. (Blinn, 1984).

Champion trees of this species are not recorded by American Forests (1996 listing).

(2)

Emeritus Florida Champion.

Size:	Circumference:	39	inches
	Height:	49	feet
	Crown spread:	46.5	feet
	Total points:	100	points

Owner / location: John A. Williams / 329 S. Bonita Ave., Panama City, Bay Co. [e. 1/2 of sec 9, T4S, R14W]

Nominator(s) / date: John A. Williams / 1980

Update: Geoffrey A. Cummings, John A. Williams / 1994

Comments: Earlier measurements: circ. = 62 in. (below low fork; 87 in. in 1994), ht. = 32 ft., spread = 50 ft. (Williams, 1980).

Lagerstroemia speciosa (L.) Pers.
Queen Crape Myrtle

(1)

☆ Florida Champion.

Size:	Circumference:	46	inches
	Height:	40	feet
	Crown spread:	39	feet
	Total points:	96	points

Owner / location: Ft. Myers Golf Course / e. side of McGregor Blvd., Ft. Myers, Lee Co. [s. 1/2 of sec 26, T44S, R24E]

Nominator(s) / date: Eric H. Hoyer, Patrick T. Fennimore / 1981

Update: Chris J. Anderson / 1994

Comments: Earlier measurements: circ. = 88 in. (below low fork), ht. = 31 ft., spread = 44.5 ft. (Hoyer & Fennimore, 1981).

Champion trees of this species are not recorded by American Forests (1996 listing).

Ligustrum lucidum Ait. f.
Tree Privet

(1)

☆ Florida Champion.

Size:	Circumference:	73	inches
	Height:	54	feet
	Crown spread:	28	feet
	Total points:	134	points

Owner / location: Univ. of Florida / Yulee Hall, campus, Gainesville, Alachua Co. [s.e. 1/4 of sec 6, T10S, R20E]

Nominator(s) / date: Michael J. Bordyn / 1980

Update: Robert T. Ing, Daniel B. Ward / 1991

Comments: Earlier measurements: circ. = 64 in., ht. = 44 ft., spread = 29.5 ft. (Bordyn, 1980).

Champion trees of this species are not recorded by American Forests (1996 listing).

Liquidambar formosana Hance
Formosa Sweet Gum

(1)

☆ **Florida Champion.**

Size:			
	Circumference:	61.5	inches
	Height:	51	feet
	Crown spread:	34	feet
	Total points:	121	points

Owner / location: Marshall A. Raff / 2202 N.W. 12th St., Gainesville, Alachua Co. [n.w. 1/4 of sec 32, T9S, R20E]

Nominator(s) / date: Robert T. Ing, Daniel B. Ward / 1992

Comments: Champion trees of this species are not recorded by American Forests (1996 listing).

Maclura pomifera (Raf.) Schneid.
Osage Orange

(1)

Florida Champion.

Size:			
	Circumference:	90	inches
	Height:	62	feet
	Crown spread:	58.5	feet
	Total points:	167	points

Owner / location: (unknown) / n. of Eestaullkee St., between Ogeohee St. & Division St., Micanopy, Alachua Co. [sec 26, T11S, R20E]

Nominator(s) / date: Michael J. Bordyn / 1982

Update: Robert T. Ing, Daniel B. Ward / 1991

Comments: Earlier measurements: circ. = 79 in., ht. = 52 ft., spread = 50 ft. (Bordyn, 1982).

National champion: Virginia (402 points).

Mammea americana L.
Mamey, Mammee Apple

(1)

☆ **Florida Champion.**

Size:			
	Circumference:	102	inches
	Height:	50	feet
	Crown spread:	63	feet
	Total points:	168	points

Owner / location: City of Key West / Firestation #3, Grinnell St. & Virginia St., Key West, Monroe Co. [s.e. 1/4 of sec 6, T68S, R25E]

Nominator(s) / date: Janet Bunch, Michael D. Brady / 1986

Update: Oneri Fleita / 1993

Comments: Earlier measurements: circ. = 96 in., ht. = 54 ft., spread = 49 ft. (Bunch & Brady, 1986).

Champion trees of this species are not recorded by American Forests (1996 listing).

Mangifera indica L.
Mango

(1)

☆ **Florida Champion.**

Size:			
	Circumference:	140	inches
	Height:	72	feet
	Crown spread:	57	feet
	Total points:	226	points

Owner / location: Gary W. Sweetman / 2019 W. Manatee Ave., Bradenton, Manatee Co. [s.e. 1/4 of sec 27, T34S, R17E]

Nominator(s) / date: Robert T. Ing, Daniel B. Ward / 1994

Comments: National champion: Hawaii (463 points).

(2)

Florida Challenger.

Size:			
	Circumference:	132	inches
	Height:	49	feet
	Crown spread:	48	feet
	Total points:	193	points

Owner / location: June Linzalone / Corkscrew Rd. (Fla. 850), 0.6 mi. e. of Koreshan State Historic Park, Lee Co. [n.w. 1/4 of sec 34, T46S, R25E]

Nominator(s) / date: Chris J. Anderson / 1994

(3)

Honorable Mention.

Size:			
	Circumference:	112	inches
	Height:	61	feet
	Crown spread:	45	feet
	Total points:	184	points

Owner / location: Roger Ensley / Corkscrew Rd. (Fla. 850), 0.8 mi. e. of Koreshan State Historic Park, Lee Co. [n.w. 1/4 of sec 34, T46S, R25E]

Nominator(s) / date: Chris J. Anderson / 1994

(4)

Honorable Mention.

Size:			
	Circumference:	73	inches
	Height:	40	feet

Crown spread: 43 feet
Total points: 124 points

Owner / location: Grace E. Clapp / jct. E. Terra Mar Dr. & Lakeview Ave., Pompano Beach, Broward Co. [sec 6, T49S, R43E]

Nominator(s) / date: Grace E. Clapp / 1991

Manilkara zapota (L.) v. Royen
= *Achras zapota* L.
Sapodilla

(1)

★ **National Co-Champion.**

Size:
Circumference:	156	inches
Height:	72	feet
Crown spread:	62	feet
Total points:	244	points

Owner / location: St. Mary's Catholic Church / 1010 Windsor Lane, Key West, Monroe Co. [s.w. 1/4 of sec 1, T68S, R25E]

Nominator(s) / date: William S. Hubard, Beverlee Wang / 1992

Comments: Acknowledged by American Forests (1996 listing).

(2)

★ **National Co-Champion.**

Size:
Circumference:	174	inches
Height:	56	feet
Crown spread:	53	feet
Total points:	243	points

Owner / location: Matheson Preserve / n.e. corner of Perrine Tract, s. of 116th St., Miami, Dade Co. [sec 7, T55S, R41E]

Nominator(s) / date: Alice Cohen, Laymond Hardy, Ron Smith / 1973

Update: William G. Miller, Roger L. Hammer, Laura Flynn / 1993

Comments: Earlier measurements: circ. = 99 in., ht. = 50 ft., spread = 29 ft. (Cohen, Hardy & Smith, 1973). Acknowledged by American Forests (1996 listing).

Melaleuca quinquenervia
(Cav.) S. T. Blake
= *Melaleuca leucadendron*, misapplied
Cajeput, Punk-tree

(1)

★ **National Champion.**

Size:
Circumference:	231	inches
Height:	62	feet
Crown spread:	28.5	feet
Total points:	300	points

Owner / location: Jane Womack / between Ft. Denaud Rd. (Fla. 78A) and Caloosahatchee River, 0.5 mi. e.

of Ft. Denaud bridge, 4 mi. w.s.w of LaBelle, Hendry Co. [s.e. 1/4 of sec 10, T43S, R28E]

Nominator(s) / date: Jeffrey S. Mangun / 1992

Comments: A destructively invasive species of the Florida Everglades and adjacent areas.

Acknowledged by American Forests (1996 listing).

(2)

Emeritus National Champion.

Size:
Circumference:	201	inches
Height:	62	feet
Crown spread:	53.5	feet
Total points:	276	points

Owner / location: Ellen Zatarain / 1136 E. Tyler St., Hollywood, Broward Co. [n.w. 1/4 of sec 14, T51S, R42E]

Nominator(s) / date: David A. Spicer / 1991

Comments: A somewhat uncertain record since the 1990 National champion (Trickel, 1983—also from Davie, Broward Co., Fla.) is a well-known tree and it seems unlikely an even larger one would be growing nearby without recognition.

(3)

Emeritus National Champion.

Size:
Circumference:	182	inches
Height:	74	feet
Crown spread:	43	feet
Total points:	267	points

Owner / location: City of Davie / Lange Park, corner of S.W. 65th Ave. & 47th St., s.e. Davie, Broward Co. [n.e. 1/4 of sec 34, T50S, R41E]

Nominator(s) / date: Robert Trickel / 1983

Update: Frank L. Zickar / 1994

Comments: Earlier measurements: circ. = 168 in., ht. = 83 ft., spread = 42 ft. (Trickel, 1983).

Tree is locally believed to be the original *Melaleuca* planted in South Florida.

(4)

Honorable Mention.

Size:
Circumference:	132	inches
Height:	81	feet
Crown spread:	42	feet
Total points:	224	points

Owner / location: Flamingo Tropical Gardens / 3750 Flamingo Rd. (Fla. 823), Ft. Lauderdale, Broward Co. [sec 25, T50S, R40E]

Nominator(s) / date: Jonathan Iles, Lillian Millman / 1983

Update: Jim Higgins / 1995

Comments: Earlier measurements: circ. = 128 in., ht. = 76 ft., spread = 34 ft. (Iles & Millman, 1983).

Melia azedarach L.
Chinaberry

(1)

☆ **Florida Champion.**

Size:			
	Circumference:	113	inches
	Height:	43	feet
	Crown spread:	31	feet
	Total points:	184	points

Owner / location: P. & G. Cellulose, Inc. / n. side of U.S. 27, 4 mi. s.e. of Perry, Taylor Co. [n.e. 1/4 of sec 3, T5S, R8E]

Nominator(s) / date: Jerry N. Livingston / 1993

Comments: National champion: Hawaii (321 points).

(2)

Florida Challenger.

Size:			
	Circumference:	90	inches
	Height:	63	feet
	Crown spread:	62	feet
	Total points:	168	points

Owner / location: Richard Sobel / 721 Terrace Blvd., Orlando, Orange Co. [sec 24, T22S, R29E]

Nominator(s) / date: John Springer / 1988

(3)

Florida Challenger.

Size:			
	Circumference:	93	inches
	Height:	61	feet
	Crown spread:	45	feet
	Total points:	165	points

Owner / location: Linda Paul / off Coral Farms Rd., Florahome, Putnam Co. [sec 34, T8S, R24E]

Nominator(s) / date: Linda Paul / 1989

(4)

Honorable Mention.

Size:			
	Circumference:	82	inches
	Height:	49	feet
	Crown spread:	40	feet
	Total points:	141	points

Owner / location: Cellon Oak Park / 0.2 mi. w. of Fla. 121, 3 mi. s. of LaCrosse, Alachua Co. [n.w. 1/4 of sec 11, T8S, R19E]

Nominator(s) / date: Robert T. Ing, Daniel B. Ward / 1993

(5)

Honorable Mention.

Size:			
	Circumference:	72	inches
	Height:	60	feet
	Crown spread:	22.5	feet
	Total points:	138	points

Owner / location: John H. Phipps / Ayavalla Plantation, Old Bainbridge Rd. (Fla. 157), 8 mi. n.w. of Tallahassee, Leon Co. [sec 29, T2N, R1W]

Nominator(s) / date: Malcolm B. Johnson / 1967

Update: Albert P. Simmons / 1988

Comments: Earlier measurements: circ. = 136 in. (incl. 2nd trunk), ht. = 60 ft., spread = 53.5 ft. (Johnson, 1967).

(6)

Emeritus Florida Champion.

Size:			
	Circumference:	74	inches
	Height:	45	feet
	Crown spread:	53	feet
	Total points:	132	points

Owner / location: Mildred Thomas / jct. S.W 4th St. & S.W. 4th Ave., High Springs, Alachua Co. [sec 3, T8S, R17E]

Nominator(s) / date: Michael J. Bordyn / 1981

Update: Robert T. Ing, Daniel B. Ward / 1991

Comments: Earlier measurements: circ. = 64 in., ht. = 42 ft., spread = 52 ft. (Bordyn, 1981).

Metasequoia glyptostroboides
H. Hu & Cheng
Dawn Redwood

(1)

☆ **Florida Champion.**

Size:			
	Circumference:	45	inches
	Height:	77	feet
	Crown spread:	30	feet
	Total points:	130	points

Owner / location: Robert K. Godfrey / 2021 Chuli Nene, Tallahassee, Leon Co. [s.w. 1/4 of sec 5, T1S, R1E]

Nominator(s) / date: Daniel B. Ward / 1994

Comments: *Metasequoia* was described in 1941 from fossil material collected in China, and was assumed at that time to represent an extinct genus. Four years later living plants were found, to 115 ft. height with trunks to 284 in. circumference (Merrill, 1948). Viable seeds reached the Arnold Arboretum, Mass., in 1948 and were provided in bulk to the National Arboretum, Washington, D.C., for growth and distribution (P. DelTredici, Nov 1994). The present tree was obtained about 1958 as a seedling from the National Arboretum (R. K. Godfrey, Mar 1994).

Champion trees of this species are not recorded by American Forests (1996 listing).

(2)

Florida Challenger.

Size:			
	Circumference:	33	inches
	Height:	54	feet
	Crown spread:	22	feet
	Total points:	92	points

Owner / location: Nellie Shattuck / s. of Fla. 20, 1 mi. e. of Bristol, Liberty Co. [n.w. 1/4 of sec 4, T1S, R7W]

Nominator(s) / date: Joey T. Brady, G. Owen House / 1986

Morus alba L.
Silkworm Mulberry, White Mulberry
Title vacant.

Size: Circumference:
             Height:
             Crown spread:
             Total points:

Owner / location:

Nominator(s) / date:

Comments: Florida trees are var. *multicaulis* (Perr.) Loudon, the true silkworm mulberry. In the late eighteenth century this variety was widely grown from the Carolinas to Florida in a futile effort to establish a silk industry.

A tree, now dead, in Eustis, Lake County, was measured in 1980 by Marc Tanner as having circ. = 128 in., ht. = 46 ft., and spread = 77.5 ft.

National champion (var. *alba*): Missouri (369 points).

Orbignya cohune (Mart.) Standl.
= *Attalea cohune* Mart.
Cohune Palm

(1)

☆ **Florida Champion.**

Size:	Circumference:	61	inches
	Height:	54	feet
	Crown spread:	30	feet
	Total points:	123	points

Owner / location: Flamingo Tropical Gardens / 3750 Flamingo Rd. (Fla. 823), Ft. Lauderdale, Broward Co. [sec 25, T50S, R40E]

Nominator(s) / date: David M. Sinclair / 1986

Comments: Champion trees of this species are not recorded by American Forests (1996 listing).

Parkinsonia aculeata L.
Jerusalem-thorn
Title vacant.

Size: Circumference:
             Height:
             Crown spread:
             Total points:

Owner / location:

Nominator(s) / date:

Comments: A tree, now dead, in Bradenton, Manatee County, was measured in 1977 by Steven Spezia and Mike Kuypers with a circ. = 56 in., ht. = 26 ft., and spread = 38 ft.

National champion: Arizona (150 points).

Peltophorum pterocarpum
(DC.) K. Heyne
Yellow Poinciana, Copperpod

(1)

☆ **Florida Champion.**

Size:	Circumference:	201	inches
	Height:	75	feet
	Crown spread:	75	feet
	Total points:	295	points

Owner / location: Flamingo Tropical Gardens / 3750 Flamingo Rd. (Fla. 823), Ft. Lauderdale, Broward Co. [sec 25, T50S, R40E]

Nominator(s) / date: John L. Dudzinsky / 1985

Comments: Champion trees of this species are not recorded by American Forests (1996 listing).

(2)

Florida Challenger.

Size:	Circumference:	132	inches
	Height:	53	feet
	Crown spread:	78	feet
	Total points:	205	points

Owner / location: Viola L. Goldberg / 940 Caloosa Dr., Sarasota, Sarasota Co. [n.e. 1/4 of sec 13, T36S, R17E]

Nominator(s) / date: Lee Barnwell / 1994

(3)

Emeritus Florida Champion.

Size:	Circumference:	111	inches
	Height:	56	feet
	Crown spread:	70	feet
	Total points:	185	points

Owner / location: Thomas Tramnell / 418 Gulf St., Venice, Sarasota Co. [sec 13, T39S, R18E]

Nominator(s) / date: William J. Schilling / 1980

Update: William J. Schilling / 1993

Comments: Earlier measurements: circ. = 66 in., ht. = 49 ft., spread = 53 ft. (Schilling, 1980).

(4)

Emeritus Florida Champion.

Size:	Circumference:	112	inches
	Height:	51	feet
	Crown spread:	47	feet
	Total points:	175	points

Owner / location: Alliance of the Arts / McGregor Blvd. & Colonial Blvd., Ft. Myers, Lee Co. [s.e. 1/4 of sec 34, T44S, R24E]

Nominator(s) / date: Patrick T. Fennimore, Eric H. Hoyer / 1981

Update: Chris J. Anderson / 1994

Comments: Earlier measurements: circ. = 127 in. (measured below low fork), ht. = 48 ft., spread = 52.5 ft. (Fennimore & Hoyer, 1981).

Persea americana Mill.
Avocado, Alligator Pear

(1)

☆ **Florida Champion.**

Size:			
	Circumference:	89	inches
	Height:	40	feet
	Crown spread:	58	feet
	Total points:	144	points

Owner / location: Frank Searle / 23 S.W. 8th St., Hallandale, Broward Co. [s.w. 1/4 of sec 27, T51S, R42E]

Nominator(s) / date: Henry Graham / 1981

Update: Frank L. Zickar / 1994

Comments: Earlier measurements: circ. = 87 in., ht. = 40 ft., spread = 57 ft. (Graham, 1981).

National champion: California (247 points).

Phoenix canariensis Chabaud
Canary Island Date Palm

(1)

☆ **Florida Champion.**

Size:			
	Circumference:	85	inches
	Height:	61	feet
	Crown spread:	26	feet
	Total points:	153	points

Owner / location: Kenneth S. Partin / 1100 Ingleside Ave., Jacksonville, Duval Co. [sec 57, T2S, R26E]

Nominator(s) / date: Kenneth S. Partin / 1981

Update: Robert T. Ing, Daniel B. Ward / 1993

Comments: This tree was designated Florida champion in 1986, then superceded by a larger tree in Lee County (Mangun, 1992 - 178 points), which has since been cut down, restoring this tree to the title. Earlier measurements: circ. = 84 in., ht. = 55 ft., spread = 26 ft. (Partin, 1981).

Champion trees of this species are not recorded by American Forests (1996 listing).

(2)

Emeritus Florida Champion.

Size:			
	Circumference:	85	inches
	Height:	57	feet
	Crown spread:	20	feet
	Total points:	147	points

Owner / location: City of Ft. Lauderdale / Las Olas Circle, e. of Intracoastal Waterway, Ft. Lauderdale, Broward Co. [n.e. 1/4 of sec 12, T50S, R42E]

Nominator(s) / date: John W. Kern / 1988

(3)

Honorable Mention.

Size:			
	Circumference:	73	inches
	Height:	48	feet
	Crown spread:	26	feet
	Total points:	128	points

Owner / location: City of Clewiston / Magnolia St., Clewiston, Hendry Co. [s.e. 1/4 of sec 9, T43S, R34E]

Nominator(s) / date: Chris J. Anderson / 1994

Phyllocarpus septentrionalis J. D. Sm.
Monkey-flower

(1)

☆ **Florida Champion.**

Size:			
	Circumference:	168	inches
	Height:	55	feet
	Crown spread:	49.5	feet
	Total points:	235	points

Owner / location: Shady Oaks Park / s. of Palm Beach Blvd. (Fla. 80), Ft. Myers, Lee Co. [n.e. 1/4 of sec 18, T44S, R25E]

Nominator(s) / date: Eric H. Hoyer, Merlin J. Dixon / 1980

Update: Chris J. Anderson / 1994

Comments: Earlier measurements: circ. = 157 in., ht. = 45 ft., spread = 39 ft. (Hoyer & Dixon, 1980).

Champion trees of this species are not recorded by American Forests (1996 listing).

Pinus strobus L.
White Pine

(1)

☆ **Florida Champion.**

Size:			
	Circumference:	92	inches
	Height:	93	feet
	Crown spread:	46.5	feet
	Total points:	197	points

Owner / location: John E. Roberts / e. of Fla. 71, near center of Greenwood, Jackson Co. [n.w. 1/4 of sec 5, T5N, R9W]

Nominator(s) / date: James A. Potts / 1983

Update: R. Bruce Turnbull / 1994

Comments: Earlier measurements: circ. = 86 in., ht. = 74 ft., spread = 41 ft. (Potts, 1983).

National champions: Michigan, two trees (400 points, 399 points).

Pistacia chinensis Bunge
Chinese Pistachio

(1)

☆ **Florida Champion.**

Size:	Circumference:	60	inches
	Height:	60	feet
	Crown spread:	47.5	feet
	Total points:	132	points

Owner / location: Univ. of Florida / n.w. corner of Mc-Carty Hall, campus, Gainesville, Alachua Co. [s.e. 1/4 of sec 6, T10S, R20E]

Nominator(s) / date: Robert T. Ing, Daniel B. Ward / 1991

Comments: Champion trees of this species are not recorded by American Forests (1996 listing).

Pithecellobium dulce (Roxb.) Benth.
Manila Tamarind, Ape's-earring

(1)

☆ **Florida Champion.**

Size:	Circumference:	188	inches
	Height:	67	feet
	Crown spread:	76	feet
	Total points:	274	points

Owner / location: St. Francis Xavier Church / n.e. of jct. Victoria Ave. & Cleveland Ave. (U.S. 41), Ft. Myers, Lee Co. [n.w. 1/4 of sec 24, T44S, R24E]

Nominator(s) / date: Eric H. Hoyer, Patrick T. Fennimore / 1981

Update: Chris J. Anderson / 1994

Comments: Earlier measurements: circ. = 174 in., ht. = 57 ft., spread = 80 ft. (Hoyer & Fennimore, 1981).

Champion trees of this species are not recorded by American Forests (1996 listing).

Pithecellobium saman (Jacq.) Benth.
= Samanea saman (Jacq.) Merr.
Rain-tree

(1)

☆ **Florida Champion.**

Size:	Circumference:	212	inches
	Height:	74	feet
	Crown spread:	121	feet
	Total points:	316	points

Owner / location: Paul Fitzgerald / Enchanted Place Apartments, 416 S.W. 4th Ave., Ft. Lauderdale, Broward Co. [n.w. 1/4 of sec 10, T50S, R42E]

Nominator(s) / date: Thomas D. Williams / 1982

Update: Frank L. Zickar / 1994

Comments: Earlier measurements: circ. = 187 in., ht. = 76 ft., spread = 112 ft. (Williams, 1983).

Champion trees of this species are not recorded by American Forests (1996 listing).

Platycladus orientalis (L.) Franco
= Thuja orientalis L.
Oriental Arborvitae

(1)

☆ **Florida Champion.**

Size:	Circumference:	39	inches
	Height:	49	feet
	Crown spread:	25.5	feet
	Total points:	94	points

Owner / location: Univ. of Florida / courtyard of Murphree Hall, campus, Gainesville, Alachua Co. [s.w. 1/4 of sec 6, T10S, R20E]

Nominator(s) / date: Michael J. Bordyn / 1980

Update: Robert T. Ing, Daniel B. Ward / 1991

Comments: This tree has a lower point total than indicated by previous records. The trunk forks at 34 in. and original circumference was measured below the fork. Present measurement, at 4.5 ft., is of the largest branch. Earlier measurements: circ. = 65 in., measured below fork (now 67 in.), ht. = 52 ft., spread = 23 ft. (Bordyn, 1980).

National champion: Maryland (123 points).

Podocarpus gracilior Pilg.
Weeping Podocarpus, Fern Podocarpus

(1)

☆ **Florida Champion.**

Size:	Circumference:	144	inches
	Height:	47	feet
	Crown spread:	42	feet
	Total points:	202	points

Owner / location: Jane Parker / 1640 Marlyn Rd., Ft. Myers, Lee Co. [s.e. 1/4 of sec 23, T44S, R24E]

Nominator(s) / date: David A. Fox / 1984

Update: Chris J. Anderson / 1994

Comments: Earlier measurements: circ. = 116 in., ht. = 66 ft., spread = 57.5 ft. (Fox, 1984).

Champion trees of this species are not recorded by American Forests (1996 listing).

(2)

Florida Challenger.

Size:	Circumference:	113	inches
	Height:	63	feet
	Crown spread:	56.5	feet
	Total points:	190	points

Owner / location: Sarasota Garden Club, Inc. / 1131 Boulevard of the Arts, Sarasota, Sarasota Co. [n.e. 1/4 of sec 24, T36S, R17E]

Nominator(s) / date: Lee Barnwell / 1994

Honorable Mention. (3)

Size:			
	Circumference:	124	inches
	Height:	45	feet
	Crown spread:	38	feet
	Total points:	179	points

Owner / location: Calvin C. Wood / 2729 Tangelo Dr., Sarasota, Sarasota Co. [s.e. 1/4 of sec 32, T37S, R18E]

Nominator(s) / date: Lee Barnwell / 1994

Podocarpus macrophyllus
(Thunb.) D. Don
Japanese Yew

☆ **Florida Champion.** (1)

Size:			
	Circumference:	86	inches
	Height:	51	feet
	Crown spread:	33	feet
	Total points:	145	points

Owner / location: Stan Harris / 2010 N.W. 7th Terr., Gainesville, Alachua Co. [n.w. 1/4 of sec 32, T9S, R20E]

Nominator(s) / date: Stan Harris / 1991

Comments: Champion trees of this species are not recorded by American Forests (1996 listing).

Florida Challenger. (2)

Size:			
	Circumference:	52	inches
	Height:	42	feet
	Crown spread:	28	feet
	Total points:	101	points

Owner / location: Ravine State Gardens / Twigg St., Palatka, Putnam Co. [s.e. 1/4 of sec 12, T10S, R26E]

Nominator(s) / date: Bill Korn, Mark Meador / 1983

Update: Ned D. Neenan / 1993

Comments: Earlier measurements: circ. = 94 in. (measured below low fork), ht. = 42 ft., spread = 35 ft. (Korn & Meador, 1983).

Pongamia pinnata (L.) Pierre
Pongam, Poonga Oil-tree

☆ **Florida Champion.** (1)

Size:			
	Circumference:	145	inches
	Height:	56	feet
	Crown spread:	78	feet
	Total points:	221	points

Owner / location: (unknown) / 29 S.W. 10th St., Miami, Dade Co. [n.w. 1/4 of sec 12, T54S, R41E]

Nominator(s) / date: Ron Smith, Albert H. Hetzell, Tom McClean / 1974

Update: William G. Miller, John T. Valenta / 1993

Comments: Earlier measurements: circ. = 116 in., ht. = 47 ft., spread = 68 ft. (Smith, Hetzell, McClean, 1974).

Champion trees of this species are not recorded by American Forests (1996 listing).

Florida Challenger. (2)

Size:			
	Circumference:	30	inches
	Height:	32	feet
	Crown spread:	33	feet
	Total points:	70	points

Owner / location: Key West Botanical Garden Society / Botanical Garden, Stock Island, Monroe Co. [n.e. 1/4 of sec 34, T67S, R25E]

Nominator(s) / date: Janet Bunch, Michael D. Brady / 1986

Pseudobombax ellipticum
(HBK.) Dugand
Shavingbrush-tree, Pachira

☆ **Florida Champion.** (1)

Size:			
	Circumference:	109	inches
	Height:	31	feet
	Crown spread:	67.5	feet
	Total points:	157	points

Owner / location: William S. Jenkins / 612 N.E. 7th Ave., Boynton Beach, Palm Beach Co. [sec 22, T45S, R43E]

Nominator(s) / date: Kevin Hallahan, Michael J. Greenstein / 1992

Comments: Champion trees of this species are not recorded by American Forests (1996 listing).

Pterocarpus indicus Willd.
Burmese Rosewood

☆ **Florida Champion.** (1)

Size:			
	Circumference:	106	inches
	Height:	76	feet
	Crown spread:	83	feet
	Total points:	203	points

Owner / location: Caribbean Gardens, Inc. / 1590 Goodlette Rd., Naples, Collier Co. [s.e. 1/4 of sec 27, T49S, R25E]

Nominator(s) / date: Chris J. Anderson / 1995

Comments: Champion trees of this species are not recorded by American Forests (1996 listing).

(2)

Florida Challenger.

Size:	Circumference:	86	inches
	Height:	55	feet
	Crown spread:	89	feet
	Total points:	163	points

Owner / location: Conservancy, Inc. / 1450 Merrihue Dr., Naples, Collier Co. [n.e. 1/4 of sec 34, T49S, R25E]

Nominator(s) / date: Chris J. Anderson / 1994

Pterospermum acerifolium
(L.) Willd.
Muchukundu, Shingle-tree

(1)

☆ **Florida Champion.**

Size:	Circumference:	40	inches
	Height:	37	feet
	Crown spread:	33	feet
	Total points:	85	points

Owner / location: Nathaniel P. Reed / Bunker Hill Rd., off Gomez Rd., Hobe Sound, Martin Co. [n.e. 1/4 of sec 26, T39S, R42E]

Nominator(s) / date: James D. Brenner / 1983

Update: Dale Armstrong / 1994

Comments: Earlier measurements: circ. = 73 in., ht. = 48 ft., spread = 38 ft. (Brenner, 1983). Much damaged by freeze in 1989, now regrowing (N. P. Reed, Mar 1994).

Champion trees of this species are not recorded by American Forests (1996 listing).

Quercus acutissima Carruth.
Sawtooth Oak

(1)

☆ **Florida Champion.**

Size:	Circumference:	75	inches
	Height:	61	feet
	Crown spread:	63	feet
	Total points:	152	points

Owner / location: Univ. of Florida / n.e. corner of Constans Theatre, campus, Gainesville, Alachua Co. [s.e. 1/4 of sec 6, T10S, R20E]

Nominator(s) / date: Michael J. Bordyn / 1980

Update: Robert T. Ing, Daniel B. Ward / 1991

Comments: Earlier measurements: circ. = 52 in., ht. = 49 ft., spread = 43.5 ft. (Bordyn, 1980).

Champion trees of this species are not recorded by American Forests (1996 listing).

Robinia pseudoacacia L.
Black Locust

(1)

☆ **Florida Champion.**

Size:	Circumference:	67	inches
	Height:	46	feet
	Crown spread:	42	feet
	Total points:	124	points

Owner / location: Alfred C. Reed / 1120 S.W. 9th Rd., Gainesville, Alachua Co. [n.w. 1/4 of sec 8, T10S, R20E]

Nominator(s) / date: Robert W. Simons / 1989

Update: Duane R. Durgee, Chad Reed / 1991

Comments: Earlier measurements: circ. = 56 in., ht. = 50 ft., spread = 31 ft. (Simons, 1989).

National champion: New York (399 points).

Roystonea regia (HBK.) O. F. Cook
Cuban Royal Palm

(1)

☆ **Florida Champion.**

Size:	Circumference:	53	inches
	Height:	80	feet
	Crown spread:	16	feet
	Total points:	137	points

Owner / location: City of Ft. Myers / Henry Ford winter home, 2400 McGregor Blvd., Ft. Myers, Lee Co. [center of sec 23, T44S, R24E]

Nominator(s) / date: Eric H. Hoyer, Patrick T. Fennimore / 1981

Update: Robert T. Ing, Daniel B. Ward / 1994

Comments: Earlier measurements: circ. = 53 in., ht. = 73 ft., spread = 15 ft. (Hoyer & Fennimore, 1981). This tree is true *Roystonea regia*, one of many trees imported by barge from Cuba by Thomas Edison in the 1920s (J. Fennen, July 1993).

Champion trees of this species are not recorded by American Forests (1996 listing).

Sabal causiarum (O. F. Cook) Becc.
Puerto Rican Hat Palm

(1)

☆ **Florida Co-Champion.**

Size:	Circumference:	89	inches
	Height:	43	feet
	Crown spread:	14	feet
	Total points:	136	points

Owner / location: City of Ft. Myers / Thomas Edison home, 2350 McGregor Blvd., Ft. Myers, Lee Co. [center of sec 23, T44S, R24E]

Nominator(s) / date: Robert T. Ing, Daniel B. Ward / 1994

Comments: This tree may have been planted in the 1890s, soon after construction of the adjacent houses.

Champion trees of this species are not recorded by American Forests (1996 listing).

(2)

☆ **Florida Co-Champion**.

Size:			
	Circumference:	84	inches
	Height:	42	feet
	Crown spread:	15	feet
	Total points:	130	points

Owner / location: Univ. of Florida / e. side of McCarty Hall, campus, Gainesville, Alachua Co. [s.e. 1/4 of sec 6, T10S, R20E]

Nominator(s) / date: Robert T. Ing, Daniel B. Ward / 1991

Comments: The last survivor of a small grove of this species planted by H. H. Hume. Date of introduction is unknown; in the 1940s this tree seemed scarcely smaller than at present (N. R. Lake, Apr 1994).

Salix babylonica L.
Weeping Willow

(1)

☆ **Florida Champion**.

Size:			
	Circumference:	84	inches
	Height:	43	feet
	Crown spread:	52	feet
	Total points:	140	points

Owner / location: Chamber of Commerce / 601 E. Howard St., Live Oak, Suwannee Co. [s.w. 1/4 of sec 24, T2S, R13E]

Nominator(s) / date: Robert W. Simons, Gary Appelson / 1993

Comments: National champions: Michigan, two trees (455 points, 453 points).

Sapium sebiferum (L.) Roxb.
Chinese Tallow-tree

(1)

☆ **Florida Champion**.

Size:			
	Circumference:	92	inches
	Height:	51	feet
	Crown spread:	55	feet
	Total points:	157	points

Owner / location: City of St. Petersburg / 4121 N. 2nd Ave., St. Petersburg, Pinellas Co. [n.e. 1/4 of sec 22, T31S, R16E]

Nominator(s) / date: Chris J. Anderson / 1994

Comments: National champion: Texas (213 points).

(2)

Florida Challenger.

Size:			
	Circumference:	87	inches
	Height:	42	feet
	Crown spread:	47	feet
	Total points:	141	points

Owner / location: Nobleton Community Church / Edgewater Ave. & 2nd St., Nobleton, Hernando Co. [w. 1/2 of sec 24, T21S, R20E]

Nominator(s) / date: Duane R. Durgee / 1982

Update: Duane R. Durgee, Daniel B. Ward / 1994

Comments: Earlier measurements: circ. = 68 in., ht. = 37 ft., spread = 43 ft. (Durgee, 1982).

(3)

Honorable Mention.

Size:			
	Circumference:	78	inches
	Height:	50	feet
	Crown spread:	40	feet
	Total points:	138	points

Owner / location: Roy Milliron / w. side of Fla. 360, 2 mi. s. of Madison, Madison Co. [sec 4, T1S, R9E]

Nominator(s) / date: Mike Evans / 1991

(4)

Honorable Mention.

Size:			
	Circumference:	68	inches
	Height:	54	feet
	Crown spread:	42.5	feet
	Total points:	133	points

Owner / location: Dorry Maine / n. side of Yelvington Rd., 1.2 mi. e. of U.S. 17, East Palatka, Putnam Co. [s.e. 1/4 of sec 9, T10S, R27E]

Nominator(s) / date: Ned D. Neenan / 1993

(5)

Emeritus Florida Champion.

Size:			
	Circumference:	40	inches
	Height:	37	feet
	Crown spread:	28.5	feet
	Total points:	84	points

Owner / location: Univ. of Florida / s.w. of Bartram Hall, campus, Gainesville, Alachua Co. [n.e. 1/4 of sec 7, T10S, R20E]

Nominator(s) / date: Michael J. Bordyn / 1981

Update: Robert T. Ing, Daniel B. Ward / 1991

Comments: Earlier measurements: circ. = (48 in., measured below fork; now 52 in.), ht. = 32 ft., spread = 35 ft. (Bordyn, 1981).

Schinus terebinthifolius Raddi
Florida Holly, Brazilian Pepper

(1)

★ **National Champion**.

Size:			
	Circumference:	166	inches
	Height:	35	feet
	Crown spread:	52	feet
	Total points:	214	points

Owner / location: Wilbur L. Martin / 601 S.W. 18th St., Ft. Lauderdale, Broward Co. [s.w. 1/4 of sec 15, T50S, R42E]

Nominator(s) / date: John W. Kern / 1990

Update: Wilbur L. Martin / 1993

Comments: Tree is still alive, but declining; not remeasured (W. L. Martin, June 1993).

Acknowledged by American Forests (1996 listing).

Sequoia sempervirens (D. Don) Endl.
Redwood

(1)

☆ **Florida Champion**.

Size:			
	Circumference:	44	inches
	Height:	60	feet
	Crown spread:	15	feet
	Total points:	108	points

Owner / location: Harold B. Bradley / 27 Linda St., West Pensacola, Escambia Co. [sec 35, T2S, R30W]

Nominator(s) / date: Harold B. Bradley / 1980

Update: Harold B. Bradley, James R. Burkhalter / 1993

Comments: Obtained as a seedling from Mt. Tamalpais State Park, California, in 1958 (H. B. Bradley, Dec 1992). Height measurement is estimated. Earlier measurements: circ. = 33 in., ht. = 31 ft., spread = 16.5 ft. (Bradley, 1980).

National champion: California (1183 points).

Spathodea campanulata Beauv.
African Tulip-tree

(1)

☆ **Florida Champion**.

Size:			
	Circumference:	103	inches
	Height:	59	feet
	Crown spread:	55	feet
	Total points:	176	points

Owner / location: Central Park, Inc. / 1400 Shadowlawn Dr., Naples, Collier Co. [s.e. 1/4 of sec 2, T50S, R25E]

Nominator(s) / date: Chris J. Anderson / 1994

Comments: National champion: Hawaii (274 points).

Spondias cytherea Sonn.
= *Spondias dulcis* Forst. f.
Ambarella, Otaheite Apple

(1)

☆ **Florida Champion**.

Size:			
	Circumference:	57	inches
	Height:	54	feet
	Crown spread:	31.5	feet
	Total points:	119	points

Owner / location: Flamingo Tropical Gardens / 3750 Flamingo Rd. (Fla. 823), Ft. Lauderdale, Broward Co. [sec 25, T50S, R40E]

Nominator(s) / date: John G. Cordy / 1983

Update: Frank L. Zickar, David Bar-Zvi / 1993

Comments: Earlier measurements: circ. = 54 in., ht. = 49 ft., spread = 32 ft. (Cordy, 1983).

Champion trees of this species are not recorded by American Forests (1996 listing)..

Sterculia foetida L.
Indian Almond, Tropical Hazelnut

(1)

☆ **Florida Champion**.

Size:			
	Circumference:	93	inches
	Height:	82	feet
	Crown spread:	51	feet
	Total points:	188	points

Owner / location: Flamingo Tropical Gardens / 3750 Flamingo Rd. (Fla. 823), Ft. Lauderdale, Broward Co. [sec 25, T50S, R40E]

Nominator(s) / date: Terry Wolfe / 1982

Update: Frank L. Zickar, David Bar-Zvi / 1993

Comments: Earlier measurements: circ. = 83 in., ht. = 60 ft., spread = 47.5 ft. (Wolfe, 1982).

Champion trees of this species are not recorded by American Forests (1996 listing).

Swietenia macrophylla King
Honduras Mahogany, Bigleaf Mahogany

(1)

☆ **Florida Champion**.

Size:			
	Circumference:	137	inches
	Height:	100	feet
	Crown spread:	78	feet
	Total points:	257	points

Owner / location: Robert C. Halgrim / 1452 Sandra Dr., Ft. Myers, Lee Co. [s.w. 1/4 of sec 29, T43S, R25E]

Nominator(s) / date: George Krauss / 1974

Update: Robert T. Ing, Daniel B. Ward / 1994

Comments: Tree was planted in 1945 (R. C. Halgrim, July 1994). Earlier measurements: circ. = 78 in., ht. = 80 ft., spread = 44 ft. (Krauss, 1974).

Champion trees of this species are not recorded by American Forests (1996 listing).

Swinglea glutinosa (Blanco) Merr.
Tabog

(1)

☆ **Florida Champion.**

Size:			
	Circumference:	54	inches
	Height:	44	feet
	Crown spread:	45	feet
	Total points:	109	points

Owner / location: Flamingo Tropical Gardens / 3750 Flamingo Rd. (Fla. 823), Ft. Lauderdale, Broward Co. [sec 25, T50S, R40E]

Nominator(s) / date: Jonathan Iles, Lillian Millman / 1983

Update: Frank L. Zickar, David Bar-Zvi / 1993

Comments: Earlier measurements: circ. = 72 in., ht. = 39 ft., spread = 36 ft. (Iles & Millman, 1983).

Champion trees of this species are not recorded by American Forests (1996 listing).

Syzygium cumini (L.) Skeels
Jambolan, Java Plum

(1)

☆ **Florida Champion.**

Size:			
	Circumference:	131	inches
	Height:	68	feet
	Crown spread:	49	feet
	Total points:	211	points

Owner / location: City of Ft. Myers / Thomas Edison home, 2350 McGregor Blvd., Ft. Myers, Lee Co. [center of sec 23, T44S, R24E]

Nominator(s) / date: Eric H. Hoyer, Patrick T. Fennimore / 1981

Update: Chris J. Anderson, Jeffrey S. Mangun / 1994

Comments: Earlier measurements: circ. = 118 in., ht. = 57 ft., spread = 48 ft. (Hoyer & Fennimore, 1981).

Champion trees of this species are not recorded by American Forests (1996 listing).

(2)

Emeritus Florida Champion.

Size:			
	Circumference:	112	inches
	Height:	62	feet

	Crown spread:	64	feet
	Total points:	190	points

Owner / location: Kenwood Elementary School / 9300 S.W. 79th Ave., Miami, Dade Co. [sec 3, T55S, R40E]

Nominator(s) / date: Karen Ross, Michael D. Brady / 1986

(3)

Florida Challenger.

Size:			
	Circumference:	119	inches
	Height:	57	feet
	Crown spread:	49	feet
	Total points:	188	points

Owner / location: First United Methodist Church / 352 W. Arcade Ave., Clewiston, Hendry Co. [sec 9, T43S, R34E]

Nominator(s) / date: Chris J. Anderson, Eric H. Hoyer / 1981

Update: Jeffrey S. Mangun / 1994

Comments: Earlier measurements: circ. = 98 in., ht. = 68 ft., spread = 60 ft. (Anderson & Hoyer, 1981).

Syzygium paniculatum Gaertn.
= Eugenia paniculata (Gaertn.) Britten
Australian Brush Cherry

(1)

☆ **Florida Champion.**

Size:			
	Circumference:	75	inches
	Height:	30	feet
	Crown spread:	31.5	feet
	Total points:	113	points

Owner / location: Ruth Hayworth / 2812 Tallevast Rd., Tallevast, Manatee Co. [n.w. 1/4 of sec 32, T35S, R18E]

Nominator(s) / date: Mark Bakeman / 1981

Update: William J. Schilling / 1994

Comments: Earlier measurements: circ. = 65 in., ht. = 46 ft., spread = 30 ft. (Bakeman, 1981).

Champion trees of this species are not recorded by American Forests (1996 listing).

Tabebuia caraiba (Mart.) Bur.
= Tabebuia argentea (Bur. & K. Schum.) Britt.
Silver Trumpet-tree, Tree-of-gold

(1)

☆ **Florida Champion.**

Size:			
	Circumference:	85	inches
	Height:	35	feet
	Crown spread:	42	feet
	Total points:	131	points

Owner / location: (unknown) / 1305 S.E. 1st St., Ft. Lauderdale, Broward Co. [n.w. 1/4 of sec 11, T50S, R42E]

Nominator(s) / date: John W. Kern / 1992

Comments: Champion trees of this species are not recorded by American Forests (1996 listing).

(2)

Florida Challenger.

Size:			
	Circumference:	78	inches
	Height:	38	feet
	Crown spread:	36.5	feet
	Total points:	125	points

Owner / location: Senior Friendship Center, Inc. / 811 S. 7th Ave., Naples, Collier Co. [s.w. 1/4 of sec 3, T50S, R25E]

Nominator(s) / date: Chris J. Anderson, Terry Fedelem / 1980

Update: Chris J. Anderson, Terry Fedelem / 1992

Comments: Earlier measurements: circ. = 65 in., ht. = 44 ft., spread = 31 ft. (Anderson & Fedelem, 1980).

(3)

Honorable Mention.

Size:			
	Circumference:	71	inches
	Height:	41	feet
	Crown spread:	39	feet
	Total points:	122	points

Owner / location: Linda Emr / 900 Coconut Circle, Naples, Collier Co. [s.w. 1/4 of sec 1, T50S, R25E]

Nominator(s) / date: Chris J. Anderson / 1995

Tabebuia heterophylla (DC.) Britt.
= *Tabebuia pallida* Hort.
Pink Trumpet-tree

(1)

☆ Florida Champion.

Size:			
	Circumference:	79	inches
	Height:	49	feet
	Crown spread:	40	feet
	Total points:	138	points

Owner / location: Edward K. Benson / 1947 N.E. 21st St., Ft. Lauderdale, Broward Co. [s.w. 1/4 of sec 25, T49S, R42E]

Nominator(s) / date: John W. Kern / 1991

Comments: Champion trees of this species are not recorded by American Forests (1996 listing).

Tabebuia rosea (Bertol.) Rose
= *Tabebuia pentaphylla* Hort.
Rosy Trumpet-tree

(1)

☆ Florida Champion.

Size:			
	Circumference:	58	inches
	Height:	71	feet
	Crown spread:	53.5	feet
	Total points:	142	points

Owner / location: Flamingo Tropical Gardens / 3750 Flamingo Rd. (Fla. 823), Ft. Lauderdale, Broward Co. [sec 25, T50S, R40E]

Nominator(s) / date: Terry Wolfe / 1983

Update: Frank L. Zickar, David Bar-Zvi / 1993

Comments: Earlier measurements: circ. = 108 in. (measured at point of abnormal width), ht. = 69 ft., spread = 31 ft. (Wolfe, 1983).

Champion trees of this species are not recorded by American Forests (1996 listing).

Tamarindus indica L.
Tamarind

(1)

★ National Champion.

Size:			
	Circumference:	167	inches
	Height:	75	feet
	Crown spread:	84	feet
	Total points:	263	points

Owner / location: Mary Immaculate School / 700 Truman Ave., Key West, Monroe Co. [s.w. 1/4 of sec 1, T68S, R25E]

Nominator(s) / date: Michael J. Cullen, David M. Sinclair / 1986

Update: William S. Hubard, Beverlee Wang / 1992

Comments: Earlier measurements: circ. = 157 in., ht. = 60 ft., spread = 82 ft. (Cullen & Sinclair, 1986).

Acknowledged by American Forests (1996 listing).

(2)

Emeritus Florida Champion.

Size:			
	Circumference:	95	inches
	Height:	44	feet
	Crown spread:	44	feet
	Total points:	150	points

Owner / location: Koreshan State Historic Park / e. side of park, Estero, Lee Co. [s.e. 1/4 of sec 28, T46S, R25E]

Nominator(s) / date: Eric H. Hoyer, Tim Eckert / 1980

Update: Chris J. Anderson / 1994

Comments: Earlier measurements: circ. = 139 in. (below low fork), ht. = 51 ft., spread = 49 ft. (Hoyer & Eckert, 1980).

Taxodium mucronatum Ten.
Montezuma Cypress

(1)

☆ Florida Champion.

Size:			
	Circumference:	45	inches
	Height:	54	feet
	Crown spread:	32	feet
	Total points:	107	points

Owner / location: Charles March / 641 N.W. 29th St., Wilton Manors, Broward Co. [n.w. 1/4 of sec 27, T49S, R42E]

Nominator(s) / date: Richard Moyroud, Frank L. Zickar / 1995

Comments: Tree was planted in 1952. Foliage is evergreen.

The largest Montezuma cypress, Oaxaca, Mexico, has a height of 40 meters (131 ft.) and a circumference of 42 meters (1653 in.). Its estimated age is 2000 years.

National champion: Texas (375 points).

Terminalia arjuna (Roxb.) Beddome
Arjan

(1)

☆ **Florida Champion.**

Size:			
	Circumference:	149	inches
	Height:	80	feet
	Crown spread:	57	feet
	Total points:	243	points

Owner / location: (unknown) / s.e. corner of Whitehorn Dr. & Pine Ct., Miami Springs, Dade Co. [w. 1/2 of sec 24, T53S, R40E]

Nominator(s) / date: Mary Ann Taylor, Irene Priess / 1990

Comments: Champion trees of this species are not recorded by American Forests (1996 listing).

(2)

Florida Challenger.

Size:			
	Circumference:	60	inches
	Height:	52	feet
	Crown spread:	54	feet
	Total points:	126	points

Owner / location: Key West Botanical Garden Society / Botanical Garden, Stock Island, Monroe Co. [n.e. 1/4 of sec 34, T67S, R25E]

Nominator(s) / date: Janet Bunch, Michael D. Brady / 1986

Terminalia catappa L.
Tropical Almond

(1)

★ **National Champion.**

Size:			
	Circumference:	135	inches
	Height:	61	feet
	Crown spread:	71	feet
	Total points:	214	points

Owner / location: Keys Title and Abstract Co. / Whitehead St. & Angela St., Key West, Monroe Co. [s.w. 1/4 of sec 6, T68S, R25E]

Nominator(s) / date: David M. Sinclair, Michael J. Cullen / 1986

Comments: Acknowledged by American Forests (1996 listing).

Thespesia populnea (L.) Soland.
Seaside Mahoe, Portia-tree

(1)

☆ **Florida Champion.**

Size:			
	Circumference:	55	inches
	Height:	31	feet
	Crown spread:	44	feet
	Total points:	97	points

Owner / location: Key Largo Hammocks State Botanical Site / n. end of Key Largo, Monroe Co. [sec 25, T59S, R40E]

Nominator(s) / date: Jeanne M. Parks / 1989

Comments: National champion: Hawaii (167 points).

Ulmus parvifolia Jacq.
Chinese Elm

(1)

☆ **Florida Champion.**

Size:			
	Circumference:	50	inches
	Height:	38	feet
	Crown spread:	65	feet
	Total points:	104	points

Owner / location: Univ. of Florida / n.e. of library, P. K. Yonge Lab School, 1 mi. s.e. of campus, Gainesville, Alachua Co. [n.w. 1/4 of sec 8, T10S, R20E]

Nominator(s) / date: Duane R. Durgee / 1987

Update: Robert T. Ing, Daniel B. Ward / 1991

Comments: This tree has a lower point total than indicated by previous records. The trunk forks into three near-equal branches at 32 in. Original circumference (74 in.; now 78 in.) was measured below fork. Present measurement, at 4.5 ft., is of largest branch (R. T. Ing & D. B. Ward, Oct 1991).

Champion trees of this species are not recorded by American Forests (1996 listing).

Ulmus pumila L.
Siberian Elm

(1)

☆ **Florida Champion.**

Size:			
	Circumference:	99	inches
	Height:	32	feet

Crown spread: 36.5   feet

Total points: 140   points

Owner / location: Frank Mills / 4025 S.W. 21st St., Gainesville, Alachua Co. [s.w. 1/4 of sec 18, T10S, R20E]

Nominator(s) / date: Robert T. Ing, Daniel B. Ward / 1991

Comments: National champion: Michigan (400 points).

Veitchia winin H. E. Moore
New Hebrides Palm

(1)

☆ **Florida Champion.**

Size:			
	Circumference:	30	inches
	Height:	70	feet
	Crown spread:	15	feet
	Total points:	104	points

Owner / location: Fairchild Tropical Garden / 10901 Old Cutler Rd., Miami, Dade Co. [n.e. 1/4 of sec 7, T55S, R41E]

Nominator(s) / date: Don Evans, Daniel B. Ward / 1995

Comments: Champion trees of this species are not recorded by American Forests (1996 listing).

Washingtonia robusta H. Wendl.
Washington Palm

(1)

☆ **Florida Champion.**

Size:			
	Circumference:	51	inches
	Height:	79	feet
	Crown spread:	8	feet
	Total points:	132	points

Owner / location: Juanita Delgado / lawn of Old Bank building, Everglades City, Collier Co. [sec 14, T53S, R29E]

Nominator(s) / date: Daniel B. Ward / 1996

Comments: The tallest of approximately 30 trees of similar height in the immediate area.

Champion trees of this species are not recorded by American Forests (1996 listing).

(2)

Florida Challenger.

Size:			
	Circumference:	47	inches
	Height:	78	feet
	Crown spread:	9	feet
	Total points:	127	points

Owner / location: City of Clewiston / Magnolia St., Clewiston, Hendry Co. [s.e. 1/4 of sec 9, T43S, R34E]

Nominator(s) / date: Chris J. Anderson / 1994

(3)

Honorable Mention.

Size:			
	Circumference:	35	inches
	Height:	73	feet
	Crown spread:	9	feet
	Total points:	110	points

Owner / location: Koreshan State Historic Park / n. side of park, Estero, Lee Co. [s.w. 1/4 of sec 28, T46S, R25E]

Nominator(s) / date: Eric H. Hoyer, Tim Eckert / 1980

Update: Chris J. Anderson / 1994

Comments: Earlier measurements: circ. = 44 in., ht. = 76 ft., spread = 9 ft. (Hoyer & Eckert, 1980); perhaps not the same tree (C. J. Anderson, June 1994).

Xylosma congestum (Lour.) Merr.
= *Xylosma senticosum* Hance
Xylosma

(1)

☆ **Florida Champion.**

Size:			
	Circumference:	51	inches
	Height:	44	feet
	Crown spread:	52	feet
	Total points:	108	points

Owner / location: Flamingo Tropical Gardens / 3750 Flamingo Rd. (Fla. 823), Ft. Lauderdale, Broward Co. [sec 25, T50S, R40E]

Nominator(s) / date: John G. Cordy / 1983

Update: Frank L. Zickar, David Bar-Zvi / 1993

Comments: Earlier measurements: circ. = 87 in., ht. = 31 ft., spread = 48 ft. (Cordy, 1983).

Champion trees of this species are not recorded by American Forests (1996 listing).

Ziziphus jujuba Mill.
Common Jujube

Title vacant.

Size:			
	Circumference:		
	Height:		
	Crown spread:		
	Total points:		

Owner / location:

Nominator(s) / date:

Comments: This tree is sparingly naturalized in the Florida panhandle. Herbarium records (FLAS, Jan 1955) indicate the species, at Deer Point Lake, Bay County, to reach a height of 15 ft., and near Quincy, Gadsden County, to attain 6 meters.

National champion: Texas (110 points).

Ziziphus mauritiana Lam.
Indian Jujube

(1)

☆ **Florida Champion.**

Size:			
	Circumference:	68	inches
	Height:	43	feet
	Crown spread:	53	feet
	Total points:	124	points

Owner / location: Fairchild Tropical Garden / 10901 Old Cutler Rd., Miami, Dade Co. [n.e. 1/4 of sec 7, T55S, R41E]

Nominator(s) / date: Don Evans, Daniel B. Ward / 1995

Comments: Three trunks, of almost equal size; the largest measured.

Champion trees of this species are not recorded by American Forests (1996 listing).

(2)

Florida Challenger.

Size:			
	Circumference:	52	inches
	Height:	42	feet
	Crown spread:	50.5	feet
	Total points:	107	points

Owner / location: Flamingo Tropical Gardens / 3750 Flamingo Rd. (Fla. 823), Ft. Lauderdale, Broward Co. [sec 25, T50S, R40E]

Nominator(s) / date: Terry Wolfe / 1982

Update: Frank L. Zickar, David Bar-Zvi / 1993

Comments: Earlier measurements: circ. = 74 in., ht. = 25 ft., spread = 55 ft. (Wolfe, 1982).

GIANTS OF YESTERYEAR

The Florida Champion Tree Survey has accumulated records of many trees that were healthy when measured and nominated, but are now dead. Of species native to Florida, nearly fifty of these deceased champions were larger in their standardized measurement than their present-day descendents. While many of these trees only slightly exceeded the current title-holders, a number greatly surpassed any known living representative of their species.

One may judge from the size of these giants of yesteryear the inherent biological potential of the different species. One may also gain a fragmentary but tantalizing image of the magnificent trees that were once common in pioneer Florida.

But one may also gain a degree of insight into the rate with which Florida is losing its old trees. Of the approximately 230 tree species native to Florida for which current data are available, 49 species, or 21 percent, are presently represented by individuals that are smaller than the individuals that exemplified the species in former years. When one considers the very brief span of years over which these data have been recorded, it is apparent that the larger trees, many of them the survivors of pre-settlement times, are vanishing far faster than present rates of growth can restore.

Part I.—**NATIVE TREES**

Aralia spinosa L.
Devil's-walkingstick

Size:			
	Circumference:	24	inches
	Height:	51	feet
	Crown spread:	23	feet
	Total points:	81	points

Owner / location: San Felasco Hammock State Preserve / n. of Fla. 232, 8 mi. n.w. of Gainesville, Alachua Co. [sec 7, T9S, R19E]

Nominator(s) / date: Robert W. Simons / 1982

Comments: Tree had died by 1990 (R. W. Simons, Oct 1991).

Avicennia germinans (L.) L.
= *Avicennia nitida* Jacq.
Black Mangrove

Size:			
	Circumference:	86	inches
	Height:	61	feet
	Crown spread:	41.5	feet
	Total points:	158	points

Owner / location: Everglades National Park / Shark River, Monroe Co. [sec?, T58S, R32E]

Nominator(s) / date: Clifford Shaw, Randy Cooley, Fred Whitehead / 1975

Comments: Exact location of tree is unknown, but all vegetation along river has been much broken down by storms; tree must be presumed dead (J. Ogden, Aug 1993).

Byrsonima lucida (Mill.) DC.
Locust-berry, Byrsonima

Size:			
	Circumference:	62	inches
	Height:	15	feet
	Crown spread:	30	feet
	Total points:	85	points

Owner / location: Lois Kitching / Caribe Lane, Sugarloaf Key, Monroe Co. [center of sec 25, T66S, R27E]

Nominator(s) / date: David M. Sinclair, Michael J. Cullen / 1986

Comments: Tree is no longer present (L. Kitching, July 1993).

Canella winterana (L.) Gaertn.
Wild Cinnamon

Size:			
	Circumference:	25	inches
	Height:	29	feet
	Crown spread:	16	feet
	Total points:	58	points

Owner / location: Biscayne National Monument / s. end of Totten Key, Dade Co. [s.w. 1/4 of sec 21, T58S, R41E]

Nominator(s) / date: Clifford Shaw, Jim Tilmant / 1975

Update: John G. Cordy, Danny Peters / 1983

Comments: Earlier measurements: circ. = 19 in., ht. = 29 ft., spread = 18 ft. (Shaw & Tilmant, 1975). Area was devastated by Hurricane Andrew, 24 Aug 1992; tree is no longer present (J. M. Parks & R. Curry, Nov 1993).

Carya aquatica (Michx. f.) Nutt.
Water Hickory

Size:	Circumference:	266	inches
	Height:	150	feet
	Crown spread:	87	feet
	Total points:	438	points

Owner / location: Carey Yates / Ocheesee Landing, w. bank of Apalachicola River, 10 mi. n.n.e. of Blountstown, Calhoun Co. [sec 7, T2N, R7W]

Nominator(s) / date: G. Owen House / 1967

Comments: Tree was once a well known riverbank landmark. It was reported blown down in 1984 (G. O. House, June 1984).

Casasia clusiifolia (Jacq.) Urban
= *Genipa clusiifolia* (Jacq.) Griseb.
Seven-year Apple

Size:	Circumference:	11	inches
	Height:	25	feet
	Crown spread:	11	feet
	Total points:	39	points

Owner / location: Biscayne National Monument / Totten Key, Dade Co. [s.w. 1/4 of sec 21, T58S, R41E]

Nominator(s) / date: Clifford Shaw, Jim Tilmant / 1975

Comments: Area was devastated by Hurricane Andrew, 24 Aug 1992; tree is no longer present (J. M. Parks & R. Curry, Nov 1993).

Citharexylum fruticosum L.
Fiddlewood

Size:	Circumference:	46	inches
	Height:	39	feet
	Crown spread:	28.5	feet
	Total points:	92	points

Owner / location: Frank Smathers / 11511 S.W. 57th Ave., Miami, Dade Co. [sec 7, T55S, R41E]

Nominator(s) / date: Crasten Clift / 1981

Comments: Tree was blown down by Hurricane Andrew, Aug 1992 (R. L. Hammer, Dec 1993).

Clusia rosea Jacq.
Balsam Apple

Size:	Circumference:	52	inches
	Height:	27	feet
	Crown spread:	28	feet
	Total points:	86	points

Owner / location: Albert D. Seymour / 119 Martin Ave., Stuart, Martin Co. [n.e. 1/4 of sec 3, T38S, R41E]

Nominator(s) / date: Wayne P. Blythe / 1980

Comments: Tree was killed in 1989 freeze (D. Armstrong, Sept 1993).

Crataegus marshallii Egglest.
Parsley Haw

Size:	Circumference:	16	inches
	Height:	33	feet
	Crown spread:	23	feet
	Total points:	55	points

Owner / location: City of Gainesville / Alfred A. Ring Park, w. bank of Hogtown Creek, between N.W. 16th Ave. & N.W. 23rd Ave., Gainesville, Alachua Co. [n.w. 1/4 of sec 36, T9S, R19E]

Nominator(s) / date: Robert W. Simons / 1973

Comments: Tree is no longer extant (R. W. Simons & D. B. Ward, Oct 1991).

Crataegus michauxii Pers.
= *Crataegus flava*, misapplied
Summer Haw, Yellow Haw

Size:	Circumference:	47	inches
	Height:	30	feet
	Crown spread:	36	feet
	Total points:	86	points

Owner / location: George H. Rowell / w. of Fla. 316, 5 mi. w.s.w. of Williston, Levy Co. [n.e. 1/4 of sec 7, T13S, R18E]

Nominator(s) / date: Buford C. Pruitt, Robert W. Simons / 1983

Comments: Tree is on ground, blown down about March 1993, date of the "Storm of the Century" (R. W. Simons & D. B. Ward, Feb 1994).

Drypetes lateriflora (Sw.) Krug & Urban
Guiana Plum

Size:	Circumference:	23	inches
	Height:	31	feet
	Crown spread:	28	feet
	Total points:	61	points

Owner / location: Snapper Creek Hammock / Coral Gables, Dade Co. [sec 7, T55S, R41E]

Nominator(s) / date: Clifford Shaw / 1975

Update: Albert P. Simmons / 1986

Comments: Tree cannot be located and is presumed dead (R. L. Hammer, Jan 1994).

Exothea paniculata (Juss.) Radlk.
Butterbough, Inkwood

Size:	Circumference:	52	inches
	Height:	45	feet
	Crown spread:	31	feet
	Total points:	105	points

Owner / location: Biscayne National Monument / Totten Key, Dade Co. [s.w. 1/4 of sec 21, T58S, R41E]

Nominator(s) / date: Clifford Shaw, Jim Tilmant / 1975

Comments: Area was devastated by Hurricane Andrew, 24 Aug 1992; tree is no longer present (J. M. Parks & R. Curry, Nov 1993).

Guaiacum sanctum L.
Holywood Lignum-vitae, Roughbark Lignum-vitae

Size:			
	Circumference:	56	inches
	Height:	37	feet
	Crown spread:	26	feet
	Total points:	100	points

Owner / location: Biscayne National Monument / s. end of Totten Key, Dade Co. [s.w. 1/4 of sec 21, T58S, R41E]

Nominator(s) / date: John G. Cordy, Danny Peters / 1983

Comments: Area was devastated by Hurricane Andrew, 24 Aug 1992; tree is no longer present (J. M. Parks & R. Curry, Nov 1993).

Hypelate trifoliata Sw.
White Ironwood

Size:			
	Circumference:	58	inches
	Height:	38	feet
	Crown spread:	35	feet
	Total points:	105	points

Owner / location: Key Largo Hammocks State Botanical Site / n. end of Key Largo, Monroe Co. [sec 24, T59S, R40E]

Nominator(s) / date: Clifford Shaw / 1976
Update: Joseph Nemec, Jeanne M. Parks / 1989

Comments: Earlier measurements: circ. = 41 in., ht. = 25 ft., spread = 24.5 ft. (Shaw, 1976). Tree is dead (J. M. Parks, May 1993).

Ilex cassine L.
Dahoon Holly

Size:			
	Circumference:	34	inches
	Height:	72	feet
	Crown spread:	22	feet
	Total points:	112	points

Owner / location: Osceola Nat. Forest / 15 mi. n.e. of Lake City, Baker Co. [e. 1/2 of sec 27, T1S, R19E]

Nominator(s) / date: Robert W. Simons / 1975

Comments: Some years ago tree was searched for, but could not be found; presumed dead (R. W. Simons, Nov 1993).

Ilex krugiana Loesn.
Krug's Holly, Tawnyberry Holly

Size:			
	Circumference:	40	inches
	Height:	55	feet
	Crown spread:	22	feet
	Total points:	101	points

Owner / location: Camp Owaissa Bauer / 17001 S.W. 264th St., 3 mi. n. of Homestead, Dade Co. [s. 1/2 of sec 30, T56S, R39E]

Nominator(s) / date: Francis Young, Elbert A. Schory / 1968

Update: Albert H. Hetzell, Ron Smith / 1973
Update: American Forests, source unstated / 1991

Comments: Earlier measurements: circ. = 15 in., ht. = 55 ft., spread = 4 ft. (Young & Schory, 1968); circ. = 34 in., ht. = 55 ft., spread = 22 ft. (Hetzell & Smith, 1973). Tree was apparently toppled and killed by Hurricane Andrew, Aug 1992; many seedlings present (C. L. Lippincott, July 1993).

Ilex verticillata (L.) Gray
Winterberry

Size:			
	Circumference:	18	inches
	Height:	26	feet
	Crown spread:	16	feet
	Total points:	48	points

Owner / location: St. Joe Paper Co. / Aspalaga Landing, e. bank of Apalachicola River, 6 mi. s.w. of Chattahoochee, Gadsden Co. [sec 35, T3N, R7W]

Nominator(s) / date: Malcomb B. Johnson, Charles E. Salter / 1967

Comments: This tree has not been seen for many years and is presumed dead (C. E. Salter, May 1995).

Ilex vomitoria Ait.
Yaupon

Size:			
	Circumference:	41	inches
	Height:	49	feet
	Crown spread:	25	feet
	Total points:	96	points

Owner / location: Ravine State Gardens / Twigg St., Palatka, Putnam Co. [s.e. 1/4 of sec 12, T10S, R26E]

Nominator(s) / date: Steven Dale / 1989

Comments: Tree is dead (N. D. Neenan, Aug 1993).

Lyonia ferruginea (Walt.) Nutt.
Rusty Lyonia, Staggerbush, Tree Lyonia

Size:			
	Circumference:	29	inches
	Height:	40	feet
	Crown spread:	21	feet
	Total points:	74	points

Owner / location: Continental Country Club / Orange Home, 3 mi. s.e. of Wildwood, Sumter Co. [s.e. 1/4 of sec 22, T19S, R23E]

Nominator(s) / date: F. C. Hester / 1971

Comments: Tree is dead, though its memory survives; stump was found in rough of golf course, alongside plaque noting the tree's championship status (J. Overby, Aug 1993).

Lysiloma latisiliquum (L.) Benth.
Wild Tamarind, Bahama Lysiloma

Size:			
	Circumference:	96	inches
	Height:	79	feet
	Crown spread:	42	feet
	Total points:	186	points

Owner / location: Castellow Hammock Park / 22430 S.W. 153rd St., Homestead, Dade Co. [n.e. 1/4 of sec 17, T56S, R39E]

Nominator(s) / date: Albert H. Hetzell, Ron Smith / 1973

Comments: Tree was destroyed by Hurricane Andrew, August 1992 (C. L. Lippincott, May 1993).

Magnolia ashei Weatherby
Ashe Magnolia

Size:			
	Circumference:	35	inches
	Height:	53	feet
	Crown spread:	36	feet
	Total points:	97	points

Owner / location: Torreya State Park / 0.5 mi. n. of Fla. 271, e. of Goodson farm, Liberty Co. [n.e. 1/4 of sec 21, T2N, R7W]

Nominator(s) / date: Jerome Bracewell, Angus K. Gholson, Joey T. Brady / 1991

Comments: Tree has recently fallen (R. W. Simons, Dec 1993).

Magnolia grandiflora L.
Southern Magnolia, Bull Bay

Size:			
	Circumference:	189	inches
	Height:	106	feet
	Crown spread:	62	feet
	Total points:	311	points

Owner / location: Wakulla Springs State Park / Wakulla Springs, Wakulla Co. [sec 18, T3S, R1E]

Nominator(s) / date: Barry A. Burch, James R. Karels / 1987

Comments: Tree was badly decayed and broke apart in 1992 (A. Whitehouse, Jan 1994).

Magnolia pyramidata Bartr.
Pyramid Magnolia

Size:			
	Circumference:	47	inches
	Height:	96	feet
	Crown spread:	25	feet
	Total points:	149	points

Owner / location: Torreya State Park / w. of campground, Liberty Co. [n.e. 1/4 of sec 17, T2N, R7W]

Nominator(s) / date: Robert W. Simons / 1980

Comments: No trace of the tree could be found (R. W. Simons, Dec 1993).

Magnolia virginiana L.
Sweetbay

Size:			
	Circumference:	157	inches
	Height:	91	feet
	Crown spread:	46	feet
	Total points:	260	points

Owner / location: St. Joe Paper Co. / 2 mi. e. of Tallahassee, s. of U.S. 27, 300 yds. w. of Southwood Plantations Rd., Leon Co. [s.e. 1/4 of sec 3, T1S, R1E]

Nominator(s) / date: George Apthorp / 1971

Comments: No trace of the tree could be found (R. T. Ing, D. B. Ward & C. E. Salter, Sept 1993).

Malus angustifolia (Ait.) Michx.
Wild Crab Apple

Size:			
	Circumference:	44	inches
	Height:	31	feet
	Crown spread:	33	feet
	Total points:	83	points

Owner / location: Paul C. Wills / foot of Sinclair St., off Meridian Rd., Tallahassee, Leon Co. [s.e. 1/4 of sec 13, T1N, R1W]

Nominator(s) / date: Charles E. Salter / 1967

Comments: Tree died in early 1980s (P. C. Wills, Sept 1993).

Metopium toxiferum (L.) Krug & Urban
Poisonwood, Florida Poisontree

Size:			
	Circumference:	63	inches
	Height:	63	feet
	Crown spread:	72	feet
	Total points:	144	points

Owner / location: Viscaya Museum & Gardens / Miami, Dade Co. [sec 14, T54S, R41E]

Nominator(s) / date: Albert H. Hetzell, Ron Smith / 1973

Update: Albert P. Simmons / 1986

Update: American Forests, source unstated / 1991

Comments: Earlier measurements: circ. = 64 in., ht. = 63 ft., spread = 72 ft. (Hetzell & Smith, 1973). Tree present; not measured (A. P. Simmons, Sept 1986). Tree is no longer present (C. L. Lippincott, July 1993).

Pinckneya bracteata (Bartr.) Raf.
= Pinckneya pubens Michx.
Fever-tree

Size:			
	Circumference:	12	inches
	Height:	32	feet
	Crown spread:	16	feet
	Total points:	48	points

Owner / location: C. G. Money / between Orange Springs Country Inn and Orange Creek, Orange Springs, Marion Co. [n.w. 1/4 of sec 30, T11S, R24E]

Nominator(s) / date: Robert W. Simons, Tom Morris / 1980

Comments: Tree is missing; site of tree is now a recently bulldozed roadway (R. W. Simons & D. B. Ward, Sept 1993).

Pinus clausa (Chapm. ex Engelm.)
Vasey ex Sarg.
Sand Pine

Size:			
	Circumference:	83	inches
	Height:	106	feet
	Crown spread:	37.5	feet
	Total points:	198	points

Owner / location: Starkey Wilderness Park / 6 mi. e. of New Port Richey, 6 mi. s. of Fla. 52, Pasco Co. [n.w. 1/4 of sec 8, T26S, R17E]

Nominator(s) / date: Raymond W. Garcia / 1990

Comments: Tree blew down in "Storm of the Century", March 1993 (R. W. Garcia, Nov 1993).

Pinus elliottii Engelm.
var. **densa** Little & Dorman
South Florida Slash Pine

Size:			
	Circumference:	156	inches
	Height:	64	feet
	Crown spread:	64	feet
	Total points:	236	points

Owner / location: Logan Smith / 4119 Camino Real, Sarasota, Sarasota Co. [sec 6, T37S, R18E]

Nominator(s) / date: Eldredge T. Carnes, Charles Robinson / 1969

Comments: Tree is now dead (W. J. Schilling, Dec 1993). This tree was *Pinus elliottii* var. *densa* (South Florida slash pine). It was the largest that has been recorded for this variety.

Pinus glabra Walt.
Spruce Pine

Size:			
	Circumference:	121	inches
	Height:	143	feet
	Crown spread:	44.5	feet
	Total points:	275	points

Owner / location: Goodwood Plantations / 1633 Physician's Drive, off Centerville Rd., 1/2 mi. n. of jct. with Miccosukee Rd., n.e. Tallahassee, Leon Co. [n.w. 1/4 of sec 29, T1N, R1E]

Nominator(s) / date: Thomas D. Beitzel, Michael Humphrey / 1985

Comments: This tree was measured 12 April 1985. It was Florida champion only until 21 November 1985 when it was downed by Hurricane Kate (A. P. Simmons, Nov 1985).

Pinus palustris Mill.
Longleaf Pine

Size:			
	Circumference:	118	inches
	Height:	88	feet
	Crown spread:	47	feet
	Total points:	218	points

Owner / location: Helen Porter / 8 mi. s.s.w. of Marianna, Jackson Co. [s.e. 1/4 of sec 18, T3N, R10W]

Nominator(s) / date: Robert C. Williams / 1983

Comments: Tree was blown down by Hurricane Kate in Nov 1985 (R. B. Turnbull, May 1994).

Prunus serotina Ehrh.
Black Cherry

Size:			
	Circumference:	192	inches
	Height:	85	feet
	Crown spread:	50	feet
	Total points:	290	points

Owner / location: (unknown) / Sugarfoot Hammock, n.e. of jct. S.W. 20th. Ave. & S.W. 62nd St., Gainesville, Alachua Co. [sec 10, T10S, R19E]

Nominator(s) / date: Michael J. Bordyn, Robert W. Simons / 1980

Comments: Tree is dead. Developer had placed fill over roots; trunk is still standing (R. W. Simons & D. B. Ward, Aug 1991).

Prunus umbellata Ell.
Hog Plum, Flatwoods Plum

Size:			
	Circumference:	40	inches
	Height:	33	feet
	Crown spread:	28	feet
	Total points:	80	points

Owner / location: Florida Audubon Soc. / Colclough Pond Wildlife Sanctuary, between Fla. 329 & Fla. 331, s. edge of Gainesville, Alachua Co. [n.e. 1/4 of sec 17, T10S, R20E]

Nominator(s) / date: Robert W. Simons / 1974

Comments: Tree is long dead (R. W. Simons, June 1991).

Pseudophoenix sargentii
Wendl. ex Sarg.
Buccaneer Palm, Sargent's Cherry Palm

Size:			
	Circumference:	30	inches
	Height:	23	feet
	Crown spread:	10	feet
	Total points:	56	points

Owner / location: Biscayne National Monument / n. portion of Elliott Key, Dade Co. [sec 18, T57S, R42E]

Nominator(s) / date: John G. Gordy, Danny Peters / 1983

Comments: Tree was snapped off by Hurricane Andrew, 24 Aug 1992 (C. L. Lippincott, Nov 1993).

Rhizophora mangle L.
Red Mangrove

Size:			
	Circumference:	77	inches
	Height:	75	feet
	Crown spread:	41	feet
	Total points:	162	points

Owner / location: Everglades National Park / Little Shark River, Monroe Co. [sec?, T59S, R32E]

Nominator(s) / date: Clifford Shaw, Randy Cooley, Fred Whitehead / 1975

Comments: Exact location of tree is unknown, but all vegetation along river has been much broken down by storms; tree must be presumed dead (J. Ogden, Aug 1993).

Rhus copallinum L.
Winged Sumac, Shining Sumac

Size:			
	Circumference:	17	inches
	Height:	44	feet
	Crown spread:	19	feet
	Total points:	66	points

Owner / location: St. Joe Paper Co. / Aspalaga Landing, e. bank of Apalachicola River, 6 mi. s.w. of Chattahoochee, Gadsden Co. [sec 35, T3N, R7W]

Nominator(s) / date: Charles E. Salter / 1967

Comments: Very old record of a short-lived species; presumed dead (dropped from 1986 Florida listing).

Rhus vernix L.
= *Toxicodendron vernix* (L.) Kuntze
Poison Sumac

Size:			
	Circumference:	15	inches
	Height:	24	feet
	Crown spread:	20	feet
	Total points:	44	points

Owner / location: Ravine State Gardens / Twigg St., Palatka, Putnam Co. [s.e. 1/4 of sec 12, T10S, R26E]

Nominator(s) / date: Steven Dale / 1989

Comments: Tree is no longer living (N. D. Neenan, Aug 1993).

Roystonea elata (Bartr.) F. Harper
Florida Royal Palm

Size:			
	Circumference:	78	inches
	Height:	80	feet
	Crown spread:	32	feet
	Total points:	166	points

Owner / location: John Berry / 275 S. Krome Ave., 1 mi. n. of Homestead, Dade Co. [s.w. 1/4 of sec 31, T56S, R39E]

Nominator(s) / date: Albert H. Hetzell, Ron Smith / 1973

Comments: Tree is no longer present (W. G. Miller, Oct 1993).

Sabal palmetto (Walt.) Lodd. ex Schult. & Schult.
Cabbage Palm

Size:			
	Circumference:	45	inches
	Height:	90	feet
	Crown spread:	14	feet
	Total points:	139	points

Owner / location: Highlands Hammock State Park / Highlands Co. [s.e. 1/4 of sec 31, T34S, R28E]

Nominator(s) / date: Harold Nett / 1965

Comments: Few palms in park presently surpass 60 ft. Rangers report tree died some years ago, but until recently a sign marking its location was left in place for tourists who were content to assume one of the numerous smaller palms in the hammock must be the champion (D. B. Ward, Feb 1992).

Salix caroliniana Michx.
Carolina Willow, Coastal Plain Willow

Size:			
	Circumference:	44	inches
	Height:	68	feet

	Crown spread:	28	feet
	Total points:	119	points

Owner / location: San Felasco Hammock State Preserve / n. side of Fla. 232, 8 mi. n.w. of Gainesville, Alachua Co. [sec 37, T9S, R19E]

Nominator(s) / date: Robert W. Simons / 1979

Comments: Tree is now dead (R. W. Simons, May 1991).

Sambucus canadensis L.
= *Sambucus simpsonii* Rehder
Elderberry

Size:			
	Circumference:	34	inches
	Height:	20	feet
	Crown spread:	14	feet
	Total points:	58	points

Owner / location: Lovett E. Williams / 2103 N.W. 40th Terr., Gainesville, Alachua Co. [n.w. 1/4 of sec 35, T9S, R19E]

Nominator(s) / date: Lovett E. Williams / 1970

Comments: Present occupant of house: "Tree has been gone for years" (R. T. Ing & D. B. Ward, Oct 1991).

Symplocos tinctoria (L.) L'Her.
Sweetleaf

Size:			
	Circumference:	47	inches
	Height:	55	feet
	Crown spread:	27	feet
	Total points:	109	points

Owner / location: Waverly Hills, Inc. / 200 ft. e. of Meridian Rd., just n. of Tallahassee city limits, Leon Co. [sec 18, T1N, R1E]

Nominator(s) / date: Malcolm B. Johnson / 1967

Comments: Tree is now only a decayed log lying on ground (R. T. Ing, D. B. Ward & C. E. Salter, Sept 1993).

Tetrazygia bicolor (Mill.) Cogn.
Florida Tetrazygia

Size:			
	Circumference:	16	inches
	Height:	41	feet
	Crown spread:	19	feet
	Total points:	62	points

Owner / location: Castellow Hammock Park / 22430 S.W. 153rd St., Homestead, Dade Co. [n.e. 1/4 of sec 17, T56S, R39E]

Nominator(s) / date: John G. Cordy, Roger L. Hammer / 1982

Comments: Tree was destroyed by Hurricane Andrew, August 1992 (C. L. Lippincott, May 1993).

Tilia caroliniana Mill.
Carolina Basswood

Size:			
	Circumference:	101	inches
	Height:	99	feet

Crown spread:	48	feet	
Total points:	212	points	

Owner / location: Andrews Wildlife Management Area / slope above Suwannee River floodplain, 1.5 mi. s. of Fanning Springs, Levy Co. [n.e. 1/4 of sec 31, T10S, R14E]

Nominator(s) / date: Robert W. Simons, Andy Andrews / 1983

Comments: Tree did not leaf out in spring of 1993 (J. A. King, Feb 1994).

Ulmus americana L.
var. floridana (Chapm.) Little
Florida Elm

Size:	Circumference:	158	inches
Height:		94	feet
Crown spread:		54	feet
Total points:		266	points

Owner / location: San Felasco Hammock State Preserve / n. of Fla. 232, 8 mi. n.w. of Gainesville, Alachua Co. [sec 37, T9S, R19E]

Nominator(s) / date: Robert Dye, Robert W. Simons / 1979
Update: Robert W. Simons / 1982

Comments: Tree was still prosperous in 1982, but later could not be located and is presumed dead (R. W. Simons, Oct 1991).

Viburnum obovatum Walt.
Blackhaw, Walter's Viburnum

Size:	Circumference:	22	inches
Height:		30	feet
Crown spread:		23	feet
Total points:		58	points

Owner / location: San Felasco Hammock State Preserve / n. side of Fla. 232, 8 mi. n.w. of Gainesville, Alachua Co. [sec 37, T8S, R19E]

Nominator(s) / date: Robert W. Simons / 1976
Comments: Tree is no longer present (R. W. Simons & D. B. Ward, Oct 1991).

Ximenia americana L.
Tallow-wood

Size:	Circumference:	16	inches
Height:		25	feet
Crown spread:		20.5	feet
Total points:		46	points

Owner / location: Biscayne National Monument / Totten Key, Dade Co. [s.w. 1/4 of sec 21, T58S, R41E]

Nominator(s) / date: Clifford Shaw, Jim Tilmant / 1975

Comments: Area was devastated by Hurricane Andrew, 24 Aug 1992; tree is no longer present (J. M. Parks & R. Curry, Nov 1993).

Yucca aloifolia L.
Spanish-dagger, Aloe Yucca

Size:	Circumference:	18	inches
Height:		15	feet
Crown spread:		4	feet
Total points:		34	points

Owner / location: Florida Div. of Forestry / Service Office, 5745 S. Florida Ave. (Fla. 37), Lakeland, Polk Co. [w. 1/2 of sec 13, T29S, R23E]

Nominator(s) / date: Eldredge T. Carnes / 1967

Comments: Tree has been gone for many years (C. Colbert, July 1993).

Part II.—NON-NATIVE TREES

Acacia auriculiformis Benth.
Earleaf Acacia

Size:	Circumference:	67	inches
	Height:	56	feet
	Crown spread:	47	feet
	Total points:	135	points

Owner / location: Terry Park / jct. Palm Beach Blvd. (Fla. 80) & Palmetto Ave., Ft. Myers, Lee Co. [s.e. 1/4 of sec 7, T44S, R25E]

Nominator(s) / date: Eric H. Hoyer, Chris J. Anderson / 1982

Comments: Tree was killed in the Christmas freeze of 1989 (J. S. Mangun, Mar 1994).

Acacia richei Gray
= Acacia confusa Merr.
Formosa Acacia

Size:	Circumference:	107	inches
	Height:	55	feet
	Crown spread:	52	feet
	Total points:	175	points

Owner / location: Flamingo Tropical Gardens / 3750 Flamingo Rd. (Fla. 823), Ft. Lauderdale, Broward Co. [sec 25, T50S, R40E]

Nominator(s) / date: Terry Wolfe / 1983

Comments: Tree was badly damaged by Hurricane Andrew (Aug 1992) and later removed (D. Bar-Zvi, Oct 1993).

Albizia julibrissin Durazz.
Mimosa

Size:			
	Circumference:	104	inches
	Height:	56	feet
	Crown spread:	47	feet
	Total points:	172	points

Owner / location: William R. Cessary / 12072 Brady Rd., Jacksonville, Duval Co. [e. 1/4 of sec 35, T4S, R26E]

Nominator(s) / date: David M. Sinclair / 1983

Comments: Original tree is dead, but vigorous off-shoots are springing from roots (R. T. Ing & D. B. Ward, Oct 1993).

Bauhinia variegata L.
Orchid-tree, Mountain Ebony

Size:			
	Circumference:	106	inches
	Height:	46	feet
	Crown spread:	37	feet
	Total points:	161	points

Owner / location: (unknown) / old sugarmill site, 1826 Leffingwell Ave., Ellenton, Manatee Co. [sec 17, T34S, R18E]

Nominator(s) / date: Eldredge T. Carnes / 1967

Comments: Tree is dead (W. J. Schilling, Mar 1994).

Brachychiton acerifolius
(A. Cunn.) F. Muell.
Illawarra Flame-tree, Flame Bottle-tree

Size:			
	Circumference:	52	inches
	Height:	47	feet
	Crown spread:	25.5	feet
	Total points:	105	points

Owner / location: Marie Selby Botanical Gardens / 800 S. Palm Ave., Sarasota, Sarasota Co. [n.w. 1/4 of sec 30, T36S, R18E]

Nominator(s) / date: William J. Schilling / 1980

Comments: Tree is now dead (W. J. Schilling, Dec 1993).

Casuarina cunninghamiana Miq.
Australian Pine

Size:			
	Circumference:	111	inches
	Height:	84	feet
	Crown spread:	40	feet
	Total points:	205	points

Owner / location: (unknown) / Meadows subdivision, Winkler Rd., just n. of jct. with Gladiolus Rd. (Fla. 865), s. Ft. Myers, Lee Co. [sec 27, T45S, R24E]

Nominator(s) / date: Michael W. Kenton / 1972

Comments: Tree is no longer present (R. W. Workman, July 1993).

Cecropia palmata L.
Yagrumo, Trumpet-tree

Size:			
	Circumference:	55	inches
	Height:	57	feet
	Crown spread:	47	feet
	Total points:	124	points

Owner / location: City of Ft. Myers / Thomas Edison home, 2350 McGregor Blvd., Ft. Myers, Lee Co. [center of sec 23, T44S, R24E]

Nominator(s) / date: Vicki King, George Krauss / 1974
Update: Albert P. Simmons / 1975

Comments: Tree was blown over in storm several years ago (R. W. Workman, June 1993).

Citrus paradisi Macf.
Grapefruit

Size:			
	Circumference:	75	inches
	Height:	35	feet
	Crown spread:	42	feet
	Total points:	120	points

Owner / location: George M. Riegler / 22506 Shirley Lane, Land O'Lakes, Pasco Co. [n.w. 1/4 of sec 30, T26S, R19E]

Nominator(s) / date: Edward L. Flowers / 1983

Comments: Tree was killed by freeze in spring 1985 (G. M. Riegler, Apr 1994).

Cordia sebestena L.
Geiger-tree

Size:			
	Circumference:	34	inches
	Height:	26	feet
	Crown spread:	27	feet
	Total points:	67	points

Owner / location: B. Hudson / 1513 Riverside Drive, Stuart, Martin Co. [n.e. 1/4 of sec 3, T38S, R41E]

Nominator(s) / date: Wayne P. Blythe, Ken Ringe / 1980

Comments: Tree was killed in 1989 freeze (D. Armstrong, Sept 1993).

Cupressus arizonica Greene
= Cupressus glabra Hort.
Arizona Cypress

Size:			
	Circumference:	124	inches
	Height:	37	feet
	Crown spread:	38	feet
	Total points:	170	points

Owner / location: Univ. of Florida / old dairy bldg., campus, Gainesville, Alachua Co. [s.e. 1/4 of sec 6, T10S, R20E]

Nominator(s) / date: Michael J. Bordyn / 1980

Comments: Tree was removed in 1987 (A. P. Simmons, Jan 1988).

National champions: Arizona, three trees (345 points, 288 points, 252 points).

Ehretia acuminata R. Br.
Heliotrope-tree

Size:		
Circumference:	76	inches
Height:	33	feet
Crown spread:	42.5	feet
Total points:	120	points

Owner / location: Univ. of Florida / n.w. corner, Museum Rd. & S.W. 13th St., campus, Gainesville, Alachua Co. [s.e. 1/4 of sec 6, T10S, R20E]

Nominator(s) / date: Michael J. Bordyn / 1980

Comments: Tree was frozen to the ground in winter 1990-1991; now re-sprouting (D. B. Ward, June 1991).

Enterolobium cyclocarpum Griseb.
Guanacaste, Ear-tree

Size:		
Circumference:	182	inches
Height:	66	feet
Crown spread:	115	feet
Total points:	275	points

Owner / location: Covenant Presbyterian Church / 2439 McGregor Blvd., Ft. Myers, Lee Co. [sec 23, T44S, R24E]

Nominator(s) / date: William D. Roesch, Chris J. Anderson / 1987

Comments: Tree had significant decay in 1991 and was removed by 1993 (C. J. Anderson, June 1994).

Eucalyptus cinerea Benth.
Silver-dollar Eucalyptus

Size:		
Circumference:	71	inches
Height:	41	feet
Crown spread:	48.5	feet
Total points:	124	points

Owner / location: Chris Regas / 8871 Yorkshire Ct., Jacksonville, Duval Co. [sec 28, T3S, R27E]

Nominator(s) / date: Gary Allen / 1983

Comments: Tree is now gone (R. T. Ing & D. B. Ward, Oct 1993).

Eucalyptus grandis Maiden
Rose Gum

Size:		
Circumference:	170	inches
Height:	74	feet
Crown spread:	79	feet
Total points:	263	points

Owner / location: (unknown) / s. of Fla. 78, w. of railroad, Ortona, 6 mi. n.e. of LaBelle, Glades Co. [sec 22, T42S, R30E]

Nominator(s) / date: Chris J. Anderson, Jerry Aiken / 1980

Comments: Tree died about 1988 (C. J. Anderson, Oct 1993).

Ficus macrophylla Pers.
Moreton Bay Fig

Size:		
Circumference:	131	inches
Height:	88	feet
Crown spread:	112	feet
Total points:	247	points

Owner / location: City of Ft. Myers / Thomas Edison home, 2350 McGregor Blvd., Ft. Myers, Lee Co. [center of sec 23, T44S, R24E]

Nominator(s) / date: Chris J. Anderson, Eric H. Hoyer / 1978

Update: Eric H. Hoyer, Patrick T. Fennimore / 1981

Update: Jeffrey S. Mangun, Chris J. Anderson / 1994

Comments: Earlier measurements: circ. = 176 in., ht. = 88 ft., spread = 84 ft. (Anderson & Hoyer, 1978); circ. = 191 in. (measured at 7 ft.), ht. = 86 ft., spread = 87 ft. (Hoyer & Fennimore, 1981). In 1994, tree was measured at 10.5 ft.; buttresses at base are flange-like, above 7 ft. in height, and extend nearly horizontally from the trunk, making measurements meaningless at 4.5 ft. Tree was badly damaged by loss of large limb in Nov 1994, with remaining limbs and trunk removed for reasons of safety in May 1996 (M. P. Carroll, June 1996).

Firmiana simplex (L.) Wight
Chinese Parasol-tree

Size:		
Circumference:	48	inches
Height:	33	feet
Crown spread:	17	feet
Total points:	85	points

Owner / location: Univ. of Florida / along Stadium Rd., n. side of Music Bldg., campus, Gainesville, Alachua Co. [s.e. 1/4 of sec 6, T10S, R20E]

Nominator(s) / date: Michael J. Bordyn / 1980

Update: Robert T. Ing, Daniel B. Ward / 1991

Comments: Earlier measurements: circ. = 40 in., ht. = 39 ft., spread = 23.5 ft. (Bordyn, 1980). Tree was removed Dec 1991 to improve access to loading dock.

Grevillea robusta A. Cunn.
Silk Oak

Size:		
Circumference:	143	inches
Height:	81	feet
Crown spread:	52	feet
Total points:	237	points

Owner / location: (unknown) / Ft. Denaud Rd. (Fla. 78A), 1 mi. e. of Ft. Denaud Rd., 3 mi. w.s.w. of LaBelle, Hendry Co. [s.w. 1/4 of sec 10, T43S, R28E]

Nominator(s) / date: Michael W. Kenton / 1972

Update: Albert P. Simmons / 1975

Comments: One of five champion-sized trees in a row, all in good shape; not remeasured (A. P. Simmons, June 1975). Five large dead trees along s. side of road (C. J. Anderson, Mar 1994).

Formerly National champion, but, following view of Little (1979) that this species is "apparently not naturalized" (correct), dropped by American Forests in 1980.

Hovenia dulcis Thunb.
Japanese Raisin-tree

Size:			
	Circumference:	96	inches
	Height:	46	feet
	Crown spread:	37.5	feet
	Total points:	152	points

Owner / location: Wesley S. Bean / 1103 N.W. 4th St., Gainesville, Alachua Co. [s.e. 1/4 of sec 32, T9S, R20E]

Nominator(s) / date: Michael J. Bordyn / 1980

Update: Robert T. Ing, Daniel B. Ward / 1991

Comments: "A big tree when I bought this place in 1942" (W. S. Bean, Oct 1991). Height and spread recently have been much reduced by lopping top and all branches (R. T. Ing & D. B. Ward, Oct 1991). Tree has recently died (D. R. Durgee, July 1993).

Earlier measurements: circ. = 92 in., ht. = 62 ft., spread = 53.5 ft. (Bordyn, 1980).

Lagerstroemia indica L.
Crape Myrtle

Size:			
	Circumference:	70	inches
	Height:	42	feet
	Crown spread:	34	feet
	Total points:	121	points

Owner / location: (unknown) / 402 N. Bronough St., Tallahassee, Leon Co. [s.e. 1/4 of sec 36, T1N, R1W]

Nominator(s) / date: Malcolm B. Johnson / 1967

Comments: Tree is no longer on property (R. T. Ing & D. B. Ward, Sept 1993).

Morus alba L.
Silkworm Mulberry, White Mulberry

Size:			
	Circumference:	128	inches
	Height:	46	feet
	Crown spread:	77.5	feet
	Total points:	193	points

Owner / location: Tanner Nursery & Garden Center / Fla. 44, 1 mi. e. of Eustis, Lake Co. [n.w. 1/4 of sec 7, T19S, R27E]

Nominator(s) / date: Marc Tanner / 1980

Comments: Tree still standing, but almost entirely dead; several basal sprouts are present (D. B. Ward & R. W. Simons, July 1993).

Tree was originally reported as *Morus rubra* (Tanner, 1980), and previously assumed to be Florida champion for that species. But the leaves (from sprouts) are clearly not that species, and appear to be *M. alba* var. *multicaulis* (Perr.) Loudon, the true Silkworm Mulberry (D. B. Ward & R. W. Simons, July 1993).

Parkinsonia aculeata L.
Jerusalem-thorn

Size:			
	Circumference:	56	inches
	Height:	26	feet
	Crown spread:	38	feet
	Total points:	92	points

Owner / location: A. Cuva / 1020 50th Ct., Bradenton, Manatee Co. [n.w. 1/4 of sec 33, T34S, R17E]

Nominator(s) / date: Steven Spezia, Mike Kuypers / 1977

Comments: Neighbor reports tree "covered whole front of house," but died about 1991 (R. T. Ing & D. B. Ward, July 1994).

Phoenix canariensis Chabaud
Canary Island Date Palm

Size:			
	Circumference:	136	inches
	Height:	35	feet
	Crown spread:	28	feet
	Total points:	178	points

Owner / location: Norman Gero / 5329 Majestic Ct., off Del Prado Blvd., Cape Coral, Lee Co. [sec 24, T45S, R23E]

Nominator(s) / date: Jeffrey S. Mangun / 1992

Comments: Tree has been cut down (J. S. Mangun, Mar 1994).

Phoenix dactylifera L.
Date Palm

Size:			
	Circumference:	60	inches
	Height:	45	feet
	Crown spread:	24	feet
	Total points:	111	points

Owner / location: Sarasota Jungle Gardens / 3701 Bayshore Rd., Sarasota, Sarasota Co. [w. 1/2 of sec 12, T36S, R17E]

Nominator(s) / date: William J. Schilling, Norman C. Easey / 1981

Comments: Tree is now dead (W. J. Schilling, Dec 1993).

Podocarpus macrophyllus (Thunb.) D. Don
Japanese Yew

Size:			
	Circumference:	101	inches
	Height:	60	feet
	Crown spread:	59	feet
	Total points:	176	points

Owner / location: Tony Wildrick / 2525 Pleasant Place, Sarasota, Sarasota Co. [n.e. 1/4 of sec 31, T36S, R18E]

Nominator(s) / date: Jack Shoestall / 1974

Comments: Tree is gone (W. J. Schilling, Mar 1994).

Podranea ricasoliana (Tanf.) Sprague
Pink Trumpet-vine

Size:	Circumference:	87	inches
	Height:	57	feet
	Crown spread:	36.5	feet
	Total points:	153	points

Owner / location: Flamingo Tropical Gardens / 3750 Flamingo Rd. (Fla. 823), Ft. Lauderdale, Broward Co. [sec 25, T50S, R40E]

Nominator(s) / date: John G. Cordy / 1983

Comments: This species is usually considered a woody vine or a "climbing shrub." Apparently here it was free-standing. No longer present on property (D. Bar-Zvi, Apr 1994).

Saraca indica L.
Asoka

Size:	Circumference:	75	inches
	Height:	25	feet
	Crown spread:	36	feet
	Total points:	109	points

Owner / location: Freeman Tilden / 2404 W. 16th Ave., Bradenton, Manatee Co. [center of sec 34, T34S, R17E]

Nominator(s) / date: David P. Utley / 1984

Comments: Tree is gone (W. J. Schilling, Mar 1994).

Spathodea campanulata Beauv.
African Tulip-tree

Size:	Circumference:	149	inches
	Height:	74	feet
	Crown spread:	38	feet
	Total points:	233	points

Owner / location: Flamingo Tropical Gardens / 3750 Flamingo Rd. (Fla. 823), Ft. Lauderdale, Broward Co. [sec 25, T50S, R40E]

Nominator(s) / date: Terry Wolfe / 1983

Comments: Tree was destroyed by Hurricane Andrew, Aug 1992 (D. Bar-Zvi, Oct 1993).

Sterculia apetala (Jacq.) Karst.
Panama-tree

Size:	Circumference:	168	inches
	Height:	136	feet
	Crown spread:	35	feet
	Total points:	312	points

Owner / location: City of Ft. Myers / Thomas Edison home, 2350 McGregor Blvd., Ft. Myers, Lee Co. [center of sec 23, T44S, R24E]

Nominator(s) / date: George Krauss / 1974

Comments: Tree is no longer present (R. W. Workman, June 1993).

Thespesia populnea (L.) Soland.
Seaside Mahoe, Portia-tree

Size:	Circumference:	86	inches
	Height:	28	feet
	Crown spread:	35	feet
	Total points:	123	points

Owner / location: Bert E. Calkins / Oleander Blvd., Palm Villa Subdiv., Big Pine Key, Monroe Co. [n.w. 1/4 of sec 23, T66S, R29E]

Nominator(s) / date: Sarah Calkins, Marjorie Terry / 1968

Comments: Tree has been down for years (T. Wilmers, June 1993).

Ulmus parvifolia Jacq.
Chinese Elm

Size:	Circumference:	58	inches
	Height:	40	feet
	Crown spread:	53.5	feet
	Total points:	111	points

Owner / location: Univ. of Florida / Rawlings Hall, campus, Gainesville, Alachua Co. [s.e. 1/4 of sec 6, T10S, R20E]

Nominator(s) / date: Michael J. Bordyn / 1981

Comments: Tree was removed about 1987 during construction of parking garage (R. T. Ing & D. B. Ward, Oct 1991).

Washingtonia filifera (L. Linden) H. Wendl.
California Washington Palm

Size:	Circumference:	76	inches
	Height:	41	feet
	Crown spread:	18	feet
	Total points:	121	points

Owner / location: (unknown) / Orange Ave. at 8th St., Sarasota, Sarasota Co. [n.e. 1/4 of sec 19, T36S, R18E]

Nominator(s) / date: Eldredge T. Carnes / 1969

Comments: Tree is dead (W. J. Schilling, Jan 1994). National champions: California, three trees (208 points, 207 points, 204 points).

Washingtonia robusta H. Wendl.
Washington Palm

Size:	Circumference:	45	inches
	Height:	83	feet
	Crown spread:	8	feet
	Total points:	130	points

Owner / location: (unknown) / Cholokka Blvd., n. of Peach St., Micanopy, Alachua Co. [sec 26, T11S, R20E]

Nominator(s) / date: Michael J. Bordyn / 1982

Comments: Tree died about 1987 (D. R. Durgee, Oct 1991).

HOW THEY DIED

Given time, it is inevitable that all trees will die. But what are the reasons they die? And how important are the different reasons? From data gathered during the Florida Champion Tree Survey it is now possible to give some exact causes and numbers.

As the records were updated for trees measured in years past, it was found that many of the old champions were no longer alive. Records were obtained as to the death or disappearance of 181 trees that had been nominated and measured in former years. In each case an effort was made to determine the cause behind the tree's death. Often the report merely read "tree gone" or "tree has been dead for some years" or some equally uninformative phrase. But in 70 cases it was possible to determine with confidence what event or action had precipitated the loss.

The most important identifiable factor in the death of Florida's champion trees is windthrow, accounting for 38 trees, or 54% of those that died from known causes. Half of these—19 trees—were blown down by Hurricane Andrew on 24 August 1992. Others were toppled in the Florida panhandle by Hurricane Kate in November 1985 and along the west coast by the "Storm of the Century" in March 1993.

The second most important identifiable factor in the destruction of champion trees is man. A further 18 trees, or 26%, were destroyed by human actions, either intentional or accidental. The state's champion parasol-tree (*Firmiana simplex*) was taken down to improve access to a loading dock. The National champion gumbo-limbo (*Bursera simaruba*) on Captiva Island was cut to make room for time-share apartments, and the nearby champion Australian pine (*Casuarina equisetifolia*) was removed as an "undesirable species." A bulldozer crushed the National champion fever-tree (*Pinckneya bracteata*) at Orange Springs. Logging in Taylor County removed the Carolina basswood (*Tilia caroliniana*), wild plum (*Prunus americana*), and Florida maple (*Acer floridana*), all Florida champions. Fill placed over the roots destroyed the National champion tough buckthorn (*Bumelia tenax*) on Amelia Island, while the herbicide Velpar, applied to adjacent *Schinus terebinthifolius*, also killed the champion Florida rapanea (*Myrsine floridana*) in the Ding Darling Refuge, Sanibel Island.

Cold weather, mostly in the form of abrupt freezes, is also an important identifiable factor, accounting for 8 trees, or 11%. Each of these trees (*Acacia auriculiformis, Albizia julibrissin, Araucaria araucana, Citrus paradisi, Clusia rosea, Cordia sebestena, Dalbergia sissoo, Ehretia acuminata*) was of a species not native to Florida. No native species was reported killed by freezes.

Fire and lightning are two forces that are well known to destroy trees. Though these factors are present in the data, they are surprisingly modest. Fire killed only 3 trees, or 4%, but of these only a sand pine (*Pinus clausa*) in the Ocala National Forest was destroyed by a forest fire; the other two were killed when an adjacent building burned. And lightning was identified as destroying only 3 trees, or 4%.

A factor that was not represented in the data is disease, either by insects or fungi. It is not known whether these organisms are really unimportant in the termination of older trees, or whether they were contributory to destruction attributed to other factors.

RATES OF GROWTH

The data gathered over the years of the Florida Champion Tree Survey have permitted estimates of the rates of growth for many tree species. Trees measured in earlier years, when remeasured in the current phase of the project, allow the determination of exact changes in dimension for individual trees that may be used as estimates of growth rates for the species.

Although data are abundant for growth rates of commercial species particularly during the earlier stages of their life cycle, no equivalent measurements are available for non-commercial species, and little information has been recorded for most tree species in the years of their full maturity.

Growth rates obtained in the present survey, however, must be viewed with caution as to their applicability beyond the individuals recorded. The number of individual trees is unavoidably low, in no case more than nine (*Quercus virginiana*) and with many species no more than one, because of the few trees measured in earlier years and the even fewer that survived to permit recent remeasurement. Further, a tree that becomes senescent, through limb loss or for other causes, will exhibit a reduced rate of growth. Even so, the paucity or absence of other estimates of growth rates for mature trees of these species justifies presentation of the available data.

Only measurements for trunk circumference are given in the following tabulation. In most cases circumference of the trunk can be measured with high repeatability even when measurements are recorded by different observers and separated by many years. Tree height and crown spread are less reliable. Height can be measured with precision by means of proper equipment and care. But height does not always continue to increase with age of the tree and may, in fact, decrease through limb-fall even though the tree remains viable. Crown spread is still more variable, in that the determination of the axes of measurement is to some extent subjective.

Changes in height and crown spread over time, if desired, may be readily determined from the INVENTORY data provided with each individual tree that has been measured more than once.

Changes in trunk circumference are presented here in the form of the calculated increase in radius per year, over the number of years that have elapsed between measurements, in both English linear and metric units.

Formula:
$$\text{radius}_{in/yr} = \frac{\text{increase in circ.}_{in}}{(\text{elapsed years})\,2\pi}$$

Or:
$$\text{radius}_{mm/yr} = \frac{(25.4)\,(\text{increase in circ.}_{in})}{(\text{elapsed years})\,2\pi}$$

Individual trees within a given species are ranked by ascending magnitude of increase in radius. Non-native species are not tabulated, but equivalent rates of increase may be calculated from data of some individuals as provided in the INVENTORY.

Measured increase in circumference, over years	Increase in radius per year
Acer floridanum	Florida Maple
Andrews & Simons, 1983	
82 in → 83 in; 10 years	0.016 in = 0.40 mm
Acer rubrum	Red Maple
Rutherford, 1986	
76 in → 88 in; 8 years	0.239 in = 6.06 mm
Acer saccharinum	Silver Maple
Marcus, 1983	
63 in → 74 in; 10 years	0.175 in = 4.45 mm
Aesculus pavia	Red Buckeye
Simons, 1979	
24 in → 27 in; 12 years	0.040 in = 1.01 mm
Alvaradoa amorphoides	Mexican Alvaradoa
Cordy & Eggert, 1983	
12 in → 25 in; 10 years	0.207 in = 5.25 mm
Amyris elemifera	Torchwood
Cullen & Sinclair, 1986	
16 in → 18 in; 7 years	0.045 in = 1.15 mm
Shaw & Tilmant, 1975	
12 in → 18 in; 20 years	0.048 in = 1.21 mm
Asimina parviflora	Small-flowered Pawpaw
Davis, 1980	
17 in → 21 in; 13 years	0.049 in = 1.24 mm
Ateramnus lucidus	Crabwood, Oysterwood
Cullen & Sinclair, 1986	
13 in → 14.5 in; 7 years	0.034 in = 0.87 mm
Betula nigra	River Birch
Andrews & Simons, 1983	
65 in → 67 in; 11 years	0.029 in = 0.74 mm
Bursera simaruba	Gumbo-limbo
Hetzell & Smith, 1973	
92 in → 97 in; 13 years	0.061 in = 1.55 mm
Canella winterana	Wild Cinnamon
Shaw & Tilmant, 1975	
19 in → 25 in; 8 years	0.119 in = 3.03 mm
Carya aquatica	Water Hickory
Rich, 1981	
219 in → 228 in; 12 years	0.119 in = 3.03 mm

Measured increase in circumference, over years	Increase in radius per year
Carya glabra	Pignut Hickory
Mould, 1980	
168 in → 177 in; 13 years	0.110 in = 2.80 mm
Beauchamp, 1982	
153 in → 161 in; 11 years	0.116 in = 2.94 mm
Castanea alnifolia	Southern Chinquapin
McGrath, 1985	
69 in → 76 in; 8 years	0.139 in = 3.54 mm
Castanea ashei	Ashe Chinquapin
Mathe, 1990	
84 in → 85 in; 3 years	0.053 in = 1.35 mm
Celtis laevigata	Sugarberry
Moore, 1980	
105 in → 110 in; 13 years	0.061 in = 1.55 mm
Simons, 1984	
115 in → 130 in; 22 years	0.108 in = 2.76 mm
Bakeman, 1984	
101 in → 113 in; 13 years	0.147 in = 3.73 mm
Marcus, 1983	
192 in → 234 in; 10 years	0.668 in = 16.98 mm
Chamaecyparis thyoides	Atlantic White Cedar
Harrelson, 1981	
120 in → 121 in; 13 years	0.012 in = 0.31 mm
Chrysophyllum oliviforme	Satinleaf
Shaw & Hetzell, 1976	
65 in → 73 in; 17 years	0.075 in = 1.90 mm
Coccoloba diversifolia	Pigeon Plum
Roundtree & Sinclair, 1986	
41 in → 45 in; 7 years	0.091 in = 2.31 mm
Nett, 1965	
66 in → 84 in; 28 years	0.102 in = 2.60 mm
Coccoloba uvifera	Sea Grape
McGarthy, 1971	
98 in → 149 in; 23 years	0.353 in = 8.96 mm
Conocarpus erectus	Button Mangrove
Schory, 1970	
63 in → 89 in; 24 years	0.172 in = 4.38 mm
Van der Hulse & Lockhart, 1974	
127 in → 174 in; 19 years	0.394 in = 10.00 mm
Cornus florida	Flowering Dogwood
Hardy, 1983	
59 in → 65 in; 10 years	0.095 in = 2.43 mm

Measured increase in circumference, over years	Increase in radius per year
Crataegus michauxii	Summer Haw, Yellow Haw
Simons, 1980	
37 in → 41 in; 14 years	0.045 in = 1.16 mm
Crataegus pulcherrima	Smooth Haw
Johnson & Salter, 1968	
23 in → 25 in; 25 years	0.013 in = 0.32 mm
Cupania glabra	Florida Cupania
Shaw & Avery, 1976	
19 in → 25 in; 17 years	0.056 in = 1.43 mm
Cyrilla racemiflora	Titi, Swamp Cyrilla
Reeves, 1980	
46 in → 51 in; 13 years	0.061 in = 1.56 mm
Diospyros virginiana	Persimmon
Andrews & Simons, 1983	
60 in → 63 in; 11 years	0.043 in = 1.10 mm
Bordyn & Simons, 1981	
59 in → 66 in; 12 years	0.093 in = 2.36 mm
Dipholis salicifolia	Willow Bustic
Shaw & Beaudry, 1975	
48 in → 53 in; 19 years	0.042 in = 1.06 mm
Erythrina herbacea	Cherokee Bean, Coral Bean
Hoyer & Workman, 1980	
38 in → 39 in; 12 years	0.013 in = 0.34 mm
Simons, 1980	
22 in → 25 in; 14 years	0.034 in = 0.87 mm
Eugenia confusa	Redberry Stopper
Hetzell & Smith, 1973	
55 in → 60 in; 20 years	0.040 in = 1.01 mm
Fagus grandifolia	Beech
Roberts, 1983	
95 in → 100 in; 10 years	0.080 in = 2.02 mm
Ficus aurea	Strangler Fig
Hetzell & Smith, 1973	
288 in → 360 in; 20 years	0.573 in = 14.55 mm
Ficus citrifolia	Shortleaf Fig
Sinclair & Zickar, 1986	
245 in → 248 in; 7 years	0.068 in = 1.73 mm
Williams, 1982	
200 in → 214 in; 12 years	0.186 in = 4.72 mm

Measured increase in circumference, over years	Increase in radius per year
Fraxinus americana	White Ash
Bordyn 1980	
128 in → 135 in; 11 years	0.101 in = 2.57 mm
Nichols, 1983	
154 in → 169 in; 10 years	0.239 in = 6.06 mm
Gleditsia aquatica	Water Locust
Saults & Livingston, 1981	
55 in → 56 in; 12 years	0.013 in = 0.34 mm
Bordyn & Simons, 1981	
90 in → 94 in; 12 years	0.053 in = 1.39 mm
Gordonia lasianthus	Loblolly Bay
Simons & Ward, 1963	
142 in → 164 in; 30 years	0.117 in = 2.96 mm
Hippomane mancinella	Manchineel
Shaw & Avery, 1976	
48 in → 56 in; 17 years	0.075 in = 1.90 mm
Hypelate trifoliata	White Ironwood
Shaw, 1976	
41 in → 58 in; 13 years	0.208 in = 5.29 mm
Ilex krugiana	Krug's Holly, Tawnyberry Holly
Young & Schory, 1968	
15 in → 40 in; 23 years	0.173 in = 4.39 mm
Ilex myrtifolia	Myrtle Dahoon Holly
Linton, 1981	
48 in → 52 in; 13 years	0.049 in = 1.24 mm
Blocker, 1972	
67 in → 74 in; 21 years	0.053 in = 1.35 mm
Fries, 1980	
30 in → 42 in; 13 years	0.147 in = 3.73 mm
Ilex opaca	American Holly
Simons, 1984	
60 in → 69 in; 9 years	0.159 in = 4.04 mm
Juglans nigra	Black Walnut
Bordyn, 1981	
88 in → 95 in; 10 years	0.111 in = 2.83 mm
Juniperus silicicola	Southern Red Cedar
Schilling, 1970	
163 in → 176 in; 23 years	0.090 in = 2.28 mm
Simons, 1976	
178 in → 195 in; 15 years	0.180 in = 4.58 mm
Simons, 1986	
196 in → 208 in; 7 years	0.273 in = 6.93 mm

Measured increase in circumference, over years	Increase in radius per year
Krugiodendron ferreum	Black Ironwood
Sinclair & Zickar, 1986	
67 in → 70 in; 7 years	0.068 in = 1.73 mm
Liquidambar styraciflua	Sweet Gum
Locklin, 1981	
139 in → 149 in; 13 years	0.122 in = 3.11 mm
Liriodendron tulipifera	Tulip-tree, Yellow Poplar
Marcus, 1983	
139 in → 140 in; 10 years	0.016 in = 0.40 mm
Magnolia grandiflora	Southern Magnolia
Simons & Bordyn, 1981	
196 in → 198 in; 10 years	0.032 in = 0.81 mm
Webb, 1980	
200 in → 205 in; 13 years	0.061 in = 1.55 mm
Crawford, 1980	
188 in → 193 in; 11 years	0.072 in = 1.84 mm
Halstead, 1980	
177 in → 183 in; 13 years	0.073 in = 1.87 mm
Rutherford, 1980	
187 in → 202 in; 14 years	0.171 in = 4.33 mm
Mastichodendron foetidissimum	False Mastic
Hetzell & Smith, 1973	
100 in → 105 in; 9 years	0.088 in = 2.25 mm
Morus rubra	Red Mulberry
Bakeman, 1981	
51 in → 60 in; 13 years	0.110 in = 2.80 mm
Nyssa biflora	Swamp Tupelo
Dale, 1989	
109 in → 110 in; 4 years	0.040 in = 1.01 mm
Nyssa ogeche	Ogeechee Lime, Ogeechee Tupelo
Simons & Allen, 1981	
162 in → 166 in; 12 years	0.053 in = 1.35 mm
Persea borbonia	Red Bay
Simons, 1986	
127 in → 130 in; 8 years	0.060 in = 1.52 mm
Newburne, 1981	
95 in → 108 in; 13 years	0.159 in = 4.04 mm
Nichols, 1983	
135 in → 152 in; 10 years	0.271 in = 6.87 mm
Pinus elliottii	Slash Pine
Courtenay, 1962	
125 in → 128 in; 31 years	0.015 in = 0.39 mm
Karels, 1985	
129 in → 130 in; 7 years	0.023 in = 0.58 mm
Loper, 1980	

Measured increase in circumference, over years	Increase in radius per year
135 in → 139 in; 14 years	0.045 in = 1.15 mm
Schilling, 1980	
112 in → 122 in; 13 years	0.122 in = 3.11 mm
Pinus glabra	Spruce Pine
Bordyn, 1980	
160 in → 165 in; 11 years	0.072 in = 1.84 mm
Roberts, 1983	
75 in → 87 in; 10 years	0.191 in = 4.85 mm
Pinus palustris	Longleaf Pine
Howell, 1981	
80 in → 88 in; 13 years	0.098 in = 2.49 mm
Pinus taeda	Loblolly Pine
Cunningham, 1982	
142 in → 146 in; 11 years	0.058 in = 1.47 mm
Beitzel & Humphrey, 1985	
137 in → 144 in; 8 years	0.139 in = 3.54 mm
Fries, 1980	
128 in → 139 in; 7 years	0.250 in = 6.35 mm
Pithecellobium unguis-cati	Cat's-claw
Spezia, 1976	
122 in → 150 in; 18 years	0.248 in = 6.29 mm
Platanus occidentalis	Sycamore
Smith & Fatic, 1981	
177 in → 186 in; 12 years	0.119 in = 3.03 mm
Reeves, 1980	
106 in → 124 in; 13 years	0.220 in = 5.60 mm
Populus deltoides	Eastern Cottonwood
Bordyn, 1985	
99 in → 109 in; 8 years	0.199 in = 5.05 mm
Prunus americana	Wild Plum
Simons, 1986	
38 in → 39 in; 5 years	0.032 in = 0.81 mm
Prunus serotina	Black Cherry
Bordyn, 1980	
175 in → 177 in; 11 years	0.029 in = 0.74 mm
Quercus alba	White Oak
Durgee & West, 1984	
51 in → 58 in; 7 years	0.159 in = 4.04 mm
Quercus austrina	Bluff Oak
Bordyn & Simons, 1981	
103 in → 104 in; 12 years	0.013 in = 0.38 mm
Andrews & Simons, 1983	
101 in → 105 in; 11 years	0.058 in = 1.47 mm
Quercus chapmanii	Chapman Oak
Simons, 1963	
50 in → 52 in; 9 years	0.035 in = 0.90 mm

Measured increase in circumference, over years	Increase in radius per year		Measured increase in circumference, over years	Increase in radius per year
Quercus falcata	Southern Red Oak		Simmons, 1981	
Bordyn, 1981			234 in → 245 in; 6 years	0.292 in = 7.41 mm
141 in → 147 in; 12 years	0.080 in = 2.02 mm		Lima, 1980	
Chauncey, 1981			235 in → 260 in; 13 years	0.306 in = 7.77 mm
279 in → 288 in; 12 years	0.119 in = 3.03 mm		Simons, 1976	
			324 in → 360 in; 17 years	0.337 in = 8.56 mm
Quercus geminata	Sand Live Oak			
Simons, 1985			**Reynosia septentrionalis**	Darling Plum
184 in → 189 in; 10 years	0.080 in = 2.02 mm		Niedhauk, 1975	
Bordyn, 1980			17 in → 20.5 in; 18 years	0.031 in = 0.79 mm
107 in → 114 in; 11 years	0.101 in = 2.57 mm			
Bordyn, 1980			**Sapindus marginatus**	Florida Soapberry
101 in → 104 in; 13 years	0.037 in = 2.76 mm		Simons, 1977	
			85 in → 88 in; 14 years	0.034 in = 0.87 mm
Quercus hemisphaerica	Laurel Oak			
House, 1980			**Sassafras albidum**	Sassafras
167 in → 171 in; 14 years	0.045 in = 1.15 mm		Clarkson, 1983	
			62 in → 81 in; 12 years	0.252 in = 6.40 mm
Quercus michauxii	Swamp Chestnut Oak			
			Simarouba glauca	Paradise-tree
Moore, 1980			Buckley, Hendrickson & Trickel, 1984	
152 in → 154 in; 13 years	0.024 in = 0.62 mm		78 in → 109 in; 10 years	0.493 in = 12.53 mm
Quercus myrtifolia	Myrtle Oak		**Swietenia mahagoni**	Mahogany
Beck, 1967			Hoyer & Eckert, 1980	
44 in → 69 in; 19 years	0.209 in = 5.32 mm		130 in → 132 in; 14 years	0.023 in = 0.58 mm
Quercus nigra	Water Oak		**Taxodium ascendens**	Pond Cypress
Locklin, 1981			Johnson, 1967	
207 in → 217 in; 13 years	0.122 in = 3.11 mm		125 in → 127 in; 27 years	0.012 in = 0.30 mm
Reeves, 1980				
180 in → 195 in; 13 years	0.184 in = 4.66 mm		**Taxodium distichum**	Bald Cypress
			Mathis, 1981	
Quercus stellata	Post Oak		548 in → 550 in; 12 years	0.027 in = 0.67 mm
Reeves, 1981			Allen, 1981	
155 in → 159 in; 12 years	0.053 in = 1.35 mm		168 in → 176 in; 12 years	0.106 in = 2.69 mm
Reeves, 1980			Marcus, 1981	
140 in → 150 in; 13 years	0.122 in = 3.11 mm		214 in → 229 in; 12 years	0.199 in = 5.05 mm
Potts & Williams, 1983			Martin, 1981	
181 in → 194 in; 11 years	0.188 in = 4.78 mm		408 in → 425 in; 12 years	0.212 in = 5.39 mm
Quercus virginiana	Live Oak		**Torreya taxifolia**	Gopherwood, Florida Torreya
House, 1980				
312 in → 314 in; 13 years	0.024 in = 0.62 mm		Neal, 1983	
Longshore, 1980			40 in → 45 in; 11 years	0.072 in = 1.84 mm
252 in → 256 in; 13 years	0.049 in = 1.24 mm			
Johnson, 1989			**Ulmus alata**	Winged Elm
248 in → 252 in; 5 years	0.127 in = 3.23 mm		Simons, 1977	
Rogers, 1980			133 in → 135 in; 16 years	0.020 in = 0.50 mm
330 in → 345 in; 13 years	0.184 in = 4.66 mm			
Serviss, 1980			**Zanthoxylum fagara**	Wild Lime
288 in → 309 in; 14 years	0.239 in = 6.06 mm		Hoyer & Byrd, 1980	
Snowden, 1967			16 in → 21 in; 13 years	0.061 in = 1.55 mm
272 in → 322 in; 28 years	0.284 in = 7.22 mm			

LARGEST AND SMALLEST FLORIDA TREES

Even within the INVENTORY of champions, some individuals stand out. They are larger—or they are smaller—than the champions of other species. And they may be larger—or smaller—in any or in all of the three dimensions whose measurements determine championship status.

The following list is a summation and ranking of the individual trees that are the largest, or smallest, in circumference, in height, in canopy spread, and in total points. For each category the twenty (or more, if of equal size) largest or smallest individual trees are listed. In the category of those largest in total points, however, the listing has been extended to fifty to accommodate the desire to place many large trees within a state-wide ranking scale.

The "largest" and the "smallest" lists are compiled somewhat differently. The "largest" trees are those individuals recorded by the Florida Champion Tree Survey with the largest measurements for the category under study, without regard to the tree's ranking (as National or Florida champions) based on total point scores. A tree that is exceptionally tall may be more modest in other dimensions and thus not be a champion. In partial contrast, the "smallest" trees are selected only among those individuals ranked as champions (or "nominees"); there is, of course, no limit to the potential number of individuals smaller than the champion.

This listing does not separate those trees that are native to Florida from those of species that have been brought to Florida for horticultural or commercial purposes. These non-native species are indicated by an asterisk (*).

Part I-A.—GREATEST CIRCUMFERENCE

1. **Ficus racemosa** *   Cluster Fig
   Circumference: **649** inches
      Flamingo Tropical Gardens / 3750 Flamingo Rd.
      (Fla. 823), Ft. Lauderdale, Broward Co.

2. **Taxodium distichum**   Bald Cypress
   Circumference: **550** inches
      Suwannee River Water Management District /
      Karst depression, 1/4 mi. n. of Suwannee River,
      4 mi. e. of Noble's Ferry bridge, 9 mi. s.w. of
      Jasper, Hamilton Co.

3. **Taxodium distichum**   Bald Cypress
   Circumference: **486** inches
      Suwannee River Water Management District /
      channel of Holton Creek, 1/4 mi. n. of Suwannee
      River, 3 mi. e. of Noble's Ferry bridge, 10 mi. s.w.
      of Jasper, Hamilton Co.

4. **Taxodium distichum**   Bald Cypress
   Circumference: **425** inches
      County of Seminole / Big Tree Park, n. of Fla.
      434, 1 mi. n.e. of Longwood, Seminole Co.

5. **Cinnamomum camphora** *   Camphor-tree
   Circumference: **422** inches
      Thomas J. Hanlon / Darby community, w. end of
      Bellamy Rd. (Fla. 578A), 6 mi. w.n.w. of St. Leo,
      Pasco Co.

6. **Bombax ceiba** *   Red Silk-cotton
   Circumference: **417** inches
      Thoroughbred Music, Inc. / 923 McMullen Booth
      Rd., Clearwater, Pinellas Co.

7. **Ficus altissima** *   Lofty Fig
   Circumference: **408** inches
      Coral Gables Federal Savings, Inc. / 3050 N.
      Federal Hwy. (U.S. 1), Lighthouse Point,
      Broward Co.

8. **Taxodium distichum**   Bald Cypress
   Circumference: **394** inches
      Florida Power and Light, Inc. / Barley Barber
      Swamp, n.e. of Port Mayaca, n.w. of Indiantown,
      Martin Co.

9. **Cinnamomum camphora** *   Camphor-tree
   Circumference: **390** inches
      Joy Trask / 6529 Farris Drive, n. of Shepherd
      Rd., s. Lakeland, Polk Co.

10. **Taxodium distichum**   Bald Cypress
   Circumference: **389** inches
      County of Seminole / Big Tree Park, n. of Fla.
      434, 1 mi. n.e. of Longwood, Seminole Co.

11. **Ficus benghalensis** *   Banyan Fig
   Circumference: **385** inches
      Holiday Inn, Inc. / 300 W. Retta Esplanade,
      Punta Gorda, Charlotte Co.

12. **Cinnamomum camphora** *   Camphor-tree
   Circumference: **384** inches
      Maurice Clavel / 311 Ohio Ave., Wauchula,
      Hardee Co.

13. **Ficus benghalensis** *   Banyan Fig
Circumference: **376** inches
City of Ft. Myers / Thomas Edison home, 2350
McGregor Blvd., Ft. Myers, Lee Co.

14. **Taxodium distichum**   Bald Cypress
Circumference: **376** inches
Florida Conference of Seventh Day Adventists /
Camp Kulaqua, head of Hornsby Run, 2 mi. n. of
High Springs, Alachua Co.

15. **Cinnamomum camphora** *   Camphor-tree
Circumference: **375** inches
(unknown) / El Rancho Village, 508 E. 44th Ave.,
Bradenton, Manatee Co.

16. **Cinnamomum camphora** *   Camphor-tree
Circumference: **369** inches
Richard J. Kinney / 40455 Otis Allen Rd. (Fla.
530), 3 mi. n.e. of Zephyrhills, Pasco Co.

17. **Ficus aurea**   Strangler Fig
Circumference: **360** inches
Bill Sadowski Park / Old Cutler Hammock, s. of
jct. of C-100 Canal & Cutler Canal, Dade Co.

18. **Quercus virginiana**   Live Oak
Circumference: **360** inches
Cellon Oak Park / 0.2 mi. w. of Fla. 121, 3 mi. s.
of LaCrosse, Alachua Co.

19. **Ficus altissima** *   Lofty Fig
Circumference: **356** inches
Hugh Taylor Birch State Park / 3109 E. Sunrise
Blvd., Ft. Lauderdale, Broward Co.

10. **Quercus virginiana**   Live Oak
Circumference: **355** inches
Jimmy Davis Enterprises, Inc. / 0.5 mi. n. of Int.
10, w. of Captain Brown Rd., 5 mi. w.s.w. of
Madison, Madison Co.

Part I-B.—SMALLEST CIRCUMFERENCE

1. **Cornus asperifolia**   Rough-leaf Cornel
Circumference: **7** inches
Prairie View Trust / Sugarfoot Hammock, n.e. of
jct. S.W. 20th Ave. & S.W. 62nd St., Gainesville,
Alachua Co.

2. **Illicium parviflorum**   Florida Banana-shrub
Circumference: **7** inches
Ocala National Forest / Morman Branch, tributary of Juniper Creek, at F. S. Rd. 71,
Marion Co.

3. **Schoepfia chrysophylloides**   Whitewood
Circumference: **7** inches
Dennis McIltrot / 3960 Ellis Rd., Ft. Myers,
Lee Co.

4. **Leitneria floridana**   Corkwood
Circumference: **8** inches
Waccasassa Bay State Preserve / near n. fork of
Ramsey Creek, 10 mi. n. of Yankeetown,
Levy Co.

5. **Agarista populifolia**   Pipestem
Circumference: **10** inches
C. G. Money / between Orange Springs Country
Inn and Orange Creek, Orange Springs,
Marion Co.

6. **Celtis pallida**   Spiny Hackberry
Circumference: **10** inches
Ding Darling National Wildlife Refuge / n. side
of Sanibel-Captiva Rd., Sanibel Id., Lee Co.

7. **Cornus foemina**   Smooth-leaf Cornel
Circumference: **10** inches
Georgia Pacific Corp. / Rice Creek Swamp, s. of
Fla. 100, 6 mi. w. of Palatka, Putnam Co.

8. **Kalmia latifolia**   Mountain Laurel
Circumference: **10** inches
John L. Dean / 821 E. 7th Ave., Tallahassee,
Leon Co.

9. **Pinckneya bracteata**   Fever-tree
Circumference: **10** inches
C. G. Money / between Orange Springs Country
Inn and Orange Creek, Orange Springs, Marion
Co.

10. **Stewartia malacodendron**   Silky Camellia
Circumference: **10** inches
C. J. Laird / s. side of Fla. 183, 8 mi. s.e. of De-
Funiak Springs, Walton Co.

11. **Suriana maritima**   Bay Cedar
Circumference: **10** inches
William R. Redman / Long Beach Rd., s. end of
Big Pine Key, Monroe Co.

12. **Halesia carolina**   Little Silver-bell
Circumference: **10.5** inches
Georgia Pacific Corp. / Rice Creek Swamp, s. of
Fla 100, 6 mi. w. of Palatka, Putnam Co.

13. **Cereus robinii**   Key Tree Cactus
Circumference: **11** inches
National Key Deer Refuge / Cactus Hammock, s.
end of Big Pine Key, Monroe Co.

14. **Crataegus opaca**   Western May Haw
Circumference: **11** inches
James Campbell \ w. bank of Escambia River, n.
of Fla. 4, 1 mi. s.e. of Century, Escambia Co.

15. **Ptelea trifoliata**   Wafer Ash, Hop-tree
    Circumference: **11** inches
        Robert W. Simons / 1122 S.W. 11th Ave.,
        Gainesville, Alachua Co.

16. **Rhus vernix**   Poison Sumac
    Circumference: **11** inches
        Ravine State Gardens / Twigg St., Palatka,
        Putnam Co.

17. **Salix floridana**   Florida Willow
    Circumference: **11** inches
        Ocala National Forest / channel of Morman
        Branch, tributary of Juniper Creek, s. of F. S.
        Rd. 71, Marion Co.

18. **Viburnum rufidulum**   Rusty Blackhaw
    Circumference: **11** inches
        Univ. of Florida / wooded slope, n. side of Mu-
        seum Rd., just w. of Fraternity Dr., campus,
        Gainesville, Alachua Co.

19. **Prunus angustifolia**   Chickasaw Plum
    Circumference: **12** inches
        Tall Timbers Research, Inc. / Fla. 12, 15 mi.
        n.n.e. of Tallahassee, Leon Co.

20. **Acoelorrhaphe**   Paurotis Palm
    wrightii
    Circumference: **12.5** inches
        Mounts Bldg. / 531 N. Military Trail, W. Palm
        Beach, Palm Beach Co.

21. **Guettarda scabra**   Rough Velvet-seed
    Circumference: **13** inches
        Biscayne National Park / s. end of Totten Key,
        Dade Co.

22. **Crataegus uniflora**   One-flowered Haw
    Circumference: **13.5** inches
        Univ. of Florida / s. edge of McCarty Woods,
        across Museum Rd. from Florida State Museum,
        campus, Gainesville, Alachua Co.

Part II-A.—
GREATEST HEIGHT

1. **Pinus taeda**   Loblolly Pine
    Height: **145** feet
        Buddy Paterson / n.w. side of Kingsley Lake, e.
        of Fla. 230, Clay Co.

2. **Pinus elliottii**   Slash Pine
    Height: **138** feet
        Laetitia Rogers / 7800 Miller Oaks Dr., Jack-
        sonville, Duval Co.

3. **Bombax ceiba** *   Red Silk-cotton
    Height: **130** feet
        Doris Vaughan / Ft. Denaud Rd. (Fla. 78A), 1.7
        mi. e. of Ft. Denaud bridge, 3 mi. w.s.w. of La-
        Belle, Hendry Co.

4. **Liriodendron**   Tulip-tree
    tulipifera
    Height: **130** feet
        Torreya State Park / n.w. corner of park,
        Liberty Co.

5. **Pinus elliottii**   Slash Pine
    Height: **130** feet
        Apalachicola National Forest / s. of Florida
        Trail, Bradwell Bay Wilderness, 8 mi. n.w. of
        Sopchoppy, Wakulla Co.

6. **Pinus taeda**   Loblolly Pine
    Height: **130** feet
        Ravine State Gardens / Twigg St., Palatka,
        Putnam Co.

7. **Pinus elliottii**   Slash Pine
    Height: **129** feet
        Apalachicola National Forest / s.e. of Florida
        Trail, Bradwell Bay Wilderness, 8 mi. n.w. of
        Sopchoppy, Wakulla Co.

8. **Liquidambar**   Sweet Gum
    styraciflua
    Height: **128** feet
        Torreya State Park / on trail s.w. from Gregory
        house, w. edge of park, Liberty Co.

9. **Quercus nigra**   Water Oak
    Height: **128** feet
        Louis Atkins / 0.5 mi. w. of Apalachicola River, 7
        mi. n.n.e. of Blountstown, Calhoun Co.

10. **Pinus taeda**   Loblolly Pine
    Height: **127** feet
        Roy Stockstill / 412 St. Dunston Ct., just e. of
        Meridian Rd., Tallahassee, Leon Co.

11. **Ulmus alata**   Winged Elm
    Height: **126** feet
        Torreya State Park / on trail s.w. from Gregory
        house, w. edge of park, Liberty Co.

12. **Pinus elliottii**   Slash Pine
    Height: **123** feet
        William S. Rosasco / 4 mi. s.s.e. of Milton, Santa
        Rosa Co.

13. **Quercus falcata**   Southern Red Oak
    Height: **123** feet
        Mark Chauncey / n. side of District Line Rd., 2.5
        mi. w. of Fla. 51, 5 mi. s.w. of Live Oak,
        Suwannee Co.

14. **Pinus echinata**   Shortleaf Pine
    Height: **122** feet
        Alfred B. Maclay State Gardens / 3540 N.
        Thomasville Rd., Tallahassee, Leon Co.

15. **Carya illinoinensis** *   Pecan
    Height: **121** feet
        Allen Bell / 9 mi. n. of Crestview, Okaloosa Co.

16. **Fagus grandifolia**   Beech
    Height: **121** feet
        Wakulla Springs State Park / Wakulla Springs,
        Wakulla Co.

17. **Carya cordiformis**   Bitternut Hickory
    Height: **120** feet
        Tall Timbers Research, Inc. / Fla. 12, 15 mi.
        n.n.e. of Tallahassee, Leon Co.

18. **Diospyros virginiana** Persimmon
    Height: **118** feet
        Torreya State Park / on trail s.w. of Gregory
        house, w. edge of park, Liberty Co.

19. **Fagus grandifolia**   Beech
    Height: **118** feet
        Anne Wright / Woodswell Farm, 7537 Proctor
        Rd., 0.3 mi. s. of s. of Centerville Rd. (Fla. 151),
        12 mi. n.e. of Tallahassee, Leon Co.

20. **Liquidambar**   Sweet Gum
    styraciflua
    Height: **118** feet
        Leland C. Thomas / 5 mi. w. of Marianna,
        Jackson Co.

21. **Taxodium distichum**   Bald Cypress
    Height: **118** feet
        County of Seminole / Big Tree Park, n. of Fla.
        434, 1 mi. n.e. of Longwood, Seminole Co.

22. **Taxodium distichum**   Bald Cypress
    Height: **118** feet
        Bayard Raceways, Inc. / along Durbin Creek, w.
        of U.S. 1, 0.5 mi. from n. edge of St. Johns Co.

Part II-B.—
SMALLEST HEIGHT

1. **Guettarda scabra**   Rough Velvet-seed
    Height: **8** feet
        Biscayne National Park / s. end of Totten Key,
        Dade Co.

2. **Baccharis halimifolia** Common Saltbush
    Height: **10** feet
        Jenkins Middle School / N. 19th St., Palatka,
        Putnam Co.

3. **Jacquinia keyensis**   Joe-wood
    Height: **11** feet
        Marsha Van Duren / w. of Egret Lane, w. side of
        Big Torch Key, Monroe Co.

4. **Kalmia latifolia**   Mountain Laurel
    Height: **11** feet
        John L. Dean / 821 E. 7th Ave., Tallahassee,
        Leon Co.

5. **Suriana maritima**   Bay Cedar
    Height: **12** feet
        William R. Redman / Long Beach Rd., s. end of
        Big Pine Key, Monroe Co.

6. **Hamelia patens**   Fire-bush
    Height: **13** feet
        Adolf Grimal / 600 Cunningham Lane, Big Pine
        Key, Monroe Co.

7. **Alvaradoa**   Mexican Alvaradoa
    amorphoides
    Height: **15** feet
        Camp Owaissa Bauer / 17001 S.W. 264th St., 3
        mi. n. of Homestead, Dade Co.

8. **Capparis**   Jamaica Caper
    cynophallophora
    Height: **15** feet
        (unknown) / n. end of Buck Key, just e. of Cap-
        tiva Id., Lee Co.

9. **Prunus angustifolia** Chickasaw Plum
    Height: **15** feet
        Tall Timbers Research, Inc. / Fla. 12, 15 mi.
        n.n.e. of Tallahassee, Leon Co.

10. **Leitneria floridana**   Corkwood
    Height: **16** feet
        Waccasassa Bay State Preserve / near n. fork of
        Ramsey Creek, 10 mi. n. of Yankeetown, Levy
        Co.

11. **Rhus vernix**   Poison Sumac
    Height: **16** feet
        Ravine State Gardens / Twigg St., Palatka,
        Putnam Co.

12. **Carica papaya**   Papaya
    Height: **17** feet
        Marie Selby Botanical Gardens / 800 S. Palm
        Ave., Sarasota, Sarasota Co.

13. **Forestiera segregata** Florida Privet
    Height: **17.5** feet
        Humiston Beach Park / Ocean Drive, Vero
        Beach, Indian River Co.

14. **Crataegus uniflora**   One-flowered Haw
    Height: **18** feet
        Univ. of Florida / s. edge of McCarty Woods,
        across Museum Rd. from Florida State Museum,
        campus, Gainesville, Alachua Co.

15. **Illicium parviflorum** Florida Banana-shrub
    Height: **18** feet
        Ocala National Forest / Morman Branch, tribu-
        tary of Juniper Creek, at F. S. Rd. 71,
        Marion Co.

16. **Sambucus**   Elderberry
    canadensis
    Height: **18** feet
         Jeri Baldwin / 1 mi. w. of Fla. 318, 6 mi. n.e of
         Citra, Marion Co.

17. **Schoepfia**   Whitewood
    chrysophylloides
    Height: **18** feet
         Dennis McIltrot / 3960 Ellis Rd., Ft. Myers, Lee
         Co.

18. **Stewartia**   Silky Camellia
    malacodendron
    Height: **19** feet
         C. J. Laird / s. side of Fla. 183, 8 mi. s.e. of De-
         Funiak Springs, Walton Co.

19. **Thrinax morissii**   Brittle Thatch Palm
    Height: **19** feet
         Fairchild Tropical Garden / 10901 Old Cutler
         Rd., Miami, Dade Co.

20. **Acacia choriophylla**   Cinnecord
    Height: **20** feet
         Phillip Elliott / Cedar Lane, Sugarloaf Key,
         Monroe Co.

21. **Cornus asperifolia**   Rough-leaf Cornel
    Height: **20** feet
         Prairie View Trust / Sugarfoot Hammock, n.e. of
         jct. S.W. 20th Ave. & S.W. 62nd St., Gainesville,
         Alachua Co.

22. **Crataegus opaca**   Western May Haw
    Height: **20** feet
         James Campbell \ w. bank of Escambia River, n.
         of Fla. 4, 1 mi. s.e. of Century, Escambia Co.

23. **Salix floridana**   Florida Willow
    Height: **20** feet
         Ocala National Forest / channel of Morman
         Branch, tributary of Juniper Creek, s. of F. S.
         Rd. 71, Marion Co.

24. **Taxus floridana**   Florida Yew
    Height: **20** feet
         Torreya State Park / near stone bridge, Liberty
         Co.

25. **Zanthoxylum flavum**   Yellowheart
    Height: **20** feet
         Bahia Honda State Park / Bahia Honda Key,
         Monroe Co.

Part III-A.—
GREATEST CROWN SPREAD

1. **Ficus benghalensis** *   Banyan Fig
   Crown spread: **191** feet
        City of Ft. Myers / Thomas Edison home, 2350
        McGregor Blvd., Ft. Myers, Lee Co.

2. **Ficus altissima** *   Lofty Fig
   Crown spread: **173** feet
        Hugh Taylor Birch State Park / 3109 E. Sunrise
        Blvd., Ft. Lauderdale, Broward Co.

3. **Quercus virginiana**   Live Oak
   Crown spread: **160** feet
        Cellon Oak Park / 0.2 mi. w. of Fla. 121, 3 mi. s.
        of LaCrosse, Alachua Co.

4. **Quercus virginiana**   Live Oak
   Crown spread: **153.5** feet
        Jacksonville Naval Air Station / Mulberry Grove
        Park, Mustin Rd., 8 mi. s. of Jacksonville, Duval
        Co.

5. **Quercus virginiana**   Live Oak
   Crown spread: **144** feet
        City of Jacksonville / 815 S. Main St., between
        Alvarez St. & Prudential Dr., Jacksonville,
        Duval Co.

6. **Quercus virginiana**   Live Oak
   Crown spread: **141** feet
        Brian Thorpe / 0.3 mi. s. of Fla. 270, 0.7 mi. w. of
        Scotland, 3 mi. s. of Havana, Gadsden Co.

7. **Quercus virginiana**   Live Oak
   Crown spread: **138** feet
        R. J. Huffman / 2850 Wilde Lake Blvd., s.w. of
        jct. Int. 10 & Fla. 297, n.w. Pensacola, Escambia
        Co.

8. **Quercus virginiana**   Live Oak
   Crown spread: **137** feet
        Jimmy Davis Enterprises, Inc. / 0.5 mi. n. of Int.
        10, w. of Captain Brown Rd., 5 mi. w.s.w. of
        Madison, Madison Co.

9. **Quercus virginiana**   Live Oak
   Crown spread: **137** feet
        Lake Griffin State Recreation Area / Fruitland
        Park, Lake Co.

10. **Cinnamomum**   Camphor-tree
    camphora *
    Crown spread: **135** feet
         Richard J. Kinney / 40455 Otis Allen Rd. (Fla.
         530), 3 mi. n.e. of Zephyrhills, Pasco Co.

11. **Quercus**   Laurel Oak
    hemisphaerica
    Crown spread: **134** feet
         Terry M. Freiberg / 14003 N.W. 150th Ave.,
         Alachua, Alachua Co.

12. **Ficus altissima** *   Lofty Fig
    Crown spread: **133** feet
         City of Ft. Myers / Thomas Edison home, 2350
         McGregor Blvd., Ft. Myers, Lee Co.

13. **Quercus virginiana**   Live Oak
    Crown spread: **133** feet
         Bulow Creek State Park / 8 mi. n.n.w. of Ormond
         Beach, Volusia Co.

14. **Quercus virginiana**   Live Oak
Crown spread: **130** feet
DeLeon Springs State Recreation Area / DeLeon Springs, Volusia Co.

15. **Quercus virginiana**   Live Oak
Crown spread: **128.5** feet
Allen R. Bush / Silver Lake Dr., e. of Fla. 19, 4 mi. s.w. of Palatka, Putnam Co.

16. **Quercus virginiana**   Live Oak
Crown spread: **128.5** feet
Gladys Johnson / 2 mi. n. of Fla. 2, 7 mi. n.e. of Campbellton, Jackson Co.

17. **Quercus virginiana**   Live Oak
Crown spread: **125** feet
Gene Yearty / 8060 Hammond Blvd., just n.e. of Devoe St., Jacksonville, Duval Co.

18. **Quercus falcata**   Southern Red Oak
Crown spread: **124.5** feet
Mark Chauncey / n. side of District Line Rd., 2.5 mi. w. of Fla. 51, 5 mi. s.w. of Live Oak, Suwannee Co.

19. **Enterolobium contortisiliquum** *   Pacara
Crown spread: **122** feet
Flamingo Tropical Gardens / 3750 Flamingo Rd. (Fla. 823), Ft. Lauderdale, Broward Co.

20. **Pithecellobium saman** *   Rain-tree
Crown spread: **121** feet
Paul Fitzgerald / Enchanted Place Apartments, 416 S.W. 4th Ave., Ft. Lauderdale, Broward Co.

21. **Quercus nigra**   Water Oak
Crown spread: **120** feet
Radford M. Locklin / w. side of Fla. 191, n. of McLellan, just s. of state line, Santa Rosa Co.

Part III-B.—
SMALLEST CROWN SPREAD

1. **Cereus robinii**   Key Tree Cactus
Crown spread: **1** foot
National Key Deer Refuge / Cactus Hammock, s. end of Big Pine Key, Monroe Co.

2. **Acoelorrhaphe wrightii**   Paurotis Palm
Crown spread: **3** feet
Mounts Bldg. / 531 N. Military Trail, W. Palm Beach, Palm Beach Co.

3. **Guettarda scabra**   Rough Velvet-seed
Crown spread: **3** feet
Biscayne National Park / s. end of Totten Key, Dade Co.

4. **Coccothrinax argentata**   Silver Palm
Crown spread: **6** feet
Bahia Honda State Park / Bahia Honda Key, Monroe Co.

5. **Thrinax radiata**   Florida Thatch Palm
Crown spread: **6.5** feet
R. A. Morcroft / 1055 N. South Lake Dr., Hollywood, Broward Co.

6. **Coccothrinax argentata**   Silver Palm
Crown spread: **7** feet
Bahia Honda State Park / Bahia Honda Key, Monroe Co.

7. **Leitneria floridana**   Corkwood
Crown spread: **7** feet
Waccasassa Bay State Preserve / near n. fork of Ramsey Creek, 10 mi. n. of Yankeetown, Levy Co.

8. **Pinckneya bracteata**   Fever-tree
Crown spread: **7** feet
C. G. Money / between Orange Springs Country Inn and Orange Creek, Orange Springs, Marion Co.

9. **Baccharis halimifolia**   Common Saltbush
Crown spread: **7.5** feet
Jenkins Middle School / N. 19th St., Palatka, Putnam Co.

10. **Cephalanthus occidentalis**   Buttonbush
Crown spread: **7.5** feet
James E. Wing / just s.e. of Santa Fe River, 1.5 mi. n.n.e. of High Springs, Alachua Co.

11. **Ateramnus lucidus**   Crabwood, Oysterwood
Crown spread: **8** feet
Key Largo Hammocks State Botanical Site / n. end of Key Largo, Monroe Co.

12. **Serenoa repens**   Saw Palmetto
Crown spread: **8** feet
Agricultural Research Center / Picos Rd., 3 mi. w. of Ft. Pierce, St. Lucie Co.

13. **Alvaradoa amorphoides**   Mexican Alvaradoa
Crown spread: **9** feet
Camp Owaissa Bauer / 17001 S.W. 264th St., 3 mi. n. of Homestead, Dade Co.

14. **Eugenia axillaris**   White Stopper
Crown spread: **9** feet
    Barnacle State Historic Site / 3485 Main Hwy., Coconut Grove, Dade Co.

15. **Thrinax morissii**   Brittle Thatch Palm
Crown spread: **9** feet
    Fairchild Tropical Garden / 10901 Old Cutler Rd., Miami, Dade Co.

16. **Kalmia latifolia**   Mountain Laurel
Crown spread: **10.5** feet
    John L. Dean / 821 E. 7th Ave., Tallahassee, Leon Co.

17. **Pisonia discolor**   Blolly, Longleaf Blolly
Crown spread: **10.5** feet
    Lignumvitae Key State Botanical Site / Lignumvitae Key, Monroe Co.

18. **Aesculus pavia**   Red Buckeye
Crown spread: **11** feet
    Foley Timber & Land Co. / e. bank of Steinhatchee River, 11 mi. s.s.w. of Mayo, Lafayette Co.

19. **Ateramnus lucidus**   Crabwood, Oysterwood
Crown spread: **11** feet
    Lignumvitae Key State Botanical Site / Lignumvitae Key, Monroe Co.

20. **Carica papaya**   Papaya
Crown spread: **11** feet
    Marie Selby Botanical Gardens / 800 S. Palm Ave., Sarasota, Sarasota Co.

21. **Eugenia axillaris**   White Stopper
Crown spread: **11** feet
    Sanctuary Golf Course / Wulfert Point, w. end of Sanibel Id., Lee Co.

22. **Viburnum rufidulum**   Rusty Blackhaw
Crown spread: **11** feet
    Univ. of Florida / wooded slope, n. side of Museum Rd., just w. of Fraternity Dr., campus, Gainesville, Alachua Co.

Part IV-A.—
GREATEST POINT SCORE

1. **Ficus racemosa** *   Cluster Fig
Total points: **775**
    Flamingo Tropical Gardens / 3750 Flamingo Rd. (Fla. 823), Ft. Lauderdale, Broward Co.

2. **Taxodium distichum**   Bald Cypress
Total points: **651**
    Suwannee River Water Management District / Karst depression, 1/4 mi. n. of Suwannee River, 4 mi. e. of Noble's Ferry bridge, 9 mi. s.w. of Jasper, Hamilton Co.

3. **Taxodium distichum**   Bald Cypress
Total points: **587**
    Suwannee River Water Management District / channel of Holton Creek, 1/4 mi. n. of Suwannee River, 3 mi. e. of Noble's Ferry bridge, 10 mi. s.w. of Jasper, Hamilton Co.

4. **Taxodium distichum**   Bald Cypress
Total points: **557**
    County of Seminole / Big Tree Park, n. of Fla. 434, 1 mi. n.e. of Longwood, Seminole Co.

5. **Cinnamomum camphora** *   Camphor-tree
Total points: **515**
    Thomas J. Hanlon / Darby community, w. end of Bellamy Rd. (Fla. 578A), 6 mi. w.n.w. of St. Leo, Pasco Co.

6. **Bombax ceiba** *   Red Silk-cotton
Total points: **506**
    Thoroughbred Music, Inc. / 923 McMullen Booth Rd., Clearwater, Pinellas Co.

7. **Taxodium distichum**   Bald Cypress
Total points: **497**
    Florida Power and Light, Inc. / Barley Barber Swamp, n.e. of Port Mayaca, n.w. of Indiantown, Martin Co.

8. **Taxodium distichum**   Bald Cypress
Total points: **493**
    Florida Conference of Seventh Day Adventists / Camp Kulaqua, head of Hornsby Run, 2 mi. n. of High Springs, Alachua Co.

9. **Ficus altissima** *   Lofty Fig
Total points: **492**
    Hugh Taylor Birch State Park / 3109 E. Sunrise Blvd., Ft. Lauderdale, Broward Co.

10. **Taxodium distichum**   Bald Cypress
Total points: **491**
    County of Seminole / Big Tree Park, n. of Fla. 434, 1 mi. n.e. of Longwood, Seminole Co.

11. **Ficus benghalensis** *   Banyan Fig
Total points: **486**
    City of Ft. Myers / Thomas Edison home, 2350 McGregor Blvd., Ft. Myers, Lee Co.

12. **Quercus virginiana**   Live Oak
Total points: **485**
    Cellon Oak Park / 0.2 mi. w. of Fla. 121, 3 mi. s. of LaCrosse, Alachua Co.

13. **Ficus altissima** *   Lofty Fig
Total points: **481**
    Coral Gables Federal Savings, Inc. / 3050 N. Federal Hwy. (U.S. 1), Lighthouse Point, Broward Co.

14. **Ficus benghalensis** *   Banyan Fig
Total points: **476**
    Holiday Inn, Inc. / 300 W. Retta Esplanade, Punta Gorda, Charlotte Co.

15. **Cinnamomum camphora** *   Camphor-tree
Total points: **470**
    Richard J. Kinney / 40455 Otis Allen Rd. (Fla. 530), 3 mi. n.e. of Zephyrhills, Pasco Co.

16. **Cinnamomum camphora** *   Camphor-tree
Total points: **463**
    Joy Trask / 6529 Farris Drive, n. of Shepherd Rd., s. Lakeland, Polk Co.

17. **Quercus virginiana**   Live Oak
Total points: **461**
    Jacksonville Naval Air Station / Mulberry Grove Park, Mustin Rd., 8 mi. s. of Jacksonville, Duval Co.

18. **Quercus virginiana**   Live Oak
Total points: **457**
    Rosemarie Permenter / 2 mi. e. of Fla. 475, 1.5 mi. n. of county line, 6 mi. s.w. of Belleview, Marion Co.

19. **Quercus virginiana**   Live Oak
Total points: **456**
    Jimmy Davis Enterprises, Inc. / 0.5 mi. n. of Int. 10, w. of Captain Brown Rd., 5 mi. w.s.w. of Madison, Madison Co.

20. **Cinnamomum camphora** *   Camphor-tree
Total points: **454**
    Maurice Clavel / 311 Ohio Ave., Wauchula, Hardee Co.

21. **Cinnamomum camphora** *   Camphor-tree
Total points: **451**
    El Rancho Village, Inc. / 508 E. 44th Ave., Bradenton, Manatee Co.

22. **Ficus nitida** *   Cuban Laurel
Total points: **450**
    City of Ft. Myers / Thomas Edison home, 2350 McGregor Blvd., Ft. Myers, Lee Co.

23. **Quercus virginiana**   Live Oak
Total points: **443**
    Brian Thorpe / 0.3 mi. s. of Fla. 270, 0.7 mi. w. of Scotland, 3 mi. s. of Havana, Gadsden Co.

24. **Quercus falcata**   Southern Red Oak
Total points: **442**
    Mark Chauncey / n. side of District Line Rd., 2.5 mi. w. of Fla. 51, 5 mi. s.w. of Live Oak, Suwannee Co.

25. **Ficus aurea**   Strangler Fig
Total points: **441**
    Bill Sadowski Park / Old Cutler Hammock, s. of jct. of C-100 Canal & Cutler Canal, Dade Co.

26. **Quercus virginiana**   Live Oak
Total points: **440**
    Lake Griffin State Recreation Area / Fruitland Park, Lake Co.

27. **Quercus virginiana**   Live Oak
Total points: **428**
    San Felasco Hammock State Preserve / n. of Fla. 232, 8 mi. n.w. of Gainesville, Alachua Co.

28. **Quercus virginiana**   Live Oak
Total points: **423**
    Gerald L. Rogers / between Santa Fe Road & Santa Fe River, s. end of Three Rivers Estates, 3 mi. w. of Ft. White, Columbia Co.

29. **Taxodium distichum**   Bald Cypress
Total points: **421**
    Apalachicola National Forest / Rock Bluff, 3 mi. s.w. of Bloxham, Leon Co.

30. **Quercus virginiana**   Live Oak
Total points: **416**
    R. J. Huffman / 2850 Wilde Lake Blvd., s.w. of jct. Int. 10 & Fla. 297, n.w. Pensacola, Escambia Co.

31. **Quercus nigra**   Water Oak
Total points: **414**
    Louis Atkins / 0.5 mi. w. of Apalachicola River, 7 mi. n.n.e. of Blountstown, Calhoun Co.

32. **Quercus virginiana**   Live Oak
Total points: **408**
    Neal Land and Timber Co. / Ocheesee Landing, w. bank of Apalachicola River, 10 mi. n.n.e. of Blountstown, Calhoun Co.

33. **Adansonia digitata** *   Baobab
Total points: **393**
    City of Hollywood / Young Circle, U.S. 1, Hollywood, Broward Co.

34. **Quercus virginiana**   Live Oak
Total points: **389**
    Ocala National Forest / 1 mi. n.w. of Mud Lake, Marion Co.

35. **Quercus virginiana**   Live Oak
Total points: **388**
    Bulow Creek State Park / 8 mi. n.n.w. of Ormond Beach, Volusia Co.

36. **Ficus mysorensis** *   Mysore Fig
    Total points: **386**
        City of Ft. Myers / Thomas Edison home, 2350
        McGregor Blvd., Ft. Myers, Lee Co.

37. **Cinnamomum**   Camphor-tree
    camphora *
    Total points: **384**
        Perkins Restaurant / n.e. of int. U.S. 19 and Fla.
        60, Clearwater, Pinellas Co.

38. **Taxodium distichum**   Bald Cypress
    Total points: **384**
        DeLeon Springs State Recreation Area / DeLeon
        Springs, Volusia Co.

39. **Khaya nyasica** *   Nyasaland Mahogany
    Total points: **378**
        IFAS Experiment Station / U.S. 441, 3 mi. s.e. of
        Belle Glade, Palm Beach Co.

40. **Quercus virginiana**   Live Oak
    Total points: **371**
        C. H. Ratliff / n. bank of Suwannee River, 2 mi.
        w. of Fla. 51, 6 mi. s. of Jasper, Hamilton Co.

41. **Quercus virginiana**   Live Oak
    Total points: **370**
        Allen R. Bush / Silver Lake Dr., e. of Fla. 19, 4
        mi. s.w. of Palatka, Putnam Co.

42. **Ficus altissima** *   Lofty Fig
    Total points: **368**
        City of Ft. Myers / Thomas Edison home, 2350
        McGregor Blvd., Ft. Myers, Lee Co.

43. **Quercus**   Laurel Oak
    hemisphaerica
    Total points: **366**
        James R. Griffith / Fla. 4, 0.75 mi. w. of Baker,
        Okaloosa Co.

44. **Quercus virginiana**   Live Oak
    Total points: **365**
        Gladys Johnson / 2 mi. n. of Fla. 2, 7 mi. n.e. of
        Campbellton, Jackson Co.

45. **Quercus virginiana**   Live Oak
    Total points: **365**
        DeLeon Springs State Recreation Area / DeLeon
        Springs, Volusia Co.

46. **Taxodium distichum**   Bald Cypress
    Total points: **363**
        Floyd Crews / e. of Fla. 135, 2 mi. s. of Fla. 6, 15
        mi. e. of Jasper, Hamilton Co.

47. **Quercus virginiana**   Live Oak
    Total points: **362**
        First Presbyterian Church / s. of jct. Lee St. &
        Second St., Ft. Myers, Lee Co.

48. **Taxodium distichum**   Bald Cypress
    Total points: **361**
        Bayard Raceways, Inc. / along Durbin Creek, w.
        of U.S. 1, 0.5 mi. from n. edge of St. Johns Co.

49. **Carya illinoinensis** *   Pecan
    Total points: **360**
        Mrs. O. V. Walker / n. side of U.S. 27, 2 mi. w. of
        Suwannee River bridge, 15 mi. s.e. of Mayo,
        Lafayette Co.

50. **Quercus virginiana**   Live Oak
    Total points: **360**
        Gene Yearty / 8060 Hammond Blvd., just n.e. of
        Devoe St., Jacksonville, Duval Co.

Part IV-B.—
SMALLEST POINT SCORE

1. **Guettarda scabra**   Rough Velvet-seed
   Total points: **22**
       Biscayne National Park / s. end of Totten Key,
       Dade Co.

2. **Kalmia latifolia**   Mountain Laurel
   Total points: **24**
       John L. Dean / 821 E. 7th Ave., Tallahassee,
       Leon Co.

3. **Leitneria floridana**   Corkwood
   Total points: **26**
       Waccasassa Bay State Preserve / near n. fork of
       Ramsey Creek, 10 mi. n. of Yankeetown,
       Levy Co.

4. **Illicium parviflorum**   Florida Banana-
   shrub
   Total points: **28**
       National Forest / Morman Branch, tributary of
       Juniper Creek, at F. S. Rd. 71, Marion Co.

5. **Suriana maritima**   Bay Cedar
   Total points: **28**
       William R. Redman / Long Beach Rd., s. end of
       Big Pine Key, Monroe Co.

6. **Baccharis halimifolia** Common Saltbush
   Total points: **30**
       Jenkins Middle School / N. 19th St., Palatka,
       Putnam Co.

7. **Prunus angustifolia**   Chickasaw Plum
   Total points: **30**
       Tall Timbers Research, Inc. / Fla. 12, 15 mi.
       n.n.e. of Tallahassee, Leon Co.

8. **Schoepfia**   Whitewood
   chrysophylloides
   Total points: **30**
       Dennis McIltrot / 3960 Ellis Rd., Ft. Myers,
       Lee Co.

9. **Cornus asperifolia**   Rough-leaf Cornel
   Total points: **31**
       Prairie View Trust / Sugarfoot Hammock, n.e. of
       jct. S.W. 20th Ave. & S.W. 62nd St., Gainesville,
       Alachua Co.

10. **Jacquinia keyensis**   Joe-wood
    Total points: **31**
        Marsha Van Duren / w. of Egret Lane, w. side of
        Big Torch Key, Monroe Co.

11. **Rhus vernix**   Poison Sumac
    Total points: **31**
        Ravine State Gardens / Twigg St., Palatka,
        Putnam Co.

12. **Gyminda latifolia**   False Boxwood
    Total points: **32**
        National Key Deer Refuge / s. of road, 1 mi. e. of
        bridge, No Name Key, Monroe Co.

13. **Hamelia patens**   Fire-bush
    Total points: **32**
        Adolf Grimal / 600 Cunningham Lane, Big Pine
        Key, Monroe Co.

14. **Pinckneya bracteata**   Fever-tree
    Total points: **33**
        C. G. Money / between Orange Springs Country
        Inn and Orange Creek, Orange Springs,
        Marion Co.

15. **Cereus robinii**   Key Tree Cactus
    Total points: **35**
        National Key Deer Refuge / Cactus Hammock, s.
        end of Big Pine Key, Monroe Co.

16. **Crataegus opaca**   Western May Haw
    Total points: **35**
        James Campbell / w. bank of Escambia River, n.
        of Fla. 4, 1 mi. s.e. of Century, Escambia Co.

17. **Ptelea trifoliata**   Wafer Ash, Hop-tree
    Total points: **35**
        Robert W. Simons / 1122 S.W. 11th Ave.,
        Gainesville, Alachua Co.

18. **Viburnum rufidulum**   Rusty Blackhaw
    Total points: **35**
        Univ. of Florida / wooded slope, n. side of Mu-
        seum Rd., just w. of Fraternity Dr., campus,
        Gainesville, Alachua Co.

19. **Crataegus uniflora**   One-flowered Haw
    Total points: **36**
        Univ. of Florida / s. edge of McCarty Woods,
        across Museum Rd. from Florida State Museum,
        campus, Gainesville, Alachua Co.

20. **Stewartia**   Silky Camellia
    malacodendron
    Total points: **36**
        C. J. Laird / s. side of Fla. 183, 8 mi. s.e. of De-
        Funiak Springs, Walton Co.

SPECIES RANKED BY HEIGHT

An important derivative of the Florida Champion Tree Survey is the ability to make quantitative statements as to the absolute and relative height of Florida's native trees, based upon a sampling of the largest known individuals of each species.

The height that trees can attain is conventionally based upon the measured vertical dimension of the tallest individual tree of the species, as recorded by the state and national champion tree surveys and other sources. However, a single tree, selected for the sole purpose of a height measurement, can give little information regarding the variability of the maximum biological potential; an aberrant individual can misrepresent its species. And generally no information is available regarding the maximum height of a population of tall trees of smaller species.

But an analysis of height based upon more than a single tree of each species must depend upon the selection of an appropriate data set, for it is obvious that the great majority of individual trees are too small to be representative of the maximum potential of the species. What is required is some agreed-upon sampling of large trees that can be used as the assumed population from which the calculations are drawn. This data set should be collected independently of its present use, and thus be unbiased.

The Florida champion tree data, collected over a period of more than twenty years, from throughout the state, and for nearly all of the native tree species, may serve that purpose. Its use requires only the assumption that each species is represented at its maximum size by those individuals nominated as champions. One must acknowledge, of course, that champion trees are nominated on the basis of trunk circumference and crown spread, as well as height, and that it is thus possible there are taller trees in the area that were not selected. And one must recognize that the recorded measurements are perhaps not accurate, and may not have been taken consistently by different observers.

But these imperfections in the data are modest in comparison to those of any other data set that is available, or, indeed, any other data set that can be realistically visualized. Therefore, with these qualifications, it is possible to calculate the mean height and standard deviation for each species and to rank the species in descending order.

The following data incorporate the available height measurements of all native trees nominated as champions within Florida, from the nominations in the 1960s to the present. Both living and dead trees are included; by the inclusion of records of now-vanished trees the set is expanded and estimates of variance are improved.

These rankings and measurements are not to be interpreted as absolute values for each species. The variances, as indicated by the standard deviation given for each species, are often quite large, a clear indication that further sampling may change both the absolute height and the relative ranking of the different species. But the present sample does provide a "best estimate" of the maximum mean height of Florida's native tree species and may serve in that capacity until some other, perhaps better, estimate is devised.

---

1. **Carya aquatica**   Water Hickory
   Mean height = 121.0   n = 3   s.d. = 25.71

2. **Carya cordiformis**   Bitternut Hickory
   Mean height = 120.0   n = 1   s.d. =

3. **Pinus taeda**   Loblolly Pine
   Mean height = 119.5   n = 8   s.d. = 17.21

4. **Pinus elliottii**
   var. elliottii   Slash Pine
   Mean height = 116.3   n = 7   s.d. = 20.80

5. **Liquidambar**
   styraciflua   Sweet Gum
   Mean height = 115.6   n = 5   s.d. = 10.90

6. **Ulmus crassifolia**   Cedar Elm
   Mean height = 112.5   n = 2   s.d. = 7.78

7. **Fagus grandifolia**   Beech
   Mean height = 112.3   n = 6   s.d. = 6.62

8. **Pinus glabra**   Spruce Pine
   Mean height = 111.0   n = 4   s.d. = 26.17

9. **Liriodendron**   Tulip-tree,
   tulipifera   Yellow Poplar
   Mean height = 108.3   n = 7   s.d. = 17.59

10. **Quercus shumardii**   Shumard Oak
    Mean height = 107.0   n = 2   s.d. = 12.73

11. **Pinus echinata**   Shortleaf Pine
    Mean height = 105.0   n = 3   s.d. = 18.68

12. **Ulmus alata**   Winged Elm
    Mean height = 104.3   n = 3   s.d. = 27.79

13. **Nyssa uniflora**   Water Tupelo
    = *Nyssa aquatica*, misapplied
    Mean height = 104.0   n = 1   s.d. =

14. **Diospyros virginiana**   Persimmon
    Mean height = 103.3   n = 3   s.d. = 12.74

15. **Taxodium distichum**   Bald Cypress
    Mean height = 103.2   n = 11   s.d. = 12.37

16. **Quercus laurifolia**   Swamp Laurel Oak
    Mean height = 102.0   n = 1   s.d. =

17. **Quercus nigra**   Water Oak
    Mean height = 101.3   n = 3   s.d. = 23.44

18. **Nyssa biflora**   Swamp Tupelo
    = *Nyssa sylvatica* var. *biflora*
    Mean height = 100.7   n = 3   s.d. = 7.02

19. **Carya tomentosa**   Mockernut
                               Hickory
    Mean height = 100.5   n = 2   s.d. = 3.54

20. **Fraxinus profunda**   Pumpkin Ash
    Mean height = 100.0   n = 1   s.d. =

21. **Quercus austrina**   Bluff Oak
    = *Quercus durandii*, misapplied
    Mean height = 99.8   n = 4   s.d. = 9.81

22. **Carya glabra**   Pignut Hickory
    Mean height = 99.4   n = 5   s.d. = 17.37

23. **Quercus michauxii**   Swamp Chestnut Oak
    = *Quercus prinus*, misapplied
    Mean height = 99.2   n = 6   s.d. = 13.60

24. **Platanus occidentalis**   Sycamore
    Mean height = 98.7   n = 3   s.d. = 6.66

25. **Pinus clausa**   Sand Pine
    Mean height = 96.9   n = 7   s.d. = 8.15

26. **Quercus falcata**   Southern Red Oak
    Mean height = 95.2   n = 5   s.d. = 17.46

27. **Quercus velutina**   Black Oak
    Mean height = 95.0   n = 1   s.d. =

28. **Pinus serotina**   Pond Pine
    Mean height = 94.0   n = 3   s.d. = 9.54

29. **Fraxinus**   Green Ash
    pennsylvanica
    Mean height = 93.0   n = 1   s.d. =

30. **Quercus alba**   White Oak
    Mean height = 91.2   n = 6   s.d. = 21.92

31. **Acer rubrum**   Red Maple
    Mean height = 90.4   n = 9   s.d. = 13.04

32. **Pinus palustris**   Longleaf Pine
    Mean height = 89.6   n = 7   s.d. = 11.91

33. **Taxodium ascendens**   Pond Cypress
    = *Taxodium distichum* var. *nutans*
    Mean height = 89.5   n = 2   s.d. = 36.06

34. **Quercus lyrata**   Overcup Oak
    Mean height = 88.5   n = 2   s.d. = 0.71

35. **Quercus**   Laurel Oak
    hemisphaerica
    = *Quercus laurifolia*, misapplied
    Mean height = 86.3   n = 7   s.d. = 11.98

36. **Fraxinus americana**   White Ash
    Mean height = 84.7   n = 3   s.d. = 9.29

37. **Magnolia grandiflora**   Southern Magnolia
    Mean height = 84.5   n = 6   s.d. = 16.75

38. **Magnolia virginiana**   Sweetbay
    Mean height = 84.3   n = 3   s.d. = 10.69

39. **Tilia caroliniana**   Carolina Basswood
    Mean height = 83.3   n = 3   s.d. = 16.01

40. **Gordonia lasianthus**   Loblolly Bay
    Mean height = 82.5   n = 2   s.d. = 17.68

41. **Prunus serotina**   Black Cherry
    Mean height = 81.7   n = 6   s.d. = 18.32

42. **Quercus pagoda**   Cherrybark Oak
    = *Quercus falcata* var. *pagodifolia*
    Mean height = 81.0   n = 1   s.d. =

43. **Quercus virginiana**   Live Oak
    Mean height = 80.3   n = 23   s.d. = 11.74

44. **Betula nigra**   River Birch
    Mean height = 80.2   n = 4   s.d. = 12.58

45. **Ulmus americana**   Florida Elm
    var. **floridana**
    Mean height = 78.2   n = 5   s.d. = 18.95

46. **Quercus stellata**   Post Oak
    Mean height = 77.8   n = 5   s.d. = 11.28

47. **Nyssa ogeche**   Ogeechee Lime
    Mean height = 75.5   n = 4   s.d. = 21.00

48. **Populus deltoides**   Eastern
                            Cottonwood
    Mean height = 75.0   n = 1   s.d. =

49. **Sabal palmetto**   Cabbage Palm
    Mean height = 75.0   n = 2   s.d. = 21.21

50. **Juglans nigra**   Black Walnut
    Mean height = 74.6   n = 5   s.d. = 24.43

51. **Quercus geminata**   Sand Live Oak
    = *Quercus virginiana* var. *geminata*
    Mean height = 74.5   n = 4   s.d. = 17.92

52. **Roystonea elata**   Florida Royal
                            Palm
    Mean height = 74.4   n = 5   s.d. = 18.47

53. **Quercus margaretta**   Sand Post Oak
    = *Quercus stellata* var. *margaretta*
    Mean height = 73.7   n = 3   s.d. = 12.58

54. **Celtis laevigata**   Sugarberry
    Mean height = 73.4   n = 8   s.d. = 12.39

55. **Magnolia pyramidata**   Pyramid Magnolia
    Mean height = 72.0   n = 3   s.d. = 21.38

55. **Pithecellobium unguis-cati**   Cat's-claw
Mean height = 72.0   n = 1   s.d. =

57. **Gleditsia triacanthos**   Honey Locust
Mean height = 71.5   n = 2   s.d. = 6.36

58. **Chamaecyparis thyoides**   Atlantic White Cedar
Mean height = 71.3   n = 3   s.d. = 15.50

59. **Sapindus marginatus**   Florida Soapberry
Mean height = 70.0   n = 2   s.d. = 2.83

60. **Swietenia mahagoni**   West Indian Mahogany
Mean height = 68.8   n = 4   s.d. = 8.73

61. **Acer floridanum**   Florida Maple
= *Acer barbatum*, misapplied
Mean height = 68.0   n = 2   s.d. = 21.21

62. **Oxydendrum arboreum**   Sourwood
Mean height = 68.0   n = 1   s.d. =

63. **Quercus laevis**   Turkey Oak
Mean height = 67.4   n = 8   s.d. = 8.03

64. **Rhizophora mangle**   Red Mangrove
Mean height = 66.5   n = 2   s.d. = 12.02

65. **Gleditsia aquatica**   Water Locust
Mean height = 66.2   n = 5   s.d. = 9.88

66. **Quercus phellos**   Willow Oak
Mean height = 65.0   n = 1   s.d. =

67. **Persea borbonia**   Red Bay
Mean height = 64.2   n = 6   s.d. = 14.23

68. **Salix nigra**   Black Willow
Mean height = 63.5   n = 2   s.d. = 6.36

69. **Acer negundo**   Box Elder
Mean height = 63.0   n = 3   s.d. = 12.12

70. **Ficus aurea**   Strangler Fig
Mean height = 62.0   n = 3   s.d. = 14.52

71. **Pinus elliottii** var. **densa**   South Florida Slash Pine
Mean height = 59.2   n = 6   s.d. = 9.95

72. **Bumelia lycioides**   Smooth Buckthorn
Mean height = 58.0   n = 1   s.d. =

73. **Ilex opaca**   American Holly
Mean height = 57.5   n = 4   s.d. = 12.12

74. **Juniperus silicicola**   Southern Red Cedar
Mean height = 56.8   n = 6   s.d. = 15.79

75. **Quercus incana**   Bluejack Oak
Mean height = 56.2   n = 5   s.d. = 4.60

76. **Ficus citrifolia**   Wild Banyan, Shortleaf Fig
Mean height = 56.0   n = 2   s.d. = 21.21

77. **Quercus marilandica**   Blackjack Oak
Mean height = 55.5   n = 2   s.d. = 12.02

78. **Ilex krugiana**   Krug's Holly, Tawnyberry Holly
Mean height = 55.0   n = 1   s.d. =

78. **Quercus muehlenbergii**   Chinquapin Oak
Mean height = 55.0   n = 1   s.d. =

80. **Prunus caroliniana**   Cherry Laurel, Laurel Cherry
Mean height = 54.5   n = 2   s.d. = 10.61

81. **Mastichodendron foetidissimum**   False Mastic
= *Sideroxylon foetidissimum*
Mean height = 54.4   n = 7   s.d. = 29.55

82. **Acer saccharinum**   Silver Maple
Mean height = 54.0   n = 2   s.d. = 13.44

82. **Dipholis salicifolia**   Bustic, Willow Bustic
= *Bumelia salicifolia*
Mean height = 54.0   n = 3   s.d. = 4.36

82. **Salix caroliniana**   Carolina Willow, Coastal Plain Willow
Mean height = 54.0   n = 4   s.d. = 10.74

85. **Prunus myrtifolia**   West Indian Cherry Laurel
Mean height = 53.0   n = 1   s.d. =

86. **Ilex cassine**   Dahoon Holly
Mean height = 52.7   n = 6   s.d. = 16.37

87. **Avicennia germinans**   Black Mangrove
= *Avicennia nitida*
Mean height = 52.2   n = 4   s.d. = 7.89

87. **Lysiloma latisiliquum**   Wild Tamarind,
Bahama Lysiloma
Mean height = 52.2   n = 4   s.d. = 18.15

89. **Morus rubra**   Red Mulberry
Mean height = 51.8   n = 4   s.d. = 8.50

90. **Sassafras albidum**   Sassafras
Mean height = 51.7   n = 4   s.d. = 16.28

91. **Quercus chapmanii**   Chapman Oak
Mean height = 51.5   n = 2   s.d. = 9.19

92. **Planera aquatica**   Water Elm
Mean height = 51.3   n = 3   s.d. = 22.37

93. **Halesia diptera**   Two-wing
Silver-bell
Mean height = 51.0   n = 1   s.d. =

93. **Metopium toxiferum**   Poisonwood,
Florida Poisontree
Mean height = 51.0   n = 2   s.d. = 16.97

93. **Simarouba glauca**   Paradise-tree
Mean height = 51.0   n = 4   s.d. = 10.95

96. **Quercus arkansana**   Arkansas Oak
Mean height = 49.0   n = 1   s.d. =

97. **Catalpa bignonioides**   Catalpa
Mean height = 48.7   n = 6   s.d. = 11.47

98. **Castanea ashei**   Ashe Chinquapin
= *Castanea pumila* var. *ashei*
Mean height = 48.5   n = 2   s.d. = 9.19

99. **Symplocos tinctoria**   Sweetleaf
Mean height = 47.7   n = 3   s.d. = 23.86

100. **Zanthoxylum**   Hercules-club,
clava-herculis   Toothache-tree
Mean height = 47.3   n = 6   s.d. = 15.77

101. **Ostrya virginiana**   Ironwood,
Hop Hornbeam
Mean height = 47.2   n = 5   s.d. = 8.58

102. **Carya floridana**   Scrub Hickory
Mean height = 47.0   n = 1   s.d. =

102. **Ilex decidua**   Possum Haw
Mean height = 47.0   n = 1   s.d. =

104. **Bursera simaruba**   Gumbo-limbo
Mean height = 46.9   n = 8   s.d. = 12.61

105. **Cercis canadensis**   Redbud
Mean height = 46.3   n = 3   s.d. = 18.34

106. **Coccoloba uvifera**   Sea Grape
Mean height = 45.7   n = 4   s.d. = 11.03

107. **Aralia spinosa**   Devil's-walking
stick
Mean height = 45.0   n = 4   s.d. = 6.98

107. **Conocarpus erectus**   Buttonwood,
Button Mangrove
Mean height = 45.0   n = 3   s.d. = 7.94

109. **Carpinus caroliniana**   Blue Beech,
Hornbeam
Mean height = 44.7   n = 4   s.d. = 4.65

110. **Cliftonia monophylla**   Buckwheat-tree
Mean height = 44.0   n = 3   s.d. = 14.00

110. **Cyrilla racemiflora**   Titi,
Swamp Cyrilla
Mean height = 44.0   n = 1   s.d. =

110. **Fraxinus caroliniana**   Pop Ash,
Carolina Ash
Mean height = 44.0   n = 2   s.d. = 19.80

110. **Rhamnus caroliniana**   Carolina
Buckthorn
Mean height = 44.0   n = 1   s.d. =

114. **Castanea alnifolia**   Southern
Chinquapin,
= *Castanea floridana*   Florida
Chinquapin
Mean height = 43.5   n = 2   s.d. = 3.54

114. **Magnolia ashei**   Ashe Magnolia
Mean height = 43.5   n = 2   s.d. = 13.44

116. **Coccoloba diversifolia**   Pigeon Plum
Mean height = 43.0   n = 2   s.d. = 8.49

117. **Quercus myrtifolia**   Myrtle Oak
Mean height = 42.0   n = 2   s.d. = 8.49

118. **Ilex myrtifolia**   Myrtle Holly,
Myrtle Dahoon
Holly
Mean height = 41.8   n = 5   s.d. = 9.39

119. **Chionanthus virginicus**   Fringe-tree
Mean height = 41.0   n = 1   s.d. =

119. **Colubrina elliptica**   Nakedwood,
Soldierwood
Mean height = 41.0   n = 1   s.d. =

119. **Exothea paniculata**   Butterbough,
Inkwood
Mean height = 41.0   n = 4   s.d. = 4.08

119. **Piscidia piscipula**   Fish-fuddle,
Jamaica
Dogwood,
Fishpoison-tree
Mean height = 41.0   n = 1   s.d. =

119. **Tetrazygia bicolor**   Florida Tetrazygia
Mean height = 41.0   n = 1   s.d. =

124. **Ilex vomitoria**   Yaupon
Mean height = 40.5   n = 2   s.d. = 12.02

125. **Cornus florida**   Flowering
Dogwood
Mean height = 40.3   n = 3   s.d. = 7.51

126. **Amelanchier arborea**   Downy
Serviceberry
Mean height = 40.0   n = 1   s.d. =

127. **Osmanthus megacarpus**   Scrub Wild Olive
Mean height = 40.0   n = 1   s.d. =

128. **Torreya taxifolia**   Gopherwood,
Florida Torreya
Mean height = 39.0   n = 1   s.d. =

129. **Hypelate trifoliata**   White Ironwood
Mean height = 38.5   n = 2   s.d. = 0.71

130. **Drypetes diversifolia**   Milk-bark
Mean height = 38.3   n = 4   s.d. = 7.18

131. **Annona glabra**   Pond Apple
Mean height = 38.0   n = 6   s.d. = 6.72

131. **Crataegus pulcherrima**   Smooth Haw,
Beautiful Haw
Mean height = 38.0   n = 2   s.d. = 11.3

131. **Persea humilis**   Silk Bay
= *Persea borbonia* var. *humilis*
Mean height = 38.0   n = 1   s.d. =

134. **Myrcianthes simpsonii**   Simpson's
Twinberry,
Simpson Stopper
= *Myrcianthes fragrans* var. *simpsonii*
Mean height = 37.7   n = 3   s.d. = 6.03

135. **Calyptranthes pallens**   Spicewood,
Pale Lidflower
Mean height = 36.5   n = 2   s.d. = 4.95

136. **Citharexylum fruticosum**   Fiddlewood
Mean height = 36.0   n = 3   s.d. = 7.94

137. **Prunus americana**   Wild Plum
Mean height = 35.7   n = 3   s.d. = 12.01

138. **Osmanthus americanus**   Wild Olive,
Devilwood
Mean height = 35.0   n = 3   s.d. = 11.53

138. **Prunus alabamensis**   Alabama Cherry
= *Prunus serotina* var. *alabamensis*
Mean height = 35.0   n = 1   s.d. =

140. **Lyonia ferruginea**   Rusty Lyonia,
Staggerbush,
Tree Lyonia
Mean height = 34.6   n = 5   s.d. = 3.85

141. **Hippomane mancinella**   Manchineel
Mean height = 34.5   n = 2   s.d. = 16.26

142. **Bumelia tenax**   Tough Buckthorn,
Tough Bumelia
Mean height = 34.0   n = 3   s.d. = 8.19

142. **Crataegus viridis**   Green Haw
Mean height = 34.0   n = 3   s.d. = 3.46

142. **Eugenia confusa**   Redberry Stopper,
Redberry Eugenia
Mean height = 34.0   n = 2   s.d. = 16.97

145. **Clusia rosea**   Balsam Apple
Mean height = 33.5   n = 2   s.d. = 9.19

145. **Myrica cerifera**   Wax Myrtle,
Bayberry
Mean height = 33.5   n = 2   s.d. = 3.54

145. **Prunus umbellata**   Hog Plum,
Flatwoods Plum
Mean height = 33.5   n = 2   s.d. = 0.71

148. **Chrysophyllum**   Satinleaf
oliviforme
Mean height = 33.3   n = 3   s.d. = 7.51

149. **Crataegus crus-galli**   Cockspur Haw
= *Crataegus pyracanthoides*
Mean height = 33.0   n = 3   s.d. = 2.65

149. **Crataegus marshallii**   Parsley Haw
Mean height = 33.0   n = 1   s.d. =

149. **Krugiodendron**   Black Ironwood,
ferreum   Leadwood
Mean height = 33.0   n = 1   s.d. =

149. **Sapindus saponaria**   Tropical
Soapberry,
Winged
Soapberry
Mean height = 33.0   n = 1   s.d. =

153. **Acoelorrhaphe**   Paurotis Palm
wrightii   = *Paurotis wrightii*
Mean height = 32.0   n = 1   s.d. =

154. **Cupania glabra**   Florida Cupania
Mean height = 31.0   n = 1   s.d. =

154. **Drypetes lateriflora**   Guiana Plum
Mean height = 31.0   n = 2   s.d. = 0.00

156. **Rhus copallinum**   Winged Sumac,
Shining Sumac
Mean height = 30.8   n = 4   s.d. = 12.69

157. **Aesculus pavia**   Red Buckeye
Mean height = 30.7   n =   s.d. = 5.03

158. **Crataegus spathulata**   Red Haw,
Littlehip Haw
Mean height = 30.5   n = 2   s.d. = 2.12

159. **Vaccinium arboreum**   Farkleberry,
Sparkleberry,
Tree Huckleberry
Mean height = 30.4   n = 5   s.d. = 6.43

160. **Pisonia discolor**   Blolly, Longleaf
Blolly
= *Guapira discolor*
Mean height = 29.7   n = 4   s.d. = 6.13

161. **Guaiacum sanctum**   Holywood Lignum-
vitae, Roughbark
Lignum-vitae
Mean height = 29.4   n = 5   s.d. = 6.66

162. **Malus angustifolia**   Wild Crab Apple
Mean height = 28.7   n = 3   s.d. = 2.52

163. **Ateramnus lucidus**   Crabwood,
Oysterwood
= *Gymnanthes lucida*
Mean height = 28.5   n = 2   s.d. = 6.36

163. **Trema micrantha**   Florida Trema
Mean height = 28.5   n = 2   s.d. = 15.98

165. **Bucida spinosa**   Ming-tree, Spiny
Black Olive
Mean height = 28.0   n = 1   s.d. =

165. **Crataegus aestivalis**   May Haw
Mean height = 28.0   n = 1   s.d. =

167. **Agarista populifolia**   Pipestem
= *Leucothoe acuminata*
Mean height = 27.0   n = 1   s.d. =

167. **Bumelia anomala**   Alachua
Buckthorn
Mean height = 27.0   n = 1   s.d. =

167. **Coccothrinax**   Silver Palm
argentata
Mean height = 27.0   n = 2   s.d. = 2.83

167. **Myrsine floridana**   Myrsine,
Florida Rapanea
= *Rapanea punctata*;
Rapanea guianensis, misapplied
Mean height = 27.0   n = 2   s.d. = 4.24

167. **Schaefferia frutescens**   Florida Boxwood
Mean height = 27.0   n = 1   s.d. =

172. **Crataegus michauxii**   Summer Haw,
Yellow Haw
= *Crataegus flava*, misapplied
Mean height = 26.7   n = 3   s.d. = 2.89

173. **Eugenia axillaris**   White Stopper
Mean height = 26.5   n = 2   s.d. = 2.12

173. **Pinckneya bracteata**   Fever-tree
= *Pinckneya pubens*
Mean height = 26.5   n = 2   s.d. = 7.78

175. **Viburnum obovatum**   Blackhaw,
Walter's Viburnum
Mean height = 26.3   n = 3   s.d. = 3.51

176. **Canella winterana**   Wild Cinnamon
Mean height = 26.0   n = 3   s.d. = 5.20

176. **Ilex verticillata**   Winterberry
Mean height = 26.0   n = 1   s.d. =

176. **Viburnum scabrellum**   Southern
Arrow-wood
Mean height = 26.0   n = 1   s.d. =

176. **Zanthoxylum fagara**   Wild Lime,
Lime Prickly Ash
Mean height = 26.0   n = 1   s.d. =

180. **Bumelia lanuginosa**   Woolly Buckthorn,
Gum Bumelia
Mean height = 25.7   n = 3   s.d. = 15.31

181. **Thrinax radiata**   Florida Thatch
Palm
Mean height = 25.5   n = 2   s.d. = 3.54

182. **Bumelia celastrina**   Saffron Plum
Mean height = 25.0   n = 4   s.d. = 2.83

182. **Byrsonima lucida**   Locust-berry,
Byrsonima
Mean height = 25.0   n = 5   s.d. = 7.97

182. **Casasia clusiifolia**   Seven-year Apple
= *Genipa clusiifolia*
Mean height = 25.0   n = 1   s.d. =

182. **Forestiera acuminata**   Swamp Privet
Mean height = 25.0   n = 1   s.d. =

182. **Ximenia americana**   Tallow-wood
Mean height = 25.0   n = 1   s.d. =

187. **Ilex ambigua**   Sand Holly,
Carolina Holly
Mean height = 24.7   n = 3   s.d. = 2.52

188. **Asimina parviflora**   Small-flowered
Pawpaw
Mean height = 24.0   n = 1   s.d. =

188. **Pseudophoenix sargentii**   Buccaneer Palm,
Sargent's Cherry
Palm
Mean height = 24.0   n = 2   s.d. = 1.41

190. **Cephalanthus occidentalis**   Buttonbush
Mean height = 23.7   n = 3   s.d. = 4.16

191. **Pisonia rotundata**   Pisonia
Mean height = 23.5   n = 2   s.d. = 6.36

191. **Reynosia septentrionalis**   Darling Plum
Mean height = 23.5   n = 2   s.d. = 6.36

193. **Alnus serrulata**   Hazel Alder
Mean height = 23.0   n = 1   s.d. =

193. **Amyris elemifera**   Torchwood
Mean height = 23.0   n = 2   s.d. = 1.41

193. **Bourreria radula**   Rough Strongback
Mean height = 23.0   n = 1   s.d. =

193. **Celtis pallida**   Spiny Hackberry
Mean height = 23.0   n = 1   s.d. =

193. **Guettarda elliptica**   Velvet-seed
Mean height = 23.0   n = 1   s.d. =

193. **Halesia carolina**   Little Silver-bell
= *Halesia parviflora*
Mean height = 23.0   n = 1   s.d. =

199. **Erythrina herbacea**   Cherokee Bean,
Coral Bean
Mean height = 22.5   n = 4   s.d. = 7.14

200. **Bourreria ovata**   Bahama Strong
back
Mean height = 21.5   n = 2   s.d. = 9.19

201. **Cornus foemina**   Smooth-leaf
Cornel, Swamp
= *Cornus stricta*   Dogwood
Mean height = 21.3   n = 3   s.d. = 1.53

202. **Carica papaya**   Papaya
Mean height = 21.0   n = 2   s.d. = 5.66

202. **Ptelea trifoliata**   Wafer Ash, Hop-
tree
Mean height = 21.0   n = 1   s.d. =

202. **Serenoa repens**   Saw Palmetto
Mean height = 21.0   n = 3   s.d. = 1.00

202. **Viburnum rufidulum**   Rusty Blackhaw
Mean height = 21.0   n = 1   s.d. =

206. **Acacia farnesiana**   Sweet Acacia,
Huisache
Mean height = 20.5   n = 2   s.d. = .71

207. **Acacia choriophylla**   Cinnecord
Mean height = 20.0   n = 1   s.d. =

207. **Crataegus opaca**   Western May Haw,
Apple Haw
Mean height = 20.0   n = 1   s.d. =

207. **Rhus vernix**   Poison Sumac
= *Toxicodendron vernix*
Mean height = 20.0   n = 2   s.d. = 5.66

207. **Salix floridana**   Florida Willow
Mean height = 20.0   n = 1   s.d. =

207. **Taxus floridana**   Florida Yew
Mean height = 20.0   n = 1   s.d. =

207. **Zanthoxylum flavum**   Yellowheart, West
Indies Satinwood
Mean height = 20.0   n = 1   s.d. =

213. **Cereus robinii**   Key Tree Cactus
Mean height = 19.7   n = 2   s.d. = 4.60

214. **Gyminda latifolia**   False Boxwood
Mean height = 19.0   n = 1   s.d. =

214. **Thrinax morrisii**   Brittle Thatch
Palm
Mean height = 19.0   n = 1   s.d. =

216. **Cornus asperifolia**   Rough-leaf Cornel
= *Cornus microcarpa*
Mean height = 18.5   n = 2   s.d. = 2.12

217. **Crataegus uniflora**   One-flowered Haw
Mean height = 18.0   n = 1   s.d. =

217. **Illicium parviflorum**   Florida Banana-
shrub, Yellow
Anise
Mean height = 18.0   n = 1   s.d. =

217. **Schoepfia
chrysophylloides**   Whitewood,
Graytwig
Mean height = 18.0   n = 1   s.d. =

220. **Forestiera segregata**   Florida Privet
Mean height = 17.5   n = 1   s.d. =

220. **Maytenus
phyllanthoides**   Florida Mayten
Mean height = 17.5   n = 2   s.d. = 0.71

220. **Pithecellobium
keyense**   Black-bead
= *Pithecellobium guadalupense*
Mean height = 17.5   n = 2   s.d. = 2.12

223. **Sambucus canadensis**   Elderberry
= *Sambucus simpsonii*
Mean height = 17.0   n = 3   s.d. = 3.61

224. **Leitneria floridana**   Corkwood
Mean height = 16.0   n = 1   s.d. =

225. **Manilkara bahamensis**   Wild Dilly
= *Achras emarginata*
Mean height = 15.5   n = 2   s.d. = 7.78

226. **Stewartia
malacodendron**   Silky Camellia
Mean height = 15.3   n = 3   s.d. = 3.21

227. **Alvaradoa
amorphoides**   Mexican Alvaradoa
Mean height = 15.0   n = 1   s.d. =

227. **Capparis
cynophallophora**   Jamaica Caper
Mean height = 15.0   n = 1   s.d. =

227. **Prunus angustifolia**   Chickasaw Plum
Mean height = 15.0   n = 1   s.d. =

227. **Yucca aloifolia**   Spanish-dagger,
Aloe Yucca
Mean height = 15.0   n = 1   s.d. =

231. **Hamelia patens**   Fire-bush
Mean height = 13.0   n = 1   s.d. =

232. **Jacquinia keyensis**   Joe-wood
Mean height = 12.7   n = 3   s.d. = 1.53

233. **Suriana maritima**   Bay Cedar
Mean height = 12.0   n = 1   s.d. =

234. **Kalmia latifolia**   Mountain Laurel
Mean height = 11.0   n = 1   s.d. =

235. **Baccharis halimifolia**   Common Saltbush,
Groundsel-tree
Mean height = 10.0   n = 1   s.d. =

236. **Guettarda scabra**   Rough Velvet-seed
Mean height = 8.0   n = 1   s.d. =

THE "AVERAGE" CHAMPION

Once data are available as to the dimensions of the large trees within an area it is possible to make calculations of the size and proportions of the "average" large tree.

Of greatest interest are those trees that have been designated Champions, either at the State or National level. The question may be asked, "What would be the dimensions of a hypothetical tree whose measurements were the average of those individuals determined to be champions of the different species?"

This question may best be addressed by separate treatment of those trees growing in Florida that have been designated National champions, and those designated Florida champions. These two categories of trees differ appreciably in size, with the Florida champions much the larger. The National champions (based upon 120 trees) averaged 65 inches in circumference and 44 feet in height, with a point value of 117. The Florida champions (based upon 99 trees) averaged 100 inches in circumference and 67 feet in height, with a point value of 179.

At first thought, trees in Florida that are the largest of their kind within the United States might be expected to exceed in size those trees that may be the largest of their species within Florida but are surpassed elsewhere in the nation. But the unequivocal contrary ranking found here is explained by differences between the species falling within the two categories. The many tree species that occur in the United States only in the tropical and subtropical areas of Florida also are found very generally throughout the New World tropics, where they reach only small to moderate dimensions; the modest size most such species attain in Florida is surely a consequence of inherent genetic limits. In contrast, the forests of the eastern United States are comprised of many species of great potential size; tree species native to Florida but also widespread northward have

opportunity in these other portions of their range to experience optimal growth under conditions that are not met within their Florida range. Thus, though there are exceptions, the geographic affiliation of Florida's champions largely determines into which category they will fall—the National champions, mostly of tropical species native (within the United States) only in southern Florida and typically of small to moderate size; and the Florida champions, of species whose ranges are largely northward and represented in Florida by individuals often of large size but still less than the largest found elsewhere.

More narrowly directed questions may also be asked. What would be the dimensions of a tree that represents the average champion oak? The average champion pine? Hollies? Palms? Are conifers as a class larger or smaller than dicots? Such questions yield views of plant groups that are unavailable by other means. And perhaps of greater value, the average measurements permit quantitative statements of absolute and relative size.

It is thus possible to say, for example, that Florida's largest conifers, as a class, are larger than Florida's largest dicotyledonous (broadleaf) tree species, which in turn surpass Florida's palms, and that the size ratio of these three groups (as expressed by point size) is approximately 3 : 2 : 1. The oaks (*Quercus*), hickories (*Carya*), ashes (*Fraxinus*), and elms (*Ulmus*), as genera, are appreciably larger than the average dicotyledonous tree, while the willows (*Salix*), haws (*Crataegus*), and buckthorns (*Bumelia*) are significantly smaller; numerical ratios may be used here also. Such relative sizes perhaps correspond closely with generally held concepts of these several genera, but it is gratifying to have a means of quantitative judgment.

Comparisons between genera may also be made on the basis of height or other measured dimensions. Some species of oak (*Quercus*) attain relatively large sizes, while others are more modest; the same is of course true for pines (*Pinus*). But what is a typical height (or circumference or crown spread) for the champions of these two genera, and how do they compare one with the other? When the champion oaks are averaged and compared with the champion pines, the pines are found to be somewhat taller (99 feet versus 87 feet). The oaks, however, exhibit appreciably larger trunk circumferences (168 inches) and crown spreads (83 feet) than do the pines (116 inches, and 54 feet). Overall, Florida's oaks, as represented by the largest individuals of each species, may be stated to be larger trees than Florida's pines (275 versus 229 points).

One must recognize that any such groupings, either of genera or higher taxonomic rank, are inherently heterogeneous, in that they are composed of different species which may vary greatly in size. The significance of any comparisons may be nullified by such variability. But where the broad concept of a genus (or other group) is deemed useful, employment of champion tree size data may permit valuable objective comparisons.

A partial compilation is provided of the average dimensions recorded in groups of interest among Florida's champions.

Florida's National Champions.
Average of all available species.

Size:	Circumference:	65.4	inches
	Height:	44.0	feet
	Crown spread:	32.7	feet
	Total points:	117	points

Comments: Based upon 120 National champions located within Florida.

Florida's State Champions.
Average of all available species.

Size:	Circumference:	100.5	inches
	Height:	67.2	feet
	Crown spread:	47.7	feet
	Total points:	179	points

Comments: Based upon 99 Florida champions (native species only).

Chamaecyparis, Juniperus, Pinus, Taxodium, Taxus, Torreya spp.
Conifers.
Average of all available species.

Size:	Circumference:	129.4	inches
	Height:	89.8	feet
	Crown spread:	47.9	feet
	Total points:	231	points

Comments: Based upon 17 trees, each the National (within Florida) or Florida champion.

Dicotyledoneae   Dicots.
Average of all available species.

Size:	Circumference:	73.4	inches
	Height:	51.1	feet
	Crown spread:	39.5	feet
	Total points:	134	points

Comments: Based upon 228 trees, each the National (within Florida) or Florida champion.

Acoelorrhaphe, Coccothrinax, Pseudophoenix, Roystonea, Sabal, Serenoa, Thrinax spp.   Palms.
Average of all available species.

Size:	Circumference:	30.2	inches
	Height:	38.2	feet
	Crown spread:	10.2	feet
	Total points:	71	points

Comments: Based upon 12 trees, each the National (within Florida) or Florida champion.

Acer spp.   Maples.
Average of all available species.

Size:	Circumference:	91.0	inches
	Height:	78.2	feet
	Crown spread:	49.6	feet
	Total points:	182	points

Comments: Based upon 4 trees, each the National (within Florida) or Florida champion.

Bumelia spp.   Buckthorns.
Average of all available species.

Size:	Circumference:	29.0	inches
	Height:	35.0	feet
	Crown spread:	25.4	feet
	Total points:	70	points

Comments: Based upon 4 trees, each the National (within Florida) or Florida champion.

Carya spp.   Hickories.
Average of all available species.

Size:	Circumference:	143.3	inches
	Height:	93.5	feet
	Crown spread:	73.7	feet
	Total points:	255	points

Comments: Based upon 6 trees, each the National (within Florida) or Florida champion.

Crataegus spp.   Haws.
Average of all available species.

Size:	Circumference:	26.9	inches
	Height:	29.1	feet
	Crown spread:	25.7	feet
	Total points:	63	points

Comments: Based upon 8 trees, each the National (within Florida) or Florida champion.

Eugenia, Myrcianthes spp.   Stoppers.
Average of all available species.

Size:	Circumference:	31.0	inches
	Height:	37.5	feet
	Crown spread:	21.5	feet
	Total points:	74	points

Comments: Based upon 4 trees, each the National (within Florida) or Florida champion.

Fraxinus spp.   Ashes.
Average of all available species.

Size:	Circumference:	116.7	inches
	Height:	82.0	feet
	Crown spread:	40.5	feet
	Total points:	209	points

Comments: Based upon 4 trees, each the National (within Florida) or Florida champion.

Ilex spp.   Hollies.
Average of all available species.

Size:	Circumference:	43.4	inches
	Height:	45.1	feet
	Crown spread:	33.3	feet
	Total points:	97	points

Comments: Based upon 10 trees, each the National (within Florida) or Florida champion.

Pinus spp.   Pines.
Average of all available species.

Size:	Circumference:	116.0	inches
	Height:	99.4	feet
	Crown spread:	54.0	feet
	Total points:	229	points

Comments: Based upon 12 trees, each the National (within Florida) or Florida champion.

Prunus spp.   Cherries, Plums.
Average of all available species.

Size:	Circumference:	68.3	inches
	Height:	40.9	feet
	Crown spread:	33.4	feet
	Total points:	118	points

Comments: Based upon 7 trees, each the National (within Florida) or Florida champion.

Quercus spp.   Oaks.
Average of all available species.

Size:	Circumference:	167.8	inches
	Height:	86.6	feet
	Crown spread:	83.1	feet
	Total points:	275	points

Comments: Based upon 22 trees, each the National (within Florida) or Florida champion.

Salix spp.   Willows.
Average of all available species.

Size:	Circumference:	33.0	inches
	Height:	43.7	feet
	Crown spread:	24.3	feet
	Total points:	46	points

Comments: Based upon 3 trees, each the National (within Florida) or Florida champion.

Ulmus spp.   Elms.
Average of all available species.

Size:	Circumference:	102.2	inches
	Height:	88.2	feet
	Crown spread:	64.0	feet
	Total points:	207	points

Comments: Based upon 6 trees, each the National (within Florida) or Florida champion.

LARGE VINES

A vine, by definition, is not a tree. It is woody, and it will generally have one stem, characteristics shared by trees. But the stem is not self-supporting, an essential trait of all plants defined as trees.

During the recent phase of the Florida Champion Tree Survey the writers were repeatedly told of giant vines, with the suggestion that they should also be included. Obviously, however, to do so would appreciably extend the original intent of recording and comparing large trees. Though a vine can be measured, its trunk is designed by evolution to minimize the amount of supporting tissue that must be produced to enable the foliage to receive sunlight, at the expense of the host tree. Thus the height, and often the spread, of a vine is very much greater than would be expected of a tree with similar trunk dimensions.

But aside from the difference in proportion, which would cause them to receive small total point scores, and the lack of precedence, there seems to be no fundamental reason why equivalent measurements of vines would not provide information that is not otherwise available. With a view to future studies it may be useful to record those species native to Florida that are known to form robust woody vining stems:

Pepper-vine	**Ampelopsis arborea** (L.) Koehne
Rattan-vine	**Berchemia scandens** (Hill) K. Koch
Trumpet-vine	**Campsis radicans** (L.) Bureau
Catesby's Virgin's-bower	**Clematis catesbyana** Pursh
Hippocratea	**Hippocratea volubilis** L.
Devil's-claws	**Pisonia aculeata** L.
Poison Ivy	**Rhus radicans** L.
Summer Grape	**Vitis aestivalis** Michx.
Muscadine Grape	**Vitis rotundifolia** Michx.
Frost Grape	**Vitis vulpina** L.

For the present, since documentation is available for only three vines, one cannot easily appraise their relative size. But in the opinion of the nominators, the following vines so greatly surpass any others of their species observed within the state that they justify inclusion in this data base.

Pisonia aculeata L.
Devil's-claws, Catch-and-Hold-Back

Florida Champion.

Size:			
	Circumference:	22	inches
	Height:	45	feet
	Crown spread:	25	feet
	Total points:	73	points

Owner / location: Collier-Seminole State Park / 20200 E. Tamiami Trail, Collier Co. [n.e. 1/4 of sec 34, T51S, R27E]

Nominator(s) / date: Daniel F. Austin, Richard Moyroud / 1995

Comments: This species usually has the form of a sprawling shrub or of a vine that sends its new stems upward through the overlying vegetation, and retains its position by means of sharp-pointed recurving branches (hence its common names).

Rhus radicans L.
= *Toxicodendron radicans* (L.) Kuntze
Poison Ivy

Florida Champion.

Size:			
	Circumference:	13	inches
	Height:	67	feet
	Crown spread:	20.5	feet
	Total points:	85	points

Owner / location: Three Rivers State Recreation Area / McMillan picnic area, 2 mi. n. of Sneads, Jackson Co. [s.w. 1/4 of sec 15, T4N, R7W]

Nominator(s) / date: Robert T. Ing, Daniel B. Ward / 1995

Comments: This giant ivy, climbing on a tall loblolly pine at the edge of Lake Seminole, is scarcely larger than others on near-by trees.

Vitis aestivalis Michx.
Summer Grape

Florida Champion.

Size:			
	Circumference:	28	inches
	Height:	68	feet
	Crown spread:	60	feet
	Total points:	111	points

Owner / location: Mike Herlong / w. side of Fla. 47, 0.2 mi. n. of jct. with U.S. 27, Fort White, Columbia Co. [n.e. 1/4 of sec 33, T6S, R16E]

Nominator(s) / date: Robert W. Simons, Daniel B. Ward / 1995

Comments: This ancient grapevine and its supporting 80 ft. laurel oak are surrounded and protected by a small park.

COUNTY TREE-FIND LIST

The following list of scientific names permits one to determine the species of living trees that have been nominated during the Champion Tree Survey for each of the 67 Florida counties. Both native and non-native species are listed; the non-natives are indicated by an asterisk (*). Further data, including location and owner, may be obtained by reference under the appropriate name in the INVENTORY listing.

This listing may serve, if desired, as the framework for preparation of big-tree "day trips," in which a route is laid out that will take interested persons on a tour of the area's exceptional trees. Such a formal tour, as prepared by local authorities, should include not only further information regarding each tree, but detailed instructions as how best to view the tree and cautions of property rights and restrictions.

The striking inequality in the number of trees nominated from the different counties is primarily a consequence of two very different factors. The climatic and edaphic uniqueness of the southernmost counties is reflected in the number of tropical and subtropical species found only in this region. Thus Monroe County, encompassing the Florida Keys and a portion of the Everglades, is not only environmentally varied but is also exceptional within the limits of Florida and the United States; 59 trees have been nominated from Monroe, of which 48 are native. To a slightly lesser extent the neighboring counties of Dade, Lee, and Broward share in this subtropical luxuriance; each has 46 nominated trees, though the number of natives (27, 17, and 12, respectively) is greatly supplemented by an abundance of non-native species.

A second factor influencing the number of trees nominated from a given county is the time and effort exerted by persons within that county to document the big trees readily accessible to them. Alachua County, with 81 nominated trees (of which 57 are native), has for many years been the home of the present investigators, as well as that of other persons professionally or avocationally interested in trees. To a lesser extent other counties, notably Duval, Gadsden, Hamilton, Hendry, Jackson, Lafayette, Leon, Marion, Putnam, and Sarasota, have been the address of one or more individuals (named in the ACKNOWLEDGMENTS) especially active in documenting big trees.

The paucity or absence of nominations from certain other counties is surely a consequence of incomplete surveying rather than limited biotic diversity. It is to be expected that future investigation will disclose these counties to contain numerous trees of impressive size, equal to or in many cases exceeding those thus far recorded.

ALACHUA COUNTY

Acer negundo	Box Elder
Aesculus pavia	Red Buckeye
Ailanthus altissima *	Tree-of-heaven
Aleurites fordii *	Tung-tree
Aralia spinosa	Devil's-walkingstick
Broussonetia papyrifera *	Paper Mulberry
Bumelia anomala	Alachua Buckthorn
Bumelia lanuginosa	Woolly Buckthorn
Butia capitata *	Pindo Palm
Carya glabra	Pignut Hickory
Catalpa bignonioides	Catalpa
Celtis laevigata	Sugarberry
Cephalanthus occidentalis	Buttonbush
Cercis canadensis	Redbud
Cornus asperifolia	Rough-leaf Cornel

Crataegus michauxii	Summer Haw	**Sabal causiarum** *	Puerto Rican
Crataegus uniflora	One-flowered Haw		Hat Palm
Crataegus viridis	Green Haw	**Salix caroliniana**	Carolina Willow
Cunninghamia lanceolata *	China Fir	**Sapindus marginatus**	Florida Soapberry
Cupressocyparis leylandii *	Leyland Cypress	**Sapium sebiferum** *	Chinese Tallow-tree
Cupressus sempervirens *	Italian Cypress	**Symplocos tinctoria**	Sweetleaf
Diospyros virginiana	Persimmon	**Taxodium distichum**	Bald Cypress
Eucalyptus cinerea *	Silver-dollar	**Ulmus alata**	Winged Elm
	Eucalyptus	**Ulmus parvifolia** *	Chinese Elm
Fraxinus americana	White Ash	**Ulmus pumila** *	Siberian Elm
Fraxinus caroliniana	Pop Ash	**Vaccinium arboreum**	Sparkleberry
Gleditsia aquatica	Water Locust	**Viburnum obovatum**	Blackhaw
Ilex ambigua	Sand Holly	**Viburnum rufidulum**	Rusty Blackhaw
Ilex attenuata *	East Palatka Holly	**Zanthoxylum**	Hercules-club
Ilex opaca	American Holly	**clava-herculis**	
Ilex rotunda *	Round Holly		
Juglans nigra	Black Walnut		
Juniperus silicicola	Southern Red Cedar	**BAKER COUNTY**	
Koelreuteria elegans *	Golden-rain-tree		
Ligustrum lucidum *	Tree Privet	**Ulmus americana**	Florida Elm
Liquidambar formosana *	Formosa		
	Sweet Gum	**BAY COUNTY**	
Liriodendron tulipifera	Tulip-tree		
Maclura pomifera *	Osage Orange	**Lagerstroemia indica** *	Crape Myrtle
Magnolia grandiflora	Southern Magnolia		
Malus angustifolia	Wild Crab Apple	**BRADFORD COUNTY**	
Melia azedarach *	Chinaberry		
Morus rubra	Red Mulberry	**Ilex myrtifolia**	Myrtle Holly
Ostrya virginiana	Hop Hornbeam		
Persea borbonia	Red Bay	**BREVARD COUNTY**	
Pinus glabra	Spruce Pine		
Pinus palustris	Longleaf Pine	**Juniperus silicicola**	Southern Red Cedar
Pistacia chinensis *	Chinese Pistachio		
Planera aquatica	Water Elm	**BROWARD COUNTY**	
Platanus occidentalis	Sycamore		
Platycladus orientalis *	Oriental Arborvitae	**Adansonia digitata** *	Baobab
Podocarpus	Japanese Yew	**Araucaria heterophylla** *	Norfolk Island Pine
macrophyllus *		**Averrhoa carambola** *	Carambola
Prunus americana	Wild Plum	**Avicennia germinans**	Black Mangrove
Prunus caroliniana	Cherry Laurel	**Bombax ceiba** *	Red Silk-cotton
Prunus serotina	Black Cherry	**Brosimum alicastrum** *	Breadnut
Prunus umbellata	Hog Plum	**Broussonetia papyrifera** *	Paper Mulberry
Ptelea trifoliata	Wafer Ash	**Bucida spinosa**	Spiny Black Olive
Quercus acutissima *	Sawtooth Oak	**Bursera simaruba**	Gumbo-limbo
Quercus alba	White Oak	**Caesalpinia pulcherrima** *	Pride-of-Barbados
Quercus austrina	Bluff Oak	**Catalpa longissima** *	Haiti Catalpa
Quercus falcata	Southern Red Oak	**Cavanillesia platanifolia** *	Cuipo
Quercus geminata	Sand Live Oak	**Chorisia insignis** *	Yellow-flowered
Quercus hemisphaerica	Laurel Oak		Chorisia
Quercus laevis	Turkey Oak	**Chrysophyllum oliviforme**	Satinleaf
Quercus laurifolia	Swamp Laurel Oak	**Clusia rosea**	Balsam Apple
Quercus michauxii	Swamp	**Coccoloba uvifera**	Sea Grape
	Chestnut Oak	**Enterolobium**	Pacara
Quercus phellos	Willow Oak	**contortisiliquum** *	
Quercus stellata	Post Oak	**Enterolobium**	Ear-tree
Quercus virginiana	Live Oak	**cyclocarpum** *	
Robinia pseudoacacia *	Black Locust		

Erythrina variegata *	Indian Coral-tree
Ficus altissima *	Lofty Fig
Ficus citrifolia	Shortleaf Fig
Ficus minahassea *	Ayumit Fig
Ficus racemosa *	Cluster Fig
Hura crepitans *	Sandbox-tree
Mangifera indica *	Mango
Mastichodendron foetidissimum	False Mastic
Melaleuca quinquenervia *	Punk-tree
Myrcianthes simpsonii	Simpson Stopper
Orbignya cohune *	Cohune Palm
Peltophorum pterocarpum *	Yellow Poinciana
Persea americana *	Avocado
Phoenix canariensis *	Canary Island Date Palm
Pithecellobium saman *	Rain-tree
Schinus terebinthifolius *	Brazilian Pepper
Simarouba glauca	Paradise-tree
Spondias cytherea *	Otaheite Apple
Sterculia foetida *	Indian Almond
Swietenia mahagoni	West Indian Mahogany
Swinglea glutinosa *	Tabog
Tabebuia caraiba *	Silver Trumpet-tree
Tabebuia heterophylla *	Pink Trumpet-tree
Tabebuia rosea *	Rosy Trumpet-tree
Taxodium mucronatum *	Montezuma Cypress
Thrinax radiata	Florida Thatch Palm
Xylosma congestum *	Xylosma
Ziziphus mauritiana *	Indian Jujube

CALHOUN COUNTY

Araucaria araucana *	Monkey-puzzle
Carya aquatica	Water Hickory
Ilex myrtifolia	Myrtle Holly
Quercus hemisphaerica	Laurel Oak
Quercus nigra	Water Oak
Quercus virginiana	Live Oak

CHARLOTTE COUNTY

Ficus benghalensis *	Banyan Fig
Pinus elliottii	Slash Pine

CITRUS COUNTY

Acer rubrum	Red Maple
Cinnamomum camphora *	Camphor-tree
Pinus palustris	Longleaf Pine
Pinus taeda	Loblolly Pine
Zanthoxylum clava-herculis	Hercules-club

CLAY COUNTY

Acer rubrum	Red maple
Carya glabra	Pignut Hickory
Ilex opaca	American Holly
Liquidambar styraciflua	Sweet Gum
Magnolia grandiflora	Southern Magnolia
Pinus elliottii	Slash Pine
Pinus taeda	Loblolly Pine

COLLIER COUNTY

Bischofia javanica *	Toog
Conocarpus erectus	Buttonwood
Ilex cassine	Dahoon Holly
Khaya senegalensis *	Senegal Mahogany
Koelreuteria elegans *	Golden-rain-tree
Pinus elliottii	Slash Pine
Pisonia aculeata	Catch-and Hold-Back
Pterocarpus indicus *	Burmese Rosewood
Roystonea elata	Florida Royal Palm
Spathodea campanulata *	African Tulip-tree
Tabebuia caraiba *	Silver Trumpet-tree
Trema micrantha	Florida Trema
Washingtonia robusta *	Washington Palm

COLUMBIA COUNTY

Castanea alnifolia	Southern Chinquapin
Cornus asperifolia	Rough-leaf Cornel
Forestiera acuminata	Swamp Privet
Nyssa ogeche	Ogeechee Lime
Osmanthus americanus	Wild Olive
Quercus austrina	Bluff Oak
Quercus virginiana	Live Oak
Vitis aestivalis	Summer Grape

DADE COUNTY

Acoelorrhaphe wrightii	Paurotis Palm
Albizia caribaea *	Tantacayo
Alstonia scholaris *	Devil-tree
Alvaradoa amorphoides	Mexican Alvaradoa
Amyris elemifera	Torchwood
Annona glabra	Pond Apple
Borassus aethiopum *	Toddy Palm
Bourreria ovata	Bahama Strongback
Bucida buceras *	Black Olive
Bulnesia arborea *	Vera
Bursera simaruba	Gumbo-limbo
Calyptranthes pallens	Pale Lidflower
Ceiba pentandra *	Kapok
Chrysophyllum oliviforme	Satinleaf

Coccoloba diversifolia	Pigeon Plum
Coccoloba uvifera	Sea Grape
Copernicia baileyana *	Bailey's
	Petticoat Palm
Cordia sebestena *	Geiger-tree
Delonix regia *	Royal Poinciana
Dipholis salicifolia	Willow Bustic
Enterolobium	Pacara
contortisiliquum *	
Eucalyptus deglupta *	Rainbow Gum
Eugenia axillaris	White Stopper
Eugenia confusa	Redberry Stopper
Ficus aurea	Strangler Fig
Ficus benghalensis *	Banyan Fig
Guaiacum sanctum	Roughbark
	Lignumvitae
Guettarda elliptica	Velvet-seed
Guettarda scabra	Rough Velvet-seed
Kigelia africana *	Sausage-tree
Lysiloma latisiliquum	Wild Tamarind
Manilkara bahamensis	Wild Dilly
Manilkara zapota *	Sapodilla
Mastichodendron	False Mastic
foetidissimum	
Persea borbonia	Red Bay
Pisonia discolor	Longleaf Blolly
Pithecellobium	Cat's-claw
unguis-cati	
Pongamia pinnata *	Poonga Oil-tree
Prunus myrtifolia	West Indian
	Cherry Laurel
Pseudophoenix sargentii	Sargent's
	Cherry Palm
Simarouba glauca	Paradise-tree
Syzygium cumini *	Java Plum
Terminalia arjuna *	Arjan
Thrinax morrisii	Brittle Thatch Palm
Veitchia winin *	New Hebrides Palm
Ziziphus mauritiana *	Indian Jujube

DESOTO COUNTY

No nominations received.

DIXIE COUNTY

No nominations received.

DUVAL COUNTY

Acer rubrum	Red Maple
Ailanthus altissima *	Tree-of-heaven
Araucaria araucana *	Monkey-puzzle
Bumelia tenax	Tough Buckthorn
Carya glabra	Pignut Hickory
Celtis laevigata	Sugarberry

Ilex ambigua	Sand Holly
Ilex attenuata *	East Palatka Holly
Juniperus silicicola	Southern Red Cedar
Lyonia ferruginea	Staggerbush
Myrica cerifera	Wax Myrtle
Persea borbonia	Red Bay
Phoenix canariensis *	Canary Island
	Date Palm
Pinus elliottii	Slash Pine
Pinus palustris	Longleaf Pine
Quercus laevis	Turkey Oak
Quercus virginiana	Live Oak
Taxodium distichum	Bald Cypress
Zanthoxylum clava-herculis	Hercules-club

ESCAMBIA COUNTY

Crataegus opaca	Apple Haw
Quercus virginiana	Live Oak
Sequoia sempervirens *	Redwood
Vaccinium arboreum	Sparkleberry

FLAGLER COUNTY

No nominations received.

FRANKLIN COUNTY

No nominations received.

GADSDEN COUNTY

Acer saccharinum	Silver Maple
Alnus serrulata	Hazel Alder
Betula nigra	River Birch
Bumelia lycioides	Smooth Buckthorn
Crataegus aestivalis	May Haw
Fagus grandifolia	Beech
Ilex decidua	Possum Haw
Liriodendron tulipifera	Tulip-tree
Magnolia pyramidata	Pyramid Magnolia
Pinus glabra	Spruce Pine
Prunus americana	Wild Plum
Quercus muehlenbergii	Chinquapin Oak
Quercus pagoda	Cherrybark Oak
Quercus virginiana	Live Oak
Rhus copallinum	Winged Sumac
Salix nigra	Black Willow
Ulmus rubra	Slippery Elm

GILCHRIST COUNTY

Betula nigra	River Birch
Fraxinus pennsylvanica	Green Ash

GLADES COUNTY

No nominations received.

GULF COUNTY

No nominations received.

HAMILTON COUNTY

Bumelia lanuginosa	Woolly Buckthorn
Carpinus caroliniana	Hornbeam
Carya illinoinensis *	Pecan
Carya tomentosa	Mockernut Hickory
Catalpa bignonioides	Catalpa
Celtis laevigata	Sugarberry
Fraxinus americana	White Ash
Gleditsia aquatica	Water Locust
Juglans nigra	Black Walnut
Liriodendron tulipifera	Tulip-tree
Magnolia grandiflora	Southern Magnolia
Persea borbonia	Red Bay
Quercus margaretta	Sand Post Oak
Quercus michauxii	Swamp Chestnut Oak
Quercus virginiana	Live Oak
Taxodium distichum	Bald Cypress

HARDEE COUNTY

Cinnamomum camphora *	Camphor-tree

HENDRY COUNTY

Araucaria araucana *	Monkey-puzzle
Bombax ceiba *	Red Silk-cotton
Dalbergia sissoo *	Indian Rosewood
Delonix regia *	Royal Poinciana
Eucalyptus robusta *	Swamp Mahogany
Eucalyptus torelliana *	Torelliana Gum
Grevillea robusta *	Silk Oak
Jacaranda cuspidifolia *	Jacaranda
Melaleuca quinquenervia *	Punk-tree
Phoenix canariensis *	Canary Island Date Palm
Roystonea elata	Florida Royal Palm
Syzygium cumini *	Java Plum
Washingtonia robusta *	Washington Palm

HERNANDO COUNTY

Sapindus marginatus	Florida Soapberry
Sapium sebiferum *	Chinese Tallow-tree

HIGHLANDS COUNTY

Carya floridana	Scrub Hickory

HILLSBOROUGH COUNTY

No nominations received.

HOLMES COUNTY

No nominations received.

INDIAN RIVER COUNTY

Aleurites moluccana *	Candlenut-tree
Bischofia javanica *	Toog
Cycas circinalis *	Sago Palm
Forestiera segregata	Florida Privet
Myrcianthes simpsonii	Simpson Stopper

JACKSON COUNTY

Carya tomentosa	Mockernut Hickory
Crataegus spathulata	Red Haw
Liquidambar styraciflua	Sweet Gum
Malus angustifolia	Wild Crab Apple
Morus rubra	Red Mulberry
Pinus strobus *	White Pine
Pinus taeda	Loblolly Pine
Quercus margaretta	Sand Post Oak
Quercus marilandica	Blackjack Oak
Quercus stellata	Post Oak
Quercus virginiana	Live Oak
Rhamnus caroliniana	Carolina Buckthorn
Rhus radicans	Poison Ivy
Sassafras albidum	Sassafras
Ulmus americana	Florida Elm
Viburnum scabrellum	Southern Arrow-wood

JEFFERSON COUNTY

Ostrya virginiana	Hop Hornbeam

LAFAYETTE COUNTY

Aesculus pavia	Red Buckeye
Betula nigra	River Birch
Carpinus caroliniana	Hornbeam
Carya illinoinensis *	Pecan
Gleditsia triacanthos	Honey Locust
Juglans nigra	Black Walnut
Magnolia virginiana	Sweetbay
Osmanthus americanus	Wild Olive

Ostrya virginiana	Hop Hornbeam
Quercus alba	White Oak
Quercus falcata	Southern Red Oak
Quercus laevis	Turkey Oak
Quercus lyrata	Overcup Oak
Quercus velutina	Black Oak
Sabal palmetto	Cabbage Palm
Ulmus americana	Florida Elm

LAKE COUNTY

Asimina parviflora	Small-flowered Pawpaw
Cinnamomum camphora *	Camphor-tree
Cornus foemina	Smooth-leaf Cornel
Pinus palustris	Longleaf Pine
Pinus serotina	Pond Pine
Quercus virginiana	Live Oak
Sambucus canadensis	Elderberry

LEE COUNTY

Araucaria araucana *	Monkey-puzzle
Avicennia germinans	Black Mangrove
Bischofia javanica *	Toog
Bumelia celastrina	Tropical Buckthorn
Bursera simaruba	Gumbo-limbo
Callistemon viminalis *	Weeping Bottlebrush
Capparis cynophallophora	Jamaica Caper
Casuarina equisetifolia *	Australian Pine
Celtis pallida	Spiny Hackberry
Chorisia speciosa *	Floss-silk-tree
Coccoloba uvifera	Sea Grape
Cocos nucifera *	Coconut
Couroupita guianensis *	Cannonball-tree
Enterolobium cyclocarpum *	Ear-tree
Erythrina herbacea	Cherokee Bean
Erythrina variegata *	Indian Coral-tree
Eucalyptus citriodora *	Lemon-scented Gum
Eucalyptus robusta *	Swamp Mahogany
Eugenia axillaris	White Stopper
Ficus altissima *	Lofty Fig
Ficus benghalensis *	Banyan Fig
Ficus mysorensis *	Mysore Fig
Ficus nitida *	Cuban Laurel
Ilex cassine	Dahoon Holly
Jacaranda cuspidifolia *	Jacaranda
Kigelia africana *	Sausage-tree
Lagerstroemia speciosa *	Queen Crape Myrtle
Mangifera indica *	Mango
Mastichodendron foetidissimum	False Mastic
Maytenus phyllanthoides	Florida Mayten

Myrsine floridana	Florida Rapanea
Peltophorum pterocarpum *	Yellow Poinciana
Phyllocarpus septentrionalis *	Monkey-flower
Piscidia piscipula	Fishpoison-tree
Pithecellobium dulce *	Manila Tamarind
Podocarpus gracilior *	Weeping Podocarpus
Quercus virginiana	Live Oak
Rhizophora mangle	Red Mangrove
Roystonea regia *	Cuban Royal Palm
Sabal causiarum *	Puerto Rican Hat Palm
Schoepfia chrysophylloides	Graytwig
Swietenia macrophylla *	Honduras Mahogany
Swietenia mahagoni	West Indian Mahogany
Syzygium cumini *	Java Plum
Tamarindus indica *	Tamarind
Washingtonia robusta *	Washington Palm
Zanthoxylum fagara	Wild Lime

LEON COUNTY

Amelanchier arborea	Downy Serviceberry
Carya cordiformis	Bitternut Hickory
Cornus florida	Flowering Dogwood
Crataegus pulcherrima	Beautiful Haw
Fagus grandifolia	Beech
Gleditsia triacanthos	Honey Locust
Halesia diptera	Two-wing Silver-bell
Kalmia latifolia	Mountain Laurel
Melia azedarach *	Chinaberry
Metasequoia glyptostroboides *	Dawn Redwood
Pinus echinata	Shortleaf Pine
Pinus glabra	Spruce Pine
Pinus taeda	Loblolly Pine
Prunus angustifolia	Chickasaw Plum
Prunus serotina	Black Cherry
Symplocos tinctoria	Sweetleaf
Taxodium ascendens	Pond Cypress
Taxodium distichum	Bald Cypress

LEVY COUNTY

Acer floridanum	Florida Maple
Betula nigra	River Birch
Carya illinoinensis *	Pecan
Cornus foemina	Smooth-leaf Cornel
Crataegus crus-galli	Cockspur Haw
Diospyros virginiana	Persimmon

Leitneria floridana	Corkwood
Populus deltoides	Eastern Cottonwood
Quercus austrina	Bluff Oak

LIBERTY COUNTY

Diospyros virginiana	Persimmon
Fagus grandifolia	Beech
Juglans nigra	Black Walnut
Liquidambar styraciflua	Sweet Gum
Liriodendron tulipifera	Tulip-tree
Magnolia pyramidata	Pyramid Magnolia
Metasequoia glyptostroboides *	Dawn Redwood
Nyssa uniflora	Water Tupelo
Prunus alabamensis	Alabama Cherry
Quercus alba	White Oak
Taxus floridana	Florida Yew
Ulmus alata	Winged Elm

MADISON COUNTY

Cunninghamia lanceolata *	China Fir
Quercus virginiana	Live Oak
Sapium sebiferum *	Chinese Tallow-tree
Torreya taxifolia	Gopherwood

MANATEE COUNTY

Callistemon rigidus *	Stiff Bottlebrush
Callitris columellaris *	Cypress Pine
Celtis laevigata	Sugarberry
Cinnamomum camphora *	Camphor-tree
Erythrina crista-galli *	Cockspur Coral-tree
Juniperus silicicola	Southern Red Cedar
Mangifera indica *	Mango
Morus rubra	Red Mulberry
Syzygium paniculatum *	Australian Brush Cherry

MARION COUNTY

Agarista populifolia	Pipestem
Carya glabra	Pignut Hickory
Chamaecyparis thyoides	Atlantic White Cedar
Cornus florida	Flowering Dogwood
Fraxinus profunda	Pumpkin Ash
Gordonia lasianthus	Loblolly Bay
Illicium parviflorum	Florida Banana-shrub
Lagerstroemia indica *	Crape Myrtle
Lyonia ferruginea	Staggerbush

Morus rubra	Red Mulberry
Nyssa biflora	Swamp Tupelo
Persea borbonia	Red Bay
Persea humilis	Silk Bay
Pinckneya bracteata	Fever-tree
Pinus palustris	Longleaf Pine
Pinus serotina	Pond Pine
Pinus taeda	Loblolly Pine
Quercus chapmanii	Chapman Oak
Quercus falcata	Southern Red Oak
Quercus hemisphaerica	Laurel Oak
Quercus michauxii	Swamp Chestnut Oak
Quercus shumardii	Shumard Oak
Quercus virginiana	Live Oak
Salix floridana	Florida Willow
Sambucus canadensis	Elderberry
Ulmus crassifolia	Cedar Elm

MARTIN COUNTY

Pterospermum acerifolium *	Shingle-tree
Taxodium distichum	Bald Cypress

MONROE COUNTY

Acacia choriophylla	Cinnecord
Acacia farnesiana	Sweet Acacia
Amyris elemifera	Torchwood
Annona glabra	Pond Apple
Ateramnus lucidus	Oysterwood
Avicennia germinans	Black Mangrove
Bourreria ovata	Bahama Strongback
Bourreria radula	Rough Strongback
Bucida buceras *	Black Olive
Bumelia celastrina	Saffron Plum
Bursera simaruba	Gumbo-limbo
Byrsonima lucida	Locust-berry
Calophyllum inophyllum *	Alexandrian Laurel
Calyptranthes pallens	Pale Lidflower
Canella winterana	Wild Cinnamon
Cereus robinii	Key Tree Cactus
Chrysophyllum oliviforme	Satinleaf
Citharexylum fruticosum	Fiddlewood
Coccoloba diversifolia	Pigeon Plum
Coccothrinax argentata	Silver Palm
Colubrina elliptica	Nakedwood
Conocarpus erectus	Buttonwood
Cupania glabra	Florida Cupania
Delonix regia *	Royal Poinciana
Drypetes diversifolia	Milk-bark
Drypetes lateriflora	Guiana Plum
Erythrina herbacea	Cherokee Bean
Exothea paniculata	Inkwood
Ficus aurea	Strangler Fig

Ficus citrifolia	Shortleaf Fig
Gliricidia sepium *	Madre de Cacao
Guaiacum sanctum	Roughbark Lignumvitae
Gyminda latifolia	False Boxwood
Hamelia patens	Fire-bush
Hippomane mancinella	Manchineel
Hypelate trifoliata	White Ironwood
Jacquinia keyensis	Joe-wood
Krugiodendron ferreum	Black Ironwood
Lysiloma latisiliquum	Wild Tamarind
Mammea americana *	Mammee Apple
Manilkara bahamensis	Wild Dilly
Manilkara zapota *	Sapodilla
Mastichodendron foetidissimum	False Mastic
Metopium toxiferum	Poisonwood
Pisonia discolor	Longleaf Blolly
Pisonia rotundata	Pisonia
Pithecellobium keyense	Black-bead
Pongamia pinnata *	Poonga Oil-tree
Reynosia septentrionalis	Darling Plum
Sapindus saponaria	Winged Soapberry
Schaefferia frutescens	Florida Boxwood
Simarouba glauca	Paradise-tree
Suriana maritima	Bay Cedar
Swietenia mahagoni	West Indian Mahogany
Tamarindus indica *	Tamarind
Terminalia arjuna *	Arjan
Terminalia catappa *	Tropical Almond
Thespesia populnea *	Seaside Mahoe
Zanthoxylum flavum	Yellowheart

NASSAU COUNTY

Bumelia tenax	Tough Buckthorn
Pinus taeda	Loblolly Pine
Quercus alba	White Oak
Quercus myrtifolia	Myrtle Oak

OKALOOSA COUNTY

Carya illinoinensis *	Pecan
Chamaecyparis thyoides	Atlantic White Cedar
Quercus arkansana	Arkansas Oak
Quercus hemisphaerica	Laurel Oak

OKEECHOBEE COUNTY

No nominations received.

ORANGE COUNTY

Ilex attenuata *	East Palatka Holly
Melia azedarach *	Chinaberry
Platanus occidentalis	Sycamore

OSCEOLA COUNTY

No nominations received.

PALM BEACH COUNTY

Acoelorrhaphe wrightii	Paurotis Palm
Albizia lebbek *	Woman's-tongue
Annona glabra	Pond Apple
Conocarpus erectus	Buttonwood
Hibiscus tiliaceus *	Mahoe
Khaya nyasica *	Nyasaland Mahogany
Pseudobombax ellipticum *	Shavingbrush-tree

PASCO COUNTY

Cinnamomum camphora *	Camphor-tree
Ilex ambigua	Sand Holly
Osmanthus megacarpus	Scrub Wild Olive
Pinus clausa	Sand Pine
Quercus incana	Bluejack Oak
Quercus laevis	Turkey Oak

PINELLAS COUNTY

Araucaria heterophylla *	Norfolk Island Pine
Bombax ceiba *	Red Silk-cotton
Cinnamomum camphora *	Camphor-tree
Dalbergia sissoo *	Indian Rosewood
Quercus incana	Bluejack Oak
Quercus laevis	Turkey Oak
Sapium sebiferum *	Chinese Tallow-tree

POLK COUNTY

Cinnamomum camphora *	Camphor-tree
Prunus caroliniana	Cherry Laurel

PUTNAM COUNTY

Acer rubrum	Red Maple
Aesculus pavia	Red Buckeye
Baccharis halimifolia	Common Saltbush
Bumelia lanuginosa	Woolly Buckthorn
Castanea ashei	Ashe Chinquapin
Cinnamomum camphora *	Camphor-tree
Cornus foemina	Smooth-leaf Cornel
Firmiana simplex *	Chinese Parasol-tree
Gleditsia aquatica	Water Locust
Halesia carolina	Little-Silver-bell
Ilex attenuata *	East Palatka Holly
Ilex vomitoria	Yaupon

Juglans nigra	Black Walnut
Liriodendron tulipifera	Tulip-tree
Lyonia ferruginea	Staggerbush
Melia azedarach *	Chinaberry
Myrica cerifera	Wax Myrtle
Nyssa biflora	Swamp Tupelo
Osmanthus americanus	Wild Olive
Pinus taeda	Loblolly Pine
Podocarpus macrophyllus *	Japanese Yew
Quercus laevis	Turkey Oak
Quercus virginiana	Live Oak
Rhus vernix	Poison Sumac
Sapium sebiferum *	Chinese Tallow-tree

ST. JOHNS COUNTY

Magnolia grandiflora	Southern Magnolia
Taxodium distichum	Bald Cypress

ST. LUCIE COUNTY

Callistemon viminalis *	Weeping Bottlebrush
Ilex cassine	Dahoon Holly
Serenoa repens	Saw Palmetto

SANTA ROSA COUNTY

Castanea mollissima *	Chinese Chestnut
Chamaecyparis thyoides	Atlantic White Cedar
Liquidambar styraciflua	Sweet Gum
Magnolia grandiflora	Southern Magnolia
Pinus elliottii	Slash Pine
Pinus palustris	Longleaf Pine
Quercus nigra	Water Oak
Quercus virginiana	Live Oak

SARASOTA COUNTY

Araucaria bidwillii *	Bunya-bunya
Brachychiton discolor *	Pink Bottle-tree
Carica papaya	Papaya
Chorisia speciosa *	Floss-silk-tree
Ficus nitida *	Cuban Laurel
Ficus religiosa *	Bo-tree
Ficus virens *	Spotted Fig
Ficus vogelii *	West African Rubber-tree
Peltophorum pterocarpum *	Yellow Poinciana
Pinus elliottii	Slash Pine
Pithecellobium unguis-cati	Cat's-claw
Podocarpus gracilior *	Weeping Podocarpus
Quercus virginiana	Live Oak

SEMINOLE COUNTY

Pinus clausa	Sand Pine
Taxodium distichum	Bald Cypress

SUMTER COUNTY

Acer rubrum	Red Maple
Ilex cassine	Dahoon Holly
Magnolia virginiana	Sweetbay
Quercus incana	Bluejack Oak
Serenoa repens	Saw Palmetto

SUWANNEE COUNTY

Celtis laevigata	Sugarberry
Chionanthus virginicus	Fringe-tree
Quercus falcata	Southern Red Oak
Quercus michauxii	Swamp Chestnut Oak
Salix babylonica *	Weeping Willow

TAYLOR COUNTY

Gleditsia aquatica	Water Locust
Melia azedarach *	Chinaberry
Ostrya virginiana	Hop Hornbeam

UNION COUNTY

Carpinus caroliniana	Hornbeam

VOLUSIA COUNTY

Carya aquatica	Water Hickory
Juniperus silicicola	Southern Red Cedar
Quercus virginiana	Live Oak
Taxodium distichum	Bald Cypress

WAKULLA COUNTY

Cliftonia monophylla	Buckwheat-tree
Fagus grandifolia	Beech
Nyssa ogeche	Ogeechee Lime
Pinus elliottii	Slash Pine
Sassafras albidum	Sassafras
Taxodium ascendens	Pond Cypress
Tilia caroliniana	Carolina Basswood

WALTON COUNTY

Quercus alba	White Oak
Stewartia malacodendron	Silky Camellia

WASHINGTON COUNTY

Carya illinoinensis *	Pecan
Cedrus deodara *	Deodar Cedar
Cryptomeria japonica *	Japanese Cedar
Cyrilla racemiflora	Titi
Ostrya virginiana	Hop Hornbeam
Oxydendrum arboreum	Sourwood
Platanus occidentalis	Sycamore
Quercus nigra	Water Oak
Quercus stellata	Post Oak
Vaccinium arboreum	Sparkleberry

NOMINATORS AND OWNERS

NOMINATORS OF CHAMPION TREES

The following 338 persons have nominated (or updated) one or more of the trees listed in the INVENTORY. The year of the nomination (or update) is also given.

John L. Accardi / 1993

Doug Alderson / 1994

Dale Allen / 1981, 1993

Mrs. Wallace Allen / 1981

Sam Allison / 1994

Jake Almond / 1990

Chris J. Anderson / 1980, 1981, 1992, 1994, 1995

Jon Andrew / 1993

Dennis Andrews / 1983

Gary Appelson / 1993

Dale Armstrong / 1994

Arden Arrington / 1996

Glen Atkinson / 1977

Daniel F. Austin / 1995

George Avery / 1976

Lynn C. Badger / 1994

Mark Bakeman / 1981

W. Wilson Baker / 1995

Lee Barnwell / 1990, 1994

Gregory P. Barton / 1992, 1993

David Bar-Zvi / 1991, 1993

Scott Bates / 1991

John A. Baust / 1979

Gary T. Beauchamp / 1982

Ralph Beaudry / 1975, 1994

Carol Beck / 1967, 1976

Thomas D. Beitzel / 1985, 1986

Amy Bennett / 1995

Catherine M. Benton / 1996

James L. Bernett / 1993

Joan Gill Blank / 1995

Virginia C. Blinn / 1984

Nelson B. Blocker / 1972

Eloise Boon / 1995

Michael J. Bordyn / 1980, 1981, 1982, 1985

Jerome Bracewell / 1986

Harold B. Bradley / 1980, 1993

Joey T. Brady / 1986

Michael D. Brady / 1986

Frank Brandt / 1993

James D. Brenner / 1983

James A. Brewer / 1980

Janice Broda / 1993

Deborah K. Brooker / 1987

David Brown / 1994

Steve L. Brown / 1988

Dana C. Bryan / 1987, 1988

Jim Bryan / 1984, 1985

Chad Bryant / 1993

Ann Buckley / 1984

Jim Buckner / 1993, 1994

Janet Bunch / 1986

Peter Burke / 1988

James R. Burkhalter / 1993, 1994

Norma Jean Byrd / 1980

Owen Cannon / 1986

Eldredge T. Carnes / 1968

Mark Chauncey / 1981

Sandy Christopher / 1991

Grace E. Clapp / 1991

Jack Clarkson / 1983

Jerry Clutts / 1993, 1994

Alice Cohen / 1973

Vincent P. Condon / 1994, 1995

Dave Conser / 1988

John G. Cordy / 1983

John David Core / 1995

John H. Courtenay / 1962

Bill Craven / 1992

John D. Crawford / 1980

Scott A. Crosby / 1991, 1992

Daniel F. Culbert / 1994, 1996

Michael J. Cullen / 1986

Clifton Cullenberg / 1989

Geoffrey A. Cummings / 1987, 1993, 1994

Joe Cunard / 1989

Glenn D. Cunningham / 1982

Michael Curtis / 1991

Steven Dale / 1989

H. Terrell Davis / 1980

Jeff Deatherage / 1986

William K. DeBraal / 1986

Richard F. Degen / 1986

Gene Dempsey / 1987, 1994

Merlin J. Dixon / 1980

Tom Donohoe / 1992

Robert Dudley / 1990

John L. Dudzinsky / 1985

Joseph E. Dunbar / 1985, 1987

Duane R. Durgee / 1982, 1984, 1985, 1987, 1989, 1990, 1991, 1994, 1995

Tim Eckert / 1980

Jim Eggert / 1983

Robert W. Ehrig / 1994

Helen Eidson / 1994

Mary Lee Eletz / 1978, 1979

David L. Evans / 1982, 1984

Don Evans / 1995

Mike Evans / 1991

Russell Fatic / 1981

Clifford Faulkner / 1984

Terry Fedelem / 1980, 1992

Patrick T. Fennimore / 1981

Larry T. Figart / 1987

John K. Fish / 1994

Oneri Fleita / 1993

Garry A. Flood / 1990

Edward L. Flowers / 1980

David L. Fogler / 1989, 1993, 1994

Larry Fooks / 1996

Steven J. Fousek / 1986

David A. Fox / 1984

Thomas Francis / 1994

Mark G. Fries / 1980

Archie W. Gaylard / 1994

Angus K. Gholson / 1993, 1995

Murdock R. Gillis / 1994

Robert K. Godfrey / 1993

Don Goodman / 1989

Richard W. Gorden / 1985, 1986, 1987

Henry Graham / 1981, 1983

J. P. Greene / 1974

Michael J. Greenstein / 1992, 1993, 1994

James Haeger / 1996

Kevin Hallahan / 1981, 1992

David E. Halstead / 1980

Lawrence J. Hamilton / 1990

Layne Hamilton / 1994

Roger L. Hammer / 1993, 1994

Ellison Hardee / 1994

Laymond Hardy / 1973

William O. Hardy / 1983

James T. Harrelson / 1981

Stan Harris / 1991

Thomas S. Haxby / 1989

Gary Hegg / 1993

Ted Hendrickson / 1984

Michael K. Hennessey / 1992

Brenda Herring / 1996

F. C. Hester / 1971

Albert H. Hetzell / 1973, 1974, 1976

Jim Higgins / 1994, 1995

Bruce Hill / 1985, 1987

Wayne Hoffman / 1990

John H. Holzaepfel / 1986

Mark Hooten / 1987

G. Owen House / 1980, 1986

Wilbur K. Howell / 1981

Eric H. Hoyer / 1977, 1978, 1980, 1981

William S. Hubard / 1992

Michael Humphrey / 1985, 1987

Stan Humphries / 1989

Jonathan Iles / 1983

Michele W. Ing / 1991

Robert T. Ing / 1991, 1992, 1993, 1994, 1995

Ed Isenhour / 1981

Ferrell Johns / 1992

Brad D. Johnson / 1993

Diane Johnson / 1989

Malcolm B. Johnson / 1967, 1968

Wayne Jones / 1993

James R. Karels / 1985, 1987

Michael W. Kenton / 1972, 1992, 1995

John W. Kern / 1988, 1990, 1991, 1992

Michael W. Kettles / 1987

Gibson T. Kiley / 1994

Vicki King / 1974

Lois Kitching / 1986

John T. Koehler / 1987

Bill Korn / 1983

George Krauss / 1974

Noel R. Lake / 1994, 1996

Winifred Lante / 1993

Roy A. Lima / 1980

Chris Linton / 1981, 1994

Carol L. Lippincott / 1989, 1993, 1994

Jason P. Livingston / 1993

Jerry N. Livingston / 1981, 1986, 1987, 1988, 1989, 1990, 1991, 1993, 1994

Donald L. Lockhart / 1974

Radford M. Locklin / 1981

Doug Longshore / 1980, 1993

Dave Loper / 1980

Vincente Lopez / 1995

Frank Loughran / 1985, 1995

Kevin W. Love / 1990

Robbie Lovestrand / 1994

S. Craig Lowe / 1994

Adriana Lupas / 1994

Owen McCall / 1986, 1987

Tom McClean / 1974

J. L. McCroan / 1986

Don McGarthy / 1971

Joe McGrath / 1985

John McMahon / 1981

Susan McMurray / 1989

Patricia L. McNeese / 1995

David S. Maehr / 1984

Jeffrey S. Mangun / 1991, 1992, 1994

Charles R. Marcus / 1980, 1981, 1983

Monay Markey / 1993, 1994

Michael J. Martin / 1981

Wilbur L. Martin / 1993

Mrs. William Martin / 1986

Norman E. Masencup / 1994

John Mathe / 1990

Joe Corbett Mathis / 1981

Mark B. Meador / 1981, 1983

Michael B. Miller / 1995

William G. Miller / 1993, 1994, 1995

Mark M. Milligan / 1990

Lillian Millman / 1983

Lisa Moore / 1995

Stuart Moore / 1980

Charles R. Mould / 1980

Richard Moyroud / 1995

Michael A. Neal / 1983

Ned D. Neenan / 1988, 1990, 1992, 1993

Joseph Nemec / 1989

Harold J. Nett / 1965

Robert Newburne / 1981

Norman Nichols / 1983

Charlotte Niedhauk / 1975

R. H. Niedhauk / 1970

David W. Norton / 1987

Joseph R. Orsenigo / 1973, 1981

Kenneth L. Oser / 1986, 1994

Stephen Oswalt / 1994

Jeff Overby / 1993

Jeanne M. Parks / 1989, 1990, 1993

Kenneth S. Partin / 1981

Linda Paul / 1989

Dodie Pedlow / 1982

Cherry W. Platt / 1993

Herb Platt / 1991

Sammy Poore / 1988

James A. Potts / 1983

Kathy Preston / 1995

Irene Priess / 1990

Wilbur C. Priest / 1990, 1994

Buford C. Pruitt / 1981, 1982, 1984, 1987, 1989

Robert Rahberg / 1986

Frank A. Rathburn / 1994

Robert W. Ray / 1991, 1994

Chad Reed / 1991

Charles R. Reeves / 1980, 1981, 1983, 1986, 1990, 1992, 1993, 1994

Niko Reisinger / 1995

Betty Rich / 1981

Debi Richards / 1980

Tony Richards / 1994

Diane Riggs / 1995

Steve Ripley / 1992

Ralph Roberts / 1983

Donald Robinson / 1995, 1996

Henry Rogers / 1980

Thomas M. Rooks / 1989

William S. Rosasco / 1990

Robert Rose / 1993, 1995

Karen Ross / 1986

Ken Roundtree / 1986

William Russell / 1987

William L. Rutherford / 1980, 1983, 1984, 1986

Jean F. St. De Croix / 1996

Charles E. Salter / 1967, 1968, 1993, 1995

Robert Saults / 1981

Mark Scheller / 1977

William J. Schilling / 1970, 1976, 1980, 1984, 1987, 1990, 1993, 1994, 1996

Elbert A. Schory / 1968, 1970

Mark W. Schwartz / 1988

Doug Scott / 1990

Sandy S. Semple / 1989

Dee Serage / 1993

Thomas H. Serviss / 1980, 1994

Clifford Shaw / 1975, 1976

A. B. Shiver / 1985

Albert P. Simmons / 1981, 1988

Erika H. Simons / 1994

Robert W. Simons / 1963, 1972, 1974, 1976, 1977, 1978, 1979, 1980, 1981, 1983, 1984, 1985, 1986, 1987, 1988, 1989, 1991, 1992, 1993, 1994, 1995, 1996

David M. Sinclair / 1984, 1986

Dee Slinkard / 1984

Alto Smith / 1994

Ron Smith / 1973, 1974

Rudy Smith / 1990

W. W. Smith / 1981

J. B. Snowden / 1967

Evelyn Somerville / 1991

Steven Spezia / 1975, 1976

David A. Spicer / 1990, 1991

John Springer / 1988

Kirk M. Stage / 1984

Brett J. States / 1986

Ken L. Stay / 1993

Claude Stephens / 1994

Dianna L. Stevenson / 1995

Perna M. Stine / 1971

Nick Sykes / 1987

Mary Ann Taylor / 1990

Walter Thompson / 1987

Jim Thorsen / 1992, 1994

Jim Tilmant / 1975

Ilke Toklu / 1993

Robert Trickel / 1983, 1984

James Truitt / 1974

Kerry Tully / 1990

Greg Turek / 1987

R. Bruce Turnbull / 1993, 1994

Allen B. Tyree / 1986

Brian Underwood / 1994

John T. Valenta / 1993, 1994

Kenneth Van der Hulse / 1974

Clay Wachob / 1993

John A. Wallace / 1986

Daniel Walsh / 1991

Bruce Walton / 1981

Beverlee Wang / 1992

Daniel B. Ward / 1963, 1985, 1991, 1992, 1993, 1994, 1995, 1996

Gordon C. Ward / 1996

Kenneth B. Weber / 1994

George Webb / 1980

Beth Weidner / 1985

Pat Wells / 1993

David P. Wentzel / 1993

Donald West / 1984

Keith Westlake / 1986

Robert C. Wilkinson / 1989

John A. Williams / 1980, 1994

Paul G. Williams / 1984, 1986

Robert C. Williams / 1983

T. Ann Williams / 1995

Thomas D. Williams / 1982

Trygve Winther / 1982

Brian J. Wittwer / 1986

Terry Wolfe / 1982, 1983

Richard W. Workman / 1980, 1991, 1992, 1993, 1995

Timothy S. Worley / 1993

Sylvia Young / 1992

Frank Zantek / 1990

Frank L. Zickar / 1985, 1986, 1993, 1994, 1995

Michael Zimmerman / 1988, 1989

Scott Zobel / 1986

Activity levels over the years of the Survey are indicated by the number of nominations (and updates) recorded annually in the INVENTORY. The numbers of nominations recorded in the early years are not fully indicative of activity of that period, in that trees are not included that have died since nomination.

1962	1	74	6	86	56
63	1	1975	5	87	24
64	0	76	9	88	16
1965	1	77	5	89	39
66	0	78	6	1990	24
67	6	79	5	91	92
68	3	1980	70	92	28
69	0	81	52	93	224
1970	3	82	14	94	170
71	3	83	34	1995	112
72	3	84	20	96	10
73	5	1985	21		

OWNERS OF CHAMPION TREES

The following 453 persons are recognized as the owners of record of one or more trees that have been nominated as champions. Where the owner is a governmental or corporate entity, a city or county location is also given.

(unknown)—20 trees

Agricultural Research Center, Ft. Pierce, St. Lucie Co.

Alandco, Inc., Ft. Lauderdale, Broward Co.

Alfred B. Maclay State Gardens, Tallahassee, Leon Co.—3 trees

Alliance of the Arts, Ft. Myers, Lee Co.

Amelia Island State Recreational Area, Nassau Co.

Mary Anderson

Andrews Wildlife Management Area, Fanning Springs, Levy Co.—4 trees

Apalachee Correctional Institution, Sneads, Jackson Co.

Apalachicola Bluffs and Ravines Preserve, Bristol, Liberty Co.— 2 trees

Apalachicola National Forest, Bloxham, Leon Co.; Sopchoppy, Wakulla Co.—7 trees

Louis Atkins—2 trees

Augusta Woods Condominiums, Naples, Collier Co.

Aycock Trust Co., Mayo, Lafayette Co.—3 trees

John J. Ayres

Bahia Honda State Park, Monroe Co.—3 trees

Jeri Baldwin

Banyon Bay Apartments, Inc., Miami, Dade Co.

Barnacle State Historic Site, Coconut Grove, Dade Co.— 2 trees

Larry Barnett

H. E. Barr

Estella Barthle—2 trees

Bayard Raceways, Inc., St. Johns Co.

Beachview Golf Club, Sanibel Id., Lee Co.

Allen Bell

Ron Bell

Bennigan's Restaurant, Clearwater, Pinellas Co.

Edward K. Benson

Uri Bergbaum—2 trees

J. A. Bielling

Bill Sadowski Park, Dade Co.

Biscayne National Park, Dade Co.— 9 trees

Bivens Arm Nature Park, Gainesville, Alachua Co.

Blackwater River State Forest, Crestview, Okaloosa Co.; Milton, Santa Rosa Co.—3 trees

Arlene Blander

Virginia C. Blinn

Boca Raton Garden Club, Inc., Boca

Raton, Palm Beach Co.

F. E. Boe

Albert Boston

Harold B. Bradley

Bradley Co., Inc., Gainesville, Alachua Co.

Moses W. Braxton

Arthur Brennan

S. L. Brothers

James Brown

Bulow Creek State Park, Ormond Beach, Volusia Co.

Allen R. Bush

Marjorie Butcko

Martin R. Butler

Elizabeth Butts

Dale Byrd

Ricardo Cadenas

Earl Cain

Mrs. Jim Cassin Corbett Camp

Camp Owaissa Bauer, Homestead, Dade Co.

James Campbell

Caribbean Gardens, Inc., Naples, Collier Co.

Carl Ivey Carter

George Carty

Castellow Hammock Park, Homestead, Dade Co.

Central Park, Inc., Naples, Collier Co.

Chamber of Commerce, Live Oak, Suwannee Co.

Steve Chappell

Charles Deering Estate, Miami, Dade Co.—2 trees

Mark Chauncey

Church of God by Faith,, High Springs, Alachua Co.

City of Apopka, City Hall, Orange Co.

City of Chattahoochee, Gadsden Co.—2 trees

City of Clewiston, Hendry Co.— 2 trees

City of Davie, Broward Co.

City of Deerfield Beach, Broward Co.

City of Ft. Lauderdale, Broward Co.—3 trees

City of Ft. Myers, Lee Co.—11 trees

City of Gainesville, Alachua Co.— 3 trees

City of High Springs, Alachua Co.— 2 trees

City of Hollywood, Broward Co.— 2 trees

City of Jacksonville, Duval Co.

City of Key West, Monroe Co.

City of Ocala, Marion Co.

City of St. Petersburg, Pinellas Co.—3 trees

City of Tallahassee, Leon Co.

City of White Springs, Hamilton Co.

Grace E. Clapp

Maurice Clavel

Mrs. H. M. Coachman

Collier-Seminole State Park, Collier Co.—2 trees

John B. Combs

Conservancy, Inc., Naples, Collier Co.

Conservation Fund, Inc., Jacksonville, Duval Co.

Container Corp., Starke, Bradford Co.

Continental Country Club, Wildwood, Sumter Co.

Coral Gables Federal Savings, Inc., Lighthouse Point, Broward Co.

James A. Corbett—3 trees

County of Alachua, Cellon Oak Park, LaCrosse, Alachua Co.— 2 trees

County of Broward, Fern Forest Nature Preserve, Pompano Beach, Broward Co.

County of Lee, Court House, Ft. Myers, Lee Co.

County of Monroe, Stock Island, Monroe Co.—2 trees

County of Pasco, New Port Richey, Pasco Co.

County of Seminole, Big Tree Park, Longwood, Seminole Co.—2 trees

W. M. Craven

Harold Crevasse

Floyd Crews

Cristopher K. Harlan Trust, Key West, Monroe Co.

D. J. Culbreth

Hugh W. Cunningham

Lamar Louise Curry—2 trees

Kenneth Curtis—5 trees

Roy Davis

John L. Dean

Richard Dean

Deer Lake School, Tallahassee, Leon Co.

Catherine Avirett Dees

George W. Dekle

DeLeon Springs State Recreation Area, Volusia Co.—2 trees

Juanita Delgado

Robert Dent

John DeSandro

Jean F. De St. Croix—2 trees

Mr. DeYoung

Lenvil H. Dicks

Ding Darling National Wildlife Refuge, Sanibel Id., Lee Co.— 5 trees

Susan Dobson

C. H. Donovan

Myrtle E. Dudley

John Dunn

Dennis Durant

Duval START Center, Jacksonville, Duval Co.

Eglin Air Force Base, Okaloosa Co.

Barbara Elliott

Phillip Elliott

El Rancho Village, Inc., Bradenton, Manatee Co.

Linda Emr

Roger Ensley

David P. Etherington

O. G. Evans

Evergreen Cemetery Ass'n, Jacksonville, Duval Co.

Fairchild Tropical Garden, Miami, Dade Co.—12 trees

Fakahatchee Strand State Preserve, Copeland, Collier Co.

Alberto Fernandez

Robert Fernandez—2 trees

Ann Fields

Thomas G. Finney

First Presbyterian Church, Ft. Myers, Lee Co.

First United Methodist Church, Clewiston, Hendry Co.

Paul Fitzgerald

Flamingo Tropical Gardens, Ft. Lauderdale, Broward Co.— 19 trees

Florida Caverns State Park, Marianna, Jackson Co.—4 trees

Florida Conference of Seventh Day Adventists, High Springs, Alachua Co.

Florida Dept. of Transportation, New Port Richey, Pasco Co.

Florida Div. of Forestry, High Springs, Columbia Co.; Chiefland, Levy Co.; Bradenton, Manatee Co.; Bushnell, Sumter Co.—6 trees

Florida Power and Light, Inc., Indiantown, Martin Co.

Florida Power Corp., Crystal River, Citrus Co.

Florida Trust for Historic Preservation, Inc., Bonnett House, Fort Lauderdale, Broward Co.

Marshall Flournoy

Foley Timber & Land Co., Mayo, Lafayette Co.

Joe Fortner

Terry M. Freiberg

Ronald Friedel

Ft. Clinch State Park, Fernandina Beach, Nassau Co.

Ft. Myers Golf Course, Ft. Myers, Lee Co.

Barbara Garcia

Charles Garrison

Georgia Pacific Corp., Palatka, Putnam Co.—2 trees

Robert K. Godfrey

Viola L. Goldberg

Gold Head Branch State Park,
    Clay Co.

Arthur Gravengood

Betty Greely

Jack E. Greene

James R. Griffith

Adolf Grimal

Donald Grubbs

Fred Guarnieri—3 trees

Robert C. Halgrim

David E. Halstead

Lawrence J. Hamilton

Sam E. Hand

Jim Hanlon—2 trees

Thomas J. Hanlon

J. O. Hannaford

Gregory Hanny

K. M. Harper

A. S. Harris

Stan Harris

Ruth Hayworth—4 trees

Robert Head

Ricky Henderson

Mike Herlong

Daniel L. Hewett

Billy Hill

Marion Holder

Holiday Inn, Inc., Punta Gorda,
    Charlotte Co.

Dixie M. Hollins

Mark W. Hollmann

Mary Homan

Tim Honderick

Mrs. William M. Hood

J. C. Horton

June Houchins

E. Hugh Howell

J. T. Howle

R. J. Huffman

Elbert Hughes

Hugh Taylor Birch State Park, Ft.
    Lauderdale, Broward Co.—
    4 trees

Humiston Beach Park, Vero Beach,
    Indian River Co.

IFAS Experiment Station, Belle
    Glade, Palm Beach Co.

Indian River Land Trust, Inc., Vero
    Beach, Indian River Co.—3 trees

Robert T. Ing

ITT Rayonier, Inc., Lawtey,
    Bradford Co.—3 trees

Jacksonville Naval Air Station,
    Jacksonville, Duval Co.

William S. Jenkins

Jenkins Middle School, Palatka,
    Putnam Co.

Jervey Gantt Park, Ocala,
    Marion Co.

Jimmy Davis Enterprises, Inc.,
    Madison, Madison Co.

John Pennecamp Coral Reef State
    Park, Key Largo, Monroe Co.

Gladys Johnson

Mrs. Malcolm B. Johnson

Ernest Jones

R. D. Justice

The Kampong, Coconut Grove,
    Dade Co.

Kanapaha Botanical Gardens,
    Gainesville, Alachua Co.

J. R. Keene

Kenwood Elementary School,
    Miami, Dade Co.

Kevin High

Key Largo Hammocks State
    Botanical Site, Key Largo,
    Monroe Co.—19 trees

Key West Botanical Garden Society,
    Stock Island, Monroe Co.—
    6 trees

Keys Title and Abstract Co., Key
    West, Monroe Co.

Kingsley Plantation, Ft. George Id.,
    Duval Co.

Richard J. Kinney

Koreshan State Historic Park,
    Estero, Lee Co.—5 trees

Koreshan Unity, Inc., Estero,
    Lee Co.

C. J. Laird—3 trees

Lake Griffin State Recreation Area,
    Fruitland Park, Lake Co.—
    2 trees

Lake Jem County Park, Astatula,
    Lake Co.—3 trees

Mr. Langley

Russell Lante

Jerry Leach

Mary Ann Lee

Lignumvitae Key State Botanical
    Site, Monroe Co.—18 trees

June Linzalone—2 trees

Forrest F. Lisle—2 trees

Michaeline I. Little

John Lloyd

Radford M. Locklin

Tony Lopez

Hattie Bell Love

Lower Wekiva State Preserve,
    Seminole Co.

Lutheran Church, Miami, Dade Co.

Artie McCall—2 trees

Martha McClellan

Paul McDowell

Dennis McIltrot

Jeffrey McInnis

J. M. McLellan

Jessie M. McNeil

Joe McNeil

Dorry Maine

Charles March

Marie Selby Botanical Gardens,
    Sarasota, Sarasota Co.—8 trees

Wilbur L. Martin

Martin Marietta Materials, Inc.,
    Chattahoochee, Gadsden Co.—
    4 trees

Mary Immaculate School, Key West,
    Monroe Co.

Bert Mason

John Mathe—2 trees

John Matheny

Matheson Preserve, Miami,
    Dade Co.

R. M. Meares

Medical Gardens, Inc., Gainesville,
    Alachua Co.

Ernie Medley

Marilyn Mesh

Fred B. Miller

Roy Milliron

Frank Mills

C. G. Money—2 trees

H. B. Moore

R. A. Morcroft

Gerald Morgan

Mound Key Archaeological Site,
    Estero Bay, Lee Co.

Mounts Bldg., W. Palm Beach, Palm
    Beach Co.

Museum of History and Natural
    Science, Tallahassee, Leon Co.

National Key Deer Refuge, Big Pine
    Key, Monroe Co.—13 trees

Neal Land & Timber, Inc.,
    Blountstown, Calhoun Co.;

Torreya State Park, Liberty Co.—
2 trees

Farrell Nelson

J. H. Nelson

Maude A. Nixon

Nobleton Community Church,
Nobleton, Hernando Co.

Northwest Florida Water
Management District, Blue
Springs, Washington Co.

Ocala National Forest, Marion Co.—
13 trees

Richard Ohmes

O'Leno State Park, River Rise,
Alachua Co.; Columbia Co.—7
trees

Olustee Battlefield State Historical
Site, Olustee, Baker Co.

Emory Osteen

P. & G. Cellulose, Inc., Mayo,
Lafayette Co.; Perry, Taylor
Co.—4 trees

Jim Padgett

Jane Parker

W. D. Parrish

Parrot Jungle and Gardens, Miami,
Dade Co.

Kenneth S. Partin

Buddy Paterson

Linda Paul

Ron J. Pavlik—2 trees

Paynes Prairie State Preserve,
Gainesville, Alachua Co.—4 trees

Perkins Restaurant, Clearwater,
Pinellas Co.

Rosemarie Permenter—2 trees

Linda J. Peterson

John H. Phipps

Michael S. Poklepovic

Patricia Powers

Prairie View Trust, Gainesville,
Alachua Co.—11 trees

Frederic Rabeler

Marshall A. Raff

Mike Ramsey

C. H. Ratliff

Ravine State Gardens, Palatka,
Putnam Co.—7 trees

William R. Redman

Alfred C. Reed

Nathaniel P. Reed

A. C. Reynolds

Robert Rice

Wayne C. Rickert

Myrtle Ripley

Riverside Day Care Center,
Jacksonville, Duval Co.

Daniel F. Roberts

John E. Roberts

Roberts Oldsmobile, Inc., Orange
Park, Clay Co.

Gerald L. Rogers

Laetitia Rogers

Rollins State Park, Ft. George Id.,
Duval Co.

William S. Rosasco

Leonard Rosenthal

Charles E. Salter

John H. Sameck

Sanctuary Golf Course, Sanibel Id.,
Lee Co.

San Felasco Hammock State
Preserve, Gainesville, Alachua
Co.—8 trees

Charles Sanford

Sanibel-Captiva Conservation
Foundation, Sanibel Id., Lee
Co.—3 trees

Sarasota Garden Club, Inc.,
Sarasota, Sarasota Co.

Ken Sargent

Jack Scott

Willard Scott

Frank Searle

Frank Sears

Samuel Senia

Senior Friendship Center, Inc.,
Naples, Collier Co.

Roy Sewell

Shady Oaks Park, Ft. Myers, Lee
Co.

Jay Shartzer

Nellie Shattuck

Silver River State Park, Silver
Springs, Marion Co.—4 trees

Robert W. Simons—4 trees

Simpson Park, Miami, Dade Co.—
4 trees

Grady Smith

Paul Smysor—2 trees

Richard Sobel

Soterra, Inc., Chattahoochee,
Gadsden Co.—5 trees

Southern Gulf West Construction
Co., Inc., Naples, Collier Co.

Southwest Florida Water

Management District, Dade City,
Pasco Co.

Southwest Forest Industries,
Chipley, Washington Co.

Jewell Springer—2 trees

St. Francis Xavier Church, Ft.
Myers, Lee Co.

St. Johns River Water Management
District, Seville, Volusia Co.

St. Joseph Land & Development Co.,
Chattahoochee, Gadsden Co.;
Bristol, Liberty Co.—3 trees

St. Marks National Wildlife Refuge,
Panacea, Wakulla Co.

St. Mary's Catholic Church, Key
West, Monroe Co.—3 trees

Dolores Standley

Starkey Wilderness Park, New Port
Richey, Pasco Co.—3 trees

Roy Stockstill

Mrs. Keith Sullivan

Sunset Cove Condominiums,
Chokoloskee Island, Collier Co.

Suwannee River Water
Management District, Jasper,
Hamilton Co., Mayo, Lafayette
Co.—4 trees

Gary W. Sweetman

Eugene H. Syfrett

Tall Timbers Research, Inc.,
Tallahassee, Leon Co.—2 trees

Tarpon Bay Marina, Sanibel, Lee
Co.—2 trees

Telford Spring County Park, Live
Oak, Suwannee Co.

Robby R. Terry

Fred Thomas

Jennings Thomas

Leland C. Thomas

Mildred Thomas—2 trees

Eartha Thompson

Thoroughbred Music, Inc.,
Clearwater, Pinellas Co.

Brian Thorpe

Three Rivers State Recreation Area,
Sneads, Jackson Co.—8 trees

Torreya State Park, Liberty Co.—
9 trees

Thomas Tramnell

Joy Trask

Diego Toiran

Ottis Townsend

Millie Tyre

Mrs. Allen B. Tyree—4 trees

Harold Tyree—2 trees

U.S. Army, Camp Blanding, Keystone Heights, Clay Co.

U.S. Dept. Justice, Miami, Dade Co.

U.S.D.A. Entomology Research Laboratory, Gainesville, Alachua Co.

U.S.D.A. Plant Introduction Station, Miami, Dade Co.

U.S.D.A. Plant Materials Center, Brooksville, Hernando Co.

Univ. of Florida, Agricultural Research Center, Leesburg, Lake Co.

Univ. of Florida, Gainesville, Alachua Co.—21 trees

Univ. of Florida, P. K. Yonge Lab School, Gainesville, Alachua Co.

Univ. of South Florida, Sarasota, Sarasota Co.

Univ. of West Florida, Pensacola, Escambia Co.

W. Lamar Upshaw

Marsha Van Duren

Doris Vaughan—5 trees

Ventura Ranch, Wildwood, Sumter Co.—2 trees

Village of Key Biscayne, Dade Co.—2 trees

John Vincent

Viscaya Museum & Gardens, Miami, Dade Co.—2 trees

Waccasassa Bay State Preserve, Yankeetown, Levy Co.

Wakulla Springs State Park, Wakulla Co.—4 trees

Ely Walker

Johnny Walker

Mrs. O. V. Walker

Harry Walsh

Ted Watrous—2 trees

William Weber

Welaka State Forest, Welaka, Putnam Co.—2 trees

Colin C. Wells

Lorine Wesley

West Jacksonville Christian Center, Jacksonville, Duval Co.

Susie Mae White

Howard H. Wilkowske

Laurel Willard

John A. Williams

Jess Wilson

James E. Wing—3 trees

Suzie Folsom Wisehart

Withlacoochee State Forest, Bushnell, Sumter Co.

Jane Womack

Calvin C. Wood

Virginia Woodward

Anne Wright—3 trees

Gene Yearty

Ellen Zatarain

ACKNOWLEDGMENTS

The Florida Champion Tree Survey has been made possible, in large part, by the enthusiastic support and skilled assistance of the county foresters and other persons who have participated in the updating of earlier tree records and the discovery and documentation of the many newly recognized champions. We are most grateful to: John L. Accardi, St. Augustine; Doug Alderson, Tallahassee; Dale Allen, Tallahassee; Sam Allison, Ft. Myers; Chris J. Anderson, Naples; Jon Andrew, Big Pine Key; George E. Apthorp, Tallahassee; Dale Armstrong, Stuart; Louis J. Atkins, Blountstown; Daniel F. Austin, Boca Raton; Lynn C. Badger, Gainesville; W. Wilson Baker, Tallahassee; Jacky D. Balkcom, DeFuniak Springs; Steve Banton, DeLeon Springs; U. Lee Barnwell, Bradenton; Greg P. Barton, Largo; David Bar-Zvi, Davie; John A. Baust, Tallahassee; Catherine M. Benton, Eustis; James L. Bernett, Port Charlotte; Joseph A. Bishop, Leesburg; Joan Gill Blank, Key Biscayne; Dana C. Bryan, Tallahassee; Chad Bryant, Marathon; James R. Burkhalter, Pensacola; Bill Cannon, **American Forests,** Washington; Carl Colbert, Lakeland; Vincent P. Condon, Marathon; John David Core, Quincy; Terrence Coulliette, Coconut Grove; Daniel F. Culbert, Vero Beach; Geoffrey A. Cummings, Panama City; Richard Curry, Homestead; Jean F. De St. Croix, Marathon; Duane R. Durgee, Gainesville; Robert Ehrig, Big Pine Key; Don Evans, Miami; Larry T. Figart, Jacksonville; John K. Fish, Perry; Oneri Fleita, Key West; David L. Fogler, Bushnell; Larry Fooks, Estero; Raymond W. Garcia, Brooksville; Archie W. Gaylard, Branford; Angus K. Gholson, Chattahoochee; Murdock Ray Gillis, Gainesville; Robert K. Godfrey, Tallahassee; Michael J. Greenstein, West Palm Beach; Layne Hamilton, Sanibel; Roger L. Hammer, Miami; Robert Heeke, Live Oak; Gary Hegg, Crawfordville; Michael K. Hennessey, Miami; Brenda Herring, Niceville; Jim Higgins, Ft. Lauderdale; Terrence Hingtgen,

Osprey; Michael W. Kenton, New Port Richey; Gib Kiley, Ocala; Noel R. Lake, Gainesville; Carol L. Lippincott, Gainesville; Ken Litzenberger, Chiefland; Jerry N. Livingston, Mayo; Doug Longshore, Jasper; Adriana Lupas, Homestead; Jeffrey S. Mangun, Ft. Myers; Monay Markey, Big Pine Key; Michael J. Martin, Sanford; Patricia L. McNeese, Summerland Key; William G. Miller, Homestead; Richard Moyroud, Delray Beach; Ned D. Neenan, East Palatka; Jim M. Niccum, Ft. Myers; John Ogden, Homestead; Kenneth L. Oser, Milton; Steve Oswalt, Blountstown; Jeff Overby, Ocala; Jeanne M. Parks, Estero; Bill Peeples, East Palatka; Cherry W. Platt, Bartow; Wilbur C. Priest, Inverness; Buford C. Pruitt, Jacksonville; Frank A. Rathburn, Madison; Robert W. Ray, Green Cove Springs; Charles R. Reeves, Chipley; Diane Riggs, Homestead; Donald Robinson, New Port Richey; Robert Rose, Lignumvitae Key; Charles E. Salter, Tallahassee; William J. Schilling, Bradenton; Thomas H. Serviss, Cantonment; Alto Smith, Ft. Walton Beach; Dianna L. Stevenson, Marathon; Larry Thompson, Marathon; Jim Thorsen, Umatilla; R. Bruce Turnbull, Marianna; John T. Valenta, Homestead; Beverlee Wang, Key West; Gordon C. Ward, Gainesville; Kenneth B. Weber, Dade City; Pat Wells, Islamorada; David P. Wentzel, Orlando; Alan Whitehouse, Wakulla Springs; T. Ann Williams, Archer; Thomas Wilmers, Big Pine Key; Carol Wooley, Dunnellon; Richard W. Workman, Ft. Myers; Frank L. Zickar, Davie; Michael Zimmerman, Lake Worth; and especially our field companion and long-active nominator of champion trees, Robert W. Simons, Gainesville. We also wish to acknowledge the wholehearted support and encouragement of the staff personnel of the Division of Forestry, in particular that of James F. Testin who has aided us immeasurably by his supervision of the Division's Champion Tree program and its integration with the present project.

SELECTED REFERENCES

The following references include not only those cited in this publication, but also others believed to be of interest or appropriate to further understanding of the Florida Champion Tree Survey.

Adams, P. 1962. Studies in the Guttiferae. I: A synopsis of *Hypericum* section *Myriandra*. Contr. Gray Herb. 189:3–51.

Clewell, A. F. 1985. Guide to the Vascular Plants of the Florida Panhandle. Univ. Presses of Florida, Tallahassee. 605 pp.

Division of Forestry. 1986. Champion Trees of Florida. Tallahassee. 34 pp.

Division of Forestry. 1990. Champion Trees of Florida. Tallahassee. 72 pp.

Godfrey, R. K. 1988. Trees, Shrubs, and Woody Vines of Northern Florida and Adjacent Georgia and Alabama. Univ. Georgia Press, Athens. 734 pp.

Kurz, H. & R. K. Godfrey. 1962. Trees of Northern Florida. Univ. Florida Press, Gainesville. 311 pp.

Little, E. L. 1979. Checklist of United States Trees. U. S. Dept. Agric. handb. 541. 375 pp.

Merrill, E. D. 1948. *Metasequoia*, another "living fossil." Arnoldia 8:1–8.

National Register of Big Trees. 1990. American Forests (special sect.) 96:1–41.

National Register of Big Trees. 1992. American Forests (special sect.) 98:1–47.

National Register of Big Trees. 1994. American Forests (special sect.) 100:3–47.

National Register of Big Trees. 1996. American Forests (special sect.) 102:12–55.

Phipps, J. B. 1988. *Crataegus* (Maloideae, Rosaceae) of the southeastern United States, I. Introduction, and Series Aestivales. J. Arnold Arbor. 69:428.

Tomlinson, P. B. 1980. The Biology of Trees Native to Tropical Florida. Harvard University, Petersham, Mass. 480 pp.

Ward, D. B. 1967. *Acacia macracantha*, a tree new to Florida and the United States. Brittonia 19:283–284.

Ward, D. B. 1968. *Acacia tortuosa* (Leguminosae), new to Florida. Sida 3:279–280.

Ward, D. B. 1991. Checklist of the trees native to Florida. Palmetto 10(4):8–12.

Ward, D. B. & J. R. Burkhalter. 1977. Rediscovery of Small's *Acacia* in Florida. Florida Scientist 40:267–270.

Ward, D. B. & A. F. Clewell. 1989. Atlantic white cedar (*Chamaecyparis thyoides*) in the southern states. Florida Scientist 52:8–47.

Ward, D. B. & R. T. Ing. 1992. Where are the Florida champions? Palmetto 12(1):3–5.

Ward, D. B. & R. T. Ing. 1992. Champion trees of the University of Florida campus. Department of Botany, University of Florida, Gainesville. 10 pp.

Ward, D. B., R. T. Ing & J. F. Testin. 1993. Florida's lost champions. Palmetto 13(4):3–5.

Ward, D. B. & R. T. Ing. 1994. How old is a silver palm (*Coccothrinax argentata*)?. Palmetto 14(2):6–7.

Ward, D. B. & R. T. Ing. 1994. Florida Champions: "Vacant title" species. Department of Botany, University of Florida, Gainesville. 9 pp.

Ward, D. B. & R. T. Ing. 1995. Florida Champion Tree Project. Palmetto 15(1):14–15.

Ward, D. B. & R. T. Ing. 1995. Florida's Ten Tallest Native Tree Species. Palmetto 15(3):6–7.

Ward, D. B. & R. T. Ing. 1996. Florida's Big Tree: Measuring the Senator, Florida's champion bald cypress (*Taxodium distichum*). Palmetto 16(2):14–16.

West, E. & L. E. Arnold. 1956. The Native Trees of Florida. Univ. of Florida Press, Gainesville. 218 pp.

Wunderlin, R. P. 1982. Guide to the vascular plants of central Florida. Univ. Presses of Florida, Gainesville. 472 pp.

APPENDIX A: WHAT IS A TREE?

Persons conversant with the English language are unfailingly familiar with the word "tree." To all, a "tree" is a large, upright, woody plant.

Perhaps the first formal definition of "tree" was that given by Leonard Fuchs in the glossary of botanical terms included within his **De Historia Stirpium,** a Latin-language German herbal published in 1542.

> A *tree* ["*arbor*" in the original Latin] is that which rises firmly and directly from the root with a simple, solitary trunk, woody and with arm-like branches.

A modern definition of trees is very differently phrased, but without change over the centuries in the essence of meaning.

> Tree: A perennial plant having a self-supporting woody main stem or trunk, and growing to a considerable height and size. [**Oxford English Dictionary,** 1933]

Technical definitions of trees usually include quantitative values. A widely accepted definition is employed by the United States Forest Service.

> Trees are woody plants having one erect perennial stem or trunk at least 3 inches (7.5 centimeters) in diameter at breast height (4 1/2 feet or 1.3 meters), a more or less definitely formed crown of foliage, and a height of at least 13 feet (4 meters). [E. L. Little, **Checklist of United States Trees,** 1979]

However their definition is worded, trees seem quite different from shrubs—shrubs are also woody, but with several to many stems; also, shrubs usually are defined without height specifications, which accommodates the many creeping or prostrate woody species.

But many of our woody plants cannot neatly be assigned to one category or the other. A number of native species—common salt-bush (*Baccharis halimifolia*), buttonbush (*Cephalanthus occidentalis*), one-flowered haw (*Crataegus uniflora*), swamp privet (*Forestiera acuminata*), sand holly (*Ilex decidua*), blackbead (*Pithecellobium keyense*), and tallowwood (*Ximenia americana*), among others—as well as non-native species such as crape myrtle (*Lagerstroemia indica*), are prone to a habit of growth that branches at or near the base of the plant, with the stems divergent but ascending.

Other species clearly have the single-stem habit of a tree, but with most individuals so slender trunked as to fail any reasonable definition of "tree." In Florida, species such as indigo-bush (*Amorpha fruticosa*), flag pawpaw (*Asimina obovata*), limber caper (*Capparis flexuosa*), wild cotton (*Gossypium hirsutum*), Archbold oak (*Quercus inopina*), smooth sumac (*Rhus glabra*), and bladdernut (*Staphylea trifolia*), among others, rarely or possibly never attain sufficient trunk girth to be called trees. But one cannot be sure that a more robust individual will never be encountered, and it is perhaps best, where all tree species within an area are under study, not to overlook the possibility that these slender-trunked woody species may also merit inclusion.

Within the limitations imposed by their variable forms, the designation of individual trees that are national and state champions requires agreed-upon numerical values for minimal trunk circumference and height. The guidelines for trees accepted as National champions (by American Forests, Washington, D.C.) follow the Forest Service definition (above); only rarely are trees admitted with more slender trunks or lesser height.

Within Florida many of the native woody plants have the form of a tree, but in size fall below the Forest Service definition. The desire to include these small but representative trees has led the present investigators to impose less rigorous measurement standards; trees accepted by the Florida Champion Tree Survey as Florida champions may have trunks as small as 7 inches in circumference (2.25 inches in diameter) and 8 feet in height.

For species with branched, divergent trunks, if one (or more) of the stems is a minimum of 7 inches in circumference, then the plant is viewed as a tree, and the largest stem selected for measurement. Woody plants with no minimum-sized stems (at 4.5 feet) must be called shrubs, and cannot be evaluated by the criteria used here.

APPENDIX B: MECHANICS OF THE SURVEY

The Florida Champion Tree Survey, as reported here, is a continuation and expansion of a project that has been ongoing since 1978 when the state's Division of Forestry began the systematic assembly of data regarding Florida's big trees. Beginning in November 1990, discussion between personnel of the Division (James F. Testin and others) and the present investigators led to realization that a joint effort could further the goals of all parties. This tentative agreement was formalized in July 1992 by a MEMORANDUM OF UNDERSTANDING (see Appendix C, below) between the Division and the Department of Botany, University of Florida, for a project that would "further the completeness, accuracy, and public awareness of champion trees in the state of Florida."

Even before signing of the formal memorandum, work was begun by the present investigators to confirm big tree data previously gathered by the Division and to expand the numbers of trees and kinds of trees represented. A computerized format was devised for transcribing field data from the Division's files. This format permitted a text-based retrieval system using specially designed macros; these macros enabled the investigators to construct print-outs of any desired content (species from any given area, any owner or nominator, or other characteristic), for their own use and for assistance to other participants in the Survey.

The Survey was structured in three phases. The first step was transcription to the computer data-base of 578 big tree nominations from former years held in the Division's hardcopy files. Transcription also involved determination of section-township-range coordinates and other information missing in many of the older files. This phase also included communication with most of the previous nominators and encouragement for them to confirm and remeasure their earlier discoveries. For those trees whose nominators were unavailable or unable to update these previous records, the present investigators assumed responsibility. By the end of this first phase, essentially all of those trees whose previous measurement was more than ten years in the past had been relocated and remeasured (approximately three-fifths of the total), or were determined to be dead. (Four trees evaded this search, all in near-inaccessible swamps, but have been retained in the INVENTORY as unranked entries, for in each case the possibility remains that the tree survives, awaiting rediscovery.)

The second phase of the Survey was begun before the first phase was completed. This was the effort to expand the study more evenly throughout the state, and to make the discovery of as many new trees of championship size, and of as many additional species, as was possible. This task rested primarily with the present investigators, who were ultimately successful in locating and measuring 146 previously unrecorded trees of large size, many of them champions. Other persons were active in submitting additional nominations and were of critical help in accompanying the investigators in the field. The extent of their help may be appraised by the many (above one hundred) persons named in the ACKNOWLEDGMENTS.

This phase also involved coordination with a similar program of national scope, the National Register of Big Trees, as conducted by **American Forests,** Washington, D.C. **American Forests** (formerly the **American Forestry Association**) is the publisher of a highly regarded eponymous magazine on forestry topics, and the sponsor of a nationwide program that since 1940 has assembled records and published listings of trees that are the largest of their species in the United States. (See SELECTED REFERENCES for recent listings.) Copies of nominations of those trees thought to be of sufficient size to be possible National champions were transmitted to **American Forests;** that organization, in exchange, routinely forwarded to the present investigators those (relatively few) nominations of Florida trees received by them that had not been transmitted through the Florida program.

At close of this phase of the Survey the computer data-base formed by these several efforts encompassed 1041 fully documented big-tree nominations. Also accumulated but not entered in the data-base was an appreciable additional number of incomplete records (largely of written or verbal reports unaccompanied by a proper nomination), doubtful nominations (mostly of trees whose identifications were dubious and could not be confirmed), or too-small trees (of non-native species, in which only trees exceeding 100 points were recorded).

The third phase of the Survey has been assembly of the present report. An unexpected, but not wholly unwelcome, complication of this third phase was the continuing flow of nominations and other data from cooperators in the field. These new data required repeated adjustments of ranking of the champions and recalculation of statistics.

As called for by the MEMORANDUM, throughout the Survey the present investigators served where possible as an information source for the media and for other persons who had need for

information regarding big trees. An appreciable number of news reports and special features on champion trees was published by writers of the state's newspapers during the years of the Survey. The investigators themselves published a series of brief articles regarding aspects of the Survey in the journal of the Florida Native Plant Society (see SELECTED REFERENCES). A "Champion Tree Newsletter" was begun in August 1993, for those individuals who were known to the present investigators to be interested in big trees. Three or occasionally four issues were distributed annually, eventually with a mailing list of about 250. These diverse publications and the "Newsletter" were valuable in bringing attention to the Survey and in enlisting assistance from knowledgeable persons in the fields of forestry, horticulture, civic history, park management, and the general public.

APPENDIX C: MEMORANDUM OF UNDERSTANDING

May 29, 1992

Agreement for a Co-operative Project regarding Champion Trees.

1. This MEMORANDUM places on record the intention of the Division of Forestry, Department of Agriculture and Consumer Services, and the Department of Botany, University of Florida, to work cooperatively in a CHAMPION TREE PROJECT to further the completeness, accuracy, and public awareness of champion trees in the state of Florida.

2. The trees of Florida are one of its most important assets. The 276 species of tree that are native to Florida and the many species of tree that are introduced to the state give it one of the most varied tree floras of any area of the United States.

3. Individual specimens of any tree species that are of exceptional size inevitably attract much interest and admiration. The very largest specimen of each species has come to be known as the "Champion." Records of such champion trees are compiled for most states and for the United States, and are utilized by the public for purposes of conservation and pride in heritage.

4. Since 1941 the American Forestry Association, Washington, D.C., has retained records and published listings of the trees that were the largest of their species in the United States— the "National Champions." (The most recent report: National Register of Big Trees, 1992 Edition). The Florida Forest Service (now the Division of Forestry, Department of Agriculture and Consumer Services) has been the A.F.A.'s

contact in Florida since the beginning of the program.

5. Since 1978 the Division of Forestry, Florida Department of Agriculture and Consumer Services, has retained records and has published listings of the trees that were the largest of their species in the State of Florida—the "Florida Champions" (The most recent report: "Champion Trees of Florida," Division of Forestry, 1990). The Division of Forestry has also forwarded to the A.F.A. records of those trees in Florida that exceed the national listings; these then also become National Champions.

6. With time, as trees age and die, and as new trees of exceptional size are located and identified, it is necessary to update champion tree records. It is desirable that these records of champion trees be based on fully documented reports, that the tree species be accurately identified, and that the scientific names be correct. It is also desirable that the public be kept aware of the program within the state of Florida to locate and record these champion trees, and that the public be encouraged to participate in the gathering of this information.

7. Specific goals of this PROJECT include: (1) Screening of the present records of Florida's champion trees, to eliminate old or dubious records, and to select those records that reflect present information of champion trees. (2) To transfer the essential aspects of these records to a data-base system that will facilitate later retrieval. (3) To expand these records by adding information regarding larger trees of species presently recorded, and to seek information regarding trees of species for which no data are currently available. (4) To encourage the active participation of the personnel of the district offices of the Division of Forestry and the general public in augmenting these records. (5) To pre-

pare for publication appropriate articles regarding Florida's champion trees. (6) To serve as an information source for the media and for persons who need large tree information for reasons of conservation and pride in heritage. (7) To update the American Forestry Association's records, thereby giving full honor and respect to those trees in the state that are National Champions.

8. The personnel who will be asked to carry out this project are: James F. Testin, Environmental Education Coordinator, Division of Forestry; Dr. Daniel B. Ward, Professor of Botany, University of Florida; and Dr. Robert T. Ing, Courtesy Assistant in Botany, University of Florida. Mr. T   s presently responsible for the Division' _nampion Trees program, and Dr. Ward and Dr. Ing are expert in the identification, classification, nomenclature, and distribution of tree species in Florida.

9. This Project shall be of indefinite duration, and shall be subject to termination by either party upon notification to the other party.

AGREED this date.

L. Earl Peterson   [signed, 16 June 1992]
Director
Division of Forestry
Department of Agriculture and Consumer
  Services
3125 Conner Boulevard
Tallahassee, FL 32399-1650

Dr. David A. Jones   [signed, 7 July 1992]
Chairman
Department of Botany
University of Florida
220 Bartram Hall
Gainesville, FL 32611

APPENDIX D: HOW TO NOMINATE A CHAMPION TREE

A big tree cannot be considered a "champion" until, first, it is nominated as such by a responsible person and, second, is so designated by an agency which has assembled documentation of other large trees and is thereby qualified to make a comparison. In the United States such a designation is provided at two levels: National champions, which are recognized by **American Forests,** Washington, D.C.; and state champions, which are determined by an agency, usually a department of forestry, within the individual states. (A few communities with exceptional affection for their outstanding trees also identify champions within their immediate area.)

The details of the documentation required for nomination differ to some extent within the different organizations. In Florida a nomination is submitted on a standardized form (Figs. 1, 2) that calls for, in addition to the measurements, the name and address of the person(s) nominating the tree; the owner of the tree and owner's address; the county in which the tree is located, with street/town/city and/or other address designations and township/range coordinates; and a sketch map of the tree's location.

Nominations must include measurements that follow the formula employed by **American Forests.** (For the Florida instructions, see Appendix E: HOW TO MEASURE A CHAMPION TREE.) Because of the variable shapes encountered among trees of different species and even within the same species, the process of measurement requires precision and thoughtful conformity to all appropriate measurement guidelines.

Correct identification of the tree is critical. In the case of species within difficult genera, either a small specimen or confirmation from a county forester or other qualified person may be required. A photograph is always welcome, but is not mandatory.

Nominations may be submitted to the: **Champion Tree Program, Department of Botany, University of Florida, Gainesville, FL 32611;** or to the **Division of Forestry, 3125 Conner Blvd., Tallahassee, FL 32301.** Upon receipt by the Gainesville office, a completed nomination will be entered into the Florida Champion Tree Survey database. For archival protection of data and for simplicity of access, all nominations received by the Gainesville office will be duplicated and the originals transmitted to the Division offices, Tallahassee. Where appropriate, a further duplicate copy will be deposited with **American Forests,** Washington, D.C., for possible listing by the National Register of Big Trees. Nominations will be acknowledged and the correspondent will be informed of the tree's status as to championship ranking.

Florida Champion Tree Record

Florida Division of Forestry
3125 Conner Blvd.
Tallahassee, Florida 32301

(904) 488-6727

Common Name:	Scientific Name:

Identification Reference (Book, Authority or Source):

Owner

Name:

Address:

Post Office: _____ ZIP:

Telephone:

Nominator

Name:

Address:

Post Office: _____ ZIP:

Telephone:

Location

County:

Sketch Map

Specific location description (address, Section-Township-Range, or distances and bearings from prominent landmarks.)

Measurements

	Measurements	Points
Crown Spread — maximum diameter: (to the nearest foot)	Feet	
Crown Spread — minimum diameter: (to the nearest foot)	Feet	Round UP from .5
Crown Spread Subtotal: (maximum + minimum diameters)		
Average Crown Spread:	Feet	
Point Conversion Divide Average Crown Spread by 4: (Round to nearest whole point)	Points	
Circumference: (to the nearest inch)	Inches	
Height: (to the nearest foot)	Feet	
Height above average ground level that the Circumference was measured:	Feet	
Date of Measurements:		Total Points

Photograph

Photographer's Name: _____ Date Taken:

Names of persons in photograph (listed, photo left to right):

Forest Education Bureau Use

Condition of Tree:

☐ Vigorous, Healthy
☐ Mature, Healthy
☐ Mature, Declining
☐ Severe Decline

Remarks:

Division of Forestry Office:

Certified By:

Signature

Figure 1

Florida Champion Tree Record

Florida Division of Forestry
3125 Conner Blvd.
Tallahassee, Florida 32301

(904) 488-6727

Common Name:	Scientific Name:
Water-elm	Planera aquatica

Identification Reference (Book, Authority or Source):	Trees, Shrubs & Woody Vines..... by R. Godfrey

Owner

Name:
San Felasco Hammock State Preserve
% Dana Bryan

Address:
Division of Recreation and Parks
3900 Commonwealth Boulevard

Post Office: Tallahassee, Florida   ZIP: 32399

Telephone: 904-488-8666

Nominator

Name:
Robert W. and Erika H. Simons

Address:
1122 S.W. 11th Avenue

Post Office: Gainesville, Florida   ZIP: 32601

Telephone: 904-372-7646

Location

County: Alachua

San Felasco Hammock Map

Bromeliad Pond

I-75

N
S

Big Water-Elm

500 yards

232

Millhopper Rd.
P

Section 12, T9S, R18E, Alachua County

It is 50 ft S. of the S. edge of the open part of Bromeliad Pond.

Forest Education Bureau Use

Measurements

	Measurements	Points
Crown Spread — maximum diameter: (to the nearest foot)	68 Feet	
Crown Spread — minimum diameter: (to the nearest foot)	52 Feet	Round UP from .5
Crown Spread Subtotal: (maximum + minimum diameters)	120	
Average Crown Spread:	60 Feet	
Point Conversion — Divide Average Crown Spread by 4: (Round to nearest whole point)	15 Points	15
Circumference: (to the nearest inch)	135 Inches	135
Height: (to the nearest foot)	41 Feet	41
Height above average ground level that the Circumference was measured:	4.5 Feet	191
Date of Measurements:	11/26/94	Total Points

Photograph

Photographer's Name: Robert W. Simons   Date Taken: 11/26/94

Names of persons in photograph (listed, photo left to right):
Erika Simons

Condition of Tree:
- [ ] Vigorous, Healthy
- [X] Mature, Healthy
- [ ] Mature, Declining
- [ ] Severe Decline

Remarks:

Division of Forestry Office:

Certified By:
D. B. Ward
Signature

Figure 2

APPENDIX E: HOW TO MEASURE A CHAMPION TREE

The concept of a "champion" tree requires that a standard method of measurement be employed. By long-standing practice, to establish some degree of equivalence between trees of dramatically different proportions, the standard method has incorporated measurement of circumference of trunk, height of tree, and spread of branches. A formula applied to these three dimensions yields a single number that can be used for comparison among individuals of a given species and among different species.

Champions are usually determined by their ranking in "point size." "Points" are calculated by applying a simple formula to three measurements:

Trunk Circumference (in inches) at 4.5 feet (or at lower point if smaller than at 4.5 feet), plus:

Height (in feet), plus:

1/4 of Crown-spread Diameter (average of largest and smallest diameters, in feet).

Total Points is the sum of the above three values.

Trees, however, are variable in form and conditions of growth, and questions often arise during measurement.

Question: Where should a trunk be measured that has a major fork just *above* 4.5 feet? **Answer:** Measure the trunk at the point of minimum circumference at or below 4.5 feet.

Question: Where should the measurement be taken if the fork is *below* 4.5 feet? **Answer:** Measure the circumference of the largest stem at 4.5 feet.

Question: When, if ever, may a trunk be measured *below* 4.5 feet. **Answer:** The *only* circumstance in which a trunk is measured below 4.5 feet is when such a measurement will yield a *smaller* circumference than at the higher point.

Question: Should the height of a fork be measured at the height of the present notch or at the height of the notch when the tree was young? **Answer:** As branch diameters increase over the years the height of the notch may move upward. But use the present height of the notch, not the (estimated) height of the notch when the tree was younger.

Question: When the trunk is inclined toward the horizontal, how should its circumference be measured? **Answer:** Measurement should be made at right angles to the axis of the trunk without regard to the trunk's orientation, but with the measurement taken at an average distance of 4.5 vertical feet above ground level.

Question: If a champion tree is toppled by windthrow, but still lives, how does one update the measurement data? **Answer:** A fallen champion is no longer a champion. Don't attempt to update the data; the tree no longer has a measurable vertical dimension.

Question: If a tree branches repeatedly from near the base, isn't it proper to measure circumference below the lowest branch? **Answer:** No. Make the measurement on the largest branch at 4.5 feet above ground. A lower measurement gives a deceptively large value in comparison with the value obtained for another tree, perhaps of larger volume, whose unbranched trunk is measured at 4.5 feet.

Question: How does one measure the trunk of a tree such as a banyan which has many secondary root-trunks? **Answer:** Snake the measuring tape around the circumference of the central trunk. If, with time, secondary root-trunks merge with the central trunk, treat the merged axis as a single trunk.

Question: If a tree has a prominent butt swell, should circumference be measured at some point above 4.5 feet? **Answer:** Measurement must be made at 4.5 feet for purposes of comparison. A second circumference measurement at a higher level may be useful in conveying a clear indication of trunk size. (Note: Certain tropical species with massive buttresses cannot be meaningfully measured at

4.5 feet; for such trees, volume measurement may be an acceptable alternative.)

Question: How is crown spread measured? **Answer:** Think of the outermost tips of the branches as forming an approximate circle, then measure its width at the point of maximum diameter and at the point of minimum diameter, and calculate the average.

Question: If trunk forks below 4.5 feet, should crown spread be measured only for the stem for which the circumference was measured? **Answer:** No. Measure crown spread for the entire crown of the tree.

Question: How is height measured when the tree is growing on sloping ground? **Answer:** Treat the surface from which height is measured as a horizontal plane centered on the base of the trunk.

Question: How is height measured in a tree such as a palm in which some of the leaves extend well above the tip of the trunk axis? **Answer:** Measure to the highest point of the most extended leaf.

Question: If highest point of tree is not directly above the trunk, at what point should height be measured? **Answer:** Measure height at highest point of crown, without regard to location of trunk.

Question: If some branches are dead, should they be included in measurement of height or crown spread? **Answer:** No. Restrict measurement to living branches.

Question: How can height be measured? **Answer:** The most accurate method is by use of a clinometer, a device that measures the angle of the top of the tree to the horizontal and converts that reading into a percentage of the horizontal distance of the device from the tree.

Question: Is any other height measurement technique available? **Answer:** The classic Boy Scout technique is always available, of placing the head at ground level and sighting across a measuring stick to the tree top, then calculating the ratio: Distance from eye to stick is to distance from eye to tree, as height of sighting point on stick is to height of tree.

Question: Can height be estimated? **Answer:** Yes. But the estimate should be under conditions that can reasonably be repeated with close conformity by different observers.

Question: Can measurement of trunk volume be considered an indicator of relative tree size? **Answer:** Under certain conditions measurement of trunk volume may be used in place of the standard formula: (a) Accepted forestry mensuration techniques must be employed. (b) The bulk of the tree must reside in a tapering near-cylindrical trunk; trees with massive spreading branches are inappropriate for volume measurement. (c) Although volume of a single tree may be of interest, volume may be used for ranking purposes only if applied to two or more trees measured by the same persons using the same mensuration technique. If ranking based upon volume differs from the "point total" ranking attained by the standard formula, the volume ranking takes precedence.

Question: Is there any general principle to follow in measuring champion trees? **Answer:** Disputes will be avoided if the effort is always made to find the *minimum* dimension under the above rules.

APPENDIX F: EVALUATION OF THE FORMULA

The familiar formula for ranking big trees, employed since 1940 by **American Forests** and accepted by all cooperating state programs, has not been revised since establishment of the National program. Its originator, forester Fred Besley of Maryland, recognized a need for a quantitative measure of trees of different proportions, and in 1925 filled that need with a simple equation utilizing the height of the tree, the circumference of the trunk, and one-quarter of the average crown spread, to create a size factor expressed in "points."

The wide acceptance of Besley's formula may be attributed in large part to the impression it gave of balance in measuring three obvious, readily determined aspects of a tree's size. The need, seen by Besley, of a single measure by which trees may be ranked as to size, is intuitively perceived as more "fair" if more than a single dimension is evaluated.

It is understandable that Besley would have used English linear measurements in his formula, for the metric system, though adopted by France in 1799 and legal in the United States since 1866, even now has not extensively penetrated American forestry practices. "Feet" for height and "inches" for circumference remain standard units of measurement within the American industry even today, as does "board feet" for volume. The units of measurement, of course, as employed in the formula, determine the weighting of the three dimensions; for example, had circumference been measured in tenths of a foot, rather than in inches, the weight given to circumference would have been reduced by 16.7%. There is no indication that Besley selected these units of measurement for reasons other than convenience, though he may have made a conscious judgment that the resulting weighting was a felicitous measure of the relative importance of height and circumference.

Besley, however, was not willing to accept "feet," unaltered, as a measure of crown spread. He has been stated (National Register, 1992) to believe that the trunk was the most important part of the tree; he thus gave the trunk's height and girth greater weight by allowing only a quarter of the spread to be included in the total score.

No quantitative evaluation of the degree of weighting of the three measurements imposed by Besley's formula appears to have been made. It is now possible, by using the amassed measurements of many hundreds of trees that are the largest of their individual species, to look at the "average" champion tree and to calculate the percentage of the "total points" derived, on average, from each component of Besley's formula. The data obtained in the Florida Champion Tree Survey lend themselves well to this analysis (see THE "AVERAGE" CHAMPION).

Before analysis, the Florida tree measurements were separated into those trees that have been designated National champions, and those designated Florida champions. The Florida champions were much the larger, with an average point score of 179, while the National champions had an average point score of 117.

No difference, however, was found between the National champions and the Florida champions in the proportions of the three measured dimensions. In each category 56% of the total points was attributable to circumference, 37% to height, and 7% to canopy width. It may be said, therefore, that the proportions of National champions and Florida champions, as determined from Florida examples, are essentially identical.

Florida's National Champions.

Average of all available species

Size:	Circumference:	65.4 inches	=	65 points	56%
	Height:	44.0 feet	=	44 points	37%
	Crown spread:	32.7 feet	=	8 points	7%
	Total points:	117 points			

Comments: Based upon 120 National champions located within Florida.

Florida's State Champions.

Average of all available species

Size:					
Circumference:	100.5	inches	=	100 points	56%
Height:	67.2	feet	=	67 points	37%
Crown spread:	47.7	feet	=	12 points	7%
Total points:	179	points			

Comments: Based upon 99 Florida champions (native species only).

But the weighting of circumference *versus* height *versus* spread in the ratio of 56 : 37 : 7 does derive appreciably more than half the total point score from the measurement of a single criterion, and allots a very minor value to the spread of the canopy. The degree of this disproportion is perhaps greater than is generally realized, and exaggerates a problem of measurement of certain species with swollen bases.

The genus *Taxodium*, the bald cypress and pond cypress, under certain Florida conditions where water level may fluctuate up and down the trunk, frequently develops into individuals whose lower trunk is massively swollen with but little increase to the trunk above the level of water exposure. In areas of the Apalachicola National Forest, Franklin County, appreciable numbers of these bulbous-based trees have developed in shallow sinkhole basins. Karst depressions near the Suwannee River, Hamilton County, hold other turnip-shaped trees, one formerly considered the Florida champion bald cypress. As described elsewhere (APPENDIX G), measurement of trunk volume, when used in place of the standard formula, yields a ranking for such trees that better reflects tree size.

Other tree species, either by environmental influence or by inherent genetic propensity, also form trunks that challenge measurement by the standard formula. The water tupelo (*Nyssa biflora*) is frequently swollen at the base; the standard formula yields point values well in excess of the scores that would be attained by a trunk of more conventional form. Even so, the practice has been to measure these trees with the standard formula and accept with resignation the resulting somewhat inflated ranking relative to other species.

But some species, with forms wholly unfamiar to Besley in his temperate, eastern deciduous forests, even more extremely challenge, or even thwart, measurement by the standard formula. The banyans—species of *Ficus*, and especially *Ficus benghalensis*, the banyan fig—characteristically develop slender, pendent, aerial roots which extend to the ground, become anchored, then by secondary growth become stout and give support to the otherwise unstable horizontal branches. By this means the canopy may expand essentially without limit, supported by a small forest of root-trunks and all interconnected by the horizontal branches.

And the baobabs, of which only one, *Adansonia digitata*, is presently in Florida cultivation, typically form trunks of enormous proportion, but of modest height and crown spread. The standard formula, were it applied to these trees in their African home—or as it will apply to Florida specimens given a few more decades of growth—will rank these trees above the largest American species of more conventional form.

But the figs and the baobabs pale in the challenges they pose to the standard formula were it applied to the many tropical species, several of them now grown in Florida, in which vertical flanges or buttresses develop on the lower trunk. These buttresses are an evolutionary modification that increases stability on soft soils and occur also with some temperate species, perhaps most notably in Florida on the trunks of the Florida elm (*Ulmus americana* var. *floridana*). But the buttresses when found on North American trees do not extend far up the trunk and thus scarcely influence measurement at 4.5 feet. The tropical species, in marked contrast, may develop buttresses that begin at a low level when the tree is young, but increasingly as the tree ages extend upward to twice the measurement level or above.

The most remarkable Florida example of a tropical tree with prominent buttresses was the Moreton Bay fig (*Ficus macrophylla*) at the Edison Estate, Lee County (recently removed, following wind damage). This tree in the 100 years since its planting by Thomas Edison first was a slender tree of conventional shape but with prominent roots along the soil surface; a rib then expanded upward along the entire length of these roots, initially to low levels that could easily be stepped over, then progressively higher. When measured in 1978 the trunk was still accessible at 4.5 feet, above the nearly horizontal flange-like buttresses; by 1981 the buttresses had extended above that point, forcing the investigator to make his measurement at 7 feet; in 1994 the buttresses were above even that level, and trunk circumference had to be measured at 10.5 feet.

Had the investigator who evaluated the Moreton Bay fig in 1994 followed the standard requirement of trunk measurement at 4.5 feet, his tape circumscribing the extended buttresses at that level would have measured a circumference in excess of 1200 inches (100 feet). This measure, combined with height and crown spread, would have yielded a point score very close to twice the total of any of the giant sequoias and many times greater than any other tree in eastern North America.

The measurement and ranking problems imposed by tree species that develop multiple trunks or basally enlarged trunks or trunks with extensive buttresses cannot be resolved in any wholly satisfactory way. If a banyan still retains its original trunk, measurement may still be made even though the increased visual impact of the multiple root-trunks is ignored. Moderately basally-enlarged trunks may be measured and used for comparison as though they are of conventional form, and the somewhat inflated score and ranking is disregarded. And trees of species that develop extensive buttresses may be measured at increasing heights on the trunk, although the resulting values are not truly comparable with trees measured at the standard level.

Volume measurement may only rarely be substituted for the standard formula because of the inherent difficulty of making those measurements, the limited number of trees whose bulk resides largely in the trunk and is thus suitable for such measurements, and the necessity of measuring volume not only of the one potential champion but of all comparable trees.

Recognition of this problem is not new. From soon after the first use of the Besley formula, questions have arisen about the suitability or even the usability of his formula for trees of unconventional form. **American Forests** (1992) has discussed this problem, though without examination of the unique problems encountered in measuring many tropical species; their conclusion was that use of the Besley formula is "simple, convenient, and no more arbitrary than any other one system."

But one simple and convenient modification could be made in the Besley formula that would diminish the impact trunk circumference has on the point score and thus the distortion caused by trees with swollen or buttressed bases. This is the elimination of Besley's casual reduction of canopy width to one-fourth of its measurement; rather, that the average spread be retained in its full measured value.

Such a "full-spread" modification of the standard formula, applied to National champion trees occurring in Florida, would change the weighting of circumference *versus* height *versus* spread from the present 56 : 37 : 7, to a more equitable 46 : 31 : 23. This change would more than triple the weighting given to canopy width, thereby assigning greater recognition to the visual impact of wide-spreading branches. It would reduce somewhat the significance of height. And it would diminish the importance of trunk girth, thereby moderating the distortion produced by trees with bases that are enlarged disproportionate to the upper trunk. A modest but not unhelpful further benefit would be the simplification of the formula and the necessary explanations of its use.

Florida's National Champions.

Average of all available species.

Size:					
	Circumference:	65.4	inches	= 65 points	46%
	Height:	44.0	feet	= 44 points	31%
	Crown spread:	32.7	feet	= 33 points	23%
	Total points:	142	points		

Comments: Refigured, with full crown spread included in point total.

But a more radical modification of the Besley formula would generate even greater benefits. Beyond the possibility of a near-term adjustment to the weightings of the standard formula lies the certainty that future pressures of scientific credibility, if not those of international commercial practice, will compel the greater use of metric values in American forestry practices. Applied to the determination of tree size, the importance of comparability with trees of other nations who use metric will eventually make English linear seem provincial and quaint.

Conversion to metric for "champion tree" evaluations has several merits. Though other countries (Australia, England, South Africa, most notably) are giving attention to the size of their largest trees, none approach the United States in the thoroughness of their surveys nor in the standardization of their measurement techniques; a system employed in the United States if denominated in metric units is likely to win acceptance, thus expanding the understanding of tree size internationally. And conversion to metric permits simultaneous re-evaluation of the weighting given to measurement factors, thereby diminishing the present distortion in ranking of trees whose trunks are basally enlarged.

An obvious, practical application of metric to the three measurements employed by Besley is the use of the meter for the height of the tree and for its average canopy width and the use of the decimeter (or the use of the centimeter times 10) for measurement of circumference. The weighting that results from this employment of the metric scale, together with use of the average crown spread (rather than one-fourth of the spread), yields a point score much smaller in total points to the presently employed Besley scale or the "full spread" scale discussed above.

But the metric scale is not grossly dissimilar in the proportionate weighting assigned to the three measured values. To reiterate, while circumference *versus* height *versus* spread is weighted by the standard formula in a ratio of 56 : 37 : 7, and the "full spread" formula is weighted 46 : 31 : 23, the metric scale weighting yields a ratio of 42 : 33 : 25. The importance of circumference, although still the largest factor, is thereby further reduced; the importance of crown spread is increased somewhat more than that of the already increased "full spread" scale; and the importance of height is increased above the values of the "full spread" scale but still below the levels of the Besley scale.

Florida's National Champions.

Average of all available species.

Size:	Circumference:	166.0	cm	=	17 points	42%
	Height:	13.4	m	=	13 points	33%
	Crown spread:	10.0	m	=	10 points	25%
	Total points:	40			metric points	

Comments: Refigured in metric, with full crown spread included in point total.

Metric scale implies one additional modification. The weighting given to circumference would be further reduced over that of the Besley scale if an adjustment were made in the height of trunk measurement. While 4.5 feet could be maintained (converted to 137 cm), a more comprehensible level would be 1.5 meters (or 4.9 feet). This small increase in measurement level, applied to a trunk of conventional taper, would slightly reduce the weighting given to circumference, and would further diminish the distortion of trees with swollen bases.

The evidence, as presented here, does show that under the standard Besley formula there is now a very heavy, arguably disproportionate, weighting toward trunk circumference, and that certain tree configurations inevitably produce bizarre and valueless point scores. Further, scientific comparability will increasingly obligate acceptance of metric values if American champion tree studies are to remain credible. This publication is not the place to propose immediate acceptance of a variance from the Besley formula, either by inclusion of the full crown spread or by conversion to metric. But discussion of these concerns and their possible resolution is now due.

APPENDIX G: A CASE OF VOLUME MEASUREMENT

Although the **American Forests** measurement rules permit substitution of volume in place of the formula employing circumference, height, and crown spread, the inherent difficulties of this alternative technique have greatly restricted its use. Following is an account (as published in **The Palmetto**, 1996) of the single employment thus far of volume measurement in the determination of Florida's champion trees.

* * * * * * *

Decades ago a gigantic Bald Cypress (*Taxodium distichum*) near Longwood, Seminole County, was recognized as perhaps the largest tree of its species surviving in Florida. As early as the 1880s visitors to the Sanford area are known to have waded through the surrounding swamp to view this tree. In 1927 M. O. Overstreet, a prominent citizen of Orlando (and State Senator, 1920–1924), gave lasting protection to the giant—thereafter known as the "Senator" in his honor—and an adjacent slightly smaller tree, the "Senator's Brother," by his donation of six acres to Seminole County. President Calvin Coolidge in 1929, during his last days in office, made a dedicatory speech beneath the tree, and a descriptive bronze plaque was placed on its trunk. In the mid-1930s the Works Progress Administration (WPA), to facilitate access, constructed a boardwalk from the nearby roadway to the base of the tree. But with access came vandalism; the bronze plaque and parts of an early iron fence were stolen by 1945. A sturdy replacement fence later placed at a small distance from the Senator's trunk has since effectively shielded the tree from overly-affectionate visitors.

Although nearly all early references to the Senator include statements of girth and height, as well as (unconfirmable) estimates of age, the first careful measurement to the **American Forests** standard was made by County Forester Mike Martin in February 1981. Mike obtained a point score of 531; this score was far above any Bald Cypress then on record, and for the moment the general assumption that the

Senator was the largest *Taxodium distichum* in Florida seemed vindicated.

But in October 1981, Joe Corbett Mathis, a Hamilton County forester, wandered into a depression north of the Suwannee River, about four miles east of the Nobel's Ferry bridge, and found a monstrous Bald Cypress shaped like a giant turnip, a hugely swollen base that tapered into a modest upper trunk. When the area had been logged for cypress, perhaps at the turn of the century, this tree was left because its lower portion was entirely hollow and its timber value, at that early date, wasn't worth salvaging. Joe measured the tree by the **American Forests** standard, which specifies the circumference be measured only at 4.5 feet, and came to a resounding 644 points. The Senator's reign as the Florida champion was over!

In 1993, with Bob Simons, we furthered the Senator's ignominy by finding a second Hamilton County Bald Cypress, on Holton Creek, that measured 587 points. This discovery placed the Senator at third rank within the state.

Also in 1993, with Bob Simons, we remeasured the Senator, as well as the then-unmeasured Senator's Brother. The Senator had a circumference of 425 inches, a height of 118 feet, and a spread of 57 feet, giving it a point score of 557, a small improvement over Mike's 1981 score of 531 but insufficient to regain even second place. The Senator's Brother came in at 491 points, the sixth largest Bald Cypress in the state.

But Simons carried the investigation further. He used a Relaskop, a complex optical device that gives diameter measurements at different levels above the ground and thus permits accurate calculation of trunk volume as a series of successively smaller cylinders. We accompanied him in measuring the volume of the Senator, the two Hamilton County giants, and, for good measure, an impressive tree known as "Old Methuselah" at DeLeon Springs Recreation Area, Volusia County.

The volume figures were just the inverse of the point scores. The Senator showed a volume of 3731 cubic feet. The Holton Creek tree had a volume of 2068 cubic feet. And Joe Mathis' tree—the Florida champion by the American Forests standard—had a volume of 1872 cubic feet. (Old Methuselah, though a beautiful, symmetrical tree, attained only 1155 cubic feet.)

So which tree is the Florida champion? Is it the Mathis tree, larger in point total? Or is it the Senator, with the larger trunk volume? One system or the other must prevail.

Simons then called our attention to a similar controversy, in California, where trunk volumes and total scores of the two largest Sequoia (*Sequoiadendron giganteum*) point in opposite directions. The General Sherman Sequoia was clearly larger in general appearance, with its massive cylindrical trunk, but the General Grant, which has a sizable butt swell and a more tapered trunk, was given a larger total point score. When volumes of the two trees were measured, the General Sherman was found to contain 52,508 cubic feet, while the General Grant contained 46,608 cubic feet. But the General Grant was scored at 1348 points, a bit ahead of the General Sherman's 1300 points.

Chaos swept the halls of **American Forests!** Since 1940, when **American Forests** began the registration of champion trees, a standard developed in 1925 by the Maryland state forester had been the agreed-upon comparator, a yardstick that permitted trees of different shapes to be matched with a single numerical scale (the trunk circumference in inches, plus the tree height in feet, plus one-fourth of the average branch spread in feet). But tree volume, even simplified as trunk volume, was an obviously logical alternative measure. What to do?

It took **American Forests** two years to decide that the standard formula was adequate, and was far easier to apply since measurements by tape and clinometer were more readily attained than those requiring sophisticated volume measurement. But in 1992 American Forests concluded that volume measure, when available, was to be used in place of the standard formula. By this ruling the General Sherman, at 1300 points and 52,508 cubic feet, was the National champion Sequoia, and the General Grant, at 1348 points and 46,608 cubic feet, was relegated to National challenger.

Applied to *Taxodium* in Florida, we must invert the ranking of the three largest trees. The Florida champion, once again, is the Senator at Longwood, Seminole County, with a volume of 3731 cubic feet. The Florida challenger is the tree along Holton Creek, Hamilton County, with a volume of 2068 cubic feet. And the Mathis tree, also Hamilton County, after its fifteen year reign as Florida champion, is now moved to third place, with a volume of 1872 cubic feet. The King is deposed! Long live the King!

But let us not be quick to accept these trees as merely Florida champions. Might the largest of them also be the National champion? By **American Forests** records, the largest Bald Cypress is at Cat Island, West Feliciana Parish, Louisiana; it has a circumference of 644 inches and a point score of 748. But the grapevine tells us it also is a "turnip," with a swollen basal trunk but little above. It cannot be displaced, of course, without volume measurements. But should it turn out to have a volume smaller than the measured Florida giants, then the Senator will become the National champion. We are awaiting records from **American Forests** and opportunity to visit and measure the Louisiana tree. Stay tuned!

Supplemental note: Volume of The Senator was measured by R. W. Simons (aided by L. D. Harris), 19 July 1993. Procedure followed the "Smalian formula," as described in **Forest Mensuration** (Chapman & Meyer, 1949): Diameters were taken at 16 ft. "log length" intervals (by use of a Spiegel Relaskop); calculation was made of sq. ft. area of log ends; average was taken for each log, multiplied by log length, and summed. (For basal log, diameter at 4.5 ft. was used, rather than at 0 ft.)

APPENDIX H: WILLIAM BARTRAM'S BIG TREES

In the mid-1770s the gentle Philadelphia Quaker, William Bartram, traveled extensively through the southeastern United States, recording in detail all aspects of its natural history. Though his fame now rests on the eloquence of the writing and the historic observations of his classic book, **Travels through North and South Carolina, Georgia, East and West Florida** (1791), it is also true that his keen eye and voluminous notes have provided the first documentation of the magnificent forests that then covered this verdant land. In Florida, as he traveled up the St. Johns River in the spring and again in the late summer of 1774, he was awed by trees of species wholly new to him and of sizes beyond any seen in the more settled lands to the north. His descriptions, with their paced measurements and estimates of height, provide a glimpse of Florida's big trees that can never again be experienced.

* * * * * * * *

"The trunk of the Live Oak [*Quercus virginiana*] is generally from twelve to eighteen feet in girt, and rises ten or twelve feet erect from the earth, some I have seen eighteen or twenty; then divides itself into three, four, or five great limbs, which continue to grow in nearly an horizontal direction, each limb forming a gentle curve, or arch, from its base to its extremity. I have stepped above fifty paces, on a strait line, from the trunk of one of these trees, to the extremity of its limbs." [William Bartram, **Travels,** 1791:84-85. Near mouth of Clarke's Creek, west bank of St. Johns River, 7 mi. s.e. of Green Cove Springs, Clay Co. Sec 8, T7S, R27E. R. Harper (1958) has noted the "fifty paces" from trunk to extremity of limbs, to be "impossible," suggesting Bartram intended the measurement to refer to the entire spread.]

"The Laurel Magnolia [*Magnolia grandiflora*], which grow on this river, are the most beautiful and tall that I have any where seen... Their usual height is about one hundred feet, and some greatly exceed that. The trunk is per-

fectly erect, rising in the form of a beautiful column, and supporting a head like an obtuse cone." [William Bartram, **Travels,** 1791:85-86. Near mouth of Tocoi Creek, east bank of St. Johns River, due w. of St. Augustine, St. Johns Co. Sec 26, T7S, R27E.]

"It is really astonishing to behold the Grape-Vines [*Vitis* aff. *aestivalis*] in this place. From their bulk and strength, one would imagine they were combined to pull down these mighty trees to the earth; when, in fact, amongst other good purposes, they serve to uphold them. They are frequently nine, ten, and twelve inches in diameter, and twine round the trunks of the trees, climb to their very tops, and then spread along their limbs, from tree to tree, throughout the forest." [William Bartram, **Travels,** 1791:86-87. Near mouth of Tocoi Creek, east bank of St. Johns River, due w. of St. Augustine, St. Johns Co. Sec 26, T7S, R27E.]

"The Cupressus disticha [*Taxodium disticham*] stands in the first order of North American trees. Its majestic stature is surprising; and on approaching it, we are struck with a kind of awe, at beholding the stateliness of the trunk, lifting its cumbrous top towards the skies, and casting a wide shade upon the ground, as a dark intervening cloud .... That part of the trunk which is subject to be under water, and four or five feet higher up, is greatly enlarged by prodigious buttresses, or pilasters, which, in full grown trees, project out on every side, to such a distance that several men might easily hide themselves in the hollows between .... From this place, the tree, as it were, takes another beginning, forming a grand strait column eighty or ninety feet high, when it divides every way around into an extensive flat horizontal top, like an umbrella, where eagles have their secure nests, and cranes and storks their temporary resting-places .... Paroquets are commonly seen hovering and fluttering on their tops; they delight to shell the balls, its seed being their favourite food .... I have seen trunks of these trees that would measure eight, ten, and twelve feet in diameter, and forty and fifty feet straight shaft." [William Bartram, **Travels,** 1791:90-92. Near mouth of Rice Creek, w. bank of St. Johns River, 3 mi. n. of Palatka, Putnam Co. Sec 24, T9S, R26E. The once-common Carolina paroquet became extinct in 1914.]

"The Palm trees here seem to be of a different species from the Cabbage tree; their strait trunks are sixty, eighty, or ninety feet high, with a beautiful taper, of a bright ash colour, until within six or seven feet of the top, where it is a fine green colour, crowned with an orb of rich green plumed leaves; I have measured the stem of these plumes fifteen feet in length, besides the plume, which is nearly of the same length." [William Bartram, **Travels,** 1791:115-116. Between Astor and Lake Dexter, w. bank of St. Johns River, Lake Co. Sec 37?, T15S, R28E. This palm is surely *Roystonea elata*, the Florida royal palm, now limited in its natural range to extreme south peninsular Florida.]

"And now appeared in sight a tree that claimed my whole attention: it was the *Carica papaya*, both male and female, which were in flower; and the latter both in flower and fruit, some of which were ripe, as large, and of the form of a pear, and of a most charming appear-ance . . . . It rises erect with a perfectly strait tapering stem, to the height of fifteen or twenty feet, which is smooth and polished, of a bright ash colour . . . . Its perfectly spherical top is formed of very large lobe-sinuate leaves, supported on very long footstalks . . . . The tree very seldom branches or divides into limbs, I believe never unless the top is by accident broke off when very young . . . ." [William Bartram, **Travels,** 1791:131-132. Ca. 6 mi. s. of Lake Dexter, w. bank of St. Johns River, Lake Co. Sec 42?, T16S, R28E. The papaya is now restricted in its natural range to hammocks of the Everglades and elsewhere in south peninsular Florida.]

"The Admiral says that he never beheld so fair a thing: trees all along the river, beautiful and green, and different from ours, with flowers and fruits each according to their kind." [Cristopher Columbus, **Journal of the First Voyage,** 28 October 1492. Written of Cuba; but reported here in apology for Juan Ponce de Leon who, on the morning of 3 April 1513, set the first European foot on Florida soil, but in his passion for gold and health-giving waters, failed to record even the slightest detail of its magnificent trees.]

INDEX TO SCIENTIFIC AND COMMON NAMES

Names listed are those included in the INVENTORY OF BIG TREES, GIANTS OF YESTERYEAR, and LARGE VINES.